The Playwright's Art

The Playwright's Art

CONVERSATIONS WITH CONTEMPORARY AMERICAN DRAMATISTS

Edited by Jackson R. Bryer

RUTGERS UNIVERSITY PRESS

New Brunswick, New Jersey

Library of Congress Cataloging-in-Publication Data

The Playwright's art : conversations with contemporary American
dramatists / edited by Jackson R. Bryer.
p.   cm.
Includes index.
ISBN 0-8135-2128-9 (cloth)—ISBN 0-8135-2129-7 (pbk.)
1. American drama—20th century—History and criticism—Theory,
etc. 2. Dramatists, American—20th century—Interviews. 3. Drama—
Technique. I. Bryer, Jackson R.
PS352. P57   1995
812'.5409—dc20   94-14070
                                                                        CIP

British Cataloging-in-Publication information available

Contents

Introduction

▶ ◀

On the evening of January 29, 1948, a new musical, *Look, Ma, I'm Dancin'!*, opened at New York's New Adelphi Theatre, marking the Broadway debut of a young playwriting team, Jerome Lawrence and Robert E. Lee, who were responsible for the show's book. Forty-six years later, Lawrence and Lee are reworking their most recent play, *Whisper in the Mind,* for a potential New York production, but the intervening decades have seen major changes in the landscape of the American theatre. Many of these changes are discussed and debated in this collection of interviews and are exemplified in the careers of the dramatists included. The range of experience represented can be seen by noting that three of the playwrights (Lawrence, Robert Anderson, and Alice Childress) began their careers in the 1940s, seven (Albee, Guare, Gurney, McNally, Simon, van Itallie, and Wilson) first attracted notice in the 1960s, four (Hwang, King, Shange, and Wasserstein) began their work in the 1970s, and one (Henley) is a product of the theatre of the 1980s. It is important to add, however, that all fifteen—as these interviews make clear—are still working playwrights. Albee, Guare, Gurney, Hwang, McNally, Shange, Simon, van Itallie, Wasserstein, and Wilson have each had new plays presented in New York within the past two years.

When *Look, Ma, I'm Dancin'!* opened in 1948, and in 1953, when Robert Anderson's *Tea and Sympathy* gave its first performance, theatre in New York essentially meant Broadway. Critic John Chapman, in his 1947–48 volume of the annual *Best Plays* compilation, mentioned only six theatres (the Provincetown Theatre, the Cherry Lane Theatre, the Greenwich Mews Playhouse, the New Stages Playhouse, the Blackfriars' Guild, and the American Negro Theatre) in his chapter on "Off Broadway"; also listed were such other "theatrical" ventures as a dramatic oratorio at Carnegie Hall, the Ice Follies of 1948 and Sonja Henie's Hollywood Ice Revue at Madison Square Garden, college productions, and children's theatres. By 1953, when Louis Kronenberger was editing the *Best Plays,* the "Off Broadway" chapter was apparently considered important enough to be assigned to a separate critic, Garrison Sherwood, who proclaimed the season just completed "Off Broadway's best year" and dealt only with dramatic presentations. Nonetheless, the chapter was brief—three pages—and covered just about a dozen groups.

It is also important to observe that, in both 1948 and 1953, the majority of off-Broadway presentations were revivals. The economics of Broadway production at that time were such that a new play by a hitherto unknown American writer could usually receive a full professional mounting in an uptown theatre (most of the off-Broadway houses were downtown, in Greenwich Village). Although Robert Anderson's first play produced in New York, *Come Marching Home* (1946), premiered at the Blackfriars' Guild, *Tea and Sympathy*, his second, received full Broadway treatment; it starred Deborah Kerr and was directed by Elia Kazan. Lawrence and Lee's first play in New York, the enormously successful *Inherit the Wind* (1955), opened on Broadway with Paul Muni, Ed Begley, and Tony Randall. And, of course, the careers of the two most important American playwrights of the late 1940s and 1950s, Tennessee Williams and Arthur Miller, took place almost entirely on Broadway.

Within a very few years, this situation began to change. By the early 1960s, there were already more options for beginning playwrights. While Neil Simon could, in 1961, receive a Broadway production for his first play, *Come Blow Your Horn* (and for every one of his twenty-two plays and five musicals that followed), Edward Albee was a much honored and quite well known figure when *Who's Afraid of Virginia Woolf?* became his first play to be produced on Broadway, on October 13, 1962. Albee's *The Zoo Story* had opened in January 1960 at the Provincetown Playhouse in Greenwich Village, had run for 582 performances, and had received Vernon Rice and Obie awards (these awards had been founded, in 1955 and 1956 respectively, expressly to recognize achievement in the burgeoning off-Broadway theatre). Albee's *The Sandbox* and *Fam and Yam* had also been produced off-Broadway in 1960; and in 1961 his *The American Dream* and *The Death of Bessie Smith* had had very successful off-Broadway runs.

Who's Afraid of Virginia Woolf? ran for 664 performances; as a result of its success, Albee, with the play's producers Richard Barr and Clinton Wilder, established Albarwild, the New York Playwrights Unit Workshop at off-Broadway's Cherry Lane Theatre. It was at Albarwild that a number of aspiring playwrights, among them Terrence McNally, John Guare, and Lanford Wilson, got early opportunities to see their work performed. These fledgling artists found other hospitable outlets for their apprentice efforts during this period. Many of Lanford Wilson's first plays were presented either at Joe Cino's Caffe Cino or at Ellen Stewart's La MaMa Experimental Theatre Club; John Guare also worked at Caffe Cino in his early career. Terrence McNally got his start at the Theatre de Lys, the

Gramercy Arts Theatre, and the Greenwich Mews Playhouse, all off-Broadway houses; while Jean-Claude van Itallie worked primarily with Joseph Chaikin's Open Theatre at the outset of his career. No longer were new playwrights dependent upon—nor even in some cases desirous of—Broadway production as a means of establishing themselves.

The major figures in the careers of American playwrights who got their starts in New York in the 1960s were not Broadway producers and directors but rather Cino, Stewart, and Chaikin, as well as Al Carmines of the Judson Poets' Theatre, Ted Mann of the Circle in the Square, Joe Papp of the New York Shakespeare Festival, Robert Hooks and Douglas Turner Ward of the Negro Ensemble Company, Richard Schechner of the Performance Group, and Julian Beck and Judith Malina of the Living Theatre. These individuals ran their theatres entirely according to their own particular tastes; they were answerable to no investors or unions. This enabled them to take risks that led to many failures but also spawned an entire generation of new American playwrights who, like their mentors, did not play by the rules or standards of the Broadway theatre. In this respect, the rise of the off-Broadway movement in the early 1960s reflected developments in the other arts and in the broader culture as an experimental counterculture began to challenge the complacency and status quo represented by the 1950s. Besides Albee, Guare, McNally, van Itallie, and Wilson, who speak so nostalgically of those days in these interviews, such major dramatic talents as Sam Shepard, Arthur Kopit, Jack Gelber, Maria Irene Fornes, Ronald Ribman, Ed Bullins, Amiri Baraka, and Megan Terry got their starts in the off-Broadway movement of the 1960s. It was at these small experimental theatres also where America was first introduced to influential and controversial contemporary European playwrights Samuel Beckett, Harold Pinter, Eugene Ionesco, and Jean Genet.

What off-Broadway afforded these artists, besides an opportunity to be heard, was a forum to grapple with subjects the mainstream theatre would not touch and to do so in unconventional styles forbidden on Broadway. Jack Gelber's *The Connection* (1959) mercilessly confronted the realities of the drug culture. Genet's *The Blacks,* produced at the St. Mark's Playhouse in 1961, is cited by many critics as the beginning of the modern black theatre in America. Although Genet himself was not black, his play inspired a movement that in turn encouraged a young black actress and part-time writer named Alice Childress to devote her full attention to playwriting. Jean-Claude van Itallie's *America Hurrah* trilogy (1966) bitterly satirized the national malaise of middle America in the Johnson years, using arresting and provocative theatrical images. Terrence McNally's *Sweet Eros* (1968) became the first serious dramatic production in New York in which an actress appeared totally nude during most of the play; and *The Boys in the Band* (1968) by Mart Crowley confronted male homosexuality far more directly and fully than heretofore, although Lanford Wilson, in his one-act *The Madness of Lady Bright*, had taken on the same subject four years earlier.

In the early 1960s, so many theatres of different kinds were springing up off-Broadway that a distinction began to be drawn that classified the smaller and more blatantly noncommercial of them (Caffe Cino, La MaMa, Judson Poets' Theatre, Open Theatre, Theatre Genesis, the Performance Group, among others) as off-off-Broadway and retained the off-Broadway designation for more established organizations like the Circle in the Square, the Phoenix Theatre, and the New York Shakespeare Festival. The off-off-Broadway movement had begun as poetry readings held in coffeehouses; these led to dramatic readings and eventually to minimally staged full productions presented on minuscule budgets often met by passing the hat after each performance. What made off-off-Broadway especially attractive for new writers was the speed with which their work could be transferred from the page to the stage: often a play submitted late one week would be presented early the next. The chief distinction between off-off-Broadway and off-Broadway was that, in the former, no one got paid. For the most part, also, the off-off-Broadway groups focused on new plays by new playwrights; and, unlike off-Broadway, where it was not unusual for a successful production to move uptown, off-off-Broadway was founded—and remained—in defiance of and as an alternative to the commercial theatre, not as a way into it.

So, while Robert Anderson, Jerome Lawrence, and Neil Simon were honing their skills with a series of Broadway successes during the 1960s, Childress, Guare, McNally, van Itallie, and Wilson were doing the same off-Broadway and off-off-Broadway. Van Itallie has never had a play produced on Broadway; McNally and Guare both had early plays fail on Broadway before returning gratefully to the relative security of off-Broadway and off-off-Broadway. McNally came back to Broadway for the successful run of his play *The Ritz* in 1975, for the quasi-successful engagement of the musical *The Rink* in 1984, and for the Tony-winning musical *Kiss of the Spider Woman* in 1992; but he has achieved his greatest success and his reputation with off-Broadway productions of *Frankie and Johnny in the Clair de Lune* (1987), *The Lisbon Traviata* (1989), *Lips Together, Teeth Apart* (1991), and *The Perfect Ganesh* (1993). John Guare's first and only successful Broadway venture, other than his 1971 book for the musical adaptation of *Two Gentlemen of Verona* (which originated at the New York Shakespeare Festival), was the 1986 revival of his 1971 play *The House of Blue Leaves*—and that revival began at the Lincoln Center Theater. Larry L. King's only Broadway ventures have been the books for two musicals, *The Best Little Whorehouse in Texas* (1978) and *The Best Little Whorehouse Goes Public* (1994). A. R. Gurney, also represented in this volume, started writing plays in the 1950s but did not see them receive professional productions until the 1960s, and he has had only one play on Broadway, *Sweet Sue* (1987). Lanford Wilson, whose first plays were done at the Caffe Cino in 1963, did not have a Broadway success until *Talley's Folly* (transferred from the Circle Repertory Theatre) in 1980 (his previous two Broadway plays, *The Gingham Dog* [1969] and *Lemon Sky* [1970], had lasted for five and seven performances, respectively).

Coinciding with the beginnings of the off-Broadway and off-off-Broadway movements in New York was the other major development that was to alter significantly the nature of theatre in America and to affect the lives and careers of the playwrights included in this volume. This was the gradual emergence of the regional theatre movement across the United States: the establishment in cities both large and small of professional nonprofit theatres that were often composed of a company of resident actors who presented a mix of classical and modern plays. As many critics have pointed out, the impetus for the regional theatre movement was virtually identical to that for off- and off-off-Broadway—a reaction against the standards, expense, restrictions, and banality of standard Broadway fare—along with a desire to offer an alternative to the road tours of past Broadway successes, which had until this time constituted the only theatrical experiences available to millions of Americans.

The three pioneers of the regional theatre movement were women: Margo Jones, who founded her theatre-in-the-round in Dallas in 1947 (she called it Theatre '47 and changed the name each year); Nina Vance, who began Houston's Alley Theatre, also in 1947; and Zelda Fichandler, who opened the Arena Stage in Washington, D.C., in 1950. They were joined in the 1960s—in an upsurge that paralleled the similarly dramatic growth of off-Broadway and off-off-Broadway at the same time—by, among many others, the Guthrie Theater in Minneapolis, the Seattle Repertory Theatre, the Trinity Repertory Company in Providence, the Berkeley (California) Repertory Theatre, the Missouri Repertory Theatre in Kansas City, Center Stage in Baltimore, the Actors Theatre of Louisville, the Hartford (Connecticut) Stage Company, the American Conservatory Theater in San Francisco, the Mark Taper Forum in Los Angeles, and the Long Wharf Theatre of New Haven. As with the alternative theatre movement in New York, most regional theatres were dominated by the vision and leadership of one individual: Jones, Vance, Fichandler, Tyrone Guthrie, Adrian Hall (Trinity), William Ball (American Conservatory Theater), Arvin Brown (Long Wharf), to name just a few. Also like the off-Broadway theatres, regional groups, which began with repertories largely composed of the classics and revivals of successful modern plays and musicals, soon began to present more new American plays. Lawrence and Lee's *Inherit the Wind* had its first performances at Margo Jones's Dallas theatre in 1955 (as had Tennessee Williams's *Summer and Smoke* in 1947). Arthur Kopit's *Indians* (1969) and Howard Sackler's *The Great White Hope* (1968) both opened at Arena Stage and went on to successful Broadway engagements, with Sackler's play winning the Pulitzer Prize. Another Pulitzer Prize winner, Paul Zindel's *The Effect of Gamma Rays on Man-in-the-Moon Marigolds*, began at the Alley Theatre in 1965.

In the 1970s, as economic conditions continued to make Broadway production of new plays increasingly risky and difficult and as the off-Broadway, off-off-Broadway, and regional theatre movements became stronger and more established, the shift that had started quite gradually now began to achieve seismic proportions. A graphic way of documenting this is to note that, in the 1960s, of the six plays awarded the Pulitzer Prize (the prize was not given in 1963, 1964, 1966, and 1968), only one (*The Great White Hope*) originated away from Broadway; while in the 1970s, only one (Albee's *Seascape*) of the eight plays so honored (no prize was given in 1972 and 1974) had its first professional production on Broadway. Three (*No Place to Be Somebody, That Championship Season,* and *A Chorus Line*) began at Joe Papp's New York Shakespeare Festival, while all the others were first produced at regional theatres: in Houston (*The Effect of Gamma Rays on Man-in-the-Moon Marigolds*), Los Angeles (*The Shadow Box* and *The Gin Game*), and San Francisco (*Buried Child*). All except *Buried Child* did reach Broadway, but the future direction of American theatre was clearly indicated. Whereas during the 1940s, 1950s, and into the 1960s, most New York–bound plays and musicals had gone through a ritual of out-of-town tryouts in traditional East Coast cities like Boston, New Haven, Philadelphia, Wilmington, and Washington (in Broadway-sized theatre spaces), now good new American plays could and frequently did originate all over the country, often in small theatres that did not present them with a Broadway production in mind but rather as part of their own subscription seasons.

This, in turn, affected the form and content of the plays that did make their way to New York; because they were no longer designed primarily for the tastes of Broadway audiences, plays originating in the regional theatres—like those from off- and off-off-Broadway—often were unorthodox and controversial. A typical case in point during the 1970s was the work of the African American poet/performer/playwright Ntozake Shange, who, for several months in 1977–78, had three pieces playing simultaneously in New York. (As an indication of the eclecticism of the American theatre in the 1960s and 1970s, in December 1966 Neil Simon had had four Broadway productions of his work running simultaneously.) One of Shange's pieces was an evening of dance, poetry, and jazz (which she called a "choreopoem") entitled *where the mississippi meets the amazon* playing at the Cabaret Space in Joe Papp's Public Theatre; another, also playing at the Public Theater, was a more traditional play, *photograph: a study in cruelty*; and the third was Shange's most successful choreopoem, *for colored girls who have considered suicide when the rainbow is enuf*, which had recently moved to Broadway's Booth Theatre. The odyssey of *colored girls* was soon to become the rule rather than the exception it was in the mid-1970s: beginning as a dramatic reading in women's bars and bookstores in San Francisco in 1974, it had come to similar venues in New York's East Village in July 1975, then to an off-off-Broadway theatre in November 1975 and to Papp's Public Theater in June 1976. It eventually ran on Broadway from September 1976 until July 1978, at the time the most unlikely of popular hits—and, not surprisingly, Shange's only Broadway experience to date.

The 1980s and early 1990s completed the shifts begun earlier. Serious theatre in the United States became more decentralized, with Broadway and even New York less and less the focus of activity. There was an increased emphasis on the development and production of new American plays in the regional theatres; Louisville's Actors Theatre and the O'Neill Theater Center in Waterford, Connecticut, pioneered the establishment of festivals of this kind of material, and similar annual events subsequently began in Denver, Washington, and elsewhere. This led to the founding of several small nonprofit professional theatres devoted entirely to new plays and musicals—among them, New Playwrights' Theatre in Washington, D.C., the Philadelphia Festival Theatre for New Plays, and Ensemble Studio Theatre, New Dramatists, and Playwrights Horizons in New York. Playwrights Horizons was instrumental in the careers of Wendy Wasserstein and Christopher Durang, two of the most important American playwrights who came to prominence in the late 1970s and early 1980s, and in the launching of three Pulitzer Prize winners of the 1980s: *Sunday in the Park with George* (1985), *Driving Miss Daisy* (1988), and Wasserstein's *The Heidi Chronicles* (1989).

The decentralization of American theatre can also be seen in the rapid expansion of the regional theatre movement. In 1961 the Ford Foundation established the Theatre Communications Group (TCG) to assist what were then 16 nonprofit professional theatres across the country; by 1970 TCG was working with 92 such theatres, and by 1992 the number had grown to 229 (this total does not include many smaller regional theatres that are not part of the TCG network). Several major cities— principally Chicago, Washington, San Francisco, and Los Angeles—now offered theatregoers a choice of several such theatres, having in a sense replicated, albeit in miniature, the off- and off-off-Broadway scene in New York. The latter has also continued to flourish: a recent issue of the

Sunday *New York Times* lists twelve off-Broadway productions and thirty-two off-off-Broadway ones. Fine durable groups have emerged off-Broadway: the Circle Repertory Company, which has presented all of Lanford Wilson's plays since its founding in 1969; the Manhattan Theatre Club, begun in 1970, which has produced the New York premieres of four Beth Henley plays (*Crimes of the Heart, The Miss Firecracker Contest, The Lucky Spot,* and *Abundance*), as well as Terrence McNally's three most recent plays; the Wooster Group; the New York Theatre Workshop; Mabou Mines; the Roundabout Theatre Company; and many others.

Of course, American theatre in the 1980s and 1990s has been subject to other changes in the cultural, social, and economic landscapes, and these are commented upon in many of the interviews. When Lawrence and Lee's *Look, Ma, I'm Dancin'!* opened in 1948, New Yorkers could watch three television channels, which were on the air essentially from 7:00 P.M. to 11:00 P.M. daily; by 1953, when Robert Anderson's *Tea and Sympathy* was on Broadway, there were already six major New York TV stations broadcasting all day and into the late evening. In 1993, when Wendy Wasserstein's *The Sisters Rosensweig* transferred from the Lincoln Center Theater to Broadway, there were fifteen commercial and twenty-four cable channels included in the *New York Times* daily listing, and many had twenty-four-hour schedules. The A. C. Nielsen Company estimates that, in January 1950, 3.8 million American homes (roughly 9 percent of the homes in the country) had TV sets; in 1960 the number was 45.2 million; in 1970 it was 60.1 million; in 1980, 77.8 million; and in 1993, 93.1 million. The Nielsen figures indicate that ever since 1980, 98 percent of American homes have had TVs, with well over 50 percent owning two or more sets. This competition for live theatre audiences— and for playwrights as well, many of whom have been lured away from writing for the theatre by lucrative assignments elsewhere—is also echoed by the proliferation of movie houses nationwide. Where previously a first-run film might be available only in selected theatres in large cities, now multiple-screen houses in shopping malls throughout the country make movies far more accessible—as do VCRs. Economic forces have had an impact, too: an orchestra ticket to *Tea and Sympathy* cost $6.00 on weekends and $4.80 during the week; *The Sisters Rosensweig* had a top ticket price of $47.50 when it opened. Another factor much discussed in these interviews is the radically altered critical situation in New York: in January 1948 Lawrence and Lee's new show was reviewed by critics from nine daily newspapers; in 1993 three remained, and only one—the *New York Times*—had any influence (its influence was so great that even a lukewarm *Times* review frequently doomed a new production; Neil Simon alone seemed immune from this rule of thumb).

Given these factors, the size of the Broadway theatre has shrunk markedly, although the number of shows playing on Broadway at any given time has remained relatively stable since the 1940s. When *Look, Ma, I'm Dancin'!* opened in 1948, it was one of thirty-four shows running; in 1962 *Who's Afraid of Virginia Woolf?* was one of twenty shows when it opened; and in 1993 there were twenty-two when *The Sisters Rosensweig* opened. But these figures are misleading and do not accurately reflect what has happened over the past forty-five years. During the 1947–48 theatre season on Broadway, according to the *New York Times*, there were eighty-five new productions mounted, of which forty-three were new plays, nine were new musicals, thirty were revivals, and four were called "miscellaneous." Among the playwrights represented that season on Broadway were Shaw (three different plays), Euripides, Shakespeare (two different plays), Ibsen (two different plays), Strindberg, and Molnar. For the 1962–63 season, the figures were fifty-three new productions: thirty-four new plays, nine new musicals, four revivals, and six "miscellaneous," among them works by Brecht, O'Neill, Shaw, Pirandello, and Wilde. In the 1976–77 season, the one that saw Shange's *colored girls* performed on Broadway, there were roughly sixty new productions, of which seventeen were new American plays (there were eight new plays imported from England) and six were new musicals; but only Shaw and Wilde among classical dramatists were performed. Through the 1980s and early 1990s, these trends continued, until the 1991–92 season saw only thirty-four new productions, many of which were presented by nonprofit companies such as Lincoln Center, the Roundabout, and the venerable Circle in the Square; only five of the Broadway productions were new American plays. The latter have virtually disappeared from the Broadway scene—to be replaced for the most part by so-called blockbuster musicals, many written by Englishman Andrew Lloyd Webber.

During this same period, the shift of American theatre away from New York produced equally striking statistics of another kind. A 1989–90 report from TCG indicated that more than 150 cities across the United States, in forty-two states and the District of Columbia, had active resident professional theatres. The report further estimated that, during that season, "these theatres collectively presented more than 50,000 performances of 2,500 productions at home and on tour, attracting an attendance of some twenty million." Among the offerings of these theatres were the very types of plays and musicals no longer generally available to mainstream New York audiences: large doses of classical plays, revivals of major plays and musicals from the modern American and European repertory, experimental multimedia and performance artist presentations, along with—in many cases—new plays and musicals by both established and unknown American playwrights and composers. With the exception of Neil Simon, none of the playwrights interviewed for this volume now open their new plays on Broadway. Most have a home at a regional, off-, or off-off-Broadway theatre where they regularly introduce their work; most do not even think in terms of a future Broadway production.

The changing face of America is also now reflected in its regional theatres and in off- and off-off-Broadway. By 1992 TCG counted among its membership organizations such as El Teatro Campesino, East West Players, National Jewish Theater, Bilingual Foundation of the Arts, Mixed Blood Theatre Company, St. Louis Black Repertory Company, Ping Chong and Company, INTAR Hispanic American Arts Center, Jewish Repertory Theatre, Pan Asian Repertory Theatre, and Repertorio Español. Another such group, the Asian American Theatre Company in San Francisco, helped launch the career of David Henry Hwang, our first significant Asian American playwright. Other talented African American, Hispanic, Chicano, Native American, and Asian American writers have begun to emerge—from the theatres that specialize in minority ethnic drama as well as from other regional theatres, some of which now annually feature a miniseries of new plays that augments their regular subscription offerings. A corollary to this emergence is color-blind casting. As theatre companies across the country have become increasingly aware of and sensitive to the large ethnic segments of the communities from which they draw their audiences, they have begun to increase the minority representation in their companies and to cast their shows accordingly. This practice, while generally accepted, has also generated some controversy, and it is addressed in a number of the interviews.

So a great deal has happened in and to the American theatre since that January evening in 1948 when Lawrence and Lee first saw their writing on a Broadway stage; but what has not changed is the theatre's perennial idealism and optimism: the stubborn belief that a great new play could open next week. A Broadway season as barren of new American plays as 1992–93 did, after all, also witness the emergence of an astonishing talent, Tony Kushner, and of his play *Angels in America*, which some of his peers consider among the supreme achievements of the post–World War II American theatre. What also has not slackened is our fascination with the process of writing and producing plays, what playwright Herb Gardner has described as "an irrational act" and "the Las Vegas of art forms," in which "one's days are spent making up things that no one ever said to be spoken by people who do not exist for an audience that may not come."

These interviews deal with the mysteries of that "irrational act," as well as with the changing face of the American theatre during the past half century. Eight of them began as programs in the Smithsonian Institution's Campus on the Mall series "Conversations with Leading American Playwrights," which I organized in the autumn of 1991. In order to give that series some coherence, a number of the same questions were addressed to each playwright. These recurrent questions also appear in the other seven interviews, which were commissioned especially for this book. I am grateful to Anna Caraveli and Binney Levine of the Smithsonian for their support and encouragement; to John Fuegi, Bonnie Nelson Schwartz, Tom Bair, and Andrew Ferguson for assistance in taping the Smithsonian sessions; and to Drew Eisenhauer for the laborious task of transcribing all the interviews. I thank the interviewers for asking challenging questions, Hap Erstein (who helped to suggest many of the recurring questions), and Kenneth Arnold and Leslie Mitchner of Rutgers University Press for their interest in the project. Once again, Mary C. Hartig improved my writing. Above all, of course, I appreciate the willingness of fifteen very talented— and very busy—artists to take the time to be interviewed, and in several cases to look through the texts after they were transcribed and make changes, corrections, and suggestions. I feel certain, however, that they would agree with me that the effort expended in putting this collection together will be more than worthwhile if it helps send a few of its readers to the live theatre and if it causes a young reader or two to consider writing a play.

J.R.B.
January 15, 1994
Kensington, Maryland

About the Interviews

Eight of the interviews originated as sessions in the series "Conversations with Leading American Playwrights," which was sponsored by the Smithsonian Institution's Campus on the Mall and took place in Washington, D.C., in the fall of 1991 as follows:

The principal questioner for the interview with Edward Albee was Laurence Maslon, associate artistic director of Arena Stage, Washington, D.C.

The principal questioner for the interview with Robert Anderson was Ernest Joselovitz, playwright and administrator of the Playwrights Forum, Washington, D.C.

The principal questioner for the interview with John Guare was Lloyd Rose, drama critic of the *Washington Post*.

The principal questioner for the interview with Beth Henley was Cynthia Wimmer-Moul, who teaches at the University of Maryland.

The principal questioner for the interview with Larry L. King was Bob Mondello, theatre critic of the *City Paper* (Washington, D.C.) and frequent reviewer and commentator for National Public Radio's "All Things Considered."

The principal questioner for the interview with Jerome Lawrence was Richard L. Coe, theatre critic emeritus of the *Washington Post*.

The principal questioner for the interview with Terrence McNally was Joy Zinoman, artistic director of the Studio Theatre, Washington, D.C.

The principal questioner for the interview with Wendy Wasserstein was Leslie Jacobson, artistic director of Horizons Theatre, Washington, D.C.

Additional questions were addressed to each of the guests in the Smithsonian series by Jackson R. Bryer, coordinator of the program, and by members of the audience.

The other interviews in the volume took place under the following circumstances:

The interview with Alice Childress was conducted in Childress's room at the Wyndham Franklin Plaza Hotel in Philadelphia at the annual conference of the Association for Theatre in Higher Education; the interviewer was Roberta Maguire, who teaches at the University of Maryland.

The interview with A. R. Gurney was conducted at the Saks Building in Chicago, where Gurney was preparing a production of *The Fourth Wall*. The interviewer was Arvid E. Sponberg, professor of English at Valparaiso University and editor of *Broadway Talks: What Professionals Think About Commercial Theater in America* (1991) and of *A. R. Gurney: A Casebook* (1994).

The interview with David Henry Hwang was conducted at the Actors Theatre in Louisville, Kentucky, where Hwang was preparing the premiere production of *Bondage*. The principal questioner was Deborah Frockt, the dramaturg for *Bondage*; other questions were addressed to Hwang by members of the audience.

The interview with Ntozake Shange was conducted via telephone; Shange was at her home in Philadelphia. The interviewer was Mary Helen Washington, professor of English at the University of Maryland and author or editor of many studies of African American literature.

The interview with Neil Simon was conducted in Simon's office in Beverly Hills, California; the interviewer was Jackson R. Bryer.

The interview with Jean-Claude van Itallie was conducted by Gene A. Plunka, professor of English at Memphis State University and author of *Peter Shaffer: Roles, Rites, and Rituals in the Theater* (1988) and *The Rites of Passage of Jean Genet: The Art and Aesthetics of Risk Taking* (1992). Questions were submitted to van Itallie, who tape-recorded his responses at his home in Charlemont, Massachusetts.

The interview with Lanford Wilson was conducted at Wilson's home in Sag Harbor, New York; the interviewer was Jackson R. Bryer.

The Playwright's Art

Edward Albee

Edward Albee was born in northern Virginia in 1928. His first professionally produced play, The Zoo Story, *was presented in Berlin in 1959. It was followed by* The Sandbox *(1960),* The Death of Bessie Smith *(1960),* Fam and Yam *(1960),* The American Dream *(1961),* Who's Afraid of Virginia Woolf? *(1962),* The Ballad of the Sad Café *(adapted from a novella by Carson McCullers; 1963),* Tiny Alice *(1964),* Malcolm *(adapted from a novel by James Purdy; 1966),* A Delicate Balance *(1966),* Everything in the Garden *(adapted from a play by Giles Cooper; 1967),* Box *and* Quotations from Chairman Mao Tse-Tung *(1968),* All Over *(1971),* Seascape *(1975),* Listening *(1976),* Counting the Ways *(1976),* The Lady from Dubuque *(1980),* Lolita *(adapted from a novel by Vladimir Nabokov; 1981),* The Man Who Had Three Arms *(1982),* Finding the Sun *(1983),* Walking *(1984),* Marriage Play *(1987),* Three Tall Women *(1991),* The Lorca Play *(1992), and* Fragments, a Concerto Grosso *(1993).* The Zoo Story *was*

awarded the Obie Award and the Vernon Rice Award; Who's Afraid of Virginia Woolf? *won the Tony Award, the New York Drama Critics Circle Award, the Outer Critics Circle Award, the* London Evening Standard Award, *and the Pulitzer Prize (the award was denied to Albee by the Columbia University trustees);* Tiny Alice *received the Tony Award and the New York Drama Critics Circle Award;* A Delicate Balance, Seascape, *and* Three Tall Women *each won the Pulitzer Prize. Albee is also the recipient of the Berlin Festival Award (1959), the Lola D'Annunzio Award (1961), a Fulbright Fellowship (1961), the Margo Jones Award (1965), the Gold Medal for Drama of the American Academy and Institute of Arts and Letters (1980), the Brandeis University Award (1987), the William Inge Award (1991), and numerous honorary degrees. This interview took place on November 6, 1991.*

▶ ──────────────────────────────── ◀

Interviewer: Why are you a playwright?

Albee: Why am I a playwright? Because it's the only thing that I can do halfway decently. If there was anything else I could do, I probably would do it.

Interviewer: Weren't you a poet first?

Albee: I attempted poetry, I attempted novels, I wrote short stories and essays—and they were all terrible. I tried to be a composer and that didn't work, I tried to be a painter and that didn't work; I even did sculpture and then there was nothing left, so I started writing plays.

Interviewer: What about being a playwright appeals to you the most?

Albee: The fact that I am one, I think. When I started writing plays, I discovered that's what I should have been doing all along. I am a playwright, therefore I write plays; it's not that I write plays and therefore I am a playwright.

Interviewer: How do you feel about the production process? Is it an impediment or is it part of the process?

Albee: The great joy is in writing the play, in the creative act itself. Seeing the play produced, if it is produced well, if it is produced honorably and honestly and to the playwright's intention, that's great. But a first-rate play exists completely on the page and is never improved by production; it's only proved by production. All these people who go around saying that a play is just there for actors and directors to turn into a work of art—that's nuts. The creative act, the writing of the play when a playwright sees it and hears it performed on a stage as he writes it, is the best production he'll ever see of a play of his that's any good.

Interviewer: You once said that *The Sandbox* was the only one of your plays that approached perfection.

Albee: No, I said it was the only one in which I thought I didn't have time to make any mistakes.

Interviewer: Because it was only fifteen minutes long?

Albee: Because it was only fifteen minutes long—and I even wrote a shorter one called *Box.*

Interviewer: Do you think that's more perfect?

Albee: Well, I made fewer mistakes in that one since I didn't have as much time.

Interviewer: "There was a time when good plays, plays that were not constructed for the mass market only but plays that were honest with themselves and also honest with the historical continuum of the theatre, there was a time when those plays could run on Broadway, if they didn't get the critical nod. That's no longer true." That statement is certainly true now, but you said it in the summer of 1963.

Albee: Well, it's even worse now, isn't it? I just think we should forget about Broadway—ignore it, leave it to the Shubert Organization and the other real estate groups, leave it to the advertising department of the *New York Times* and just ignore it, turn our backs on it completely. The American theatre is in pretty good shape; it exists in the minds of its playwrights, it exists in the majority of its regional theatres, at least those who haven't turned into tryout houses for the Broadway theatres. It exists in the experimental off-Broadway theatres, and it exists in university theatres. Let's just ignore Broadway; it doesn't have anything to do with anything anymore.

Interviewer: To what degree was that quote true in 1963? We usually think of that as some golden time.

Albee: We playwrights are supposed to think ahead a little bit and see trends. Even then it was getting clear to me that trouble was about to happen. The star system, the economics of the theatre, the desire of people who were putting on plays to make them as safe and ersatz as film and television: all those forces were beginning to get deeply rooted. The fact that now they have completely taken over the commercial theatre in the United States is sad, but a lot of us saw it coming back in 1963.

Interviewer: When you had your first successes in the sixties, it seemed that America was starting to ask some more questions. Do you think we've lost that edge as theatregoers?

Albee: The early sixties were very interesting because off-Broadway had its birth around 1960. We were a society that asked a lot of questions about ourselves then. We've certainly gone away from that. At least for over twenty years now we seem to want our theatre more and more to lie to us: to tell half-truths, to be escapist, to be comforting, to say that "we are fine" rather than hold the mirror up to us as it's supposed to and ask the tough questions. God knows, film and television can't do it in this country anymore. Because of economics, the theatre can, and it's a pity that it's being discouraged from doing that.

Interviewer: Your work confirms the fact that you are a very provocative playwright who likes to prod the audience into using their head. Is that job tougher for you now?

Albee: No, I keep right on doing it. It's not tougher for me. Apparently it's tougher for the audience, which indirectly, I suppose, makes it tougher for me, since I like to eat as much as anybody else does. But no, I don't find it any tougher to do. As a matter of fact, I find more of a need to do it.

Interviewer: Since we're in Washington, and since many find the way we fund art in America pretty reprehensible, have we gotten the sort of artistic support that we deserve?

Albee: The amount of money that is funded for the education of the public in the arts is ludicrously small, and the attempt on the part of both the know-nothings and the cynics who know better to try to cut that funding is criminal. We have so much waste in our government. There is so damn much pork barrel legislation which transcends the minimal amounts we give to the arts. We would be much better off to support the arts until people couldn't stand it anymore. We should support the arts to such an extent that participation in the arts becomes as natural as breathing.

Interviewer: As an inveterate museumgoer, do you think that theatres should have the kind of accessibility that museums do—with ticket prices that allow more people to attend?

Albee: This whole thing about ticket prices is so confusing. The fact that people are willing to spend seven dollars and fifty cents to see appalling movies leads me to conclude that maybe you could charge a little bit more to see a play by Chekhov. I don't know. Maybe people should be willing to pay a little bit more to see a great play than a lousy movie, but God knows there is something wrong with our serious culture in this country when our theatre is more often than not in the possession of the upper middle class which happens to be white. Most of our arts are, as a matter of fact, in possession of that group, and we are a far more diverse society than that. The fact that we have not been able to make our more serious arts broader in scope is deeply troubling to me. That's only partly economic, and it's partly educational as well. It has to do with the double social standard we have in this country.

Interviewer: You've funded different foundations to support artists yourself and are supportive of artists in general. Are there different ways we might go about funding artists in our society from the way we do it?

Albee: My foundation doesn't fund artists. It provides a place where painters and sculptors and writers and composers can come and live and work and have some freedom to do their work without financial pressure and also have the opportunity to intermingle with people in the other arts, which they don't normally get the chance to do. In an ideal society we wouldn't need to be funding our creative artists, but the vast majority of the money that goes into the support of the arts in the United States does not go to the support of the creative artist. It goes to things. It goes to buildings; it goes to existing organizations which may or may not be interested in producing the work of living creative artists. I bet no more than 5 percent—and I would say that is maybe a generous figure—of the money that goes to the support of the arts in this country goes to the support of the creative artist individually. I've sat on grant-giving councils all over the place, including the National Endowment and the New York State Council on the Arts, and in both places (although it may have changed in the National Endowment by now) it was assumed that money should be spread around. It should be spread around to institutions, in the Dakotas as well as in more urban areas, on the assumption that, for example, there must be as many first-rate composers of string quartets in Dubuque as there are in New York. I worry when I see millions of dollars of New York State music grant money going not to support worthwhile composers but to support a symphony orchestra somewhere up near, but not in, Buffalo. I'm not sure that we have our priorities correct.

God knows, we should try to make the arts available to all people, but we should not use any kind of federal funding, any grant funding, to lower the standard of the arts, which is quite often what we do, on the assumption that to bring the arts to a large number of people you've got to lower the standard of what is brought to the people. There is a corruption in that that should be avoided. We're talking about such a small amount of money. We're talking about, what, for the National Endowment, $126 million a year, when our deficit this year is going to be $350 billion, and our budget is $2 trillion or some preposterous sum? The amount of extra money that it would cost to do proper funding for the individual creative artist is so tiny, it's almost absurd to have to talk about it.

Interviewer: In the eighties, there was a lot of work and time spent in workshopping plays and developing plays.

Albee: That's a term I hate—the verb "to workshop." When did that become a verb, by the way?

Interviewer: Back in the sixties you started Playwrights Sixty-Six, where you worked with up-and-coming playwrights.

Albee: We did the first productions of an awful lot of young playwrights including Terrence McNally, Lanford Wilson, Sam Shepard, LeRoi Jones, Adrienne Kennedy, and on and on and on. But one thing we did not do is "workshop." We assumed that these plays were just fine as they were; we liked their rough edges. Most "workshopping" rounds the rough edges of plays so that they can't stick into anybody's mind. It rounds the edges and shaves them down and makes them accessible and acceptable. Plays are meant to be tough and jagged and wrong-headed and angry and all the things that "workshopping" all too often destroys. So we didn't workshop plays. We took angry, tough, imperfect plays, and we put them on the stage, and everybody had a good time.

Interviewer: Have directors become too collaborative in that process, do you think, over the years?

Albee: Let's put it this way: as a metaphor or a simile, whichever you like, for a play let us take a string quartet composed by a composer. Let's go back to Beethoven's time, okay? Nobody workshops a string quartet. The first violinist doesn't get together with the second violinist and say, "You know, the composer wrote a C-sharp there; we don't like that, do we? Let's make that into an F." Everybody—directors and actors and producers and dramaturgs and theatre owners and theatre managers—feels that a play is there to be collaborated upon. A play is a work of art, for Christ's sake! You shouldn't do a play that needs to be collaborated upon; you should do a play that you respect and want to do to its total virtue. The idea of directors feeling that they are creative artists rather than interpretive artists, and of actors feeling that they are creative rather than interpretive artists, is so much bullshit. And it's done serious damage to our theatre. We get critics who think that they have the right to be collaborative artists as well—and then we're really fucked up.

Interviewer: Have we lost the ability to trust a playwright?

Albee: I don't think we've lost the ability to do it. Somewhere along the line it's become the assumption that the playwright is there to be worked upon instead of letting the playwright work his magic upon other people.

Interviewer: Is that the lack of strong producers who have had commitments to works?

Albee: No, it's the fault of strong producers who feel it is their property. Unless you're going to do improvisatory theatre, you can't do it without the playwright. Playwrights, generally speaking, are given a pretty hard time these days. They're not being treated with—I hate the word "respect," but it's a good one. You hear it too infrequently in the arts these days. They are not being given the respect that they deserve.

Interviewer: You were lucky, as you've said in print, that you had a director in your early career, in Alan Schneider, who respected your work.

Albee: Alan once said to me that only on two occasions in his professional life (and neither was with a play of mine, I'm happy to say) did he direct a play that he didn't respect. This led him to respect an awful lot of unpopular plays by Beckett, by me, by various other people—but Alan did respect the play. He did not believe that a play should be rewritten during the rehearsal period, did not believe that a play should be rewritten to accommodate the taste of the audience or to accommodate the diminished talents of the actors. If they were diminished talents, he felt that the play was there to be served. Alan did something very, very interesting that taught me a lot both as a playwright and when I became a director as well. Alan would come to me weeks before rehearsal began on a new play of mine with hundreds of questions that he wanted to ask me about my intentions—about the characters, who they were, what their background was. We had several sessions of hundreds of questions each, and it was useful to me because I discovered that I really did know things about my plays and about my characters that I hadn't known because nobody had asked me before. It also indicated to me that he was not going to wing it, that he was going to do what the playwright intended—and that was a very, very good lesson for me.

Interviewer: It's got to be more than mere coincidence that you and Alan Schneider met over a Beckett play.

Albee: It is a coincidence that we met over a Beckett play unless you want to assume fate. What are you getting at?

Interviewer: Beckett's been an author you've admired, an author you've been influenced by?

Albee: Oh God, yes! Sam Beckett invented twentieth-century drama and made all sorts of amazing things both possible and impossible for the rest of us. Possible because he opened up so many doors and windows for what could be done, and impossible because we all realized we couldn't do it as well as he did. Meeting Alan was nice, but meeting Beckett was much more important.

Interviewer: Do you think that Beckett has been well assimilated, now that *Godot* has become a classic?

Albee: I wish you wouldn't say *Godot.* I don't think it's his best play; everybody else does, but I don't. What does "assimilated" mean?

Interviewer: That he's become acknowledged at least by critics and scholars and students to be one of the major playwrights, if not *the* major playwright, of the twentieth century. Gradually, we've been able to incorporate him and understand him better.

Albee: We certainly don't produce him very much, I'll tell you that. I think if you assimilate someone into your culture you give them the respect of producing their work from time to time. I teach down at the University of Houston, and I work quite a lot at the Alley Theatre there, which is a good regional theatre. Last winter I directed a double bill of two of Beckett's plays—*Krapp's Last Tape* and *Ohio Impromptu*—and I discovered in the history of the Alley Theatre it was the second time they had done a production of Beckett's plays, which is astonishing. We were talking about Broadway earlier. You think about the number of playwrights who are not produced in what is meant to be the American theatre in any one given season, the number of playwrights who are not on Broadway this year (well, there aren't any playwrights on Broadway this year), the number of playwrights who regularly do not get produced in our commercial theatres: like Sophocles and Aristophanes and Euripides; and maybe Shakespeare now and again if it's set in Spanish Harlem maybe. Or if the right TV star wants to do it. And Racine, Molière, Beckett, Chekhov, Ibsen, Pirandello—these people are not performed in our commercial theatre. In our theatre consciousness as a theatregoing public, I don't think we've assimilated any of the great playwrights.

Interviewer: But since 1963, when you made the quote that I mentioned earlier, those playwrights are being done. They aren't being done in New York, but they are being done in resident and regional theatres on an ongoing basis. If you take your first statement, which is let's forget about New York anyway, then is it just as well that they are being done around the country?

Albee: When I went to Berlin in 1959 for the world premiere of my play *The Zoo Story,* I noticed what was being done on the Broadway stages of West Berlin of that time, and it was interesting. It was Brecht, it was Beckett, it was Goethe of course; it was the great playwrights. Maybe that's what prompted those remarks that I made, because I noticed that that wasn't happening in those days on Broadway, from which we took guidance as to what the nature of theatre was. What a bizarre country we are, where our commercial theatre does not concern itself with great art. I'm delighted that those regional theatres that aren't behaving like tryout houses for Broadway are living up to their responsibilities and are doing some of the great plays, balanced nicely with more easily salable stuff usually. I think that's fine. It's the very least they can do, but I don't think that doing the very least they can do is ever enough.

I also have a theory—I've had it for a long time; I've probably been wrong for a long time, but I still have it—that there is nothing innately corrupt about the taste of the American people. It is that they are not given the opportunity of choice, of being able to choose between that which is really good and that which is mediocre. I'm convinced that if not only our Broadway theatres but our regional theatres were secretly funded so that a group of very, very good people (I'd like to be in the group, of course) could decide what plays would be done, and these were the plays that the American audience had access to for a period of ten or fifteen years, I'm convinced that that would probably become the taste of the American theatregoing audience.

I had a long talk with Walter Kerr one night many years ago. He pointed out to me that something really terrible has happened to American taste because back in the Greek days, and in Shakespeare's day, everybody was pouring in to see plays by Sophocles. And I said that there wasn't anything else to do; that's the only entertainment they had; they had to do that. And he said, "Well, what about the Globe Theatre in Shakespeare's day?" And I said that there were three entertainments available to people in Elizabethan England: there were executions, there was bear-baiting, and there was *King Lear*. The people who couldn't get in to the bear-baiting and the executions went to see *King Lear*. Translate bear-baiting and executions into movies and television today. The people who can't get in to the bear-baiting and who can't get in to the executions go to the live theatre.

Interviewer: When you first started writing, you were labeled as part of the group of writers known as the Theatre of the Absurd, but you have an active dislike of labels.

Albee: Only when they are inaccurate. When Martin Esslin coined the name Theatre of the Absurd, it was a philosophical concept; but somehow very, very quickly it got translated into being stylistic. So a Theatre of the Absurd play was not a naturalistic play, and that made the whole thing ridiculous. That's when I stared getting fussy about it.

Interviewer: Someone once asked John Gielgud, a man who should know, what style was, and he said, "Style is simply knowing what play you're in."

Albee: Exactly. All plays are naturalistic and all plays are highly stylized, because there is no such thing as naturalism except for maybe Paddy Chayevsky and a few other people.

Interviewer: If people walked into a theatre and didn't know it was your play playing there, what would you like them to notice about it to indicate to them that it was your play?

Albee: If they knew my work, perhaps there is a sound that my plays make; maybe there is an Albee sound, but I can't find it, I'm not aware of it. Maybe some of my preoccupations and concerns about how we lie to each other—the truths we tell, the evasions—would be prevalent in the play. Beyond that I don't know. I'd like to think that if they're willing to be engaged they'd have an involving time and maybe, possibly, come out changed, conceivably even for the better.

Interviewer: You've often described yourself as the most eclectic playwright who ever wrote. You've tackled all sorts of different kinds of characters and situations. Is there an Albee style? Or does that change from play to play?

Albee: I don't know. People tell me to go see a play by this or that new playwright, that it sounds exactly like me; so I go to see it and I don't know what they're talking about. Style is a matter of form and content that co-determine each other. You don't try to take a subject matter that wants to be handled in a fantastic way and stick it in a naturalistic framework. The two relate to each other. There are degrees of stylization in all of my plays. None of them is naturalistic; some of them give the illusion of being more naturalistic than others. There must be a way my characters speak that defines an Albee play to an audience, but I don't know what it is because I don't think about myself in the third person.

Interviewer: Don't actors and directors often make the mistake of erring on the naturalistic side of plays and not enough on the stylized side?

Albee: You can't. When you act a play, no matter how stylized a play is (and I've learned this as a director too), all you can act and all you can direct is the moment-to-moment literal naturalistic truth of what is happening to the character at that particular moment. You can't act stylized unless you're a lousy actor. Even if you're in a highly stylized play, you're still acting naturalistically within that play. All of my plays are naturalistic no matter how highly stylized they are, so it's a very tricky matter. You can't act style, in the same way that you can't act metaphor. You can't act meaning; you can only act what is happening.

Interviewer: Let's talk about *Seascape,* a 1975 play that is set, geographically, on a beach on Long Island, isn't it?

Albee: The beach in *Seascape*? No, but I assumed that it has seasons, so it's probably somewhere in the North.

Interviewer: And a middle-aged couple is visited by another middle-aged couple who share some problems with each other, except the second couple are a pair of lizards who come from the sea. That's certainly not a "naturalistic" situation.

Albee: Yes, it was absolutely naturalistic. Those weren't metaphorical lizards, those weren't symbolic lizards, those were real lizards, real beach, real humans. It's the old thing with most people and comedies. Most people in comedies don't know that they are being funny. If the actor knows that he's being funny, then the play won't be funny.

Interviewer: Another thing about *Seascape* that's interesting is that it had an additional act at one point.

Albee: Yes, it did. It was a three-act play at one time. It was about as long as *Parsifal,* not quite as funny but almost as long. I took one act out because, although I had it in at the first rehearsal and I enjoyed it, it was totally unnecessary. The fact that I could remove that entire act overnight like a tooth without any damage to the sense of the play indicated to me that maybe I was being a little bit self-indulgent. So I took it out; but it was staged at some point by some people who got hold of it. Somebody did the whole damn thing in Holland, I believe. The original second act took place at the bottom of the sea. It was nice; I have it somewhere. It made a few problems for the set designer, of course, but he solved them. That was Bill Ritman, who solved them nicely.

Interviewer: You've talked a lot in print about how music has influenced you. How have the fine arts and design influenced you as a writer?

Albee: When you write a play, at least when I write a play, when I'm putting it down on paper anyway, and even when I'm thinking about it before I put it down on paper, I see it and I hear it. But I don't see it and hear it in some kind of amorphous general area. I see it and hear it as a performed stage piece, which saves me an awful lot of time in that I don't have to do as many rewrites as other people do, because I see it being performed on the stage. Since I see it and I hear it, I have a fairly comprehensive visual sense of what it should look like and what it should sound like as well as what it should mean. Therefore, I like to work in great detail with the set and lighting and costume designers, not insisting on this or that particularly but having a sense, because I have a sense of the specific environment. I want the set and costume and lighting and sound designers to have that same sense.

Interviewer: Does your interest in modern art influence the way you consciously or unconsciously put a play together or the way you see it visually?

Albee: No, I usually try to have a set that is, as Thurber put it, a container for the thing contained. I don't like to sit in the theatre and watch the set. I like sets to be efficient, and I like them not to call any attention to themselves beyond being proper containers for what's happening. As much as I admire twentieth-century art, and while I do like to see it employed both in dance and in opera even far more than it is, sometimes it can get in the way of theatre.

Interviewer: Boris Aronson said the best sets you should notice for two seconds.

Albee: About that. There was a time when in every play that Jo Mielziner, who was a very famous set designer, designed the following would happen: the curtain would go up, we'd be in some kind of murk, and lights would very, very slowly start appearing all over the set, and the set would start appearing, and damned if the audience didn't applaud. The set got applauded. Now that's wrong, totally wrong. Aronson's quite right; you should notice the set and then it should go away. Everything should go away in the theatre. You shouldn't be aware of acting, you shouldn't be aware of directing, you shouldn't be aware of playwriting either. You should be aware of the reality of the experience that's happening to you; all of that stuff has got to vanish. If any of it is terribly noticeable to you, then somebody has done his job wrong. And it makes no difference whether it's a naturalistic play or a highly stylized one.

Interviewer: In terms of music, you once said that one day your plays would get to the point where they would have to be conducted.

Albee: I write very precisely and carefully. I learned from Chekhov and I learned from Beckett to write very, very carefully and precisely, and I also learned that drama is made up of two things: sound and silence. Each of them has its own very specific duration. Playwrights notate sound and silence, loud and soft, just as precisely as a composer does. There is a profound difference in duration of pause between a semicolon and a period, for example, and a wise playwright knows that, in the same way that a composer knows the difference between durations. I discovered that writing a play is very similar to writing a piece of music. The psychological structure of a play is similar to that of a string quartet. You attempt simultaneity of speech the same way the instruments are playing, although you can't very often do simultaneity because it's easier with instruments. But you are composing in a sense, and I have watched other directors (I was going to say conductors), as well as myself, directing me, directing Beckett; and at a certain point in the rehearsal, the director, off somewhere so no one will see that he has gone quite mad, is standing there not looking anymore, but he is indeed conducting. A play that is written very carefully and very precisely and accurately can be conducted. It is sound and silence; it's a matter of durations, and if you write that carefully you do end up being conducted. When I go back to a play that I've directed (one of mine or Beckett's or anybody's) a week or so later, I don't have to watch the production because I know the actors are going to be standing where they are supposed to be, sitting where they are supposed to be. That's just directing traffic; if you've done that right, then you forget about it. All I have to do is listen and I can tell whether the production is where it should be or whether it's getting sloppy and falling apart and so I go back in and reconduct.

Interviewer: Do you listen to music when you write your plays?

Albee: No, I listen to music before I write. I prefer to listen to the music of what my characters are saying when I write. I think everybody should begin the day by listening to a couple of Bach fugues. It sort of gives a sense of order and coherence to the day. Maybe that's a good way to start—after the oatmeal, some Bach. My own musical tastes in what we call serious music go from Obrecht and Gilles right on up to Elliott Carter, so I don't have any problem anywhere there. I have a little problem with some of the second-generation romantic composers like Respighi and people like that.

Interviewer: Can you talk a little bit about your writing process? It sort of goes in two parts for you, doesn't it?

Albee: Three. My writing process is in three parts. There is what I assume is going on in my mind creatively without my being aware of it. That must take a fair amount of time because I have never said, with the exception of one play (*The Death of Bessie Smith*, which I wrote because of my rage at what I believed had happened to her in 1937 in the South), "I must write a play about this or that." I have never been aware of getting an idea for a play; a number of critics would agree with this, but not the way I mean! I become aware that I have been thinking about a play. When I become aware of a play that I have been thinking about, it's already gone a certain distance; it's already quite nicely formed in my head. The characters are already there, the destination is there generally. Generally, the environment of the play is already there when I become consciously aware of it. That's part one.

Part two is, again as Thurber said, let your mind alone: leaving all of that alone, not writing the play down instantly when I'm aware that I have been thinking about it, but letting it develop, mutate, letting it do things, letting it take its own time. I will play tricks to see how well I know the characters that are developing in my head. I will figure out some scene that cannot be in the play, and I will take a walk and improvise dialogue with these characters for a scene that will not be in the play to see how well I know them. I can keep a play in that condition in my head anywhere from four or five months to six or seven years. I always have two or three or four of them sort of floating up there ready to land, in a holding pattern above the airport of my desk. Oh God, I didn't know I was going to say that!

Then comes the time when I decide it is now time to write the play down on paper, to get it out of my head because it's taking up too much space. I haven't the vaguest idea of what the first two, three, four lines of dialogue are going to be; I have no idea of what any of my characters are going to say. That's called writing the play down on paper, where you discover and articulate everything you've been planning. That's the third part of writing, and that for me never takes more than two or three months. I can write a play down in two or three months, but I might have thought of it for, God knows, two or three or four years before I was aware of it. I write one draft, I make pencil corrections, and that's what I go into rehearsal with. I think I do most of my rewrites in my mind before I'm aware of the fact that I'm doing them, so I don't have to do them on the page.

Interviewer: There's an idea for a play that you've mentioned in interviews over the years as being imminent. It's about Attila the Hun.

Albee: I still have that play up there; it's still floating around along with a few others. I may get to that. Interesting guy, Attila. Do you know much about him? Very interesting guy. Did you know that Attila the Hun was one of the most educated men in Europe? Did you know that Attila the Hun was raised in the Roman court, as sort of a hostage, and that the Roman emperor's son was raised in Attila's father's camp, so that Attila was one of the most educated men in Europe? Did you know that one of his boyhood friends from when he was living in Rome became Pope Gregory, who was pope when Attila laid siege to Rome? It was the two boyhood friends meeting outside of the walls of Rome, and Pope Gregory somehow persuaded Attila to lift the siege of Rome. That's a good scene to write, let me tell you. Most people don't know these things. It struck me as very interesting that one of the most educated people in Europe would try to destroy civilization. As I watch history, it's not the most novel idea in the world, I suppose, but it certainly is an interesting one. Also, a nice thing about writing that kind of historical play is that there weren't too many journalists around in those days, so there's not too much written and I can make up my facts.

Interviewer: You don't get enough credit for the wonderful parts you write for actors. Do actors as part of the process help you or hinder you?

Albee: When I'm writing a character, I don't concern myself with anything except the reality of the character. I would never think about a specific actor for a role, because then I wouldn't write a character; I'd write a role. I don't start thinking about actors until I finish the piece. I try to make the characters as real and as three-dimensional as I possibly can, which maybe, if I succeed, is why actors like to work on them.

Interviewer: Have there been specific moments where actors might have contributed something you hadn't expected that helped you turn a play a certain way or added something to your perspective on a play?

Albee: When you write something, you're working both from your conscious and your unconscious mind, and you don't necessarily always know what you have done until somebody points it out to you; so an actor can indeed reveal a facet of a character that I've written, a depth of the character, that I wasn't consciously aware of. But if the actor's done a proper job, the actor is revealing what was there, something merely that I didn't know about. I've evolved a nice rule: If an actor or a director does something to a play of mine which diminishes it, which makes it less interesting than I thought it was, they're wrong, and I will not take any responsibility for it; if, on the other hand, a director or an actor finds something in a character of mine or a play of mine that makes it far more interesting than I have consciously known that it was, I instantly take credit for it. I've never had an occasion where an actor has suggested that things be in the character that were not there and then I've gone ahead and put them in. That's never happened. The actors that I've worked with—and I've worked with some pretty good ones—maybe had their hands full with the characters as written. There have been one or two occasions where I've been unfortunately stuck with a star whose competence was less than tolerable, who tried to simplify a role down to that particular tiny talent that the actor had. Those have been unhappy experiences, but generally the finest actors have been very busy with the characters I've written. They seem happy with them, or if they're not they don't tell me.

Interviewer: You make a distinction in a lot of your interviews between interpretive artists and creative artists. Does directing your own plays help you eliminate the middle man, get closer in contact with what's going on in the play with the actors?

Albee: The only reason, I think, that I became a director was to direct my own work with as much accuracy toward what I saw and heard when I wrote the play as I possibly could, on the assumption that that might be useful to somebody, to see what was really going on in the author's mind. The nice thing about directing your own work if you're the playwright is that there are two salaries. That's by far the nicest part. And you have double control over choice of actors, and I like that too. I suspect that when I'm directing a play of mine I'm far more willing to make cuts and changes than I would permit any other director to suggest. Maybe this is because I have greater confidence in myself, and maybe that is because my level of boredom is far lower than most people's.

I think I've probably learned a good deal about playwriting from directing, and probably a good deal about directing from playwriting. The idea put out by the Society of Stage Directors and Choreographers that playwrights should not direct their own work is put out merely because they want to have all the jobs available for the members of their union. It's based on the notion that the playwright shouldn't direct his own work because he understands it. Or perhaps he knows too much about it. Some playwrights can never be objective about their own work and shouldn't direct their own work. Some playwrights shouldn't be allowed in the theatre when their plays are in rehearsal because they will take anybody's suggestion and rewrite and quite often destroy their own work or do serious damage to it. Look what happened with Tennessee Williams and so many of his plays. Elia Kazan changed them. Tennessee always had his commercial success afterwards with Gadge's version, but he would then publish his original version along with it so that he had it both ways.

Interviewer: You once said that one of the reasons you like directing is that when you're not, you watch directors and actors fight over what the subtext is, and when you are, you know what the subtext is because you wrote the subtext.

Albee: Yes, but I've also discovered as a director that the author's subtext has nothing to do with the subtext that two different actors will need for the same role. I've directed fifteen or twenty different productions of *The Zoo Story* in the past thirty years. For one of the first productions I directed of it, a young actor—now recently dead, alas—named Ben Piazza was playing the role of Jerry. All you have to know to follow this is that in the play the character Jerry has a rather profound relationship with his landlady's dog. On the second day of rehearsal Ben came up to me and said, "When Jerry was growing up, did he have a dog?" This was obviously something Ben the actor needed to use to understand how the character related to his landlady's dog, and I tried to think back to the subtext that I had in my mind when I created the character of Jerry. I couldn't remember, so it occurred to me, let's see, what will be most useful for Ben Piazza to use to create this character? I said, "Oh yeah, Jerry grew up on a chicken farm his father had in New Jersey about fifty-seven miles from New York." I was making all of this up totally. "And there were lots of animals. Not only were there these awful chickens around, there were goats and sheep and two horses and six dogs." And I named the dogs for him, told him what brand they were, and I told him of a couple of the adventures that Jerry had had as a kid with the dogs. Ben nodded, we went

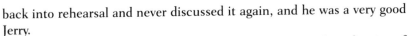

back into rehearsal and never discussed it again, and he was a very good Jerry.

Twelve years after that I was directing another very good production of *The Zoo Story* somewhere else with totally different actors. This doesn't happen too often, but it happened this time. The actor playing Jerry came up to me the third day of rehearsal and said, "When I was growing up [by "I" he meant Jerry], did I have a dog?" And of course I thought back to what I told Ben Piazza, but then a bell went off and I said, "This actor will work better through deprivation." So I said to him in answer to his question, "No, you weren't allowed to have any pets when you were growing up. You wanted pets very badly, but your father hated dogs. You sneaked a puppy into your room when you were six years old, and your father drowned it." So he nodded, he went back, and we had a very good production of the play. The question is, which is true? Which subtext is true? Both. Because the subtext that each actor needs is the subtext that is valid, that will allow the actor to become the character. I learned as a director that subtext is there not to force but to become the character. If you hired the right actor, an intelligent talented actor, 90 percent of your work is done—if you've written a halfway decent play. I discovered that most problems that actors seem to be having in a scene have less to do with the writing of the scene than they have to do with subtextual choices that have been made.

Interviewer: Who are some of your favorite actors?

Albee: I've been very lucky, with the exception of a couple of actors that I would never work with again in my life. I've worked with some extraordinary performers, both English and American, and in foreign languages. Just to mention a few of the ones that I've been lucky enough to work with: John Gielgud, Paul Scofield, Peggy Ashcroft, Colleen Dewhurst, Jessica Tandy and Hume Cronyn, and I'm going to forget a lot of them now. I've worked with some awfully good actors and had a good time working with them. When I first started writing plays and getting involved with actors, I believed what everybody else did: that actors were not necessarily bright or sensitive people. I found that this is quite often true, but the very best are both enormously intelligent and sensitive and deeply caring people. I was very relieved and pleased to find that to be true.

Interviewer: Can you tell us about your most recent play, *Three Tall Women*?

Albee: *Three Tall Women* had its world premiere at the English Theatre in Vienna this past June. I directed it. There are four actors in it: three tall women and one fairly tall man. It's in two acts. You need more? I'm very bad about talking about the work. I don't like to tell the stories of plays. All right. In the first act, a ninety-two-year-old woman is in conversation with her fifty-two-year-old sort of nurse-companion and a twenty-six-year-old assistant. The play is basically this old woman rambling variously about her past, about her hates, about her vengefulness, all the things that when you get to ninety-two you seem to get very fond of talking about. She is not senile, but she lives in a past that did not exist quite often. She has a stroke at the end of Act I which silences her.

When Act II begins, the stage is empty except she is there in the bed with an oxygen mask. The fifty-two-year-old woman and the twenty-six-year-old woman come in looking and seeming somewhat different from who they were in the first act, and they stand over the bed of this comatose woman, and then the woman herself comes in and obviously it's a dummy on the bed. We understand fairly quickly that the three women are really the same woman at different ages: at ninety-two, fifty-two, and twenty-six. We learn a great deal more about that woman. We learn a great deal more about how we view life at twenty-six, how we view life from the top of the mountain looking both backward and forward at fifty-two, and how we view ourselves at both twenty-six and fifty-six when we are ninety-two, and how we imagine we are going to be behaving when we are ninety-two when we are both fifty-six and twenty-six. As usual in my plays, not a great deal happens; but all of that happens. The English Theatre in Vienna is very interesting. A lot of the audience speaks far less English than it pretends to, and this includes some of the critics. But the ones who seemed to understand the play were quite fond of it, and those who seemed bewildered were not.

Interviewer: Could you say something about the film version of *Virginia Woolf*?

Albee: As Beckett says, it was better than a kick in the teeth. When I sold the rights of that play to Warner Brothers, they promised me Bette Davis and James Mason, who were both exactly the right age for it at that time. Bette Davis was fifty-two, and James Mason had always been forty-six, so it was just dandy. Then it was decided that Richard Burton and Elizabeth Taylor were big stars, and so they became Bette Davis and James Mason. I suppose the only problem was that Elizabeth Taylor was thirty-two. She was trying to play a fifty-two-year-old woman, and I don't think she quite convinced me that she was fifty-two. I think they pretended that she was forty-five, which made the nonexistent child no longer on the eve of his twenty-first birthday but younger, which destroyed one of the metaphors of the play for me. Another thing about the film bothered me a little bit, although it's a lot better than a lot of films of plays have been. I wrote the play in color, but for some reason they made the film in black and white. I don't understand that. Maybe that's because black and white is more serious. I don't know. It certainly messed up the video cassette sale, I'll tell you that.

Also, the play is both very serious and very funny. I found the film, maybe because it was not a live experience, very serious but not particularly funny. I also found the film not as claustrophobic as I intended the play to be. The play is meant to be set in one room. I didn't even like them going up to the bedroom or to the kitchen, and when they went out to that ridiculous roadhouse I thought it was doing serious damage to the claustrophobic intention of the play. I imagine that I had been influenced to a certain extent by Jean-Paul Sartre's play *No Exit*, but I also think I probably wrote the play as an answer to another claustrophobic play by Eugene O'Neill called *The Iceman Cometh*. *The Iceman Cometh* postulates that you have to have pipe dreams or false illusions in order to survive, and I think *Virginia Woolf* was written to say, maybe, that you have to have them but you damn well better know that they're false illusions and then survive knowing that you're living with falsity.

I much prefer the film that was made of my play *A Delicate Balance* that had Katharine Hepburn, Paul Scofield, and Kate Reid and a number of other very good people in it, directed by Tony Richardson. I thought that was a somewhat better film. In neither case, however, and this is interesting, was there a screenplay used. I'm told there was a screenplay written for *Who's Afraid of Virginia Woolf?*, and indeed it says, "Screenplay by Ernest Lehman," the producer of the film; but as I look at the film (and I've seen it seven or eight times now), as far as I can see he wrote two sentences: "Let's go to the roadhouse," and I believe the other one was something like "Let's come back from the roadhouse." I'm told he paid himself $350,000 for writing the screenplay, so that's $175,000 dollars a sentence, which is pretty good.

I'm told that there was a screenplay that he did write, in which (and I hope this is apocryphal) the nonexistent child had become a seriously retarded child, a real child, and was kept upstairs. Well, so much for historical political metaphor. Anyway, I'm also told that when Burton, Taylor, and Mike Nichols read the screenplay, after their laughter died down they said, "If we have to use this screenplay, we will not make the film," and so they went back and went into rehearsal as if it were a play for a couple of weeks and used my text. They cut about fifteen or twenty minutes out of it; they cut out almost all of the historical political argument, and they unbalanced it slightly, making it more Taylor's film than Burton's film.

The film of *A Delicate Balance* was a better film. It was part of that ill-fated American Film Theatre project, where serious films of serious plays were made rather well, as often as not, and then shown without much advertising in places that people could not get to at hours when they would not go. *A Delicate Balance* was also rehearsed as a play and was shot in sequence. They shot that movie from the beginning of the play until the end, five days for each act. The only other play of mine that was made into a film I have not seen. That was the film of my adaptation of Carson McCullers's *The Ballad of the Sad Café*. I saw some rushes and I saw some shooting of that, and I did not want to see it. I heard it was fairly literal and not very good.

Interviewer: There is a story about *Virginia Woolf*—that Henry Fonda's agent got the script but didn't tell him about it, and he was furious forever after.

Albee: Yes. This is to say nothing against Uta Hagen and Arthur Hill, who were both superb in their roles, but neither of them was the first choice. Henry Fonda, whom I had seen onstage and whom I respected as a stage actor, was offered the role of George in *Who's Afraid of Virginia Woolf?* in the 1962 production. His agent did not show it to him and said, "Mr. Fonda is not interested." Whether he would have taken the role or not, who knows. He said he would have taken the role, but he might not have. I think that was the end of that particular agent for him anyway! We offered the role of Martha originally to Geraldine Page with the agreement both of me and Alan Schneider, who had been hired to direct the play, and Gerry Page was very excited about doing it. But she said in her tiny voice that she would have to talk to Lee Strasburg about it first. She came back a couple of days later with the information that Lee was going to allow her to do the role, and it was okay if Alan Schneider directed it but that he, Lee Strasburg, would have to be at all rehearsals as a sort of éminence grise. And that is why Geraldine Page did not play Martha on Broadway in *Who's Afraid of Virginia Woolf?*

Interviewer: Do you think it's possible that any of your female characters are actually male homosexuals in disguise? Do you think homosexuality plays a part in much of your work?

Albee: Well, let's see, I've got about three plays where there are characters who are gay, so I suppose to that extent that it does. What I've never done is write a male character as a female or write anybody who was gay as straight or straight as gay. There's a difference you may have noticed between men and women, and it would be very very difficult to lie in that particular fashion, and playwriting is not about lying. I don't know how that story about *Who's Afraid of Virginia Woolf?* got started that, somewhere along the line, it was written about two male couples. You never know what's going on in the deepest recesses of your mind, so I asked a number of actresses who were playing Martha if they thought they were playing men. I asked Uta Hagen; it had never occurred to her. When I directed it in 1976 with Colleen Dewhurst, I asked her if she thought that she was playing a man, and I asked Ben Gazzara if he thought he was playing a gay man. It had never occurred to either of them. It had never occurred to Elizabeth Taylor that she was playing a man, and it never occurred to me. I don't think all that game playing and role playing are necessary.

There was a disgraceful article written in the *New York Times* by the then drama critic, one of the several they have gotten rid of although they have not gotten rid of all of them that they should have, a man named Stanley Kauffmann. He wrote an insidious and slimy and disgusting article not naming the names of any of the playwrights he was talking about but saying that we all knew, nudge, nudge, did we not, that a number of our most famous American playwrights were homosexuals, and did we not also know, nudge nudge, that they were really writing about males when they were writing their female characters? It was appalling and disgusting and the sort of thing that infiltrates far too much of our criticism. He was talking about Tennessee Williams primarily then, and Tennessee never did that, and I can't think of any self-respecting worthwhile writer who would do that sort of thing. It's beneath contempt to suggest it, and it's beneath contempt to do it. These critics who suggest it ought to grow up or ought to go into another kind of butchery, hog slaughtering perhaps.

Interviewer: You've always had harsh words about critics. What is a good critic?

Albee: A good critic is one who likes my work. A bad critic is one who does not. All playwrights feel this way. Some of us are honest enough to admit it.

Interviewer: It's been said that some of your plays, perhaps most notably *Virginia Woolf* and *Tiny Alice*, reflect your own experience of being adopted. Do you believe that?

Albee: I was adopted and I am real. The child in *Who's Afraid of Virginia Woolf?* was metaphorical, so I don't think there's too much relationship there. In *Tiny Alice*, I don't think there's any relationship to adoption whatever. The one play where it might be suggested that there is some biographical input in the play is *The American Dream*, but even there it is so metaphorical and so highly disguised that I'm not so sure even there. I'm not one of these playwrights who writes about himself very often, maybe because I find my characters much more interesting than I am. And I also find the characters that I can invent are a good deal more interesting than the people that I know. Even in the play *The American Dream* the character Grandma, of whom I'm very fond and who's a very, very interesting character, was, I suppose, infinitely more interesting than my maternal grandmother, upon whom it was partially based. I wish she had been as interesting as the character that I wrote, but alas, she was not.

I also think that character is based partially on Beulah Witch. Those of you who are old enough to remember "Kukla, Fran, and Ollie" will remember Burr Tillstrom, whom I knew. Burr would invite me over to his apartment in Chicago for an evening and he would say, "Excuse me, there's somebody who wants to talk to you." And he would disappear into another room, and all of a sudden I would hear this great cackling voice of Beulah Witch say, "Edward, come here!" And I'd go into that room, and there would be a little puppet stage, and Burr would have disappeared behind it, and there would be Beulah, and she and I would sit and have a half-hour conversation. As a matter of fact, I told Burr that *The American Dream* should be performed by him and the Kuklapolitan Players, that the play could be done very nicely by all of them. Oliver J. Dragon, of course, could play the American Dream; and Beulah Witch, of course, could play Grandma; and it would have been a nice experience.

I always write about myself in the sense that my characters are limited by my perceptions, though sometimes I think that they can imagine things that I cannot imagine. I'll tell you one thing: they have read things that I haven't, because I can read a book and within six weeks or less completely forget everything about the book. I've started reading books a second time, only realizing three-quarters of the way through that I've read this book before. I forget everything that I read, but twenty years after I've read something and forgotten about it I'm writing a character in a play and the character will quote from something that I cannot remember the experience of having read. I don't write about myself very much. Every character I write is limited by my perceptions but is also basically invented by me from people I've known and from people I've observed plus the particular kind of invention or creativity that we're supposed to do as writers. I've not written many memory plays. I've not written many plays about me or my family.

Interviewer: You once added up the names, didn't you say, of all the writers who influenced you?

Albee: Once, back in the middle sixties when I was very interested (much more interested than I am now) in critical evaluations of me and my work, I started noticing that critics, with this particular type of shorthand that passes for critical thought, were saying that Albee's work resembles this one or that one or that one. I was quite pleased by the good list of writers that I'd clearly been influenced by. I made a list of twenty-five contemporary playwrights that I was supposed to have been influenced by. And I looked at a lot of them and I thought, yeah, sure I'd been influenced by them, I would have been a damn fool not to have been. But there were six or seven playwrights on that list that I was supposed to have been influenced by whose work I didn't know. I thought that was going to be the neatest trick of the week, and then I went and read these people's work, and I realized that, of course, I had been influenced by them because we both had been influenced by the same sources.

Everybody, unless he's a self-conscious primitive or a damn fool, is going to be influenced by his predecessors and his betters. It's our responsibility to be; we don't want to reinvent the typewriter. We don't want to be so ignorant that we get a bright idea to write a play about a young man who comes back to the city after having been away since he was a kid and he falls in love with a female mayor of the city who happens to be twenty or twenty-five years older than he and they get married and then he discovers that it's his mother. If we've read *Oedipus Rex* we're not going to do that. But it was interesting to me that there were these playwrights that I was supposed to be influenced by that I hadn't known. Of course I'd been influenced by them because we had been influenced by the same people.

Interviewer: What terrifies you?

Albee: Not being asked wonderful questions.

Robert Anderson

Robert Anderson was born in New York City in 1917 and received under-graduate and graduate degrees from Harvard University, where he began writing for the stage. His plays include Come Marching Home *(1945),* The Eden Rose *(1948),* Love Revisited *(1950),* Tea and Sympathy *(1953),* All Summer Long *(1954),* Silent Night, Lonely Night *(1959),* The Days Be-tween *(1965),* You Know I Can't Hear You When the Water's Running *(1967),* I Never Sang for My Father *(1968),* Solitaire/Double Solitaire *(1971),* Free and Clear *(1983), and* The Last Act Is a Solo *(1991). He adapted* Tea and Sympathy *and* I Never Sang for My Father *for the movies; for the latter he received a Writers Guild of America Award. He also wrote the screenplays for* Until They Sail *(1957),* The Nun's Story *(1959), and* The Sand Pebbles *(1966) and is the author of two novels,* After *(1973) and* Getting Up and Going Home *(1978). In 1980 he was elected to the Theater*

Hall of Fame, and he was awarded the William Inge Award in 1985. This interview took place on December 11, 1991.

▶ ─── ◀

Interviewer: Why did you become a playwright?

Anderson: That's a long story. I had other things in mind. Somebody once said life is what happens while you're making other plans. My father was a businessman. If you know *I Never Sang for My Father*, that is essentially my father's story. He was an orphan kid who one day saw an advertisement for a free course in typing and shorthand at the Underwood Typewriter Factory. He took the course, became a stenographer at about the age of seventeen, and worked his way up to being vice-president of the biggest copper company in the world. He retired in the unfortunate year of 1929 and lost all his money. He never wanted us (I have an older brother) to be businessmen, and I didn't want to be a businessman either, listening to what went on at our dinner table. He wanted us to have professions. I must say my poor father never thought my writing was a profession. I wrote poetry; I was the Harvard class poet. I also was a singer; I was a soloist with various glee clubs. I thought I was going to be a musician, but my parents took care of that. They had some important musicians in to hear me sing one Sunday afternoon. They said, "It's a very nice voice, but it's not worth giving your life to," so that was the end of that. I don't even sing in the bathtub now!

   I was acting in undergraduate plays at Harvard, and one day a fellow student said, "How would you like to go across the river to Boston and try out for a part in a play at a girls' school?" I felt that was wonderful. I had been very lonely my freshman year at Harvard. So I went over, and lo and behold, I fell in love with the director, who was ten years older than I was. She was a graduate of the Yale Drama School and had attended the Royal Academy of Dramatic Arts in London. I found my life and my wife in one fell swoop. We started on a scandalous relationship; Harvard didn't care as long as I got her out of my room by eight o'clock. They somehow thought we couldn't do before eight what they assumed we were going to do after eight! She had a very lovely apartment on Beacon Hill. I acted in all her plays, and I sang. She did some lovely operettas, like the American premiere of Offenbach's *La Vie Parisienne*; I had a good enough voice to sing in that. But she said I was a better writer than I was an actor or a singer—and she said acting is a miserable life for a man anyway. It's a sexist remark, but she made it. I guess the assumption in those days—I'm talking about the thirties now—was that if a woman didn't make it by her mid-twenties or thirty she could marry, but a man by his mid-thirties, if he hadn't found his career it was pretty tough to switch.

We were married after I got my master's degree, and I began my moon-lighting. I taught at Harvard, I taught at girls' schools. I was writing plays, I was being a husband, I was learning how to be a cook and all those things. I took my orals for my Ph.D. the night before I went away to war; I think they passed me on the assumption that I wouldn't be coming back. But I did come back, and here's where my playwriting career really began. I had been writing plays all along—during the summers and in a creative writing course. I wrote a play somewhere between Iwo Jima and Okinawa, how I don't know. I was more interested in what was going to happen to me after the war than whether or not I was going to be killed. I did not want to go back and finish my Ph.D.; I did not want to write a thesis. Harvard in those days made you write on something at least one hundred years old, and I didn't want to go back. I won a prize for the best play written by a serviceman overseas, and received an NTC–Rockefeller Grant to write plays. After I came back I was asked to teach a playwriting course at the American Theatre Wing, and I said, "I've never taught a course in playwriting," and they said, "You've taught and you've written plays, put them together." So I learned that if you want to learn some-thing, teach it. I'd rush into class every night and say, "Guess what I found out about third acts or first acts or whatever!" Then I got a job writing radio shows, and finally in 1953 *Tea and Sympathy* was produced on Broadway.

Interviewer: You also wrote television in that period, didn't you?

Anderson: Yes. I suppose I was part of the "Golden Age of Television." While I was still in the Pacific, *Come Marching Home,* the play that won the award, was done at the University of Iowa. E. C. Mabie was the big guru in drama in the Middle West in those days, and he did it; and then it was done at the Blackfriars' Guild, a Catholic theatre (a very good Catholic theatre) off-Broadway.

Interviwer: You also worked with Hallie Flanagan, didn't you? For those of you who don't know, Hallie Flanagan ran the Federal Theatre Project during the Depression.

Anderson: We never worked together. I was overseas when my play won the prize (she had been one of the judges), and I was overseas when it was done at Iowa; but she and my first wife, Phyllis, went out to Iowa to see the production, and the director took sick, and Hallie and my first wife directed it. The Rockefeller Grant was worth two thousand dollars, a lot of money in those days. I was in touch with her all during that time. I was having a terrible time writing a new play. She had been instrumental in giving me the two thousand dollars, and she wrote me these very comforting letters saying, "We really don't expect a play; just write. We're investing in your talent."

Interviwer: You went to work with John Gassner?

Anderson: That was part of the deal. The fellowship required that I had to check in with some professor. John Gassner was teaching at the New School for Social Research, and I took a course under him. He became my mentor actually. He said something very important to me once. He was also story consultant for Columbia Pictures, and I used to go to his office in New York, and he'd lie down on his couch, a short little man only about so big, and he said, "You know, you're not angry enough about anything. That's the problem with your plays; you're not passionately enough involved." Columbia Pictures was not interested in any of my work, but he was a staunch supporter, and he put three of my plays into his *Best Plays* anthologies.

Interviwer: He later on went on to be a professor at the Yale School of Drama for a long time, didn't he?

Anderson: Largely because of my wife. My wife and Mollie Kazan, who had both been Yale graduates, campaigned for him, and he became the Sterling Professor of Playwriting.

Interviwer: Could you talk about that period of time, the late forties, early fifties, when you were doing television? What was the role of the writer in those days? Have you been writing television recently?

Anderson: A little bit, yes.

Interviwer: What were the differences? You just did a special. Compare that to what you were doing then.

Anderson: The special I did, *The Last Act Is a Solo,* was a one-act play done on Arts & Entertainment Television on a program called "General Motors Playwrights' Theater." Television in the early fifties was very much like Andy Hardy, like "let's do a show." It was very informal. It was live television, as you know (those of you who are old enough). Live television was extremely exciting because you were watching it on your tube but you knew that somebody might fall dead on camera and sometimes did. I remember I was talking to Princess Grace much later, and we were comparing days in early television because she was an early television star. She was doing something at NBC where the set was shaped like a football field and the cameras roamed up and down the center. All along the side were the sets. If I were going to have a person in one scene and then in another scene, I had to be careful they had time to change their costumes. She said one day she was changing down to the buff. Why she should have to change down to the buff, I have no idea; but there she was in the buff, and she looked up and there was an NBC guided tour: "Hi, Grace!"

Live TV was done much more as you would do a play. First of all, we rehearsed it for two or three weeks, the same way we would a stage play. Then the last couple of days the camera people came in and got their camera angles. Then we rehearsed it live, and then it was finally shot. It was pretty scary, I'll tell you. One week I had the Lunts in a play, Margaret Sullavan in another, and Kim Hunter and Lloyd Bridges in a third. It's extraordinary for a young writer. I got out of the war at about twenty-eight, but that's young to be working that way. As to nowadays, I recently had a show done called *Absolute Strangers,* which was a big show done on CBS this spring about abortion. I had nothing to do with it except to write the script. It's all being done "over there." You can't see what's going on.

I remember, when I was doing *The Sand Pebbles* with Robert Wise, he was screen-testing a girl. I looked at her (I was far enough away so I couldn't be heard) and I said, "What are you wasting your money on her for?" He said, "Wait until you see her on film." And she was marvelous on film. So there's no sense in the writer watching a setup; you don't know what it's going to look like with a camera here, a camera there, another camera somewhere else. I can't step up to the director and say, "You know, I don't like the angle of that shot." There's no time, in the first place. That television show that was done this spring by CBS cost four million dollars, so there's no time to do that. The other show was done on what's called tape. *The Last Act Is a Solo* with Olympia Dukakis was very much like old-time television because you were sitting in a large closed-in room with five or six screens in front of you. The actors are someplace way down the hall, and each one of these screens represents a camera. You can rehearse; we rehearsed for two weeks the same way you would rehearse a play. Then the director can say, "Well, camera one, camera two." It's just like a play.

Interviwer: You've written for radio, for television, for movies, for theatre; you were also a novelist.

Anderson: I wrote a musical once, too.

Interviwer: Oh, that I didn't know. Some of your plays have been adapted; you've adapted some of your own. *I Never Sang for My Father* was a play, then adapted as a movie. What were the differences with your own plays? That one you conceived of first as a movie, but it was done as a play first and then as a movie. What were the differences in your writing of it, between the stage and the movie?

Anderson: *I Never Sang for My Father* was conceived of as a movie because I was tired of the theatre at that time and had had no luck in it for a while. I wrote a movie about my father called "The Tiger"; I always thought of my father as a tiger. I gave it to Fred Zinnemann, with whom I'd done *The Nun's Story* with Audrey Hepburn; he flew with it to London and called me from the airport. He said, "This is the best thing you've ever done; I'm going to do a movie with Spencer Tracy playing the old man." Of course, that pleased me no end, and Spencer Tracy read it and said he didn't want to play the old man. Then I gave it to Kazan, who had done *Tea and Sympathy*; he was in Europe making a movie and he said, "This is the best thing you've ever done. Will you turn it into a play for Lincoln Center?" They were just getting going. When he came back he said, "We have nobody to play the old man." Then John Frankenheimer, a very fine movie director who did *Seven Days in May* and *The Manchurian Candidate,* said he would like to do the movie with Freddie March playing the old man. That delighted me. But he didn't do anything about it for months, and then finally he said, "I can't do it." So I sat down and wrote the play myself.

Nobody wanted to do *I Never Sang for My Father;* they said it was too shattering. Who wanted to go see a play about old age and what you do with an old father and a father loving a son and so forth? It was finally on the point of being done when suddenly Martin Manulis, who produced "Playhouse 90" in the early days of television, said CBS had asked him to come back to do a television show and he wanted it to be "The Tiger." I said, "'The Tiger' is no longer 'The Tiger'; it's now *I Never Sang for My Father,* and we're about to go into production." He said, "Wait till you hear the cast, and they've all agreed. Spencer Tracy will play the father, Katharine Hepburn will play the mother, Richard Widmark will play the son." He assumed that my wife Teresa Wright would want to play the daughter. My producer said, "With a cast like that, let it go." Manulis called me back in two weeks and said CBS turned it down as "too shattering"—so there you are.

I'll tell you some of the problems that developed as we went along. The new wife is in the movie; she was in the original movie, but she is not in the play. She got eliminated from the play, but when we came to do the movie we wanted her back in again. The director felt she opened the story more; that's a phrase they use a lot. The ending of the play did not work as written. The actors played it through, and Hal Holbrook, one of the actors, Alan Schneider, the director, and my producer, Gilbert Cates, said, "Bob, it doesn't end right." It ended with the new wife there, and they had given the father, who was now a widower, a birthday present, pajamas or something. As she gave it to him, she kissed him on the cheek, and he said, "On the lips, my dear, on the lips." At that point, the son turned to the audience and said, "That night I left my father's house forever," because this was castration. Always during the story and during my father's life, I was the little boy. I drank Dubonnet while he drank six-to-one martinis. I didn't know about life and so on.

Now, nobody can *tell* the playwright to change anything. It's in our contract. I *did not* change the story. The son still left the father. I went home that night and by the grace of God, about three days from the opening in Philadelphia, maybe a few more days, I sat down and I said, "Okay, Dad, let's have the scene we never had," and I wrote the scene that saved the play, the confrontation scene between the father and the son, which is a twenty-minute scene at the end of the play. Then I had to go and tell the actress that she was no longer in the play, that we had cut her out, which was a terrible thing to do. The producer wouldn't do it, the director wouldn't do it; she was my friend, so I had to do it. Her name was already on the billboards.

I've only had a few movies of my own work done. *Tea and Sympathy* was nowhere near as good a movie as it was a play because of censorship problems. We had the same cast: we had Deborah Kerr and John Kerr and Leif Erickson. Movies lose the humor. *I Never Sang for My Father* has a great deal of humor in it. That character is a very funny character, in addition to being a rather terrifying character. Melvyn Douglas gave a marvelous performance, but it's different. Audiences laugh at him in the play, and it gets very quiet when it's important to; but the movies don't do it. *Tea and Sympathy* has a lot of humor that never came across.

A play exists halfway between the stage and the audience, and that's why the show is different every single night. Brooks Atkinson used to say people get out of a play what they bring to it. If you bring the problem of a father and a son or the *Tea and Sympathy* problem or the bed problem in *You Know I Can't Hear You When the Water's Running* or any of those problems, you contribute, you're part of the show. The French have a phrase about going to the theatre; it's assister au théâtre. Assister is to be present at—but I like to translate it as "assist." The movie goes on whether you're there or not, and you know it, so you go to sleep; you're not participating at all, whereas you are important to a play.

Interviwer: When you were writing about your own father, what kind of changes were you going through? How were you affected emotionally then and later during the rehearsal period?

Anderson: To tell you the truth, it's more difficult for me to see it than it was for me to write it. I have a very hard time seeing that movie, and a very hard time when I see revivals of the play, because I get very emotionally involved. Obviously I was emotionally involved when I wrote the famous last line: "That night I left my father's house forever. What did it matter if he never loved me or I never loved him. Perhaps she was right but when I hear the word 'father' it matters." The difficulty in the writing of it is having these very strong emotions and channeling them into your craft. You bring up something which we should discuss. I went into analysis when my first wife died, and I said something very significant to the doctor. I said, "Don't take my longing from me." I wanted the pain removed; it wasn't, of course. When we were doing *I Never Sang for My Father* (the movie), we took it around to show to people before we released it. I would talk about my father, and obviously I'm still moved by him and I was moved then, and somebody said, "How long ago did your father die?" I said, "About ten years," and they said, "And you're still moved by it?" I said, "I hope I always am." I'm moved by my wife's death; I'm moved by all the things that have happened to me, because this is what we write about.

It's hard for me to re-create what I really felt during all the writing and rewriting of the play. I certainly know that when I wrote that last scene I was very upset because it released a great many things that I had never said and he had never said to me. I knew that he might have said them, and I knew that I might have said them to him, so that was a catharsis in a certain sense. The important thing is emotion recollected in tranquility, as Wordsworth says. At the same time, Robert Graves says, "Tranquility is of no creative use." The important thing is to be able to back away and to make you cry. My crying is not important. I have cried; the important thing is for me to make you cry.

My first wife produced a play called *Come Back, Little Sheba*, by Bill Inge. It was his first play on Broadway, and it was dedicated to her. Shirley Booth played it, and she was magnificent in it. There's one great scene where after her husband goes after her with an ax and leaves the house, she calls up her father and asks if she, a middle-aged woman, can come home; it's a terrifying scene. There would be times when we'd go and be so moved that we couldn't go backstage and see Shirley for a while. When we'd finally go back, she would say, "It was terrible tonight, wasn't it? A dry night." At other times, we weren't moved at all, and we would go back and she would say, "You can't come in." She had moved herself. Hemingway said something terrific; he said, "The first draft the writer gets everything, and the reader gets nothing. The second draft the writer gets a little, the reader gets a little. Every draft after that, the reader gets everything and the writer doesn't get anything."

Interviwer: Don't you have more control over what happens on the stage because it's word-centered and you're the one who has control over the words? There's no camera, and there's no technician up there colorizing it or doing whatever they're doing, and there's no musical background.

Anderson: You get your vision much more. Let me give you an example which is not word-oriented. At the end of *Tea and Sympathy*, the woman comes up to the boy in the dormitory. He has been called homosexual, and he has gone to the town whore to try to prove that he isn't, and so forth. She comes up there to his little bit of a room. He has a lovely scene with her where he says, everybody knew it, now I know it, and so on. Finally she gets up to leave, and she sees how desperate he is. He's lying on his bed, a little cot, and she turns and realizes that something has to be done; so she closes the door and bolts it. The boy turns around when he hears the bolt. Deborah stood by the bedside and held out her hand with her palm up. The boy turns and looks; he's stunned, and very slowly he reaches his hand up and takes hers as she unbuttons the famous three buttons. When Joan Fontaine took over, I was sitting alone with Kazan in the audience while they were doing rehearsals. Joan Fontaine held out her hand with her palm down and I said, "It looks like Queen Victoria: 'Kiss my hand.'" That's the sort of thing you work on. It's like old radios used to have three dials and you were constantly switching those dials. If you changed this, then you had to change that. A little thing like that makes a big difference in the climactic moment in the play.

Interviwer: You much prefer theatre to the other media, don't you?

Anderson: You have more control, not in the sense of more power, which you do have also. As I mentioned earlier, the Dramatists Guild contract gives the author complete control over casting and choice of director; nobody can change a line. That's news to a number of people. They don't know that the author has that much power. But you also have control over your work. You have four weeks of rehearsal with the entire play, with the cast in front of you, and let's say a scene becomes tedious. You can say, "Well, I'll cut that scene and take the information that's in it and put it someplace else." When you're doing a movie, first of all a movie is not shot in sequence. They may do the last scene first and the first scene last. They might be working in a set that's very elaborate, and you see the scene and you say, "I wish we could cut that." It's too late; you can cut it, but you cannot take the information out of that scene and put it someplace else. I remember when Bob Wise and I were doing *Sand Pebbles* with Steve McQueen, at the opening he came up to me and said, "My God, can't we get ten minutes out of it someplace?" It's too late.

Interviwer: What about a play as opposed to a novel?

Anderson: Of course, in a novel you have complete control. I just like the play form best. I've always liked the play form. I only wrote two novels when I was dealing with subject matter which I thought I couldn't get into the theatre. A lot of scenes took place in bed, which we haven't yet been able to master in the theatre. I love dialogue; I think I fell in love with dialogue first. I remember my brother, who is four years older than I am, came home one Christmas vacation and he left a book. I took it to my mother after I'd seen it and I said, "What is this?" She said, "That's a play." I'd never seen a play in script form before; I'd seen Shakespeare, that's about all. She said, "That's a play," and I became fascinated by dialogue.

Interviwer: What about the initial production process? Do you find that a hindrance to you as a playwright or a help?

Anderson: It's very exciting. When Marc Connolly, a marvelous play-wright who wrote a wonderful play called *Green Pastures,* was ninety years old and was on his deathbed, he was in a coma. He came out of this coma for one second and he said, "We've raised the money. We're going into rehearsal tomorrow." There's that sort of excitement about going into rehearsal, in this day and age particularly. The production problem is very difficult because you have to find the people who will realize your play, and if you have the wrong director, or the director is not doing the same play you wrote, you're in trouble.

Interviwer: What is the importance of actors of a high caliber for the play in concept, in rehearsal, and in its artistic success?

Anderson: It's never important in terms of concept because I've never written a play for an actor. A lot of people thought I wrote *Tea and Sympathy* for Deborah Kerr, but I didn't. A lot of people say, "I want an actor. I don't want a star." I want stars who are actors, and I think the people I've been fortunate enough to have in my plays are all stars and they're all actors. I would not be interested in a play just for star value to bring in an audience—because if they're not good the play would be a failure. My friend Pete Gurney, a neighbor of mine who wrote *The Dining Room* and *Love Letters* and a number of other fine plays, says, "Why do you want stars? Get somebody else." Well, I noticed when he did *Love Letters* he got more stars than anybody else has ever had in the American theatre, be-cause those parts did require stars. My plays are obviously done by non-stars after they get through with the major runs, but I've just been very lucky. As I said, the playwright has absolute control over casting, so we can get fine actors. I've never had to compromise on an actor; that's a very lucky thing for me to say, but I've worked very very hard on it.

Let me give you a small example. When we were doing *Tea and Sympathy,* my first play on Broadway, I knew Elia Kazan because, as I said earlier, he had gone to Yale Drama School with my first wife. He did not want to use Deborah Kerr, and Deborah Kerr did not want to do the play. I had sent the play to Deborah because I did a radio show with her. As I told you before, I wrote a program called "The Theatre Guild on the Air" where we did adaptations of plays, novels, and movies for such actors as Helen Hayes, Rex Harrison, Richard Burton, Ingrid Bergman, and Deborah Kerr. That's where I learned to love stars. When she left to go back to Hollywood, I said, "Someday I'd love to do a play with you" and she said, "Well, I'm going to Hollywood forever, so we'll see." So I wrote *Tea and Sympathy,* and I sent it to her immediately. This was long before I had a production. I thought she would just be perfect in this part, and she wrote back and said that she thought it was a lovely play but that she thought it was the boy's play, not the wife's play. I disagreed with her, and then, of course, when the Playwrights' Company came to do the play, I told Kazan that I would like Deborah Kerr. He said that he did not want Deborah Kerr because, he said, "I want this to be the discovery of you, the playwright, not a Hollywood star"—which was very generous.

We saw everybody else, all the actors he had worked with, all very fine actresses like Kim Hunter and Patricia Neal and Julie Harris and so on, and I kept saying, "I want Deborah Kerr." We finally had cast everybody else and he said, "What are we going to do?" And I said, "I wish you'd go out and meet Deborah." I got in touch with Deborah, and she said yes, she would have tea with him. She had tea with him, and he sent me a telegram saying, "You're absolutely right and she's going to do the play." The play would have been quite different without her. Even though Ingrid did it in Paris and it was done by some other very fine actresses, Deborah put a stamp on that play. In terms of production, in terms of rehearsals, it's marvelous to work with stars. Deborah played that play for two years, and it was always perfect. She played it intensely every night; nobody dared clown around, nobody dared say, "Why don't we do it this way or that way?" That's the way it was played. The star of the play sets the stamp on the production. She did one year in New York and one year on the road. I've had no problems with stars at all.

I had one problem with Henry Fonda, and it is a great story. In *Silent Night, Lonely Night,* we were in Boston, and we came back one time from the theatre and he said, "I'm having a terrible time with that long speech. It's very hard for me to say." So I said, "What's the problem?" And he said, "It's difficult." I said, "It's supposed to be difficult. It's supposed to be a difficult speech." He said, "Well, listen, I've been a very good fellow. How about easing it up for me?" I would never do that for anybody else, but Hank had been a very good fellow, so I eased it up for him, and that night he played it that way. He came back and he said, "You're absolutely right. It should be difficult for me to say." That's a good actor. I've never had any bad experiences with a star in the theatre.

Interviwer: When you're working with an actor, have you ever made changes—or have you ever learned something from an actor in a rehearsal process that has opened up something about your play?

Anderson: People always say, "Weren't you absolutely thrilled to have the various stars and performers that you've had?" And I say, "I always visualized them as perfect productions anyway, so they didn't surprise me at all when they did it brilliantly; that's what I had expected." I always trust what an actor says. If an actor says, "I'm having trouble with a line," I worry about it. You have to listen to actors. They have an instinct for what they can say, what they are, what they're doing. I have not had too many of them come up and say, "I'm having trouble." I remember when we started rehearsing *Tea and Sympathy* with Kazan we had a reading which was thrilling, sitting around on chairs, and then he said, "You get lost for about two or three days. I didn't watch you make your mistakes, I'd rather you not watch me making mine." So I came in after the first three days and he said, "We have some things to talk over with you," and I began to tremble, even though, as I say, we have a contract. When I used to teach playwriting, I used to say half the job of being a playwright is writing a play, the other half is getting along with people. Which is true in life, right? So I thought, here it comes. They wanted to change things like a syllable, "I didn't come in" to "I did not come in." It was ridiculous. That's how much Kazan protected that script, and also I have to tell you the actors loved the script, and we did very, very little work.

Marty Balsam gave us a little trouble. He's a wonderful actor; he won the Tony Award for *You Know I Can't Hear You When the Water's Running*. But Alan Schneider, the director, had trouble with him. He kept trying to improvise the lines, and Alan said, "You know, we like the lines." Philip Barry, a famous playwright of some years ago, was auditioning somebody, and they started to make up the lines, and he stopped them and he said, "The lines have already been tested for sound." Finally, although if Marty were to talk to you he'd probably tell you he invented all the lines, he came back to doing the lines as written.

There's another funny story which I sometimes tell about Alan Webb, who played the father in *I Never Sang for My Father*. It was a brilliant performance; he was nominated for a Tony that year, but Marty Balsam beat him out. My father always thought he was very manly, and he would always order a very dry martini, six to one, with a twist. About the fourth day of rehearsal, Alan Schneider said to me, "Alan doesn't want to say 'with a twist.' Do you want to make a problem of it?" I said, "I don't want to make a problem of it, but I'm just curious. He doesn't lisp." (I've had very good actors that I've had to work on lines with because they lisp.) Schneider said, "No, he just doesn't want to say it." I said, "It's all right with me if it's 'a very dry martini, six to one.'" So that's the way he rehearsed it, and that's the way he played it on the road. We came in on opening night in New York and he said, "I'd like a very dry martini, six to one, with a twist." Actors sometimes have to feel that they make the part their own, that they do something that puts a stamp on it, whatever it is. And you have to go along with that.

Interviwer: What terrifies you?

Anderson: What terrifies me sometimes is not having anything to write about; that terrifies me. I think there's always a sense of stage fright when you really start to write the dialogue. I spend months going over material. I call it fishing with my thoughts or my ideas. Every day I sit down to see what fish I draw up out of the water and I never look at the fish of the day before. Then I say, "Okay, I'm going to write the dialogue," because I don't like to rewrite very much. I have rewritten, of course; we all have to rewrite, but the first time is very important. It terrifies me if I get it wrong the first time; that's scary. Also, opening night terrifies you, and reading the reviews terrifies you; but there's nothing you can do about it. I think a playwright is terrified, has stage fright (whatever you want to call it), when he says, "I'm about to try to dredge something out of me that I don't even know is there, and I hope to God it's good."

Interviwer: *Tea and Sympathy* was produced in 1953 by the Playwrights' Company, which was started by five or six of the leading playwrights of the thirties, who by that time had been writing less and had aged.

Anderson: The company when I joined it was Maxwell Anderson, Robert Sherwood, Elmer Rice, Roger Stevens, and John Wharton.

Interviwer: Roger Stevens had come in and basically revitalized it, hadn't he?

Anderson: Well, he brought money.

Interviwer: And leadership—financial leadership—and brought you in.

Anderson: The sad thing is, I am their age now. As a matter of fact, I'm older than Bob Sherwood was when he died. As you get older, it's difficult, it doesn't always work. I'm struggling with a new play right now, and it's extremely difficult. None of them had a good play on while I was a member. *The Bad Seed* was on, and that was a thing that Max Anderson didn't pay much attention to; he was rather ashamed of it. It was a success; it got him out of some very serious tax problems. Sherwood did not have a play until we did one posthumously. Elmer Rice had a poor play called *The Winner.* They hoped that I would bring young writers in. I couldn't find any young writers who wanted to come in, because by that time the Dramatists Guild had the contract that I was telling you about: control over casting, no words changed. The playwrights had formed the Playwrights' Company because they couldn't get the control they wanted. The Theatre Guild, which was a very good producer, wasn't giving them the control; so they formed the company for themselves. I could bring nobody else in. I wrote *Tea and Sympathy, All Summer Long,* and *Silent Night, Lonely Night,* but by 1960 Elmer and I were the only surviving playwrights in the company—so we disbanded.

Interviwer: Let's talk about your process of writing. How do you start out, once you have your idea for a play?

Anderson: Creativity is very difficult to talk about. I can talk about it ex post facto: this is the way I must have done it. It's pretty hard to remember exactly how I did do it. As to *Tea and Sympathy*, I came across a note in an old notebook of mind the other day which said, "Let's try the older-younger love story again." Obviously, I was in love and had married a woman ten years older than I was; it was a potent story, and I wanted to tell it in some terms. I did not originally tell it in terms of the present *Tea and Sympathy*. I told it in terms of a boys' school, but the woman was the professor's daughter, not his wife. The conflict was between a young student and a young master who had come back from the war very much embittered. It was quite a different play except for the general background. It was the McCarthy period; people forget about that. I had had a number of friends who had gone through the grinder and been called dirty names. How does a person prove he's not? Also, it was my father. My father was very macho. He was not macho in build; he was a slight man, a little shorter than I. But he believed in the tough guy and the hard hitter, and I guess somewhere along the line I wanted to write a play about, as Laura says in the last act of *Tea and Sympathy*: "Manliness is not just swaggering and swearing and mountain climbing; manliness is also tenderness and gentleness and consideration." That was news in 1953. I think it's still news to a certain extent. The scene in the play where the roommate tries to teach the boy how to walk happened to me at Harvard. It was the reverse; I was teaching another boy how to walk. He was in my house at Harvard, and he was being taunted, and he came and knocked on my door one night and I said, "I don't know what they're all talking about. Maybe it's the way you walk." Can you imagine? So out of my trying to teach him how to walk came that wonderful scene. The bits and pieces come from everything.

Interviwer: Could you talk about the daringness of *Tea and Sympathy* at the time that it was written?

Anderson: It was turned down by every producer in New York City saying it would be a succès de scandale. The Theatre Guild, to whom I owed a great deal because I had done their radio and television shows, thought it was a fine play, but they were scared to death of it. My agent didn't like the play, and she handed it back to me and said that it was out to one other company. That was the company that did it, the Playwrights' Company, a very distinguished company. There were always people who walked out. During the last scene, which nowadays is still a very delicate scene, on the road coming in we'd get little titters, a little laughter, and Deborah Kerr and John Kerr were very upset by it. Kazan said, "You are talking about things on stage that most people don't talk about in their own bedrooms, so you've got to expect it." The nervous laughter died out pretty soon when people knew the play and knew its quality. I didn't think it was daring. Nothing happens onstage.

The biggest problem was when we came to make the movie. Every movie company wanted to make the movie, and the censors wouldn't let them make it. The censoring organization was called the Breen Office in those days. Samuel Goldwyn pleaded with me to change this, change that; finally Metro-Goldwyn-Mayer decided to do it. I don't know if you've seen the movie, but I'm a little bit embarrassed by it. It's still an important movie; we devised a prologue and an epilogue. It was about to open at Radio City Music Hall and the Legion of Decency, a group of Catholics who determine what you may see and what you may not see, said they would give us a condemned rating and it could not open at Radio City Music Hall. They sent me around to talk to the Legion of Decency, some monsignors and some lay Catholic people, and they said, "You have to write in the word 'sin' someplace." I said, "I can't do it, that's not what the play is about." They said, "She committed adultery," and I said, "Of course she committed adultery, but the marriage was destroyed." They went on and on and on, and so finally I said, "I have to make sure you understand. When he thought he was homosexual he went to the town whore and he failed. And he found a knife and tried to commit suicide and failed." I said to them, "Which would you rather have, her commit adultery, or him commit suicide?" They said, "Oh, he wouldn't do that." I said, "That's for me to say, not for you to say; it's my character." So they backed down.

They're thinking constantly of making it over again and bringing it up to date. You don't have to bring it up to date; it's very up to date right now with all the gay-bashing that goes on around New York. I go to schools and they tell me that the play is still very apropos. Ten years ago I represented the American screen artists at the Moscow Film Festival, and I thought that when you signed on for the film festival, you signed on for the duration. But a lot of other Americans came for their picture and left. So I was taken up by the Norwegians, who had done many of my plays. The Russians took us out every morning to see the children's villages and the collective farms and so on—propaganda. One morning we were on one of these buses and I heard one of the Norwegians behind me say, "*Tea and Sympathy?*" And I thought, "Well, obviously, someone has asked who I am." The rest of that bus trip, people came up the aisle and said, "*Tea and Sympathy?*" in various languages, shook my hand, and left. It must have been the movie, because it was not produced that widely on the stage. *You Know I Can't Hear You When the Water's Running* is a much more shocking play.

Interviwer: Do you sit down and get an idea? Do you sit down and just start writing the dialogue?

Anderson: Let me tell you two stories. When we did the movie of *I Never Sang for My Father,* we shot part of it in an old studio in uptown New York City, and Melvyn Douglas, Gene Hackman, and I were driven back and forth by a taxi driver, actually a transport worker's union driver. On the third day, when we dropped Mel and Gene, he said to me, "I know what those two fellows do. What do you do?" I said, "I wrote the script." And he said, "Imagine knowing all those words!" Isn't that a marvelous phrase? Sidney Kingsley, who wrote *Men in White* and *Dead End* and a number of plays, had been working on a play for a long time; so I said, "Sidney, how is the play coming?" and he said, "It's almost finished. I'm going to start to write the dialogue tomorrow." Playwriting is spelled w-r-i-t-i-n-g and a playwright is spelled w-r-i-g-h-t; in other words, to construct. I always hesitate to talk about this because people think it's like filling in a coloring book.

I do not know my play completely when I sit down to write, but I know my ending. I know what I'm building up to. As with *I Never Sang for My Father,* the ending is still the same; in other words, the emotional effect is still the same, because the son leaves the father under basically the same circumstances. The plot changes. The story is the relationship between the characters and how it changes, the plot is what changes it, and my plot at the end changed just for that one scene. I keep journals. When I feel I want to write a play, have time to write a play, have something urgent to say, I look through my journals. I make notes from them. I will day after day throw my idea or my enthusiasm or whatever it is essentially at my desk, and I'll put those aside and I won't look at those notes again. I may do that for a month or two until something crystallizes in story form—a beginning, a middle, an end. Let's say I know I'm going from Boston to Washington; I don't know whether I'm going to go by way of New York or some other town that you can go through, but I know generally that's where I'm going to go.

I don't write any dialogue, because that's the fun of it. The fun of it is: I've got a man here and he's got to fall in love with this woman by the end of the scene. I may know vaguely what they're going to talk about, but I could write a great love scene about a piece of soap. I did this in the bed scene in *You Know I Can't Hear You When the Water's Running.* It's called "The Footsteps of Doves." Years before, my wife and I were trying to choose beds, after we had been married a certain number of years; and in a bed store I heard this couple talking about which bed to buy. Their whole lives were revealed by what beds they wanted: a single bed, or a double bed, or a large bed. So I said, "Someday I'll write that," and I did. This whole marriage was revealed humorously, funny but also sad, in the choice of which one wanted the double beds, which one wanted to go with the single beds, and so forth.

Let me tell you the origin of one of the other stories in *You Know I Can't Hear You When the Water's Running*. They're four "dirty" one-act plays which nobody wanted to do. It's my greatest success; it's playing in repertory at the Czech national theatre and so on, but nobody wanted to do it. My first wife died, and three years later I married Teresa Wright, who had been married before. Her daughter lived with us. We kept her house in California, because in the summertime she'd go out to do a movie and I'd go out and do something. One morning at breakfast in New York, I said, "Teresa, how would you like to go? We can go out the southern route, the northern route—any way you'd like to go. We have plenty of time to drive." And she said, "I don't know, but let's make sure we go by way of Denver and stay at that hotel where we had that great night together." And I said, "I've never been to Denver in my life." Of course, she blushed and called me a bastard and a few other things, and I said, "If you had mentioned any smaller city, but about the big cities I've got a pretty good idea." So I went to my study that day and I said, "You know, I bet if we were old enough"—close to the age I'm approaching now—"I would have said, 'Oh, Denver, that was great.'" In other words, I would have become all the men in her life and she would have become all the women in my life.

There is the creative leap, the hip-hop from what was said at the breakfast table to making it into something which is more meaningful. It's only a fifteen-minute play. I wasn't writing a play about people who can't remember anything, I was writing about that idea. These two old people sit in rockers. It's the play of mine that is done most in the world: it's simple, all you need is two rockers. They chatter on and they can't remember who they were married to, who they had their children by, who were their lovers, where they lived, and so on. One minute one person remembers, and the next minute the other person doesn't remember. It's like a Bach fugue; you can't have them forget just anything. He's got to forget what she remembered two speeches ago and so on, and at the end they say, "Let's be quiet for a moment." They rock quietly, and they take each other's hands, and he says, "I remember Venice." (I used Venice instead of Denver.) So that is how a story materializes.

Interviwer: Those are one-act plays, and you've written some wonderful one-act plays as well as full-length plays. Isn't writing one-act plays very, very hard? A full-length play has its own difficulties, but because one-act plays are basically short doesn't mean they're easier. Aren't there some writers who can write one-act plays extremely well but can't write longer ones?

Anderson: It's the same with short story writers. John Cheever was a brilliant short story writer but he couldn't write a novel.

Interviwer: Do you always know when you've got a one-act play or when you've got a longer play?

Anderson: I didn't pay too much attention to one-act plays after my learning period. Everybody starts out with one-act plays, of course. I didn't come back to them until the sixties with *You Know I Can't Hear You When the Water's Running* because nobody wanted to do *I Never Sang for My Father*. Jerry Lawrence and his partner Bob Lee set up an organization called the American Playwrights Theater. The idea was to get the plays of established playwrights into the regional theatres before Broadway rather than after. Mine was the first play done. It was called *The Days Between* and was done in Rochester, where my brother was dean of the medical school. I had gone to the opening night on a Friday, and it went very well. I didn't see it Saturday night, but I called them before I left and said, "How did it go on Saturday night?" There was some hesitation on the other end of the phone and I said, "Don't worry. Nobody has ever liked my plays on Saturday night." They said, "Well, it didn't go so well. People had been drinking. They had been at football games." Nobody liked to play my plays on Saturday night. I was traveling down to Baltimore, where I had a talk at Center Stage the next day, and I was trying to think why people don't like to see my plays on Saturday night. I hate to be called a sensitive writer, just like I don't want my obituary to say "Author of *Tea and Sympathy* Dies" when there are other plays. I remembered something that John Gassner had said in an introduction to a play of mine called *Silent Night, Lonely Night*. He said, "Robert Anderson is a gentleman in an age of assassins."

I got up to give my talk at Center Stage, and I started to talk about that and I said, "I guess you don't want to go out with a gentleman on Saturday night, so my next play is going to be about this guy standing in his bathroom door naked and telling his wife, 'You know I can't hear you when the water's running.'" Laughter—so I went home to write what I first called "Four Plays for Saturday Night," but nobody wanted to do them. Nobody has ever wanted to do any of my plays. They didn't want "Four Plays for Saturday Night" because they thought the audience would think they only played on Saturday night. In those days people were not doing one-act plays, so they didn't want to emphasize that. That's how *You Know I Can't Hear You When the Water's Running* was born.

I'd never written plays like those before, fifteen-minute plays. I think you just have to plan them more. George S. Kaufman was a famous playwright and director in the thirties and forties, and somebody asked him to read a play because they were having trouble with the last act. He said, "I'll tell you the trouble without reading it; it's the first act." I've been called in as a play doctor. I've never doctored a play, but a lot of my friends who were having trouble on the road would say, "Would you come up and look at the play?" I'd say, "There's nothing I can do." They say, "Fix the ending," and I say, "I cannot fix the ending because there is nothing to build to." Lloyd Richards, who directs August Wilson's plays, has another phrase. He says that the audience should have an appointment at the end of the play. You're leading toward a payoff in very common terms. Structure is storytelling, and you are building toward something at the end of the play. That's why I don't write until I know what I'm going to do some way or other at the end of the play.

Interviwer: Is it difficult getting young playwrights not to be mechanical and to allow their own surprises, to have a sense that dialogue is defined by the action that is taking place?

Anderson: I say I write to find out what I didn't know I knew, to find out what I didn't know I felt. I was blocked after my wife died, and I had lunch with John Steinbeck. I said, "John, you've been blocked; what do you do?" He said, "I write poetry to find my emotions. I'm not a poet, so I throw the poetry away and I write my novel." I went to London, and of course I knew I was going to write something about my wife, because I was devoted to her; so I wrote some poetry about her, and then I wrote *Silent Night, Lonely Night*. In the process, I burst into tears in one scene because it talked about a moment when I had not liked her, and I had never consciously known that there had been such a moment.

I'm in the process now of something interesting. I just finished giving a series of talks and lectures, and I'm going to continue them. But when I sit down to work, something in my subconscious is saying, "I'm not going to open up for you; you're not going to give me full time." It's when you can sit there and say, "I have nothing to do for the next whatever," and then you suddenly write something that makes you cry, and you never knew. That last scene in *I Never Sang for My Father* never happened—it is pure fiction—but it is based on my knowledge of myself, my knowledge of my father, his resentments, and my resentments. I was letting myself go; that scene was written in one night, and that's what happens. I knew what I had to do; I knew that I had to write a scene so that the son would leave the father at the end of the scene. I say that it is an unconscious act within a conscious framework. It cannot be too conscious; you have to allow yourself suddenly to do things.

Interviwer: You said it's important to be passionate about what you write about. Would you care to follow up on that?

Anderson: Yes. Very definitely. I know how to write a play. That's no problem. What I have to wait for or find is something that I'm passionately involved in. Somebody once said that all you need in the theatre is two planks and a passion. All you need to be a playwright is a pen, paper, and a passion. You have to have a story or a feeling or whatever it is that says, "I want you to hear this story." The trouble with a lot of plays is that they are not enough of anything: they are not sad enough, tragic enough, exciting enough, or funny enough. They are a little bit of everything. I don't think you go to the theatre to be *interested*. You go to be passionately involved.

I had a student I was teaching many, many years ago, right after the war. He was a very talented, skillful student, but I was not going to move him to the advanced class. He came down to my apartment and begged to be advanced, and for some reason or other, perhaps I had pictures around my house of my family or whatever, he started to talk about his father. At the end of the hour he said, "Are you going to let me stay on?" I said, "Yes, if you write a play about your father." He said, "My father? He's not interesting." I said, "You've just held me spellbound about your father." He wrote a play about his father that made him a fortune. It's called *A Hole in the Head*, and it played in New York for two years, it played on the road for two years, Frank Sinatra made a movie of it, they made a television series of it, and they made a musical of it. He had a real problem with his father. Tennessee Williams said he wrote about what bugged him.

Interviwer: Have you ever experienced writer's block, and how do you overcome it?

Anderson: I experienced it, as I say, after my first wife died. I think that was for emotional reasons. I'm experiencing it to a certain extent now, although I can't call it writer's block now because I've worked at it for a year. I don't call it really blocked until I go over my hundreds of notes and I say, "Well, that was interesting. I felt that, but I wonder if I still feel that way about it." Everybody has their own way of doing it if they can do it. When I wrote *The Last Act Is a Solo*, I had a writer's block then. I wasn't moved by anything; I really was dead. Finally I said, "Well, does that disturb you?" It did disturb me, so I got up enough emotion about being dead, or feeling dead, and I wrote what I think is one of my best plays, about a woman who wants to commit suicide, an old actress. It's very funny, too.

Interviwer: Do you find it difficult to write women's dialogue, and do you find yourself being conscious of whether or not it's true to a woman's thoughts?

Anderson: I have no problem at all. If I'm famous for anything, I'm famous for women's dialogue. Somebody once said it's as though you're taking dictation. The character is really speaking. I've been around an awful lot of women, as we all have, and I just seem to write women very well. Certain types of men I probably can't write very well because I haven't known them that well. Arthur Miller said he's in every play; well,

I'm in every play. I'm not necessarily the character in every play, but my voice is in every play. I have no problem with dialogue. What I have problem with is story and structure. That's what most people have problems with. If you have the story you assume that the characters are going to talk.

Interviwer: Isn't it difficult getting yourself into a character? It's not sounding like a character; it's the emotion and the life of a character. Isn't getting into a woman like getting into a foreign country?

Anderson: Sometimes when I'm writing, I go away someplace, maybe take a few notes with me; then I write, and I will write the entire play in two or three weeks. I don't go back and correct; that's why I can't use a word processor. I write longhand, and I'm getting arthritis in my hands or something's happening. I don't stop. The important thing is to get the scene going, get them talking, get them working. You can always go back and fix it. I've pushed away from the desk so many times and said, "Nobody is ever going to understand what I've just written because it's so personal." That's exactly what they do understand. There is a price to pay. Ingrid Bergman came over to see a play of mine called *Solitaire/Double Solitaire* and she said, "If I'd been married to you, I would have divorced you." I had a friend who wrote a novel, and his wife came in and saw the manuscript when she shouldn't have. She just read the top two pages, and when he came back she said, "I have to read that novel." He said, "I'm working on it. I don't want any comment." She said, "I have to read it. I won't give you any comment." She read it, and she handed it back to him without any comment, with her wedding ring on top of it. I had somebody that I loved very, very dearly who said, "I cannot live with the intimacy of your writing. I respect you for it, I admire you for it, but. . . ."

It is really getting into the unknown. In the Middle Ages they drew maps of what they knew. Around the edges of what they didn't know they said, "Beyond here are monsters." That's the area in which a good writer is writing. I have to allow myself to write in those areas which are going to offend people or upset people. I would never have written *I Never Sang for My Father* with my father alive, that I can tell you, because that's such a close picture of him. I have never written a nasty picture of anyone, and yet some people say, "That's me, isn't it?" Five women told me after *Solitaire/Double Solitaire*, "I see you finally got me in a play." You use a word from one, a phrase from another, you use something from the family background of another. It is that business of daring. Gertrude Stein wrote something which is very strange because she mixes her metaphors. She said, "Write as though nobody's listening." If you can do that, it takes a lot of courage.

Interviwer: Could you talk about writing the film of *The Nun's Story*?

Anderson: Before my wife died, she had seen a review of *The Nun's Story* and said, "This looks like something you'd be interested in doing." About six months after she died, Fred Zinnemann asked me to read the book of *The Nun's Story.* People wonder how I did it because it's an internal story. I thought it was a beautiful book, and I found it not difficult at all. We did research in the Congo; we went to Belgium and stayed near convents. We would drive Dame Peggy Ashcroft, who played one of the mothers superior, and Audrey Hepburn in these Cadillacs down the back alleys of Paris and let them into convents for the night. Audrey would stay on her knees on the cold floor for eight hours; she was a marvelous role model. Then the next day we'd come and pick them up in the Cadillac and they'd go home, bathe, and we'd take them out to great French restaurants! It was a marvelous experience. They were very happy with the first and second drafts, but I didn't go to the Congo when they shot it. I was writing *Silent Night, Lonely Night* in London. I came back when they came back to Rome and stayed around a while. A writer on the set of a movie is useless, as I tried to explain earlier. It costs thousands of dollars for every shot. The writer can't say, "Hey, wait a minute, I've got a new line" or "Wait a minute, I think that this should be done this way." It's the director's picture from then on.

Interviwer: What ideas would you have for plays today that would be more shocking than *Tea and Sympathy?*

Anderson: We can never have sex onstage. You might as well face that; you simply can't. John Cheever was asked why he didn't have more sex in his short stories and he said, "We all know what happens, don't we?" We don't know what happens. That's why I wrote two novels, one called *After* and the other called *Getting Up and Going Home.* I don't know exactly. There are adulterous relationships, there are people living very happily with husbands that have a lover, there are men very happy with wives who have lovers. A lot of people muddle through with these crazy mixed-up relationships. I was addressing some group once and somebody said, "You're really in favor of adultery, aren't you?" I seem to have written, starting with *Tea and Sympathy,* some stories and plays about adultery. It's a subject that interests me, and I think we could do more with it. If I ever write another, I'll let you know. I hope you will know. I hope you'll hear about it all over the world.

Interviwer: Could you talk a bit about Elia Kazan?

Anderson: I'm very close to him. He's eight years older than I am, but he's my closest friend. He's gone through some terrible situations. Two wives have died, his grandson was killed in a head-on collision (an accident, no drinking involved), and now his son on the West Coast is dying at the age of fifty. He always wanted to be a writer. He told me that when he stopped directing plays and he concentrated on movies, because after my play he did quite a number of movies. He said, "I'm realizing your work in the theatre. In the movies, it is, more or less, my work." That's the legend—that the movie is the director's work, and to a certain extent it is, there's no question about that. I was stunned that the opening night review of *Tea and Sympathy* mentions his name once and mentions my name in about five different paragraphs, whereas he had really dominated the whole rehearsal process. Not so in the movies. Then he made the final jump to wanting to be by himself and write. He was extremely successful. He says, "I know none of you like my novels, but I love sitting morning after morning after morning with the typewriter." He always wanted to be a writer.

Interviwer: Have people forgiven him?

Anderson: I don't think it's a matter of that. Dear God, if they haven't, they ought to stick their heads in a bucket. Yes, there are people who have not, of course. Some people won't talk to me because they know he's my best friend. He has his reasons. I don't know if you've read his autobiography. It's a long, difficult book, but it's marvelous. And he had his reasons.

Interviwer: Could you speak a little more about the writer's voice?

Anderson: Each writer is looking for his own voice. Arthur Miller doesn't sound like Tennessee Williams, doesn't sound like Neil Simon, doesn't sound like Beckett, doesn't sound like Sam Shepard. One of the most difficult things is to find your voice. Several people have said to me, "You haven't written any plays recently." I say, "I'm struggling for a story." They say, "We don't care about the story. We want to hear your voice." It's my response to a situation, my response to a *Tea and Sympathy* situation, my response to an *I Never Sang for My Father* situation. I don't mean this in any arrogant sense, but there is nobody else writing about men and women, I think, as intimately as I write about them. The last scene in *Double Solitaire* is much braver and bolder than *Tea and Sympathy*.

I took a course with Robert Frost once, and he read some of my poetry, and then we had a conference and he said, "Don't be first, be second." Hollywood wants to be first to be second. The minute anything's a hit they make ten like it. With the poet or the writer, it's his own voice. We all start out imitating somebody, because that's what draws us into it. I started out imitating Clifford Odets, Noël Coward, and about four other people because of the dialogue. Finally—and this is what John Gassner was telling me—it doesn't matter, if you're not passionate about something. In other words, you're not writing about something that matters to you. Arthur Miller writes about moral subjects which matter to him; Tennessee wrote about very personal offbeat subjects that mattered to him. It's our choice of material that's part of our voice, and our dialogue. You could never confuse David Mamet with Arthur Miller; it's the voice. You never confuse a Rembrandt with a Renoir or a Miró. It's that special thing that the artist tries to find.

Alice Childress

Born in Charleston, South Carolina, Alice Childress was the great-grand-daughter of Ani, a slave who was freed at age twelve in Charleston on "Juneteenth," or Final Freedom Night, one year after the Emancipation Proclamation. She was raised in New York City by her grandmother Eliza White, who encouraged her to write. Childress wrote stage plays, television dramas, screenplays, and novels, as well as numerous essays. She wrote her first play, Florence, in 1949, while a member of the American Negro Theatre. Her other plays include Just a Little Simple (1950), which was an adaptation of Langston Hughes's Simple Speaks His Mind; Gold Through the Trees (1952); Trouble in Mind (1955); Wedding Band (1966); Wine in the Wilderness (1969); String (1969); Mojo (1970); and The African Garden (1970). She also wrote many plays with music, including Young Martin Luther King (1969), Sea Island Song (1979), Gullah (1984), and Moms (1987), which was based on the life of comedienne "Moms" Mabley.

Among her other writings were Like One of the Family *(1956), a compilation of her newspaper pieces written from the perspective of a domestic worker; the young adult novel* A Hero Ain't Nothin' But a Sandwich *(1973), for which she also wrote the screenplay; and the adult novel* A Short Walk *(1981). She was the recipient of numerous awards and distinctions, including a Tony Award nomination for her performance on Broadway in* Anna Lucasta, *an Obie Award for* Trouble in Mind, *and a Pulitzer Prize nomination for her novel* A Short Walk. *In 1966 she was awarded a two-year Harvard appointment at the Radcliffe Institute for Independent Study. She graduated from the program in 1968; in 1984 she received a Radcliffe Alumnae Graduate Society Medal for Distinguished Achievement. Additionally, she was awarded the first Paul Robeson Medal of Distinction from the Black Filmmakers Hall of Fame in 1977 and a Lifetime Career Achievement Award from the Association for Theatre in Higher Education (ATHE) in 1993. This interview took place on August 6, 1993. Alice Childress died on August 14, 1994.*

► ———————————————————————— ◄

Interviewer: This afternoon in the workshop you gave you spoke a fair amount about what you've written and why you've written it, but what specifically attracted you to write for the theatre?

Childress: I guess I explained in the workshop that my grandmother worked seemingly, without realizing it, with the Montessori Method. We didn't have money—I think I touched on our not having money—and yet she found ways to live positively and to creatively experience life. She was very creative in thinking up things: finding swatches of sample materials, feeling tweed and satin and silk and saying what she thought of it, asking what I would make out of that if we had ten yards of it. We'd get lost in thought for a long time. We used to sit at the window and watch the snow on winter nights. Once when a man was passing by she said, "Oh, it's so cold. Poor man, look at him, his coat is open a bit. Where do you think he's going?" I said, "Home." And she asked, "Does he have a family?" We were constructing a story, a play. I answered, "Yes, he has a wife." "Why didn't she sew his button?" "Maybe she didn't have a button." "Oh, they don't have a button. How many children do they have?" And I told her. And she asked, "What are their names?" We didn't call this anything, but we were creating.

Then when I went into grade school, they had plays. The teachers were always amazed at my acting and speaking, but I had been doing it with my grandmother at home. I didn't know it was anything special, you see. I knew in church—she'd take me to church—there were people who did Sunday afternoon recitations and readings, and sometimes I saw little playlets; but in school it had a name: drama, plays, make believe, and imagining. A friend of mine—I talked to her the other day; she has grown children, grandchildren—she and I made costumes and would put these improvised costumes on in each other's homes. Maybe you've seen pictures of old Russian theatre where people at holiday time—that was the aristocracy, I guess, did that—put on a play, in the house, with a curtain and the sets and all that? Well, we did that . . . in Harlem.

Interviewer: And how old were you?

Childress: Maybe from ten on. Then someone would play music; my friend's mother had a player piano. We lived in Harlem, 118th Street, between Lenox and Fifth avenues. Our people didn't let us go out and play in the street. So we had to play, right? We sang "La Paloma" and did the Spanish dance. We improvised Spanish costumes and hair combs. We were doing theatre. I remember my grandmother sometimes making newspaper curls and pinning them in my hair—to be like Alice in Wonderland. So it began with my grandmother. Her sense of drama was very strong.

Interviewer: She passed her creative ways on to you?

Childress: Yes. But she never said, "Be a writer, be an actress." We'd just do it. I saw some of that in Truman Capote's lovely Christmas piece—did you ever see that story? In that I saw the same spirit: His aunt said, "Let's make cakes" and "Let's trim a tree." It wasn't "Here's some money—go buy some ornaments—we'll put up the tree." It became a *doing*. The people Capote was writing about, like my grandmother, were people who have what I always call the inborn creative spirit. People who are seekers. People who have such a good time.

Interviewer: So theatre has been almost second nature for you?

Childress: Yes.

Interviewer: Your real entree into theatre and performing was with the American Negro Theatre, right?

Childress: It was a concentration, yes.

Interviewer: How did the ANT come about? How did it happen? I have read in other pieces about you that you were a founding member of that company.

Childress: No, it actually started a year or two before I joined it. I think the founders, Abram Hill and Frederick O'Neal, felt there should be a serious theatre, even though it was amateur theatre—it was not Broadway or off-Broadway theatre—in Harlem. They got together actors and directors; Abram Hill was the primary director. It was a small acting company, and they obtained space in the Schomburg Library; the library was named for a black Puerto Rican historian. The ANT encouraged acting, writing, and directing. I had never had such a concentrated time of theatre study, and I hadn't been around black theatre in school, only in Harlem's churches—Salem, St. Martin's, St. Phillip's, and so many others.

Interviewer: While at the ANT, didn't you write plays for the group because they said, "We need plays"?

Childress: *Florence* happened that way. We had very little material that was written for black actors. *Anna Lucasta,* for example, which went to Broadway, was a white play by Philip Yordan adapted for a black cast. So when they said, "Alice, write us a one-act play," I wrote *Florence,* and we performed it. But most of the time I was studying with the director, Abram Hill. He sometimes asked me to help direct by coaching, if an actor might be having a hard time with a scene. When Abram Hill had to go on with the play, he would say, "Take this actor for a while and work on this scene." In the American Negro Theatre a part of our purpose was to have every member perform every function in the theatre at some time. We had to help stage-manage, clean the theatre, do mailings, costumes, and put in time making up actors and directing. Everything that happened in theatre, you had to do some of it. Of course, major time went into what we did best. But that was a very good experience.

Interviewer: Total immersion.

Childress: We learned what a director goes through, so we had a better understanding of direction. We also had to go around the neighborhood selling tickets door to door, ringing neighborhood doorbells, asking people to come to the theatre.

Interviewer: That's a challenge.

Childress: The only job I escaped—no one said anything and I never brought it to their attention; I consider it one of the hardest jobs in theatre—was stage-managing.

Interviewer: So do you think you learned most of what you know about playwriting through that experience with ANT in the 1940s?

Childress: Greatly. I was there for eleven years, four nights a week, whether I was in a play or not. You see, the artists worked in the day, and every night we had to report whether in a production or not. That's how we learned these things—makeup, lighting, props, scene design, etc.

Interviewer: How about the other theatres that have done your plays? How was your experience at Greenwich Mews, where *Trouble in Mind* was originally performed?

Childress: It was a good experience, but it was also rough. That was where I ended up directing the play. I had to go in because there was a problem with the actors; they felt the director and the play weren't working. The leading lady wasn't working, so the original director took over her role and I went in to direct. I like to direct, but not especially my own work. I like to act in my own plays even less. I acted in *Florence* once in an emergency. I feel it is necessary to be out front looking because onstage, in the one experience when I was acting in my play, I found myself watching the other actors, watching how the scene was going. I felt I could direct my own work better than I could play in it.

Interviewer: About *Trouble in Mind,* I've read that the production at Greenwich Mews had a happier ending than the one that is published in Lindsay Patterson's book, *Black Theatre.*

Childress: Yes, it had two or three endings, but I tell you, I never agreed with that happy ending. You know what happened? They wanted a happy ending where the whole cast—black and white—came together and walked out on the show together. And that was the one thing that critics—a couple of the critics—had said: "This claptrap at the end." The producers had told me, "We're not going to do it unless you change the ending." They didn't say that when they got the play. But by this time the actors were employed, we were close to opening—and that was when they said that we're not going to do it unless you do this ending where everyone sticks together and wins, united. I disagreed with it because I saw nothing of this sort happening anywhere in the commercial theatre. I think they thought this is what *ought* to happen. Wouldn't it be wonderful if people stuck together? But they weren't doing it! I couldn't wait to get my play back to undo that. I always hated myself for giving in and changing the ending.

We did *Trouble in Mind* in London in October 1992. One critic thought I *had* made changes to suit the audience. Remember the Irish American doorman? One said, "I wish she hadn't thrown in the Irish man who admired the rebellion"—he thought I did it just a while ago because we were in London. They were having all these demonstrations and explosions and all at the time of the play's opening in 1992. Eight bombings that week. But that was the original script! Still, they thought, "Ah, you've come to England so you're going to put the Irish thing in."

In the original company at the Mews the actor playing the part of the doorman, though, did want some changes. He was threatening to go unless a certain line was changed. "Okay, I'll change that line," I said. Then he wanted something else, "Or I'll go," he said. I said, "That's up to you." I wasn't going to participate further in "We'll close this show if you don't write this" and "We'll leave if you don't do this." A changed ending was enough.

In that first production they felt, "We're giving you the opportunity to do this—a black protest play. And we're the ones putting it on, and you're going to do what we say about its outcome." Ever after that I resented that change. The producers got very quiet when a couple of critics said, "A clap-trap kind of ending," or something like that. In London, I rewrote the ending again. I changed it some from the published ending.

Interviewer: You don't end it with Wiletta reciting Psalm 133?

Childress: I did, but I had a little scene where Manners, the director, came back out, and he had one last ploy to pull to get her to do it his way, and she didn't, and he just sat there and watched her go through this thing she did at the end. So you did feel, "Who knows, maybe they'll come together." That was not the happy or unhappy ending. It was more open-ended. People always want things to end their way on racial things. Then, at the Greenwich Mews, they got more worried about outcome with an interracial cast.

Interviewer: Who is "they"?

Childress: Producers! At the Greenwich Mews, they felt, "We want to show a positive image to the public of black and white working together, so they should *all* come together and say, 'None of us are going to work unless—.'" I haven't known of any Broadway company where they all walked out because some actress or actor felt a certain way. I totally disbelieved the ending they wanted.

Interviewer: Especially when it's set at a particular historical moment when I don't think anybody would have.

Childress: I don't think they'd do it even now. We haven't gotten there yet. But I have heard of actresses of many different races rebelling. Sometimes they'd have to fire someone or just quietly replace her—"Get rid of this nuisance."

Interviewer: Were those stories the basis for *Trouble in Mind?*

Childress: My experience acting in *Anna Lucasta* on Broadway contributed a lot. I based Wiletta on Georgia Burke, someone who had also played in *Anna Lucasta.* Georgia Burke was a person like Wiletta who went along, went along, went along. Some days she said, "I'm tired of it." And I thought, "She has the spirit that could be Willetta's." She didn't go through what I wrote, but she had the right spirit. So the character of Georgia Burke became very influential in the writing of *Trouble in Mind.*

Interviewer: Also on the subject of rewriting, I wanted to ask you about *Wedding Band.* The stage version, as I read it, focuses so much on the backyard community, while the television version doesn't. You've talked a little bit about this before—that when you go to another medium, the focus will change. But so much more emphasis was on the relationship between Herman and Julia in the television version, as opposed to Julia finding her "black self," which dominates the stage version. Were the reasons for the revisions you did for the television production entirely because of the medium?

Childress: Some of it was Joe Papp, who was directing the television version: "Yeah, I want this new scene, I want it," he would say. He was spending a gang of money—and plus, Joe Papp wanted more than anything in the world to be a director. He produced *Wedding Band* because he wanted to direct it. When we were getting ready to begin rehearsals for the production at the Public Theater in 1972, I suggested three or four different directors. He said, "Unacceptable. Unacceptable"—and these were good directors. I said, "Joe, I don't personally know any more directors." I was selecting directors who had directed readings of it; one had directed the Chicago production. He said, "I want you to direct it." Joe wanted to step in, and he figured—you'll still have the play. So that's what happened. That explains some of the changes made in the production at the Public and in the one on television: Papp wanted them. There's a book called *Enter Joe Papp*. The author, who sat in on Public Theater rehearsals, says that when Joe walked in on the show to direct, it was never the same again. It broke my heart to see Joe change the direction of our production. You know when he came in? He did not come in until we were into the third or fourth night of previews with a standing ovation every night. He said, "If it's going to be like this, I want to be in it. So I'm going to direct." Again, you've got a whole cast sitting there. You can say, "I won't allow it," or you can keep plodding on and open. It was not a mistake to go on and open.

One thing Joe Papp had was a magnificent perseverance: if he said he was going to put it on television, he would. He was doing three plays on television in 1974. So he said, "Which do you want, first, second, third?" I said, "It doesn't matter." He said, "Always go first, get in early." I said, "Why?" He said, "In case they cancel, yours will have been done." But when it got closer he said, "I can't put you first. I'll put you second." Do you know, they canceled the third one. I heard they really wanted to cancel after the first because *Sticks and Bones* was controversial material. He would handle controversial material when others wouldn't, and he respected my writing. But then he comes in to direct—he's been in on I don't know how many productions as a director—he would get lost in too many effects; sets—he loved them. In *Wedding Band*, he thought, "I'll reconstruct Charleston." But if he said something was going to be done, he would do it. And he didn't care about being criticized for doing "controversial work." What got in his way as a director was that, in my opinion, Joe was stronger than the play characters; they could not have their way with him. They began to take on his way of thinking and doing. But—I loved Joe's fearlessness. So many plays would never have seen a stage anywhere if he had not lived and become the mentor of new creative ideas. He was not afraid to defy spoken or unspoken rules.

Interviewer: With *Wedding Band,* you said it was due to go to Broadway, and I've read that a number of Broadway producers had taken options out on it for a number of years but that nobody had the nerve finally to do it.

Childress: Some of them, I think, had the nerve, but not the money. It frightened them because some of the people they went to for money said, "What about that ending? What about this? I want a happy ending and I want this and I don't want Herman to die." Joe told me, "You know, we'd be on Broadway, Alice, if it wasn't Julia's play—if it became more of Herman's play." Then he began making it neither one nor the other—playing both of them back and forth evenly where I wrote a starring role for Julia. He felt the ending had to be changed to make it a Broadway show: "If he doesn't die, he leaves her. It must be his decision. She goes north or she doesn't and they break up, but it's his final decision."

You see, white leading ladies have this to contend with, too. You know how they say there aren't many leading ladies, unless you go way back to *A Doll's House* when the woman made a sole decision—then she was a leading lady. Lillian Hellman's *Little Foxes*—the woman, for better or worse, *is the lead.* But in a black-white situation, if the woman is the decision maker as in *Wedding Band,* it is assumed the man has lost his manhood . . . because what happened was her decision.

Interviewer: Do you think we could get *Wedding Band* done on Broadway today? Have we come far enough that we could do that?

Childress: I don't know. At the time I wrote it I didn't think in those terms. I thought if a play was well crafted and done well that it would succeed. You know how people laugh at a well-made play? You don't say that when you go to have a suit made, or when you go to have a heart operation, that you don't want anything well made. It's just with plays. But they also have a criterion with women: "Do you know how to *construct* a play?" Lillian Hellman demonstrated: "I'm going to show you, I'm out there with the best of them, and I'll stand up." Then they began to ridicule something being well made. It was like the old thing where black voters, when they gained the right to vote in the South, had to take an exam; you had to pass the exam before you could go and cast your vote. The examiners would read two pages of the Constitution and say, "Now, explain what that means." Answer: "It means you don't want me to vote." Well, with women it meant "You can't participate." Either it's too well made or it's not made well enough. Damned if you do and damned if you don't.

Interviewer: You have said that Broadway is an important measure of a playwright's progress in the theatre, not because of the content or form of the works, but because they're more regularly reviewed and so become universally known.

Childress: Also they make money; I didn't put that in. You're financially recognized. If you put a work of stature out there and it also makes money, that's international progress.

Interviewer: At some time, at some point, do you wish to have something on Broadway?

Childress: Oh, sure. I've also turned down some things where they've said we could go to Broadway with it. Either I didn't see how they were going to do it, or as they talked they were really saying, "Let's don't do this. Let's take your general idea and make it something else." I don't feel precious about writing. If you can show me a scene is too slow and it's not working—I have given in and conceded and rewritten. But I don't want to go to Broadway and end up doing what I did on *Trouble in Mind*— changing the ending when I *knew* I was doing the wrong thing.

I knew I was doing the wrong thing, but at the same time I shakily felt, "Maybe I could be wrong." When everyone around you is saying, "This is wrong," you can grow uncertain. They may be right—or wrong. After a while, you may say, "Okay, let's do it," when you feel it's wrong. And then you feel maybe that you'll never do what you want to do because something's always wrong with what you want to do. But I know better than that. I'm not alone. I've known of many writers who have told me they regretted making changes—people with hits. You can feel that way even though a show is running—mad as hell because the main thing you truly believed in has been changed. When you hear "We're not going to do it" and "We're going to close down early because of one thing," and all the actors have studied and learned their parts, you don't know if you have the right to snatch the play. I made no money on *Trouble in Mind*. We had standing room only, but I made about forty dollars a week as a writer. But we were trying for rep—our reputation. We were very idealistic about all we'd done . . . and we were happy for trying our best and having good audiences.

Interviewer: How about today? How hard is it for you to get a good production of one of your plays today?

Childress: It's hard. I may find out just how hard in the next season because there are a couple of plays that people want to do. There are a lot of people who have wanted to do productions in basements and lofts and places around of work of mine that hasn't been done before. But I now want a better first production of my work. When you know what it needs—it doesn't have to be that expensive, but it has to have basic things, what it really needs.

Interviewer: You've said you prefer writing plays, even though it is so hard to get something good done, to writing anything else—although you've written novels for both adults and children, and you've written essays and newspaper columns. Why do you prefer writing plays?

Childress: Because I feel at home—and it's more of a challenge. You have to get an awful lot of things going in a play. In the theatre, it is so very different from writing a novel. You need a producer, you need the house, you need the lighting designer. Simplicity is what you need very much. Sometimes I feel that if I produce, direct, write—some writers have done the whole thing themselves—that it'll be right. It's not a matter of a surefire hit or anything, but you're sure fired up to looking at what you meant it to be. To see that work.

Interviewer: So you're saying that the collaborative aspect of the theatre can at times be a frustrating experience?

Childress: Yes. You may have people in a group who don't like each other. I can't tell other people's truths for them, but a writer once told me that for his first play he had a name star whose requirement was that the writer never be allowed in the theatre during a rehearsal. The writer felt wretched. The actor wanted to freely dabble with lines. They had a good run. The writer said he felt a little better when he was able to take his wife and child—they had been very poor—on a grand vacation.

The theatre has made artists crawl. There seems to be a growing resentment against the first creative source. When you write a play, the producer may say, "It's mine now. What do you think I'm putting it on for? You've expressed yourself. Now I have to be expressed, too." And meanwhile the director says, "I see this play another way." Sometimes you can convince them otherwise, but you go home weary.

Interviewer: When you do write a play, and you get it to a theatre and rehearsals begin, how much of your play is completed?

Childress: Oh, mostly you're there all through rehearsals and the previews, and sometimes there are changes made after opening, during the actual run. But certainly, by opening night, the critics have either cheered or jeered or it's surviving a while on its own. But you're working and should be on call to work. A great director wants you on hand through the whole rehearsal period. Sometimes he'll come out and say, "I can't do anything with this" or "It needs something else." So you have to be there to correct your own errors, or to make a scene more playable, or to squeeze down and cut for time.

Interviewer: On some occasions have you profited when you've brought the play to production, seen when it's up there that it's just not working, and then you reworked it?

Childress: If it's not working and you have to rework it—that's one problem. But the difficult thing is if someone says, "I just want the man to be more the lead." It's not because something is wrong with the play, it's because society would like the male role to be the main one. Many actresses complain about Hollywood films because they have so few good lead parts. They try to equalize roles when possible. Or else they try to portray the downtrodden woman. But the stand-up woman—the winner—they consider that unwomanly . . . or perhaps hard to sell. A serious woman character is harder to sell than a serious man.

Interviewer: That brings me to something else that I wanted to ask you about. You write extraordinary moments in ordinary—real—women's lives. But it seems to me that when I've gone back and read what critics have written about your plays, their comments suggest that they have missed that.

Childress: Yes. Sometimes they deliberately miss certain things. "We like your writing, but this is too political," when we're living in the middle of politics every day! You turn on the news: business is going to fail—whatever—but don't mention that, because it makes people unhappy. In *Wedding Band,* I included the Calhoun speech that Herman gives. Those were actually Calhoun's words. Not one critic has ever mentioned that scene when Herman gives the John C. Calhoun speech. They say, "Herman creates a scene in the backyard." They never have mentioned the speech. Many many many many reviews of *Wedding Band,* not one has opened his mouth—"It's a racist speech that he was forced to learn"— they have not mentioned it in any review. "There's a difficulty in the backyard when he's ill," they say. They just put the conflict between Julia and Herman's mother; they do not say it's triggered by the speech he gave to the group. They don't even mention his father's membership in the Klan, the Knights of the Gold Carnation.

Interviewer: That's difficult to understand.

Childress: I associate that with a certain disapproval: "Why do you do things like that?" I think I had read somewhere—I think I still have old clippings from many years ago—about some man who used to have his child read racist speeches (like some skinheads or people in the Klan today) at a picnic. Children don't know what they're saying. Grown-ups rehearse them, give them the speech and a sign to carry. But I never saw any mention of this speech in a review. I kept looking, but nothing. "A turbulent scene in the backyard" was what they usually said. However, many productions were done in regional areas, colleges, where I did not see the presentation. I've never seen two productions that looked the same. All have been different.

Interviewer: I remember also in one review of *Wedding Band* the critic talked about "overwriting." In that play, which strikes me as such a tight play, there's no room for overwriting.

Childress: There were certain things they didn't want discussed; that was the "overwriting." Then I felt, "We just need to be clearer." Sometimes I would try to clarify and clarify.

Interviewer: They just weren't prepared to get it?

Childress: A writer told me once, "Alice, you have to tell them what you're going to do, then you have to say, 'Now I'm doing it,' and then you have to say, 'Now I'm finished with it,' in order for them to say, 'Oh, that's what you meant.'" You know, the kind of writing where Lula would come out and say, "Boy, I got mad when I heard him give that old John C. Calhoun speech in the backyard—that racist who said so-and-so." That way you *explain* the play. But if you have Herman just do it and his mother says he won this money, they may not get it.

Interviewer: So you do not have too high a regard for critics?

Childress: To the contrary, the best critical writing shows the power of observation, the ability to see and hear something and then *analyze* it. Critics are also writers. We only wish more critics had that keen power of observation, no matter if it is pro or con. Critics too often develop a flippant attitude toward writers, to play to their own audiences. There is a laxity in newspapers; often they will hire someone with no experience or ability to evaluate theatre. We speak of a "good" or "bad" review— meaning only that a critic liked or didn't like a play. Good criticism is really worthwhile reading when it shows an understanding of theatre.

Interviewer: When you start working on a play, how much of it do you know right off the bat? Do you know how it's going to end? Do you outline first?

Childress: I usually know my opening and my ending fairly well. I also know the story. When I get to how to do it, then there's a lot of outlining that has to be done—how to make it dramatically move, keep pushing forward—besides getting the story down. That goes for books, too. I usually know the opening and the closing—where I'm going, and some idea of how to get there. Even though you know the story, you can't just "story" and go on through. It has to have its ups, its downs, its different levels, the why as well as the how of it.

Interviewer: Does a character ever start to take over when you're writing?

Childress: Yes, characters often take over. Sometimes it's good, sometimes it's not. Right now I have one character running off with a book because she flows—she's not the lead—and your own common sense tells you it can't be that way. I'll have to rein her in.

Interviewer: I'm wondering, in *Mojo,* if perhaps the character of Irene might have taken over when you were writing that play. She is such a strong presence.

Childress: She did in a way, because she was very real. I met her in several people, including a little of myself. She flowed. I find a deep sense of romance in the lives of women like Irene that is seldom talked about. A black woman is seldom considered a romantic figure if she is strong. Irene was passionate as well as strong. She felt she couldn't *afford* to love. So often black women are seen as defeated, unloved figures—good at taking the hard knocks of life, stereotypically stalwart. Irene was not that. She sacrificed too much and came to realize she had been unfair to herself— by assuming a false hardness which was not her own.

Interviewer: Do your plays, then, take twists and turns in places you didn't really expect?

Childress: Yes, particularly in places where things won't move according to your specifications. As people and events come to life on the page, they escape your mind-set and begin to seek their own direction.

Interviewer: Can you think of a particular play where it went a lot differently than you originally expected it might go? In *Wedding Band,* for example, did you know Herman was going to die?

Childress: Yes. Some people saw that as his defeat. I don't like to see birth or death as defeat. We live in a world where we say "under God this and this" and religions teach absolute faith in God, and yet we are terrified by the idea of death. We speak of but don't believe in the happy hereafter. When a lead character dies the play is considered "tragedy." I ask, "Are we going to our just rewards, or not?" However, I wasn't thinking of any rewards before or after death when I was writing *Wedding Band.* Even in his death throes, Herman had the strength of determination. He didn't "give up" and die.

I figure they are very strong people who try to live true to themselves up to the end. Herman had unfinished business to complete. Sometimes it's even hard for an actor to see that's why he came back to Julia's, to say: "*I should have handled our lives another way.*" This is what he's saying: "I'll leave my deathbed to undo this." He is not saying, "I wish I had this to do over again"; he said, "I was *wrong*, I shouldn't have done that to you." We also have to understand his strength. He'd be a pretty weak man to walk out on his mother and sister—they had no way to make a livelihood. For him to walk off and say, "I'm in love, too bad about you, but I borrowed your money and you don't have any left." As he told Julia, "I owe them something. I used their money." He was talking at a time when commitment really meant something; one didn't walk out on a mother and sister—and leave them penniless. And where was he going? To a relationship outside of the law—the illegal relationship with Julia.

I thought Herman was a strong person. Julia thought so, too, at the end when she gave him a peaceful scene. She made him forget about dying. She said, "Look at the friendly people on the shore, they're waving good-bye, and they ask us to 'Come back,' but we're going, going, we're going." She meant we're going to be free of heartache and stress. She made a happy death for him. We're used to people who just drop their heads to one side and say, "Carry on, dear" or something. But Julia and Herman kept fighting to the end. He wasn't quite dead when the curtain came down. She said, "Yes, yes, at last we're living for ourselves." When she closed the door against others and said, "No one comes in my house. Go away, win the war, represent the race, go to the police. Do what you have to do," she's giving them their freedom, not hers. Herman and Julia were arguing all through the play and loving each other, but they were arguing about their condition of life—their helplessness.

Interviewer: Julia, by getting back to her beginnings, her heritage, is able to overcome that helplessness.

Childress: Yes.

Interviewer: Herman's acknowledging his own heritage also enables Julia and Herman to forge an honest relationship.

Childress: Look at Herman's mother at the end—at the very end. She says, "I've tried but I can't understand it." That's about as honest as she could get. "You see me standing here before you." In that line she means she's defeated. "I stand here and just tell you—I don't know what this is about"; because she sees it was a huge thing with Herman. Julia wasn't just his little fun-girl. That was common, having a woman on the side—whatever color she was. Men would "sow their wild oats," but he was making it a life-and-death issue. There's always been good response to the play, even though there's been this trouble about how it ought to end. Producers want things solved. That's safer ground. As phony as it would be, I think they'd prefer the mother or Annabelle to come in and take Julia in, as if to say, "We've been wrong." Even kindly white supremacy is made of "sterner stuff."

Interviewer: In the stage production, you do have Annabelle come close to Julia's house and listen to Julia's words to Herman, which you didn't have in the television production.

Childress: I felt that was as far as they could go before it became unbelievable to me. I'm not sure they would have gone that far. They might have remained at home and shut the door, but I could go that far as a writer. I could believe that much, but I couldn't believe it wrapped up nicely and neatly and them having a little chat together. Papp said, "We could have had a hit show." He said, "People want to feel good about something." I think I am forced to write things that people are disturbed about, annoyed about. The state of society is such that it makes observers feel frightened when things are not wrapped up. Take *A Hero Ain't Nothin' But a Sandwich.* They changed the ending in the picture. Oh, they changed it here, here, here, and here, so much—and *I* wrote the screenplay! They did two endings, one where he didn't show up at his drug rehab place—that's my ending. They did another one, him showing up and them hugging one another. I wanted the actor—Paul Winfield—to look straight out at the audience at the end of the film and say, "Benji, I'm waiting for you." I felt that covered any Benji anywhere. That was what I meant. No, they had to have the real Benji running around the corner, running and then hugging. I was moved by it but didn't believe it. They had other places like that all through the script—they were changing meanings. The script was weakened—to make the leads more lovable. They did do good things also. But they were going to ban the movie anyway, despite all the changes; there were two hearings on banning it even after it was weaker. People said, "Who'd want to write about drug addiction in kids?" That was seventeen or eighteen years ago. Some asked, "Why write about a child drug addict when there are so many positive things?" I saw them in the street. Now it is safer to write and produce scripts about children addicted to drugs.

Most people don't want their children to become writers. They want them to be doctors and lawyers or to become president of something. They don't say, "I want my child to grow up to be a writer." African American writers commonly write in defiance of society. If they make some big bucks happen, someone says, "Well, well, well, I always knew he had it in him."

Interviewer: With the screenplay of *A Hero Ain't Nothin' But a Sandwich* you had less control than in the Greenwich Mews production of *Trouble in Mind* or the Public Theater production of *Wedding Band,* didn't you?

Childress: According to our guilds and unions, the playwright is in a stronger position than the screenwriter. No one has the right to change your stage play. But your screenplay or a TV play, they can do what they want after you sign the contract. Banks lending film money do not want a writer or actor to have the final say. The producer is the one who borrows the money. The producers are money-responsible for everything. They get the first draft out of the first writer and the second draft out of the second writer, and so on, and on.

Interviewer: It also seems that in your plays and in *A Hero Ain't Nothin' But a Sandwich* that you've always been a bit ahead of the curve and people have said, "Why are you writing about this now?"

Childress: Well, I didn't conceive of *A Hero Ain't Nothin' But a Sandwich.* I wrote some short pieces on kids on drugs, and Ferdinand Monjo, an editor at Coward, McCann & Geoghegan, called me up. I met Ferd, who was originally a playwright at New Dramatists. He said, "I read a piece you wrote about a drug-addicted child and another piece you wrote about a woman whose son was drug-addicted called 'Happy Mother's Day.' Why don't you just write a young adult book about it?" I said, "Why should it be a young adult book? It seems to me it should be an adult book that may be about a child." He said, "It's a young adult book because I'm vice-president of the young adult division." He was a wonderful editor.

Interviewer: How do you think the state of the American theatre is now, in general, and for blacks in particular, in comparison, let's say, with the 1960s?

Childress: Just more, I guess, could mean better; but first, there aren't enough plays out there talking about black events, and second, when you put it all together for something considered black theatre, there are very few confrontational plays between blacks and whites. You have black family plays, where blacks confront each other: "Yeah, they'll buy that. Let's see you folks fight it out," you see. *A Raisin in the Sun* was about a mother-son relationship—somehow *she's* stopping him from being a man. Take the film—and it wasn't a black film necessarily—*Guess Who's Coming to Dinner,* which they keep showing and showing and showing. At the bottom line of *Guess Who's Coming to Dinner,* Katharine Hepburn tells off the black mother about her racism. The message becomes "I can accept this, but you, the black woman, are the racist." What black people do to each other is very popular. What whites are doing to us and each other is dramatically a black-white conflict. It has been going on since long before the Civil War. It is an uncomfortable subject.

Interviewer: Do you think there's some point where we can get beyond that?

Childress: Those who insist will push it along, and then maybe someone's work will be done. But you take the common TV stories we have—the cop stories where they have a black and a white sidekick working together—they might have a little point once in a while, but mainly they catch a black criminal and then they catch a white criminal. They think that makes a positive, balanced statement: "We're getting along." We're not, though. This is the problem. Society is getting more and more divided because we lie about the situation. Anything that deals with true conflict between the races leads to discomfort for those selling products. The commercial sponsor! The contradictions—all this goes to make up the drama. Today someone asked what I thought of realism. What I should have said is, realism can be worrisome at its best or trite at its worst.

Interviewer: We're not yet done with realism in the theatre, then, in your opinion?

Childress: No. We don't allow realism to gallop ahead. It's always, "This isn't quite the right time for that approach" or "We want to accomplish just a little bit." This is what I say in *Trouble in Mind.* You have the director and others saying, "If we could just make people feel lynching is wrong." I thought, "If they didn't know that was wrong when they entered the theatre, we're dealing with idiots."

Interviewer: And we're in trouble.

Childress: In deep trouble.

Interviewer: So we probably haven't gotten to the point where the label "controversial" could be dropped from your work?

Childress: Not yet, but it gets better. Controversy only means disagreement. I know what drama feels like. It goes right to the root of the subject. Why couldn't Joan of Arc ask some nice gentleman to lead her soldiers for her? This way she could avoid controversy—and drama. Why did she have to run out there? What's she going to win? When her headstrong action happens onstage, we say, "Damn, that's drama."

Interviewer: In light of that, which playwrights do you think have influenced you or taught you, or which playwrights have you particularly admired?

Childress: I wasn't really reading that much of the work of other playwrights when I was first writing. I just went in and did it. I didn't think, "Now I want to write plays." It was just something I did, something my grandmother and I had started. I began reading other playwrights long after I had started writing plays. The writers I later read and admired included Lillian Hellman and Paul Laurence Dunbar. Dunbar wrote wonderful books and poetry. I find you can watch a dancer or listen to a piece of music and be inspired to write a play. I've been more moved to write in a certain way by things like that rather than by other playwrights. A sunset or a rainstorm or sudden stillness may tap the creative spirit.

Interviewer: If you had a canon of black plays, if you had to construct that right now, what would you include?

Childress: Do you mean plays that have been written or plays that you think should have been written?

Interviewer: Plays that have been written.

Childress: I don't know, because I've enjoyed lots of plays. They don't have to be what I think in terms of controversy. I've enjoyed the work, but I feel there's a certain angle that never gets there. Take *Purlie Victorious*. What was his victory? It's sort of a comedic-serious play. It's about Purlie getting the Bethel Baptist Church, winning it for his people away from a man with a slave-master mind. At the end of the play, they get the Bethel Baptist Church, but master's son gives it to them. Purlie had told the people he fought for and won it; then they find out it is given to them by the *son* of the oppressor, who becomes liberal enough to give it to him. They said, "But Purlie, you didn't win it," and he said, "Well, I should have. It should have been that way. That's what should have been." The white audience feels relief that master's son gave it to him and so won for the blacks. I'm talking about very good writers, but somehow the plays stop short on the question of black-white conflict. What about *A Soldier's Play*? What happens at the end of that? This isn't saying it's not true, but we are led to believe that a white man has killed a black man. Right? In the end we find out it was a black who killed another black. In the film a black and a white man go off together with a sense of admiration and under-standing for one another because they had uncovered this black-on-black murder. In each play, what happens is the blacks must criticize them-selves.

I had one producer tell me—a black producer—"No more confronta-tional plays—we don't want them." Now, how does this enter regional theatre—not only regional but semipro theatre? It has to do with grantsmanship and success. What kind of message is found in produced controversy? Can you get a grant for a militant play? I don't even call militant what some people call militant. If you disagree with something, it isn't necessarily militant. I call militant an outright fighting to win—that kind of militancy. But they call your *attitude* too militant if you question the status quo.

Interviewer: Theatre is often described as the most conservative of the art forms. Do you agree with that?

Childress: It's more conservative than it used to be. It's moving more toward conservatism. Of course, there were things considered controversial, such as Nora slamming the door in *A Doll's House*. That was very controversial in its time because then the audience said, "What are you saying? A discontented woman should walk out and slam the door? This is marriage?" It was objectionable. A woman did this. Ibsen might have known someone who did this in life. Or maybe he was saying she ought to walk out. A man saying it is more acceptable. The woman could not champion herself as freely.

Women have rarely had the opportunity to be the strong characters in drama. Could you picture *Oedipus* as the mother's play, with Oedipus's mother playing the full lead instead of Oedipus? Would he put his eyes out and all of this kind of thing about having been his mother's lover? Perhaps she would not put hers out because she could not show the *passion* and intellectual sensitivity that Oedipus had. What about the end of Oscar Wilde's *Salome*—"Kill that woman!" Again, the woman becomes the villain even though a man ordered and had John the Baptist's head severed. The man had promised the female dancer anything she wanted. She wanted the head of John the Baptist. A man had given his word to reward her with whatever she desired. He had another man's head chopped off, brought it on a platter, and presented it to the female dancer. His word and pledge were intact. I don't believe his honor. If he was honorable I felt he would say, "For the first time in my life I will break my word; I'm not going to decapitate this innocent." She becomes the villain because he cuts it off, and then he says, "Now I'm going to kill you." So it is always, always an argument with a woman figure as evil or conniving or weak or overbearing.

Interviewer: Have we gotten very far beyond that?

Childress: Do you know how long it took for the Catholic Church to change its mind about the burning of Joan of Arc? Wasn't it about four hundred years? Then they made her a saint. It was a big change, but it took a long, begrudging time.

Interviewer: Yes, but as a priest once told me, for the Catholic Church, a century is hardly any time at all. Why do you think the American theatre is more conservative now?

Childress: Reining in is the last lashing of the wounded lion's tail. The American theatre is in trouble with minorities and women, I think. You take the superpatriots. I haven't written about this, and neither am I going to. But you take the flag-waver, in Congress or wherever: "America, America, America—I love America, and we're not going to let these blacks, foreigners, and women and whatnot run this beloved country." These are the people who have foreign bank accounts! No matter how hard they wave the flag, I ask, "Why'd they go and put their money in foreign banks where superpatriots stash away secret accounts?" If the country goes down they plan to have another place to go and spend. I wonder what kind of "patriot" could plan such a thing. If you put this in a play, they'd say, "Now, did you have to bring that up? It makes people uncomfortable, especially people you have to go and ask for money." Not that words correct situations. They're not going to stop doing anything because we make mention—but I feel that's the drama we're living. I don't say let's go out and save anything—the worst name you can call anyone in America is a do-gooder, right?

Interviewer: So you're writing what you see?

Childress: I write what I see, hear, and feel. I think this is the only realism that some fear. I'm not writing about somebody sitting on the front porch knitting an afghan. Power people really don't seek a woman president unless she's Margaret Thatcher, who can agree with men first.

Interviewer: If it's the last lashing of the lion's tail . . . ?

Childress: What they mean—I do believe it came out of Africa—is the lion is most vicious when it's desperately fighting for its life.

Interviewer: That could be a good sign, couldn't it?

Childress: Oh, sure. There was anger like that over the outcome of the Civil War. The fury of the losers. But then the wounded nation went on. If we didn't have it then, we'd have had a Civil War later. It was something inevitable. It wouldn't have happened when it did if it wasn't so dividing to have two USAs, a North and a South. Lincoln had to sign for emancipation to avoid dividing the country into two parts. It didn't go on mainly about slavery.

Interviewer: The historical points are always very important for you in your plays. What role does the research play in your writing?

Childress: Drama is the controversy of life, the contradictions in history. If you write about characters living at a particular moment, you have to know something about the times in which they live. Research keeps opening up for you more of the things that people must have experienced. In *Wedding Band,* Julia was a dressmaker because that was one of the honorable things a woman could do as a lady in Charleston in 1918. Woman's work, in general, was for common women—washwoman, governess. A few could work as a waitress. A seamstress could work in her own home. Very often women needed money and didn't want to work outside the home. Some women made candy, like Mattie, or cooked and delivered cakes, etc. But there was a certain honor in being a dressmaker or caring for small children.

Interviewer: Julia Augustine, when she's with Lula, the next morning before the parade—she and Lula do this strutting, a "dimly remembered" African folk dance.

Childress: Yes.

Interviewer: How would Julia, who initially seems to have no remembrance of tradition, ancestry, and heritage, know that dance?

Childress: It is passed down. Julia follows Lula's example. How would *I* know it? I know it from watching my grandmother. This is how people just pick it up. It was not hard to do. It is an easy thing. It was commonly done. You can't stop in a historical play and account for everything—but it was not an unusual dance for working-class women. Hands akimbo (on your hips), hold your head high, and dance the other down.

Interviewer: I guess it would be harder for her not to know it.

Childress: Yes. If they had a birthday party, they might jump up and start that dance. Some people would watch it and clap—others would jump in the middle of it. It was recognizable. See it once and it's remembered. However, some danced better than others.

Interviewer: Do you ever write with a particular actor or actress in mind? I think about Ruby Dee in particular.

Childress: No. Sometimes I might picture someone in something, but I usually picture the characters and not actresses. I picture people I know or people I have heard of. Once the actor or actress is playing the role, sometimes I rewrite based on the performer, or change something because I see what would be better for that interpretation.

Interviewer: When you write a play, do you picture an audience? Who do you write for?

Childress: When I write, I see the stage. I don't think of an audience looking at the play. I'm taking the place of an audience. I also see the characters, and sometimes I see them in their right places; if it's a home scene, I see them in their real home, that room, etc. This is for character development. I don't write for one particular audience, but I do write for actors, from the perspective of a writer-actress-director, according to the needs of the moment—that is, when we are in rehearsal, which is rewriting time again.

Interviewer: How would you describe your writing process? Do you write in longhand or on a computer?

Childress: I do both—longhand and computer. At times I do longhand and then put it on the computer. Sometimes for what I'm writing I decide the computer would be better. Regular typing I no longer do. You can't correct easily. You can correct longhand faster than typewritten copy.

As for my writing process, I generally follow the advice I give newer writers: try not to polish up front. You have worked yourself to death. Keep going, keep going. If it's poorly written, too bad. Keep going. When you have an end, you've got something whole. Then rewrite, rewrite. Polished incomplete things wear you out.

Some writers sit down and write every day, regardless. I am not that disciplined. It is something I positively envy. Early on when I was writing, I didn't have the opportunity to be disciplined, to write at a set time. I had to work; I had to take care of my daughter. Many women writers are wearing so many hats—they work, have to care for the children, pick them up from school—they write when they can. Discipline can come with grants. For me, the appointment to the Radcliffe Institute from 1966 to 1968 was wonderful because then I *could* close a door and write. Like most women, I didn't have a workroom of my own at home. Today I write at night, in the day, in the middle of the night. It would be nice to have set hours like 11:00 A.M. to 4:00 P.M., but that's a dream thing. When it hits me, I do it.

John Guare

John Guare was born in 1938 in New York City and educated at Georgetown University and the Yale School of Drama. His plays include The Loveliest Afternoon of the Year *and* Something I'll Tell You Tuesday *(1966),* Muzeeka *(1967),* Cop-Out *(1968),* Kissing Sweet *(1969),* A Day for Surprises *(1971),* The House of Blue Leaves *(1971),* Marco Polo Sings a Solo *(1973),* Rich and Famous *(1974),* Lydie Breeze *(1982),* Gardenia *(1982),* The Talking Dog *(adapted from a story by Anton Chekhov; 1986),* Six Degrees of Separation *(1990),* Women and Water *(1990), and* Four Baboons Adoring the Sun *(1992). His book for the musical adaptation of* Two Gentlemen of Verona *(1971), for which he also wrote the lyrics, won a Tony Award and a New York Drama Critics Circle Award.* The House of Blue Leaves *won the Los Angeles and New York Drama Critics Circle Awards and an Obie Award. He has written the screenplays for* Taking Off *(1971),* Six

Degrees of Separation *(1993), and* Atlantic City *(1980), for which he received the New York, Los Angeles, and National Film Critics Circle awards, as well as an Academy Award nomination. In 1989 he was elected to the American Academy and Institute of Arts and Letters. This interview took place on October 16, 1991.*

▶ ──────────────────────────────── ◀

Interviewer: It's nice to have you back in Washington, where you belong.

Guare: It's wonderful to be back. I went to Georgetown, and in 1957 they had a one-act play contest, and I wrote a play for it (Donn Murphy directed it), and I wrote a play every year after that. The last year I was here, in 1960, I wrote a musical called *The Thirties Girl,* and then I went to Yale Drama School. A number of years later I wrote *The House of Blue Leaves* about a songwriter, and I used the songs from *The Thirties Girl.* When I was at Yale Drama School, I won a prize in a D.C. play contest which Richard Coe was the judge of; so I always feel that, even though I'm from New York, my beginnings came from here and how fortunate I was to go to school here and to live here from 1956 to 1960. I checked coats and sold orange juice at the National Theatre and ran the Lost and Found and took care of the posters. I'm glad to be here tonight as a playwright because playwriting is my job, my way of working in the theatre; but if I couldn't write plays, I would work in the theatre some other way.

Interviewer: How did you begin? Did you see theatre as a boy and fall in love with it?

Guare: Yes, I was lucky. It was one of the great things about growing up in New York City. My parents liked to go see shows, and I went to see plays every time there was a birthday or a holiday. I also had two great-uncles who had toured in vaudeville from about 1880 to 1917 when the act folded. There were sixteen plays that they toured in in stock, plays with names like *Pawn Ticket 210* and *The Old Toll House* that had scenes like, where my great-uncle would come out as the old man and say, "Twenty-five years ago this very night my son took the money. He did not know it was rightfully his. Oh, if I could only see him again to right that wrong." They always celebrated Christmas in the middle of the summer, at the end of July, because that's when they were home. It all just seemed tremendously romantic. My uncle, my mother's brother who had been in the act, then became an agent and was head of casting at MGM from 1934 to 1956. So there always was a sense that it was just there, it was all possible; the theatre was something very possible.

My father worked on Wall Street and really despised it. He hated his life and he said, "Whatever you do, John, don't get a job." It was the best advice that anybody could ever have, because I knew, when I was at Georgetown, probably after 1957 after the freshman-year play contest, that that's what I wanted to spend my life doing. When I was eleven I had done a couple of plays, and the newspapers on Long Island had done a story about an eleven-year-old playwright, and that just seemed to be perfect: there I was in the paper—"John Guare, Eleven-Year-Old Playwright." I saw it and I said, "There it is, my identity." For my twelfth birthday my parents gave me a typewriter because I was a playwright, and I still use that typewriter. They honored that; it wasn't a fantasy. I was very, very lucky in having tremendously supportive parents.

Also, my timing was very lucky. When I went to Yale Drama School in 1960, the off-off-Broadway movement was just starting, and it was a remarkable time. It was a time when you could write a play on a Thursday and bring it over to a theatre and it would open on Monday. Edward Albee was a saint; he did something that truly demands canonization. With the money that he made from *Virginia Woolf*—and *Virginia Woolf* in a certain sense was the last great international blockbuster—he took a lease on a theatre in Vandaam Street and for six months did a new play every weekend, full productions! It was just a remarkable time. You'd go to La MaMa and you'd go to Caffe Cino. There was a man named Joe Cino who was a Sicilian steam presser by day. He worked from 7:00 A.M. to 4:00 P.M. as a steam presser, and then he would go to Cornelia Street. Now it's a real estate office. It was a little place, probably about as big as this stage, very narrow and long but filled with Christmas tree lights and every imaginable piece of junk in the world; it was just extraordinary. That's where Lanford Wilson began. I saw some remarkable things there; they were unlike anything I'd seen.

So I brought my plays in there when I got out of the air force. And he said, "I'm very sorry, but we're only doing plays by Aquarians." I said, "I'm Aquarius, February fifth. I swear to you, I'm an Aquarius." He looked at my driver's license and he said, "All right." He checked his chart and he said, "These are the dates when you'll open, and you run for two weeks because of Saturn, and I think we'll give you a one-week extension," and we ran three weeks. I don't know what would have happened if I'd been a Virgo, but that is where I began. It was a remarkable time because there were no critics; you would just stop by to see what was there.

One night my father came down to see a play there, and he was sort of shocked that we would pass the hat afterwards. The rule was that there had to be more of you onstage than them out there, but we'd play for one or two people. My father said, "I've got an idea. Why don't you write a hit Broadway musical, and then you can go back to the Caffe Cino?" He was right, and that's exactly what I did. In 1965 I got a letter one day from a place called the Eugene O'Neill Theater Center in Waterford, Connecticut, that was trying to begin which said, "We're trying to begin a theatre center. What do playwrights want?" The people who ran this theatre up in Connecticut wrote around to different theatres and to agents and other people, and they picked the twenty writers who appeared the most. So one day in July 1965 we went up there—Lanford Wilson, Leonard Malfi, Sam Shepard, Terrence McNally, and I—and we just had a great time. It was sort of like a Fresh Air Fund Camp in this great house that O'Neill had written about in *A Moon for the Misbegotten*. They were going to tear it down; they were going to use it for firemen's training in the New London area until George White got hold of the house, which is right on Long Island Sound. We talked up there for about three days about what did playwrights want, and that was it; we went home and were dumped off the bus in Times Square. And a year later they said, "We're ready now; the theatre's going to be, and you said you wanted your plays done, and so July 18 will be your day." We were all assigned a date, and I wrote the first act of *The House of Blue Leaves* for that first year of the O'Neill. It was just an amazing time because it was just about doing; it was about the fun of doing.

Interviewer: Why are you a playwright? Why not a novelist or a poet?

Guare: Because to be a playwright means that you belong to a whole world. When you finish a novel, you hand it to the editor and get it back, and then one day it appears in the store and that's it. With a play, you have that solitary experience of living with your material, and then you give it over to a producer and a director. A play is finished when it's produced; it is the construction of a whole world. It literally is a world that you move into. It's a remarkable experience belonging to the theatre, which is almost a planet unto itself. That's what I love about it. Writing is my job—to work on a play, to work on the production of a play.

Interviewer: But don't you lose it when it goes into production? Don't you give it up to other people?

Guare: Willingly. That's my job. What you want to do is, you want to produce it onstage to have an effect on the audience.

Interviewer: How much control do you get over the production? How can you be sure it's the effect you wanted to get?

Guare: Thanks to the Dramatists Guild contract, nothing can be put onstage without your permission. The producers cannot choose a director against your wishes; they can't cast somebody against your wishes. The difference between writing plays and writing for films is a key one; it's all about the copyright. When you write a movie, the movie company owns the piece. They own the work, and they can cast whoever they want in it, they can bring in as many writers as they want to to change it; and you're paid up front for that, in exchange for giving up your copyright. In the theatre, in exchange for holding on to the copyright, you get paid after the fact. But it makes all the difference in the world, because you own your material, because everything that's on that stage is playwriting. If there's an actor miscast, generally if it's a new play they don't say, "God, that actor was terribly miscast." They just say, "God, what a rotten part." To be a playwright you've got to know about every aspect of what's on that stage— the lighting, the costumes, and the set—because that's the visual way in which the audience will enter the world of your play. Thanks to the Dramatists Guild, the organization that represents the interest of seventy-five hundred playwrights, lyricists, and composers in America and Great Britain, we have that power, if we choose to use it.

Interviewer: You once said if you're going to be in the theatre you have to be naive, primitive, or you have to know as much as you can.

Guare: That's right, and you can only be naive once. You only get to be a virgin once. After that you just have to know everything that's happening on that stage. The horrible thing is you're not allowed to say, "Well, I didn't know any better." If you want to make mistakes, they have to be educated mistakes. They have to be your own mistakes, not mistakes out of ignorance.

Interviewer: So that's what challenges you about playwriting, as opposed to writing a novel where all you're responsible for is the words on the page and then it just goes into a bookstore?

Guare: That's right, yes. The thrill of working with actors, that collaborative process of working with actors and a director, is remarkable. They once asked Peter Brook what is the great aesthetic problem, and he said, "The greatest problem is once you've discovered a laugh, how do you repeat the laugh." Those are the great problems in the play: when you say, "God, they laughed last night. Why aren't we getting it tonight? What did we do? How did we get that laugh? How do we find the correct music of the play, so that the audience has generally the same response every night?"

Interviewer: In the introduction to the new edition of *The House of Blue Leaves* you say you write so that the original wound never goes away. Is that one of the reasons?

Guare: Yes.

Interviewer: So, even if you write about a black man pretending to be Sidney Poitier's son, you're still writing about yourself?

Guare: You can't write about what you can't imagine.

Interviewer: Is there some aspect of John Guare's wound in that play?

Guare: Why not?

Interviewer: As much so as in plays that actually depict your experience?

Guare: The material of *Six Degrees* had been sitting inside me for a number of years, working its way out, working its way in and then out.

Interviewer: How does your own creative process work?

Guare: I get up in the morning and I go to work. It's as simple as that. I love to work. If I don't work I get sick. I work on the dining room table until about one or two, and then I do other stuff. Before I go to bed at night, I like to sort of look over what I've written, when I finish, just to give myself a task to start with the next day; so that when you wake up in the morning, you're not just saying, "What do I have to do?" Last night there was a documentary on PBS about the Dead Sea Scrolls, and it was just like playwriting because they had this long table all filled up with these little fragments. This guy (he ultimately went nuts, this Harvard professor; it was just a tragic story) said, "I look at that piece and that piece, and I study all the pieces, and when I go to bed at night, I'll wake up in the morning and I'll say, 'Yes, forty-four fits with ninety-three, yes.'" And he said, "I have to have a great memory because I have to have all the fragments to figure out what can go with what." I said, that's like playwriting where you have all these fragments in your head, rag-tags of lines, and moments and scenes, and we don't know what connects with what. And you have to give yourself a problem to trust your unconscious with, and your unconscious will solve it during the night, so when you wake up in the morning you can go right to it.

Interviewer: In writing *The House of Blue Leaves,* didn't you write parts of it quite a time apart?

Guare: In 1966 I wrote the first act very, very quickly. There's just three people in it, and I couldn't find anybody who understood the way it should be played, so I read the lead, Artie, at the O'Neill. I knew what I wanted the second act to be. I mean I knew what the events were, but it took me from 1966 until 1971 to develop the craft to deal with nine people onstage and to deal with the rigors of farce. I also wrote about eight drafts, literally eight or nine drafts, of the second act of the play, always with the same general events. There was a starlet in it who comes from California in the second act, and it drove me crazy because the second act began and this person had to come in and everybody had to tell her everything that happened in the first act because she was going to unravel everything.

Sometimes Corinna Stroller would be horrible, she would be a cheap tramp, and then in the next version she'd be grand and generous and wonderful, and in the next version she'd just have all these identities. I didn't know how to take hold of the material, because the people in the first act had to tell this vision from California the problems of their life. I said one night to the producer, "I don't know why I have to waste all this time telling them, because nobody listens to anybody else anyway; she might as well be deaf." I said, "Oh!" The minute that I knew she was deaf I realized that nobody in the play was paying any attention to anybody else anyway. That was the key to it: by making her deaf and not having to say anything, the door opened up and air went through. I had been working with a director who was taking the play in a very naturalistic tone and wanted to explore the material in a very naturalistic psychological way that I wasn't interested in. At the cost of a friendship, I didn't want him to be with the play, and Mel Shapiro came on as the director. I knew what I didn't want the play to be, and it took me four years to hear myself say, "She might as well be deaf," and I could just write the second act very quickly.

Interviewer: Since you've spent over a quarter of a century in the theatre in New York, how would you say that the off-Broadway and off-off-Broadway situations have changed since you were first in them?

Guare: It all ended one day. Two things happened. In 1967, right about there, the papers started seriously reviewing off-off-Broadway. Suddenly, it wasn't daring. Once things got reviewed there was sort of a recklessness and a sense of it being underground that went out of it. Then literally one day in 1969 in Edward Albee's theatre, a play was done for a weekend called *The Boys in the Band* by Mart Crowley, and that play took off. It moved uptown where it played a thousand performances. When Mart Crowley's play moved and became such an enormous success, it was in a sense the end of off-off-Broadway. Also, one horrifying day Joe Cino stabbed himself to death eighty times, and it just ended. I don't know whether it was drugs or life or the sixties, but Joe died, and that was when the sixties was starting to turn in on itself.

Interviewer: In recent years you've found a home at Lincoln Center, haven't you?

Guare: Yes. When I worked at the Public Theater, when you had a new play you were the key member of that theatre. Then you went into casting and rehearsals and preproduction, and opening night was a very, very sad time. You realized you were expelled from the theatre because after the play opened you had no role in the theatre. So in order to be a citizen of that world, you had to write a play to earn a passport back into that world of the play. What was extraordinary when Lincoln Center started, when Bernie Gersten and Gregory Mosher started their run in 1985, the people who worked there worked there. The day after a play opened, you'd be brought in and asked, "Well, who should we cast in the next play, or what play should we do?" Everybody who works there feels that they belong there. In the six years that I've worked there, I've had two plays done. The first was a revival of *The House of Blue Leaves*. Originally, they were going to do *Gardenia,* but because the cast that Gregory Mosher wanted wasn't available to him, he said, "Well, let's do *House of Blue Leaves,*" and that eight-week run went on for a year, which was wonderful. In that time, I also became the editor of a newspaper because we felt that there were a lot of issues that were not being dealt with in any of the papers around New York, so we started a newspaper. Then a musical I had worked on in 1968 with Jerry Robbins, Leonard Bernstein, and Stephen Sondheim came back to life. It was an aborted musical, and we worked at a workshop of that for six months at Lincoln Center, and we did five performances of it. It's still incomplete for various reasons. Then I wrote *Six Degrees* and gave it to them, and we just went into production with it. Another play that we did a reading of a short while ago, *Four Baboons Adoring the Sun,* we're going to do as soon as we get a director. Jerry Zaks, who did the last two plays, is doing a revival on Broadway of *Guys and Dolls* and is not available. I feel that I'm just at home; you're involved in the theatre there, not just as a playwright but for one's knowledge of the theatre. You know you belong there, and that makes an enormous difference.

Interviewer: What would you say are the qualities, from your experience and from the point of view of a beginning playwright, that make a great producer?

Guare: Somebody who understands the story that you want to tell. What makes a good production is that everybody involved in it is trying to tell the same story, is after the same effect. A great producer is somebody who understands what the play wants to be and will help assemble the director who will most answer the challenge of the demands of that play, the best set designer for it, the best costume designer who will know. Anybody can open a play. Amateurs open plays; they just say, "I'll get a play and hire some terrific people and put it on." A producer's job begins the day it opens, because what reviews are are a handful of cards that are dealt to you. No play gets all raves which just say, "Wow, this play sells itself." A good producer knows how you make the play run, how you give the play realistic life. It's not enough just to open. A producer's job in a sense begins when everybody else's ends. The producer assembles everybody and makes sure they are working under optimum conditions, and then on opening night when the reviews come out the producer's real job begins—to say, "How do I get the people in to see this play?"

Interviewer: How do they?

Guare: Well, that's why there are very few new producers. Where are the people who find the visionary way of doing theatre? I'm not a producer but that's what there's a sore lack of.

Interviewer: Do you consider yourself a political writer—with a small *p*?

Guare: I think you're political if you're trying to show that people are the products of more than just psychological conditioning. I think that, generally, naturalistic writing is apolitical, because naturalistic writing is about sheer behavior and kitchen-sink truth. I think that when you're trying to work on an antinaturalistic level, you're trying to bring the whole world into it. You're trying to have more energy on that stage than the simple frustrations between two people.

Interviewer: Do you think that because theatre is by nature social—that is, you're watching it with a group of people—that that makes it more necessary that it be political?

Guare: I think so, yes.

Interviewer: Whereas a novel you read by yourself.

Guare: It's that people come out of their homes to go to a communal place to experience it, and they have to come out of that theatre and return home. You have to go out into the street in the city to see theatre generally, and I think that going to the theatre begins the minute you leave home.

Interviewer: What terrifies you?

Guare: The blank page; you have to fill it up. An empty stage, the first day of rehearsal, when you're auditioning people, the unknown—am I making the right choice? In the theatre, you make a decision on a whim and say, "All right, we have to jump into it, make that decision right now," and it's a decision that you'll live with for the rest of your life.

Interviewer: What do you feel the status of the playwright is in American society today?

Guare: Nobody quite knows what playwrights do. An audience still thinks actors make up the lines, and they think that the director obviously had all the ideas. In the last twenty-five years, the playwright has generally been treated as somebody who supplies a number of lines, but then the director shapes them and supplies the true meaning to them. Any time that playwriting is considered part of literature is to be applauded. Plays are not reviewed when the book is published. The book section will say, "Well, that play has already been reviewed by the theatre section. It doesn't have any interest to us; it doesn't belong to our world." So playwrights find ourselves not knowing quite where we belong, whether we are in show business or literature; it's a very odd place where we belong. But it's okay by me because I like being in never-never land.

Interviewer: You've worked in the movies as well as for the theatre, and the cliché about screenwriting is that all you are doing is providing a blueprint and that after you've provided it people just take off with it and you get no credit. A playwright gets a little more respect from his peers, doesn't he?

Guare: Well, you use the words "take off." The first movie I worked on was a picture called *Taking Off.* It was Milos Forman's first American movie, and it was just a great experience. It was a lot of fun, working with Milos. One had to respect the way Milos worked; he didn't even like actors. It was quite remarkable the way he worked, not letting people see the script and deciding on the lines in his own original form of English. It was extraordinary, this wonderful movie that I don't think anyone ever saw. Buck Henry and a woman named Lynn Carlin were the leads in it. Milos would say things like, "All right Buck, now you say, 'Why do you a-think she run away?' And Lynn, you say, 'Because she phones, she phones, she always phones!' Okay, got it? Roll 'em. 'Why do you think she ran away? Because she would've phoned. She always phones.' Okay, print it. Now you say. . . . " Ten years later I wrote a film for Louis Malle, *Atlantic City,* and I was there every day. Louis said the immortal words to the producers who were shocked that they had to pay money to the screenwriter to show up. They asked, "Why is he there?" And Louis said the immortal words that should be carved over every studio wall. He said, "If you have somebody here for the hair, why not somebody here for the words?"

The cliché is you're just being a prostitute to work in the movies, that theatre is perfect and Broadway is horrible, and off-off Broadway is even more pure. The only time I've ever felt horrible, that I did something horrible, was off-Broadway where I did something against my own wishes to keep an actor. It all comes down to who you work with. I feel that the script for *Atlantic City* is as much mine as a play is. It's Louis's, it's our job; we all did our work. Milos Forman and Louis Malle are two guys who treat a writer terrifically, and they respect him, but the copyright for *Atlantic City* is owned by two people up in Montreal. A developer can do anything he wants to it; he can bring a writer in to change the ending. That's the producer's right—and you're paid up front for that, for selling the copyright to your work, as I said earlier.

Interviewer: Do you approach screenwriting differently from writing a play? Has your filmwriting informed or affected your playwriting?

Guare: Working on a movie is very much like working on a musical, in that when you're working on a musical you have to say, "Well, this part will be okay because the music will take care of this. I don't have to write this scene because the choreographer will do this part." When you write a play, the audience needs so little, a crumb, to make the setting. *Women and Water* had thirty-five scenes in it, and it could take place on a bare stage. No matter what problems the play had, the audience never said, "I didn't know where I was"—and that was an extraordinary lesson for me. That's the great thing, for me, writing for movies: that it got me out of the one set. That's been a great liberation. But working on a musical and working on a film are very similar in that in a musical you just say, "The composer will take care of this part" or, in a film, "The camera will take care of this amount of energy."

Interviewer: I don't know if you'd agree with this, but in the movies a director or sometimes even a fantastic performer can make the film even if the screenplay isn't quite there, but I've never seen a production in which I thought the script was weak that the director or the actors could get very much above.

Guare: I disagree with you.

Interviewer: You do?

Guare: Yes. For example, Sarah Bernhardt and Eleonora Duse toured around for years in some turkeys. I think that a star is somebody who makes us want to look at them. We don't want to look at them in anything, but I think that, because plays have become fewer and far between, that time of the stage vehicle when we would go see a great star doesn't exist anymore. But I think that there are people that the camera either likes or doesn't like. It was interesting seeing somebody like Madonna onstage in David Mamet's play. She did a very, very solid job, but it just didn't have any sense of the majesty of her, whatever manipulated aura is on film. A star is a star; a star is somebody you just want to look at.

Interviewer: When you finish a play, do you feel it's complete?

Guare: No, it's incomplete. It's a team. You go out and you say, "Who is the best person to do this? Who should direct this?" When we were first doing *Blue Leaves* we couldn't find a director for it. John Lahr, who was working at the Guthrie Theater, said, "There's a director here named Mel Shapiro who's just done a brilliant production of *Merton of the Movies,* and I think you should see him." He was coming to New York to do a production of a Vaclav Havel play, and I went to see the play at the small theatre in Lincoln Center. This production of the Havel play had a feeling that I wanted. There was an energy in the air that that play generated, and I said, "That's what I want my play to be." There was something that I recognized, a haunting quality that that play had. I met the director, Mel Shapiro, and the star that played in that play, Harold Gould, and they both came and did *Blue Leaves* the next year.

The same thing happened when we were trying to do the revival of *House of Blue Leaves.* I went down to the Public Theater to see a Chris Durang play called *The Marriage of Bette and Boo,* with Chris Durang in it. It was so funny but reached a level of psychic pain. At the end I went to Jerry Zaks and I said, "Would you please do my play?" He said, "Strangely enough, I did the play at Dartmouth ten years ago, and I've always wanted to do it again." So that was that.

It's about recognizing sensibilities; that's why I said before you've got to see everything. You just say, "Oh, I like the way that designer works. I like the way that that designer does something. I like the way those costumes were designed. I like the way those people look." You've got to be aware of everything on that stage, because everything on that stage is going to be called playwriting. You see plays that in a bare room, a rehearsal room, are beautiful, and they get onstage and, oh God, the floor is wrong. I remember there was a production out in Chicago in 1976 for the Bicentennial; they were trying to discover lost American plays and were doing a farce by William Gillette called *Too Much Johnson* about very strait-laced people going into the jungle. Jack Gilford, a great clown, was in it, and in rehearsal it was spectacularly funny. You really felt that a play was going to be restored by this production. Then in dress rehearsal they put the costumes on, and they looked so beautiful, but they were in very, very stiff material. You couldn't see the actors' bodies when they fell down; it was a production that was baffled and destroyed by the material of the costumes, but everybody said, "What a rotten play!" It was a key lesson for me to say you really have got to know everything. You've got to know if it's a comedy, you've got to know the questions to ask the designer.

In the current production of *Six Degrees,* I told the set designer, "All I know is, it's got to move fast, because I just did a production of a play at Yale and the scenery looked pretty as a picture, but it took thirty seconds or a minute to change each scene, and in a farce that's an eternity." Tony Walton understood that, and he and Jerry Zaks wanted the play to move quickly. One of the problems of that stage at Lincoln Center is it's not in the round but it's a thrust, and the entrances and exits are very, very far away, so it's terribly hard to make a quick entrance and exit. Jerry Zaks wrestled with it for five weeks before he said, "Everybody is telling stories"—one of the lines in the play is "Oh, have I got a story for you"—

and he said, "Stories sitting around a campfire," so he put the actors in the front row so they could just appear. That was people working together, where you become part of a team. Being a playwright acknowledges our reliance on other people, and that's one of the joys of it, that it is a world. I've very rarely had a play done that hasn't created some sort of relationship, some sort of new event in my life. Each production that you do opens up a new door; some new person enters your life, or you take a turn in your life that you never expected. A play is a world.

Interviewer: Can you tell the story about your mother seeing the first scene of *Bosoms and Neglect* on TV?

Guare: Oh, it was a nightmare.

Interviewer: Would you prefer not to tell it?

Guare: I don't even know how to say it. There's a play called *Bosoms and Neglect,* and the first scene in the play was a challenge for me to write because it happened word for word. An event happened to me, and I came out and wrote it down because I didn't know what to do with it, it was so shocking to me. It was incredibly personal, and it was shocking. I was not emotionally prepared for it, and I said, "Here is something I don't know what to do with—it terrifies me, it scares me, it challenges me. I don't know what to do with this event." And so I said, "I'm going to write a play about it." Using this real event as a springboard for a play to see what would happen: that was my challenge. You've got to be prepared for everything. My mother knew nothing of what the play was about. She'd say, "Oh, what's it about?" And I'd say, "Oh, nothing. It's not about anything. It's just nothing." She said, "I've never heard you say this about a play before." And I said, "It's just about nothing. It wouldn't interest you." She turned on the reviews, and they had a section from the play there on all the channels. The scene they elected to show was the word-for-word reportage of what had happened to her. So not only were the reviews on television horrible, but it was like a nightmare that she turned on the television and there was one of the secretest, darkest moments of her life. That's the story. As we say, it was a learning experience. Anne Meara, who had been Bunny in the original production of *Blue Leaves,* went to my mother and explained to her that it was all right; so I've always been grateful to Anne Meara for calming my mother down. It's one of the dangers of having an artist in the family. You don't quite know whether what you're going to say is going to end up where, but there you are.

Interviewer: Can you explain the title of *Six Degrees of Separation*? Also, what about the racial issues in the play?

Guare: The title comes from a statistical theory that's gone around for a number of years that there are 5.8 people between every other person on this planet. I was just sort of fascinated by that, and it seemed that "5.8 Points of Separation" didn't seem to be a good title, so I just rounded it off. About the racial issue, I think that race is still the one issue that we live with every day that is so hot that we still don't know what to do with. I was fascinated by this story because it's about what white people want black people to be, what black people think white people want them to be, what our self-image is. I wanted to try to strip those away and see what I felt about them. Does that answer the question? I can't speak in any doctrinaire way about the racial issues, because I didn't go into it with a program. I went into it to find out how I felt about it and how we deal with it. It was an issue I wanted to deal with—to whatever degree of success, I can't answer. It was a world I wanted to enter.

Interviewer: Are there any endings, especially happy endings, that you find inappropriate for the modern stage?

Guare: Well, yes, I think a play that ends with a legless hero going "Yeah!" or a blind person overcoming all. I mean any ending that just shows "you can do it," that is, the things that belong to TV movies, where you say, "God, leprosy isn't bad, it will just make me a better person for having this." Yes, I think that any ending that just says that no matter what, if you want it enough, you'll get it and you deserve it and God loves you. I think that we have to have endings that say, "You know what? God doesn't care, and chances are if you win it he'll take it away in about five seconds anyway." I think that the lines are very clearly drawn now between television and theatre and that the theatre is someplace you go for some degree of truth. If you've committed yourself to television, then you can't play a character that's got a rough side to him, because the viewers might go to another channel; and if you're a writer you can't have something that might end bleakly, because the advertisers will say, "Sorry, we don't like that." I think that we have to recognize the freedom of the theatre. It's the one place in this likeable world where we can go where we don't have to be likeable, where we can listen and find a new entry into an old situation.

Interviewer: Could you enlighten us about *Marco Polo Sings a Solo*?

Guare: I can't even enlighten myself about it! That's a play that I started writing when I left London on an airplane, and I said that I was going to finish the first act of it by the time I got to Kennedy Airport in New York. It's a play that there are about fifteen different drafts of, and I realized with that play—it was so much fun to work on that I kept writing and rewriting it, or making it do what I wanted, that I realized that you can't spend that much time on rewriting a play. A play for all its faults is going to be that. There's no such thing as a perfect play; every play has got its broken back somehow, and I must move on to other plays. It was great fun working on that, mainly because it got me to Nantucket where part of my life really began.

When we were doing it up in Nantucket, Jimmy Woods, a wonderful actor who was in the original production, came out onstage and gave this long monologue which wasn't in the play at all. I had thrown it out the day before, and I went back to Jimmy and I said, "Where did that come from? What are you doing?" And he said, "Well, I went to your room to pick you up, and you were out, and I saw that your door was open, and I went through your garbage can to see what was there, and I saw all these papers rolled up, and I said, 'I like this. I can say it'"—so we put the speech in and it stayed! It was a play that was so freeform that you could put anything into it. It was a play that got me realizing that structure was not a cage. I understood from that play—not about me, but I understood that Ibsen was a great playwright because he made the machinery work in a poetic way rather than being formulaic. There are so many layers of the play for me, so many versions of the play, that I see it and I sort of can't see it clearly. It was personally, in a growing way, one of those plays I learned an extraordinary amount from.

Interviewer: Could you tell us about how Joseph Papp worked with writers in a "fatherly way"?

Guare: Joe and Bernie Gersten are wonderful producers because they make the impossible happen. They figure out a new way to do things. They figure out a way for people to work at their optimum, and they challenge people to go beyond themselves. They push actors further than they have gone. They make people find new parts of themselves.

Interviewer: Who are your two favorite characters and why?

Guare: Oh, Clytemnestra. Mama Rose in *Gypsy* because she takes all those elements which belong to musical comedy and pushes into new psychic areas. I don't know. A couple of years ago, I saw an actress named Fiona Shaw do *Mary Stuart* in London, and it was just wonderful. It was just a play where you saw a great character. Are you thinking of great performances? Maggie Smith's Hedda Gabler. In my own work? You don't have favorite characters, because you just want somebody to carry the plot. I like Bunny in *The House of Blue Leaves* because she moves the plot, because you can rely on her to come in and cut to the chase. I like characters that help the plot along and keep it moving and let us know where we are.

Interviewer: And the others you just tolerate?

Guare: I'm always in a sense more admiring of the ringmaster. They're controlling, telling the audience where to look. The Wallendas can fly, but it's got to be the ringmaster who sets up the atmosphere for the Wallendas, to say, "Watch out, if they fall they'll fall further than anyone has ever fallen. And you'll be seeing something which you've never seen before." I like the character of the ringmaster better than the Flying Wallendas. You expect the Wallendas to do something beautiful, but I think that I like the characters in the play that tell the audience what it is they're to feel as opposed to what is actually onstage.

A. R. Gurney

A. R. Gurney was born in 1930 in Buffalo, New York, was educated at Williams College and the Yale School of Drama, and taught literature for many years at the Massachusetts Institute of Technology. He is the author of three novels, The Gospel According to Joe *(1974),* Entertaining Strangers *(1977), and* The Snow Ball *(1984), and of the plays* The Rape of Bunny Stuntz *(1962),* The Comeback *(1965),* The Open Meeting *(1965; revised, 1990),* The David Show *(1966),* The Golden Fleece *(1968),* The Problem *(1968),* The Love Course *(1970),* Scenes From American Life *(1970),* The Old One-Two *(1973),* Children *(1974),* Who Killed Richard Cory? *(1976),* The Middle Ages *(1977),* The Wayside Motor Inn *(1977),* The Dining Room *(1982),* What I Did Last Summer *(1983),* The Golden Age *(1984),* The Perfect Party *(1986)* Another Antigone *(1986),* Sweet Sue *(1986),* The Cocktail Hour *(1988),* Love Letters *(1989),* The Snow Ball *(1990),* The Old Boy *(1991),* The Fourth Wall *(1992), and* Later Life

(1993). He has received the Vernon Rice Award (1971), a Rockefeller playwright-in-residence award (1977), a National Endowment for the Arts award (1981), an American Academy and Institute of Arts and Letters Award of Merit (1987), a New England Theatre Conference award for greater achievement (1987), a Lucille Lortel outstanding production award (1989), and honorary degrees from Williams College (1984) and from the State University of New York at Buffalo (1992). This interview took place on February 24 and March 24, 1993.

▶ ─────────────────────────────────── ◀

Interviewer: How much of a struggle is it, still, for you to get a new play produced?

Gurney: I think it's less of a struggle than it used to be, possibly because I've learned to write rather simple and easily doable plays, with good parts, which is one of the secrets of getting your play done. It's not simply making it inexpensive—small casts, simple sets (they don't have to be one set)—but they certainly have to be simply conceived. Also I'm learning more and more that all the parts have to be interesting. You can't write any extraneous parts. You can't get actors to stand around and hold spears anymore. So getting produced has gotten easier, which doesn't mean it's terribly easy. It still involves an awful lot of luck: whether there is a slot available here or there, and so forth.

Interviewer: Where does a Broadway production rank in your set of goals? Is it still a final test of a play's viability for you, or has the scene in America changed so that regional productions are sufficient to validate a play?

Gurney: Well, I suppose it should be a goal for me, but it really isn't as much. I'm not even sure it ever was. The Broadway audience, as I perceive it when I go to a Broadway play, doesn't really seem to be my audience. I've had one play on Broadway, *Sweet Sue*, and another sort of on Broadway, *Love Letters*, and the economic pressure on you and on the whole production seems to me somewhat inhibiting artistically. So I don't really write for Broadway any more, if I ever did. I feel lucky enough to have a play done off-Broadway or elsewhere in the country. I don't have a yearning to see my name in lights on Broadway. I simply don't.

Interviewer: Your career has been built mainly in what we would call the nonprofit theatre and off-Broadway, and you have worked with those audiences. Have you formed a clear distinction between the advantages and disadvantages of working in that realm of theatre?

Gurney: Of course, there's something about a New York audience, and I think particularly a New York off-Broadway audience, which is very sharp, fresh, and "with it." Audiences in regional theatre can be that way, but they tend to be less invested in the theatre than New York audiences are. You don't have that final ping of excitement and acceptance in the regional theatre. But, on the other hand, what I like about regional theatre audiences, resident theatre audiences, not-for-profit audiences, is that some of them are there from a sense of responsibility to the *idea* of theatre. You do at least have a sense of common values in those audiences, not that those values are all good. But at least there's a kind of coherent community you're speaking to or against, which I find exciting. With a Broadway audience, the assumptions are different. They're there to be entertained and to get their money's worth. I don't think you get that in the regional theatre. There they're interested more in being enlightened, and in celebrating this theatre they've probably subscribed to.

Interviewer: Bringing this to your particular plays—and you have had a good deal of experience not only with Broadway audiences but with New England audiences, and with Southern California audiences because you've done a lot of work with the Old Globe—can you think of moments in the plays that scored, or got different responses, from the Hartford audiences and from the Old Globe audiences?

Gurney: There are certain solid laughs that occur no matter where you are. And then there are certain audiences that seem to get a kick out of one aspect of the play in the West where they might not so much in the East.

Interviewer: Can you think of a specific instance?

Gurney: I can't, offhand. I suppose I could if I looked up my rewrites, my comments, or my notes on a production. But no, at the moment I can't.

Interviewer: Do you define even more sharply than you already have the audience member that you're writing for?

Gurney: I think I tend to see myself writing for a kind of ideal, educated middle class, but not necessarily a white middle class. I sort of have an ideally democratic audience in my mind.

Interviewer: With a small *d*?

Gurney: With a small *d*, yes. Not for a political party! I assume a certain amount of education on the part of the audience. And I try to assume that they're there, again, as I said earlier, not simply to be entertained but to sort of work with me as a playwright toward some kind of a communal sensibility.

Interviewer: If I'm remembering right, *Love Letters* has been optioned by a motion picture company.

Gurney: That's true.

Interviewer: And you've completed the screenplay.

Gurney: That's true also.

Interviewer: Could you talk a little bit about the changes that you had to make, contrasting the playscript with the screenplay?

Gurney: Obviously it was a tough adjustment because the play thrives on, depends on, its simplicity. It's simply two people sitting at a desk reading letters back and forth. The fun of going to the play is letting the audience imagine the events they write about. With the movie, of course, you have to show all that, which means you have to change the thing. The whole adult love story becomes much more important in the movie because in order to interest stars in doing it, you can't simply make it, say, 50 percent adult, 30 percent adolescent, and 20 percent children, which is the way the play is. You have to really make it 80 percent the adult story with a few flashbacks, maybe, into earlier periods. So the whole form changed because of that.

Also, we had to bring it up to date, in a sense. The play *Love Letters* is about two people who were born in the early thirties. Well, for various reasons, again, if you're going to interest stars in doing it today, and those stars are going to ultimately go to bed together, you've got to really make them a little younger than the characters in the play. So these characters are born right after World War II, which changes a lot of the details of their lives and the events of their lives. It really became a very different thing. The screenplay is about letter writing to some degree, but we don't have too many shots of people sitting there writing; that's not terribly interesting. So we established the idea that they communicate through letters, but most of the time we use dialogue and voice-overs to show the events of their lives.

Interviewer: I've heard that *Love Letters* was the first play that you wrote on your new computer. Is that true?

Gurney: That's true.

Interviewer: So you took a twenty-first-century piece of technology and immediately revived an eighteenth-century art form!

Gurney: That's true.

Interviewer: That's marvelously rich. I think that's great.

Gurney: I think that happens a lot with me, and I suspect with other writers. You think about, write about, what you don't have. It was the very fact that I'd always written with a pen, liquid ink on lined paper, and it was the very fact that I was no longer using that particular instrument, that made me, for better or worse, write about pens and paper on a machine which has nothing to do with either. It was the same thing with *The Dining Room*. We were living in Newton, Massachusetts, at the time, and because of the energy crisis, we'd turned our dining room into a living room and cut off the living room part of our house. So suddenly I was living in a house with no dining room, and it made me want to write a play about the implications of a dining room.

Interviewer: Could you point to other aspects of your process of writing that have changed because of your move to a computer?

Gurney: *Love Letters* began just by sort of playing with the computer, but with the plays after *Love Letters*, I normally do start the initial draft with pen and ink and paper. I get halfway into it, and when I feel I'm on a roll, then I shift to the computer because the computer makes it much easier to revise, go over, change. And of course, that can be bad as well as good. I think sometimes you tend to iron out some of wrinkles in your writing when you're working with a computer, because it's so easy to revise and go over and review. And sometimes the wrinkles in one's writing, the inconsistencies and odd little quirks that are not quite explicable, are the ones that give it a particular life. That's a trap you have to watch when you're using a computer.

Interviewer: I know that people who are going to be reading this are going to be curious about this. What hardware and software do you use?

Gurney: I use an IBM PC simply because it was given to me by my father-in-law, who was very much interested in computers. Every time he gets a new one he gives me his old one.

Interviewer: Is he in the computer business?

Gurney: He's a retired gentleman of eighty-some years, but he fell in love with computers. Just by giving me one and teaching me to use it, he persuaded me to switch—and I've stayed with it.

Interviewer: This runs counter to American mythology. It's supposed to be your children that introduce you to computers. In this case it was your father-in-law!

Gurney: That's right. That's interesting, isn't it? I know I shouldn't, and I'm going to change, but I'm still on the old dinosaur of a program, WordStar 2000. I'm either going to change to WordPerfect or Word. I get conflicting advice from different people on which to change to; maybe this summer I'll finally change.

Interviewer: Is there software for playwrights that puts it in a script form for you?

Gurney: There isn't. I devised my own formatting, and that's very easy. I don't think any programming has resolved the problem of making sure that the character who speaks is on the same page as his or her dialogue. Once you make one little change, one little rewrite, then the whole formatting goes off and you find the name of the character at the bottom of the page and his or her dialogue at the top of the next page. I don't think that problem has been resolved.

Interviewer: I have had a good deal of pleasure reading your novels. I think *Entertaining Strangers* is one of the best academic novels. I think you just got it absolutely right from page one to the end. And I think *The Gospel According to Joe* is fascinating and completely absorbing. I have been recommending that to my colleagues and friends. I know we have talked about this before, but I am more interested than ever that you find the play form attracts you so strongly. Why are there only four novels by A. R. Gurney?

Gurney: There really are only three published ones. There's a fourth one which I kind of withdrew. I started sending it around, but it was obviously incomplete. I withdrew it, and ultimately, at least parts of it turned into *The Fourth Wall.*

Interviewer: Tell me more about that. In *Broadway Talks,* you said, "Well, if I can see the floor plan of the stage, if I know how the characters get on and off, then I think I'm working with a play. But if I can't see those exits and entrances, then maybe it's a novel." Has anything about that changed in ten years?

Gurney: Not really. I would make that a little more specific now. If I'm clear about the stage space (and it doesn't have to be a room, it could be a universe), but if I can see the space and the space is limited in the sense that it's workable onstage, then I seem to want to write a play. *Entertaining Strangers* obviously has certain theatrical things about it. It's the old *Tartuffe* plot, after all, transposed to academia. I remember starting it in a faculty room, then trying to do a kind of multiple-set play, but there were just too many characters, too many spaces that it wanted to take place in. I just decided that, even if I tried to wrench it into a play, it would never really be done; it would be too expensive. So I said, "What the hell, let me try to make it into a novel."

The same with *The Snow Ball*. Again, that started as a play. I said, "Nobody's going to put this on." So I turned it into a novel. Then, after I had gained some reputation, Jack O'Brien from the Old Globe said, "Let's think about that in terms of a play." So I tried to. Whether I succeeded or not, I don't know. I might have been trying to put the toothpaste back in the tube, yet I'm kind of proud of the way I did it. It's different from the novel, the play version; it is quite elaborate. And I think I'm more at home in plays, possibly because I've done more of them. The emotional payoff from drama is obviously more immediate. With a play, you know where you are with an audience, for better or worse, very quickly. With a book, you don't. Maybe I'm just more at home with that kind of immediate gratification.

Interviewer: When you were growing up in Buffalo, obviously your imagination must have been deeply stimulated by the novels and the stories that you read. I know you were taken to plays in Buffalo, but somewhere along the line the pull of the stage must have begun to overwhelm the power of the novel form that attracts so many others.

Gurney: Well, yes, I liked to read a lot. I liked to read novels when I was little. But whenever I had a school assignment for a composition—and in those days we were always assigned compositions—I remember a number of times I'd say, "Can I write a play instead?" I always seemed to like the dialogue form. I remember as a little kid I used to hate what I called "I books," books that were told in the first person. I always felt as a kid that that was such a limited perspective. I liked the third-person narrative where you had an outsider. Now, that's not necessarily dramatic. You can have a third-person narrative without going into drama, but the reverse is certainly true; it's very hard to write a play from an individual perspective. You can try. Tennessee Williams tries in *The Glass Menagerie,* but in the end that's not what it's about. The most significant scene in *The Glass Menagerie* takes place when the narrator isn't there.

In any case, something about my sense of perspective made me veer toward drama too. And of course, when I was at college, playwriting in America was very celebrated. The reviews of Miller's plays, of Wiliams's plays, of Inge's plays, or of any plays seemed much more exciting than book reviews. To be a playwright at that time seemed to me to be much more exciting than to be a novelist. Yes, Cheever and Updike were beginning to write, and of course, Norman Mailer and Salinger had already been writing, but I didn't see myself as them. I wanted to be a playwright and to have a play on Broadway, because at that time there was no off-Broadway.

Interviewer: What do you think of critics? Have you ever learned anything from them?

Gurney: It's a very complicated thing. Some critics I've learned a lot from.

Interviewer: Would you care to name some names?

Gurney: When I was first starting out in Boston, when I was teaching at MIT (I'd started out before that, but by then I'd begun to take myself a little more seriously), Elliot Norton was the critic at the *Boston Herald*. He was a very intelligent man, and I was in a summer workshop up at Tanglewood where he was the critic in residence, and I listened to him very carefully. He was very helpful and very encouraging. Harold Clurman was very encouraging to me as well. He was also involved in this summer program. I went there twice. Both those critics were very influential on my writing and my sense of what plays are all about.

Interviewer: When were those sessions?

Gurney: I think '67 and '70. It was the Boston University workshop at Tanglewood. I had a play done each year. *Scenes from American Life* was '70, and both Clurman and Norton were involved in that one. The earlier one, in '67, was a play which then was called "David and Goliath"—it ultimately became *The David Show*—and that was again Clurman. They taught me to take myself seriously as a writer. Since then, it's been very tricky. Yes, you certainly can't write for the critics, and they can be very hurtful, and destructive, and mean-spirited, some of them. I don't like to read them very much for that reason. But others—Bill Henry or Edith Oliver—have been very supportive and helpful over the years. But because many critics can be so mean-spirited, it's very hard for me to read them even if I wanted to learn something; so I've kind of made a point of not reading the reviews.

Interviewer: Do you ever hear from audience members? Do people write to you?

Gurney: A lot.

Interviewer: Do you save those letters, the theatre historian said, hopefully?

Gurney: Oh, I've saved all those letters. Some are critical, some are not. And I try to answer them, although maybe not immediately. If someone's going to take the time to write me and think about what I've written, I can certainly take the time to write back.

Interviewer: Has anything an audience member written to you changed your angle of vision in the next project or suggested an idea for a play?

Gurney: Not that I'm aware of. If they have, or if they changed a perspective or changed an attitude, I think the suggestion must have been absorbed in such a way that by the time that the change came out, it would have been very hard to say, "I made that change because of that letter." I'd like to think I respond to what people tell me and learn from life, but I also know that the creative process is a very complicated thing, and it's very hard to attribute it to one particular source.

Interviewer: How involved do you get in the mounting of a first production?

Gurney: I try to get as involved as I can, and that's very involved. I certainly pick the director.

Interviewer: Did you pick the director for *Fourth Wall* here in Chicago?

Gurney: Yes, David Saint. He took it out on a kind of minitour this summer—Westport, the Cape, and Cambridge. He and I met beforehand. We talked about it. The playwright, with the producer, of course, always picks the director and participates in the picking of the technical staff, the set, and the costumes. You go over the set very carefully, the costumes as well, the lighting, and certainly the casting, which is a huge element of the play. I try to sit in on a lot of the rehearsals. With this one (*The Fourth Wall* in Chicago) I'm not going to be here every minute because I think I've done most of the groundwork already, but I'll certainly come back during previews and try to get it right.

Interviewer: Then, during the run, if you're in New York and the show is running, do you stop in?

Gurney: I like to drop in and just take a look at it and say hello to the actors. I find it very difficult to sit through one of my plays once it's done and out and reviewed. I don't know why that is. I can see part of it, I can stop in and see a particular scene I'm worried about; or if I haven't seen it in a year, I can stop in. But it's very painful for me just to go in and sit in the theatre. I can listen to it over the intercom; I can talk to the actors about it afterwards. If I have something specific to do, if the director isn't in town and we've gotten word that the actors are getting off course, then I'll go and look at it very carefully. But just to go and be there and enjoy it is impossible.

Interviewer: Why do you think that is?

Gurney: Because I've seen it, I've done it. There's nothing more for me to do. If there's something to do, fine. But I've written it as well as I can. The audience is now responding to it. With *Love Letters,* of course, it's different because it may have a different cast. It is terribly interesting to see how they do it. But, oh, just to sit there! Some writers love to do that. But I can't.

Interviewer: How much of a play do you know when you're writing it? Do you get it all blocked out? Chekhov is apparently famous for having it all worked out in detail before he set down line one. Other playwrights take the Pinter method and just listen to the voices in the head and follow them where they go—or at least he says he does. Where do you fall along that continuum?

Gurney: I think I'm somewhere in between. In order for the story to tell itself, to present itself, I really have to have some idea of where I want it to end up. I might not end up there, but I start off at least with that in mind. Then sometimes the characters do take it in an entirely different direction, and that magnificent climax or ending that I was working for doesn't seem to want to be there anymore. I find the characters either going into another play or, if I'm in trouble, they shuffle off entirely and there's no play at all. It really depends on the play, but in general I have a vague sense of shape in my head, particularly where I want it to end. I do believe that drama is about what happens next, and if I don't know what's going to happen next, or have some instinct of what I want to have happen next, then I don't think the play will have the necessary momentum.

Interviewer: Could you point to one of your plays where this sense of being taken over was particularly strong?

Gurney: Many of them. *The Dining Room* would be an example. I didn't know where it was going to end. All I knew was that I wanted to have a play that took place in one room during the course of a day. It had to get more exciting, and something important had to happen toward the end of the day. What could you have take place in a dining room as the light is beginning to wane? I suppose it had to be something about death, which has become a kind of penultimate scene in *The Dining Room,* as the table is being set for the final dinner party, the ultimate scene. So that seemed like a kind of logical outcome of the form.

At other times I find myself sort of straining to get to a climax, and those aren't normally as good. Recently I wrote a play called *The Old Boy* which builds to a certain speech. I've sold it to the movies, and I know the guy who's doing the screenplay, so I think that speech will be right, but I never got it right onstage. It felt strained to me. It needs the cutting back and forth between speaker and audience in response. I tried to do that in one draft, but it didn't work onstage. I never got the climax for that play quite right.

I just finished a play called *Later Life,* which is going on at Playwrights Horizons this spring. There I had a very specific climax in mind, and what I thought was a wonderful ending. The first draft had that ending in it, but the second draft went in an entirely different direction, toward a different climax. I hope it works.

Interviewer: Can you give me an idea about what the ending was without telling the whole story?

Gurney: I don't think I could. I think the best thing to do would be to talk about that after you have seen the play. Otherwise I'd waste your time and my energy telling the plot.

Interviewer: How much writing and rewriting do you do before and during rehearsals and out of town?

Gurney: That depends on the play, but normally quite a lot. Once the actors seize it, you want to write for them, too. I envy those playwrights, like Shakespeare and Molière and, I suspect, Sophocles and Pinter, who worked with companies, and who could see and hear particular actors every day and sometimes even act with them. They did all that work in their head that I can do only when I get into rehearsal.

Interviewer: Is this something that you go to with eagerness? When you go back to the hotel tonight, are you going to sit down with your laptop?

Gurney: At this point with this play, *The Fourth Wall*, I think it's probably a mistake to make any more major adjustments. I spoke to the actress playing Peggy, and I did a little rewriting earlier, just two lines, while she and I were talking. Certainly that's happened. When I can see where a problem is, I'm eager to solve it. But I think with this play I've done most of that work in the tryout this past summer.

Interviewer: I know from prior conversations and from talking with some of the people who have acted in your plays that you have a great deal of affection for actors, and the actors in your plays have a lot of affection for you and your work. What was the curve of your learning about actors and about writing for actors? What do you know now about writing for actors that you didn't know in *The David Show* back in the late sixties?

Gurney: I think I know a little more about acting technique; I know the instruments better. It's like writing, when I first started playwriting, I mean. I had gone to the Yale School of Drama, so I'd worked with actors there, gone to classes with them, and done a lot of workshops with them. So I knew actors, but the more you work with them, the more you realize that they are artists. Their instincts are something to listen to very carefully. You should not get into an adversarial relationship with them, because we're all working on the same property, we're all trying to get the same effect. I've learned immeasurably from them. The rhythms of lines, for instance, I've learned from actors. The rhythm of writing is so important, and you learn from how actors read and act a line. The importance of pauses, all those things that make a play work and live onstage, you learn from actors. So I think it's very important for people who want to write for the stage or for television to work very closely with actors.

Interviewer: A theme that I keep seeing, that I think that you continue to place in the plays, is the question of education, the question of what is the common ground on which your audience can stand so that it can appreciate your play or any play, the sense of community that comes in. If one of your grandchildren comes to you in the next year or so and says, "I've written this little play, Grandpa, and I think I want to become a playwright like you"—let's say this grandchild is about fourteen—what would you recommend for the aspiring playwright as a pathway to develop the dramatist's skills, given the climate in America now?

Gurney: It's very different from what it was, in some ways; in some ways it's the same. Just as an aside before I answer that question, let me say that there is an awful lot of creative energy in drama in America right now. It's not necessarily on Broadway. That's not where it's happening, but off-Broadway and in the resident theatres. An awful lot of people are writing plays. Maybe they're not making a living doing it. Maybe they also have to write for television or do something else. Yet a lot of younger people are turning to the dramatic form to say what they want to say. So it's not quite as obsolete a form as I thought it was, as I would have thought, say, ten years ago.

I would say to my grandchild, "Get the play done." How do you get a play done? First, I'd say, "You're fourteen, you've written this play. See if you can get some friends of yours to read it in class. Just get the sense of performance. Get the idea of making the thing public. Let's not you and I sit and talk about whether it works or not. Because I'll say something and I know you won't believe me. But you will believe it when you just get three or four of your friends and you Xerox the script, put in in their hands, and have them read it in class. Then, if you can, get it done again. Persuade your drama teacher to do it for the school. Get people to come to it. There you'll either begin to be bitten by the bug, so that's all you want to do, or you'll say, 'This is not for me. I don't like my words being made fun of. I don't like the collaborative aspect of theatre. I don't want to have to argue with an actor about what a line says or means.'" Some people hate it, and some people never rise to the bait. So I would say to anybody starting out, do anything you can to get the play public and to get the collaborative experience going.

Interviewer: I wanted to ask you about the professors that you've put on the stage. There have been four or five of them, going back to *The Old One-Two,* I think. Tony in *A Perfect Party* has been a professor; and there are Professor Lesser in *The Fourth Wall* and Harper in *Another Antigone.* Have I left anybody else out? Professors in their private and public aspects also figure in *Three People, The Love Course, The Problem,* and *Later Life.* And in *Entertaining Strangers* the whole story is about professors. This is perfectly natural because of your long connection with academe; you've been a professor yourself. You're writing about what you know. Professor Lesser is probably the most a figure of fun. Harper is pretty serious.

Gurney: Yes. He and the professor in *The Old One-Two* are pretty much the same guy. They're both classical scholars. The professor in *The Old One-Two* is the less serious version of Harper. Yes. He's serious. He's supposed to be a good man, Harper.

Interviewer: Other than that you don't specify occupation too much.

Gurney: Well, there are stockbrokers, lawyers, and Richard Cory runs a business. I don't show many people in the workplace, except for professors. That's a workplace that I know pretty well. I don't have many office scenes; with the possible exception of *Richard Cory*, I don't have many scenes about men at work. I guess there are a few in *Scenes from American Life*. But I think the explanation for that is obvious: I don't know those other worlds very well.

Interviewer: In *Sweet Sue*, I think you deal for the first time with a woman who has a profession. She is an illustrator, and her move from illustrator to artist forms a key thread in the story. In *Another Antigone*, the dean is a woman, and her position and responsibilities as a dean figure very much in the play. But aside from those two characters, women in your plays are wives and mothers concerned with the well-being of the community, the sustainers of the community.

Gurney: I want to argue with you a little on that. Take Melissa in *Love Letters*: she is hardly a sustainer of the community. Peggy in *The Fourth Wall* has been a social worker; that doesn't do it for her anymore. Certainly the women in *The Cocktail Hour* have sat on hospital boards and done all that, and they are sustainers of the community in that sense. So in general you're right, but there are certainly exceptions to that.

Interviewer: There have been more exceptions recently, so I'm wondering if you connect this in your own mind to what's happening today?

Gurney: I'm trying to.

Interviewer: Having made that sociologically reductive kind of statement, I also hasten to add that the actors report that, all the way through, the women characters strike them as more complex and interesting, on the whole, than the men. Peggy and Julia in *The Fourth Wall* are more vital and complex and psychologically and spiritually attuned to their environment than the men are.

Gurney: I think that's a valid observation. I don't know what it says about me, but I think perhaps it says more about American society that the men, at least as I see them, tend to be more rigid. They tend to frame the world in a more rigid way and are less eager to adapt, to respond, to change. I'm writing about cultural change—that's what I'm really writing about all the time—and women seem to be able to respond to change in a way that men can't. Men tend to be obsessed with the past, with their own constructs, their own ideas. I think of *The Fourth Wall* because that's currently on my mind. Roger brings his piano with him from Buffalo and wants to play Cole Porter and really wants to go home. He's got to watch sports on television, and he's got his life all arranged, whereas the women are reaching. Even Julia is ultimately resilient. She'll go anywhere, do anything. And Peggy is yearning for some kind of newer world.

Interviewer: Even Floyd, who fancies that he is attuned and on top of things, is so in this very artificial and completely serious kind of way.

Gurney: That's right.

Interviewer: He ends up missing a good deal of what's going on and misinterpreting what's going on and misinterpreting what he could do possibly to affect it at all.

Gurney: And of course he and Julia can't go through the wall at the end. They end up locked in an old-fashioned domestic comedy. They're stuck.

Interviewer: You've always spoken of the desire for community. We've talked about that in connection with just about everything that you've written. And you have talked about the need to justify the use of the theatre, how this becomes an issue for you. You want to be sure that everything that you do as a writer for the theatre makes use of the theatre's genuine qualities.

Gurney: Communal aspects. Very much so.

Interviewer: You feel there's so much out there in the way of other options for people—television and film—that attracts us all strongly but that does not strike to the heart of the community the way the theatre can. You want to be sure that we're using what the theatre can do as much as we can.

Gurney: Right. Absolutely.

Interviewer: Could we put some definitions to the virtues that the theatre strives to sustain beyond community? If community is the goal, what are the objectives that we try to achieve on the way to that goal?

Gurney: Well, in the first place, the theatre is live and immediate. It's not on film or on tape. Every performance is new and fresh and different. You have the immediacy of *life,* of three-dimensional human beings who are onstage. It gives you a sense of *life.* Also it's traditional. It's an old, old medium. You are not simply putting on a play, but you are putting on a play in a tradition which goes way back to when the caveman first told a story around a fire. You are hooking your audience and yourself and your actors into a very old ceremony, which I like.

It's free. I don't mean that it doesn't cost money. But the writer is free to say things that he or she wants to say, which is not true in the movies or television, where every word is vetted and changed, or thoroughly questioned by the various executives who are in control. So there's much more of an opportunity to make a kind of personal statement in the theatre, an individual statement, for the writer and for the actors. The actors are freer onstage than they are in the movies or television. Thy don't end up on the cutting room floor. Their performance is something they create. Every night, it's there. The camera doesn't look away from them. They might not have every scene, but they are there.

So all those things—the immediacy, the sense of community, the sense of continuity, the sense of freedom—all these things appeal to me.

Interviewer: How much do the practices of theatre today assist achieving those virtues, and how much do they trip up the progress toward those goals?

Gurney: That's a very good question. If you're talking about the Broadway theatre, the economics involved, and the number of producers who have to get involved because of economics, you're moving more toward something like Hollywood or television. You simply have more people adjusting the product, telling you to take out that scene or put in this star. Freedom is jeopardized. You're not as free when you're writing for Broadway. I learned that with *Sweet Sue*.

The critical picture today is very tricky. The playwright, particularly if he or she wants to succeed beyond the local community, still has to go through New York. A New York success is still the imprimatur of theatre success in this country. And when I say that, I'm thinking of the *New York Times*. You can survive a bad review by the *Times*. Some writers do. Herb Gardner does. Neil Simon has. But nonetheless, for a young writer coming up, it's very hard. A young writer has to be approved by the *Times* in order to really succeed and get out there in the world. And that's unhealthy, the fact that one individual's opinion, no matter how bright he is, should so determine one's fate. That's not freedom, when you are at the mercy of one opinion.

The third problem is that your actors, more and more, are unwilling to commit themselves for very long to a play. It's not that they don't want to. It's simply that they need more money. They need to live. Fortunately for them, they have many other opportunities now, not simply in the movies and television, but soaps, commercials, voice-overs. So they don't have to be in plays. It's a tough thing, when you consider *The Fourth Wall*, to get four actors to commit four months of their lives to perform in Chicago.

What about their pets? What about their children? That's tough. Even in New York it's hard to get them to commit for very long, so the tools of the trade are less available these days. You no longer can call on actors even in New York. Many have moved to California. So those are the problems.

I keep thinking of the younger writers. They don't have the opportunity today to cut their teeth—as I did—with one-act plays, with workshops and coffeehouses and all those little places where we put on these plays, not for critics, just for audiences who wanted to go there, where we learned how to do it.

Beth Henley

Beth Henley was born in Jackson, Mississippi, in 1952. She received her undergraduate education at Southern Methodist University and did graduate work at the University of Illinois. Her first professionally produced play, Crimes of the Heart *(1979), won the New York Drama Critics Circle Award and the Pulitzer Prize. Her other plays are* Am I Blue *(1972),* The Wake of Jamey Foster *(1982),* The Miss Firecracker Contest *(1984),* The Lucky Spot *(1984),* The Debutante Ball *(1988),* Abundance *(1990),* Signature *(1991), and* Control Freaks *(1992). This interview took place on October 23, 1991.*

Interviewer: Why did you become a playwright?

Henley: My mother was an actress (she still is an actress); so I started going to the theatre when I was very young, and I always loved reading dialogue. She picked plays for the season at the theatre in Mississippi, and I would read the plays. I read plays early, and I loved the kind of magic of the theatre. I don't know; I just grew up with it.

Interviewer: Did you go to the rehearsals and get involved in the actual production of the plays by watching what was going on?

Henley: Yes. Seeing them tear down the sets afterwards, going back to the dressing rooms, and helping her learn her lines; it was a sanctuary for me, and it still is really.

Interviewer: Now that you're writing plays, are you still a large part of the play in the rehearsal process, or is the rehearsal process where you're letting go? Do you enjoy the rehearsal process?

Henley: Yes, I do. I love the rehearsal process because that's what theatre is about. It's this collaborative art, and you get to see other people enhance your work. Sometimes they "de-hance" your work, but it's just thrilling when someone throws an insight into something that you didn't know was there or when the melody of the lines goes together exactly right. Everybody is so passionate about it; it's always exhilarating to be around people that are filled with passion about what they're doing.

Interviewer: How old were you when you first started writing, and were plays the first thing you wrote?

Henley: I remember being really small, and I had a book where you're supposed to draw pictures and write a story, and I remember being so frustrated—I must have been very small—because I had so much to tell and I couldn't figure out how to tell it. I wrote a play in sixth grade, a musical called "Swing High, Swing Low" that I tried to produce with some friends. We included boys, and that was just hopeless because then it got way out of hand. Nobody would rehearse, and I was not very good at being a dictator. Then I took a creative writing class in which I wrote a story and had to read it in front of the class. It wasn't completed, and I hated it so much that I scrunched it up and threw it down and ran out of the class, but I didn't get in trouble. I was always shocked that I didn't get in trouble for behaving so hysterically.

Interviewer: How do you usually start when you write a play?

Henley: I always start with a blank page and a lot of exasperation and self-loathing because I haven't written anything in so long. I've got inner turmoil; it's like a dam which is about to break.

Interviewer: What gets you started?

Henley: I wish I could figure out how not to get started this way, but really it seems like it's some sort of explosion or pain or desire to understand something.

Interviewer: Do you get an idea for a character first, or do you begin with a plot, something you want to see happen on the stage so you want to write a play around it?

Henley: It varies. Most of the plays I wrote early were based on a situation. *Crimes of the Heart* is based on the situation of a sister shooting her husband, and everyone has to come back in this traumatic event and deal with old wounds. *The Miss Firecracker Contest* is obviously based on a beauty contest and the events around that; *The Wake of Jamey Foster* is about a wake; *The Debutante Ball* is about a debutante ball; *The Lucky Spot,* my next play, was about the opening of a taxi-dance hall in the sticks of Louisiana in the Depression. Oftentimes it has been around an event. I figure out who would be there, and what they would want, why they would want to be there or not want to be there, what their dreams would be in this situation, and what this event could mean to them. My later plays, like *Signature* and *Control Freaks,* aren't so centered in an event, I guess. *Control Freaks* is about these people who try and open up Furniture World and end up murdering each other.

Interviewer: Do you write from an outline?

Henley: I have basically a lot of the theme, images, or dialogue, and I'll have "sister's dialogue" (things I think this one particular character may say) or things I think another character may say. Then I have miscellaneous dialogue, things that I don't know who says, or I don't know if anybody says them.

Interviewer: How do you do rewriting?

Henley: I'm good at rewriting because it's so much easier than writing the original thing. I like to do rewrites after hearing the play read or seeing it in previews. Previews are great because you can do the play at night and then you have five hours the next day to rehearse it and make changes. Oftentimes if you leave a piece alone for a couple of months and come back to it, cuts are obvious, or ways to fix things become really clear that you were stuck on in production.

Interviewer: Did that happen with *The Debutante Ball?* You worked on that over a period of time, didn't you?

Henley: Yes. That's the most torn-apart-and-put-back-together play I've written, because I wrote it over a long period of time. I didn't sit down and write it all in four months or whatever. I had a production of it done in

California, and then I had a whole other production done in New York—and my rewrite between the production in New York and the one in California was really bad. It wasn't either this or that, and then I had to go to really changing it to make it more like that.

Interviewer: Do you start with a title?

Henley: Not necessarily, although my titles, as you can see, are sort of bland: *The Debutante Ball, The Miss Firecracker Contest, The Wake of Jamey Foster, The Lucky Spot.* I kind of got on a roll—and then *Abundance.* I saw a boat called *Abundance* and I thought, "Isn't that the most beautiful word?" Who ever has an abundance? Of course, it's meant ironically, I guess, in the play. With *Signature* I did, too. That's a good question. I never knew it, but I do usually have a title when I start, sort of.

Interviewer: What format do you use if you don't really have an outline, and how do you maintain the discipline to keep working?

Henley: Writing the first line is always so scary, because I think in the first page you've got to have tone, you've got to have character. There are just immeasurable amounts that you need before you can write one line and let the characters start talking. Although I don't have an outline, I have done much preparation, and I may well have an outline for the first scene. I will say, "Okay, there is going to be a scene between Lenny and Chick. We're going to get that there is a problem with Babe. A gift's going to be given, and here is a couple of lines that might go in that scene." Then I'll say, "Doc comes, a horse is dead, and then so-and-so comes in." That's all I know: so-and-so is going to come in. It gets less and less specific until I really don't know anything until I've written that first scene.

How do I have the discipline? Sometimes it's very hard. You have to allow yourself to be idiosyncratic, and if you want to walk around and pick up lint off the carpet, just understand it's part of your process. I can understand why a lot of people don't write, because it's hard to have the discipline. If you do it for a long time, sometimes you get to where you like to be alone. It's sort of frightening, too; but I've always liked to be alone. Sometimes you have to sit there in a chair for two hours and not know what to do. You just think about the play. Because a play is so small, it's like a little chess puzzle, and you can't really go too far askew or you're going to be off the beam. It takes a lot of discipline just going in there every day even if you don't write. I've spent times when I couldn't write and I would just make myself sit there for five minutes with a blank sheet of paper, and then the next day ten minutes with a blank sheet of paper, and then the next day it would be fifteen minutes and I would draw some zigzags. You have to be willful.

Interviewer: Can you talk more about your preparations before you write the first page?

Henley: It's different for each play. With *Abundance,* I had to do so much research because it takes place in the nineteenth century and it deals with Indians and all sorts of things I was completely ignorant about. With *The Lucky Spot,* I had to do all this research on taxi-dance halls and the Depression; but with *Control Freaks* I just really had to enter my own psyche. With *Control Freaks* I would write pages and pages without even thinking about what I was writing, pages and pages where nothing has to make sense, and then go back and say, "Well, this character may say this" or "This might be said in the kitchen" or "This would be said in the yard" or "This would be seen." I went back and categorized it like that, still without putting any pressure on myself to have answers—like an actual plot or a story or interconnections.

Interviewer: So you don't necessarily know exactly what the message is prior to writing the first page?

Henley: Not even prior to the last page. I don't believe in a message. I think it would be disastrous if you could say what the message of *Hamlet* was. Even with a minor play, everyone is going to come away with something different depending on if they've just left their lovers or if they've just had a child or if they've just been fired. You're going to connect with the work in your own way. If you're too cold or if you're hungry, you'll get a different message. I think that's inevitable and sort of wonderful.

Interviewer: You've lived in California for quite a while now. Has that changed the kinds of plays you write? The early plays were very much about the South. Do you see yourself moving away from the South dramatically at all, or do you still feel that because your roots are there you will always write about the South?

Henley: Well, my last three plays have not taken place in the South, so I feel like I am probably moving away from that a bit as a locale for my work.

Interviewer: Do you miss the South?

Henley: In a personal sense, desperately yes.

Interviewer: How do you think your life in the South affected your writing?

Henley: I'm from Jackson, Mississippi, which is the capital of Mississippi and is in the center of the state, and I think it had a very profound effect. My first play takes place in Hazelhurst, which is where my father's family is from; the second one takes place in Brookhaven, where my mother's family is from; the third one takes place in Canton, where I went to camp;

the next one takes place in Hattiesburg, where my aunt and uncle and cousins live. It was a mysterious world, and it was the first world I was familiar with.

Interviewer: You once said that writing helps you not to feel angry. Do you think that's still accurate, that that's one reason you write—so you don't feel angry about something?

Henley: Sometimes when I'm writing about something I get in a rage. The last time I was writing I was screaming at my typewriter and I was getting very angry, but I think it's a good kind of anger because it's focused and alive; it's not in on yourself or destructive to other people.

Interviewer: Why do you write?

Henley: Why do I write? I write because it makes me feel like I'm alive.

Interviewer: How did you get into playwriting?

Henley: I started at a university in a theatre program in which I was majoring in acting. That was invaluable because I took a lot of theatre history classes where I read plays from all times, and also style classes where you would do Restoration plays and you would have to study art from the period and dances from the period. You would have to memorize lines if you were in a play. If you were in *A Midsummer Night's Dream*, even if you had a tiny part you would hear that poetry over and over again, the structure of it. If you had one little speech, you'd have to memorize each word of that speech. I think I only took one playwriting class. The only good thing about that is that it gives you this time set aside to write a play. Also you were onstage and you realized that it's easier if I have props, or it's not easier if I have props, or I don't have time to change from this costume to the next—just very practically about getting people on and off. You learned how to think about a character very specifically, like what do I want in this scene and why am I here?

Interviewer: Was the play you wrote in playwriting class *Am I Blue*? If so, where did you get the idea for *Am I Blue*?

Henley: Yes, it was *Am I Blue*. I remember I was taking summer school and staying in a dormitory and I was studying Shakespeare. I remember getting some idea about a play I wanted to write. I really can't tell you exactly what the genesis of the idea was. I just thought something about a girl who was sort of wacky and not invited to her senior prom and a young boy who has been given a pass to a prostitute. I just remember thinking, "I have this idea," and I couldn't stop thinking about it and putting images together. I remember thinking, "I've almost got this written in my head; I should take this course because that would be an easy job. That will be one less thing I'll have to do." I'm sorry, but I can't exactly quite recall. I know I'd been to New Orleans and I was enchanted and mystified by the city.

Interviewer: What terrifies you?

Henley: Doing interviews.

Interviewer: Creatively, what terrifies you?

Henley: It has terrified me a couple of times when I haven't been able to work. I generally say it's part of the process, but it's very debilitating not to be able to write.

Interviewer: Would you rather be heard through the plays than through interviews?

Henley: Definitely, absolutely.

Interviewer: Do you feel that the plays have in them certain things you have repressed in your own dealing with other people? Has being a playwright enabled you to write about certain things that you've repressed in your own life?

Henley: I don't know. I write about things I'm concerned with, that are troubling me; and I suppose some of what you write is unconscious and subliminal. That's sort of where the magic comes from; it's not plotted logically like "This is something I want to explore." But it does come from inside you.

Interviewer: Is it still hard for you to get your plays done, now that you've had a Pulitzer Prize and some commercial success?

Henley: It's pretty hard. I had to go to Poughkeepsie and live in a dorm for my last play. It's difficult if you write a play that's not something that immediately makes sense to people as commercial. I certainly send out many plays that get rejected from theatres as well, but at least they will generally read them.

Interviewer: Your last play to be produced was *Signature*, wasn't it?

Henley: Yes, that was the one done in Poughkeepsie.

Interviewer: It's about the future, isn't it?

Henley: Yes. It takes place in the year 2052 in Los Angeles. It's about Boswell, who is an art philosopher who finds out he is going to die and goes to a graphologist who tells him he can change his life by changing his handwriting. It's really about what is your signature, what do you leave in life, what's important that you've done or haven't done—or is anything important? It's sort of uncommercial; that's why it was done in Poughkeepsie.

Interviewer: Do you think it's easier for women playwrights to be produced now than it was ten or twelve years ago?

Henley: It seems to be, actually. There seem to be more women playwrights, and I have no idea why. I may be completely mistaken.

Interviewer: Do you think that the non-profit theatre network like Poughkeepsie is a good place to try out your plays? Do they give you a chance to develop them?

Henley: Yes, because a lot of times you can get very good people to come out of town, and that's the most important thing—having an excellent cast and a good director. I think with *Abundance* I probably pushed it to New York too soon before I had gotten to see enough various productions to find exactly what tone I wanted and everything. *The Debutante Ball* has never been produced in New York, and it has had more productions than some plays that have gotten to New York right away and have been slaughtered. Sometimes if you keep something out of New York, it enhances its life.

Interviewer: Can you speak about *Abundance*?

Henley: I spent a lot of time working on *Abundance* because it takes place in the nineteenth century. It's about two mail-order brides who come out West for adventure, and it takes place over a twenty-five-year period. It really is about how insidiously people's dreams are taken away from them. You come out here with all this hope and energy and desire, and suddenly you sell yourself out for a warm cup of coffee without really realizing you've done it. I loved working on that piece because I loved doing research on that period.

Interviewer: It's set in Wyoming?

Henley: It takes place in the Wyoming Territories. Most of my plays have been very classically structured and all take place over a twenty-four-hour period. This is the first one which is much more fragmented. That was really exciting, to see if I could put the essence of ten years into one scene. It was a challenge.

Interviewer: I found the relationship between the two women fascinating, especially how it changed over the twenty-five-year period.

Henley: Yes. It's about how somebody starts out with somebody else looking up to them and how that power can corrupt a relationship. When the second banana suddenly becomes even more powerful, one sees all the resentment that goes with that. Suddenly the person that used to be your lackey is now in a position of power; so it was also about shifts in power and how important it is, if you are going to maintain long-term relationships with people, that you be able to change. People shouldn't shrivel; people should let each other grow and face the consequence that maybe they won't need you if they grow.

Interviewer: Do you think that Broadway is some kind of final testing ground for a play? When you write a play, do you always want it to go to Broadway?

Henley: Yes, I want it to go to Broadway and be made into a major motion picture and win Academy Awards and Tonys and Pulitzer Prizes! That's really what I do want; but usually that doesn't happen.

Interviewer: It did once!

Henley: I love Broadway theatres. It's so great if it plays in a Broadway theatre; there's just nothing cooler, except for seeing your play done well.

Interviewer: How do you feel about critics? What kind of job or function do they perform, and have you learned from them when you've read things that they've said?

Henley: I don't want to get started on critics. H. L. Mencken said that asking a playwright what he thinks of critics is like asking a lamppost what he thinks of a dog.

Interviewer: When you're writing, do you have a particular audience in mind?

Henley: I know this may sound pretentious, but I do try and write for myself, because anyone else is too hard. If you're writing to please someone else, it's too hard to be alone that much. I must write about something that really really concerns me, that I'm desperately passionate about or interested in or upset about; but I do always fantasize that it will be well received.

Interviewer: What's your writing process?

Henley: Do you mean when do I write?

Interviewer: Yes.

Henley: This is so boring. I write on spiral notebook paper. I don't have a computer, so then I'll type it up on a typewriter and Xerox it and make changes and turn it over to a typist. I usually write from about eleven in the morning till four or five in the afternoon, unless I write in the evenings. I usually don't know where my piece is going. I never know where it's going, but I do a lot of preparation before I write the first line. It's very important to me to do a whole lot of work on the characters and the situation and the ambience, the atmosphere.

Interviewer: One of the biggest movements in theatre now is toward multicultural and color-blind casting. Have you had to take that into account in writing your more recent work?

Henley: *Signature* takes place in the future, and the stage directions read that this is best done with a multiracial cast because I want to get the feel of a cosmopolitan future. The only stipulation is that the two brothers should be of the same race, but their race isn't important; they could be Asian or Afro-American. I feel that way with *Control Freaks* as well, but I haven't consciously decided to do that. It depends on the type of play you're writing. If you're doing something like *Waiting for Godot,* where we don't know where those people are coming from or where they are going, it's all right; but if you're writing about a specific time or place, as in *Crimes of the Heart,* then obviously race is important because there is a segregated bigoted thing going on. I just think it depends on how specific you're being about the character's background as to whether that's an issue.

Interviewer: When you're writing a character, how much of their history do you know? Do you feel that you really know where they come from and their surroundings and how they were educated?

Henley: Very much, because I write each character as though I were playing them, as if I had to perform them, and I really want to know. Every character has a secret, every character has a reaction to the other characters, every character has a greatest fear, and every character has a greatest dream; and I want to know what their sense of humor is and what their sexuality is and how they dress and how they talk. It's great because you can play all these parts you'd never be cast in.

Interviewer: Do you merge with your characters when you're writing them?

Henley: Yes. You have to look at things from their point of view. They do not judge themselves in the same way the people reading the play may or may not judge them. They have objectives that are so strong, like these people that murder people. It's so scary to write about evil people. *Control Freaks* is the first play I've written about evil people. I really wanted to understand the banality of evil, and you have to find it in yourself, I think, to portray it.

Interviewer: Isn't it hard to merge with that kind of mind-set when you're writing it?

Henley: Yes, it's challenging and it's hard, but I like things that are hard.

Interviewer: What do you think will keep the American theatre active and healthy?

Henley: I don't know. I feel so bad because this theatre I love in Los Angeles just closed. It was the Los Angeles Theatre Center and it closed last week. A friend of mine was in a play running down there at the time, and they had the most brilliant production by Rosa Abdul, who's really a theatre genius. It just broke my heart to see this theatre close, and I feel so helpless.

Interviewer: Is it finances?

Henley: Yes, finances. That's something that's so troublesome to me, but I don't worry about it because I figure the most I can do is to keep working. I don't know how to fix that problem, that the arts are just dying.

Interviewer: There are easier and more lucrative ways that you can make a living, even as a writer. Why do you write plays rather than novels or movies or TV scripts?

Henley: I've also written screenplays. I don't believe I can write novels; they seem so big. If you write a play, then there are at least some times when you're not alone. The reason I love the theatre, as I said earlier, is because it always felt like such a sanctuary to me from the real world. It was such a magical world where everyone was passionate about something; they felt so alive when they were there, and they really cared that their water be set exactly here and not here. It made you not think about dying. As a playwright, you maintain your copyright; you have so much more control than you have in the movies. Screenwriters sell their copyrights. They can fire you, they can have somebody rewrite you; it's really a director's medium. It's not your vision, whereas I think a play is so much more the author's vision. It's more of an actor's medium as well, because they can't cut things that you did. I love to go to the theatre so much more than movies because generally you see much more of a personal vision in plays because you only need a hundred people out there. In movies, you have to open wide, you have to sell the video; so a bunch of people at a table sit down to figure out what will sell the most. Theatre is just more interesting to me.

Interviewer: You have just finished doing a screenplay of *The Lucky Spot*, but you were asked to do that, weren't you?

Henley: Yes, and I certainly didn't turn it down. My last play was not a big financial boon. *The Lucky Spot* was slammed in New York, and it kind of disappeared and then was done in this tiny little theatre in London. A director came to see it, really loved it, and he wants to make it into a movie; so I've just finished the screenplay. Who knows if it'll get made into a movie, but they pay you ridiculous amounts of money. I was literally sitting there with scissors and tape—here's some good lines; paste them in there. It's so easy, and now that will give me some money to go work on another play. I'm going to take *Signature* to Chicago in March, and I won't have to worry about how to pay the rent for my expensive hobby.

Interviewer: Besides doing screenplays, are there other things that you write?

Henley: No. I've done a couple of screenplay adaptations. I did a Reynolds Price book called *A Long and Happy Life* and a John Kennedy Toole book called *A Confederacy of Dunces.* I think doing that has helped me a little better with prose. You see how beautifully they can stretch it, and you study it so you can understand their mind-set and their tone and the way they do dialogue. I feel like they taught me that and paid me, but they never made the movies.

Interviewer: Do you think Hollywood respects playwrights?

Henley: No, Hollywood has an unmitigated disregard for writers in general, but that's why I live in Hollywood. The good thing about being in the theatre world in Los Angeles is that there really is none, so you don't feel disturbed that you're not a success and that you're not "with it." You just go and do your work. It's been really good for me to be able to go to New York and have a play that's a hit or a play that's a flop and just go back and say, "Okay, that's done, that's good; now I'll go start again." That's what really ends up making you find life bearable anyway.

Interviewer: Do you think that your plays have suffered in their transfer from the stage to the big screen?

Henley: No, I think I've been extremely lucky. I don't feel like there has been a definitive version of any of my plays that I've seen. I think I've seen what I feel to be definitive performances by actors, but it's never all come together in this one wholly perfect experience. I think that's okay because it's still alive, and maybe it'll be perfect somewhere somehow years from now or maybe not, but that's why I don't expect the film to be perfect either. In the movie versions of *Crimes of the Heart* and *Miss Firecracker* there are really great lines and really creative moments. It's exciting for me to see how those two directors saw the works, and I felt like they were both sincere to the spirits of the pieces on different levels.

Interviewer: You were satisfied with the film version of *Crimes of the Heart?*

Henley: Yes, I was happy with it. I can't watch it because it hurts me to watch my own things, but I really was when I saw it. I was very moved and very pleased; I have it on video, and someday I'm going to watch it again.

Interviewer: How do you go about structuring your work when it's intended for the stage as opposed to for the screen?

Henley: A screenplay, I think, is much easier to write, because you can virtually have as many characters as you like and go so many places compared to the stage. In *Control Freaks*, she's standing on the balcony and she's talking to her dress; then she drops her dress down, it floats downstage, and he picks it up and starts dancing with it. Somehow that's very theatrical, but it's not something you would do in a movie. People actually get to see the dress fall, and they know it might hit the ground, and there's something about that that's alive and fun. Sam Shepard is great at that. He'll have toasters all over the stage, and then the toast starts coming up. Then you smell the toast and see the toast and it's a surprise. The audience is delirious. If you did that in a film, it just wouldn't be the same.

Interviewer: Cutting a lemon onstage you would smell the lemon.

Henley: You'd smell the lemon, you'd see the juice come out, you'd see the knife, you'd see him wipe off the knife, you'd see that there was a knife between them that was real. It's interesting.

Interviewer: Is there one play you've written that you think you've learned the most from?

Henley: *Control Freaks.*

Interviewer: That's your most recent one.

Henley: I'd probably say that about any of my most recent ones, but I do feel that now at least.

Interviewer: What kinds of things did you learn?

Henley: It's very succinct; it's about an hour and a half, and it's all in one shot. It starts and doesn't stop. It starts very controlled, and it unravels until everything is just insanity. It was very challenging because you had to be extremely succinct and everything had to build exactly structurally right. I was so afraid of the chaos coming because how can I write chaos? I really had to let go; it was extremely exciting and scary. Also, writing about these evil people was challenging because they weren't people I loved. In all my other plays, even though people behave very badly, I love them. I didn't love these people, but they were real; so that was interesting.

Interviewer: Do you have any favorites among your characters that are special to you?

Henley: Boswell in *Signature* and Popeye in *Miss Firecracker*.

Interviewer: I always wondered why Popeye was given the gift in the first scene.

Henley: Those earrings?

Interviewer: Yes.

Henley: I don't know if it's just in the South—this happened to me in Hawaii as well—but people give you things because they have such a desperate need to be liked. Later in the play, the character reveals that she hated those earrings; they pinched her ears, and she was glad to get rid of them. Something that appears to be a generous act—I'm trying to make myself look good by giving you something that I really don't like—the duplicity of that act, I think, reveals something later about Elaine. It's also the magic that a gift like that would hold for a character like Popeye. How extraordinary that would be, to have something hanging off your ears! For somebody who's never had something hanging off their ears and who hears voices through their eyes, it seems completely unbelievable.

Interviewer: Is there anything you would like to do besides write plays and screenplays?

Henley: Ski.

Interviewer: What appeals to you about skiing?

Henley: You asked what I wanted to do and I said I wanted to ski; I've never skied in my life.

Interviewer: What do you expect?

Henley: I just love the existential idea of nothing but white and going down at breakneck speed. I think you would feel so alive. I think it would make me laugh and laugh if I did that.

Interviewer: Is there anything in theatre that you'd like to do? Do you want to direct?

Henley: I'd like to direct. To direct you have to have a sense of self, and I so often want to hide what I'm thinking that to be able to talk to people and tell them what you want would be a challenge. I always want to make people feel good; I always tell actors, "You did great," and then I go to the director and say, "Would you fire them!" I always think it would be a challenge to learn to interact more forthrightly with people, so I'm thinking of maybe directing *Control Freaks*.

Interviewer: Is *Control Freaks* the one you wrote the part for Holly Hunter in?

Henley: Yes.

Interviewer: Can you tell us a little bit about that part and why it was for her?

Henley: Holly Hunter was in *Crimes of the Heart* on Broadway; she was in *The Wake* on Broadway; she was in *Miss Firecracker* off-Broadway; and she did the first production of *The Lucky Spot* at Williamstown. She's just an actress that I feel an extreme affinity for. I'm working at this small Equity theatre in Los Angeles that Holly is a part of; so I thought, "I want to write a play for her." I don't generally do that—write a play with an actress in mind—but I wrote this part for her. This part is basically a woman who is not integrated, so instead of playing one part she is sort of several people. Basically she's two people: one person that's violently enraged all the time, and the other person that's real sweet. Holly has this real range; I know Holly has the technical facility and the emotional guts.

Interviewer: Have you always been interested in those split images, the two sides that you were just talking about?

Henley: Have I always been interested in that? It's hard to think of what you've always been, but I know I've always had a fascination with darker images because they frighten me so much. I think I'm always confronting myself with them. I remember I made this glass hand with a knife, and I would drip red candle wax over it all the time; I don't know what that comes from. I think it's sort of the complexities of life that I find most real. If you get things that are just Disneyland, it doesn't seem real to me. The six o'clock news is real, and that's got a lot more grotesque things in it than my plays.

Interviewer: Your favorite holiday is Halloween, isn't it?

Henley: I love Halloween. The autumn is my favorite season, and Halloween is my favorite holiday.

Interviewer: Are you going to dress up for Halloween?

Henley: I think so.

Interviewer: How do you put the humor in your plays?

Henley: I don't know. It's not deliberate exactly.

Interviewer: Do you think they're funny?

Henley: When I saw *Crimes of the Heart,* I was really amazed at how funny it was to people. I just think it's the way your mind works. Coming from the South, people didn't have much patience with you embracing your own pain, groveling in it. It was always, "So big deal, the house is burned. There goes Atlanta, sorry." I think it's a part of the country that has been destroyed and has had to have this sort of grip from another part of you. They face it much more front on. People are just almost ostentatious about their pain.

Interviewer: In so much of your work you have the dark side and the comic side together like two halves of a split image. You've said that you first saw that in Chekhov. Is that so?

Henley: Yes. A moment in theatre that changed my life happened when I was in New York—I must have been nineteen or so. *Three Sisters* was going to be produced at the university I was going to, and I said, "*Three Sisters,* great! Parts for women; I'll read this." I kept reading it, and I didn't get it. What is this? Who are these people? Then I went to see an all-black production of *The Cherry Orchard* starring James Earl Jones and Gloria Foster, and I started to get it. It was like a satori when James Earl Jones as Lopakhin came back in after buying the cherry orchard and said, "I bought it." It was the greatest day of his life because he was no longer a serf, but also it was the worst day in his life because he had betrayed his dearest friend. All through that speech he was zing, zing, zing, back and forth between despair and joy, madness and sanity, and regret and not caring. I was screaming in the theatre; I thought I was going to be evicted. I started crying and laughing and I couldn't stop. Then, after he leaves, Gloria Foster falls out of her chair and has to be carried off. It was just absolutely a revelation about how alive life can be and how complicated and beautiful and horrible; to deny either of those is such a loss.

Interviewer: Do you think that *The Debutante Ball* is your most daring play?

Henley: No, *Control Freaks* is.

Interviewer: I haven't had a chance to see that one yet; but in *The Debutante Ball* there are some really daring moves that you make. Tell us a little bit about the play's production history and about why it's daring.

Henley: It's very Jacobean. It has everything thrown in it. There's a beautiful ballroom with a balcony but also a bathroom onstage. The essence of it all is these people trying to look beautiful for this ball, but they're like animals and they're going in and having to pluck out hairs and shave their legs. Their facades cracking is really what it's about. The debutante slices her face with a razor; then, later, her mother beats her up and she has a miscarriage onstage in her debutante gown. There is the deaf cousin who has a lesbian affair with the sister. The last scene is just the mother getting into the bathtub with psoriasis on her skin and the daughter bathing her. These people have so many scars, and are trying to be so beautiful, and have so many secrets. It's about secrets as well.

Interviewer: Would you say that's the focus of *The Debutante Ball?*

Henley: Secrets? One of them, I think.

Interviewer: Any others that come to mind?

Henley: Secrets and lies.

Interviewer: Can we talk about *Crimes of the Heart* a little bit?

Henley: Sure.

Interviewer: What are the crimes?

Henley: I guess Babe's crime is shooting her husband because he hurt someone who was innocent. I guess her mother's crime was killing herself and leaving her children because she could no longer bear the pain of being left by her husband. Meg's crime was being so afraid of Doc she left him with his broken leg saying she would marry him and went off to Hollywood. Lenny's crime is more of a crime to herself in that she won't tell the truth to the man she is in love with because she is afraid if he knows the truth he won't love her so she just chucks the whole thing. I guess a lot of it is them coming to terms with their crimes and trying to unshackle themselves from the past.

Interviewer: Do you think there is a way in which each of the sisters experiences a freeing from the expectations of the society that they were in, and of their family, during the play?

Henley: Yes, I think so. Lenny calls up her boyfriend and she tells him the truth, that she can't have children, which is her secret. She was afraid he would leave her; in fact, it turns out that he hates kids! Meg, I think, feels reconciled with Doc, even if they're not together; and Babe gets so desperate that she tries to commit suicide. But one of the things that plagued her was why their mother killed herself and hanged the cat; then she realized she hanged the cat with her so she wouldn't be alone; and Babe realizes she is not alone. All three of the sisters have really kept their most precious pains a secret from the other sisters; they've been ashamed or afraid to share them; and by the end of the play, I think, they—like it or not—have had to share these secrets. Babe never told anybody her husband beat her, Meg never told how bad she felt not being a success and how bad she felt about leaving Doc, and Lenny hasn't revealed to them her great wish not to be alone. She has made it seem like it was okay that she took care of Old Granddaddy.

Interviewer: You've talked elsewhere about when you were going to write the ending of *Crimes of the Heart* and you thought Babe was going to die.

Henley: I had gotten to Act III, and I just had images. I knew there was going to be a birthday cake, and I knew there was going to be a rope or a suicide. Then I discovered it was Babe and I said, "Oh no, Babe's going to die? Oh well, you have to keep writing! This is really going to be a tragedy. I thought this was kind of being comedic, but no, it's a big tragedy, and they're going to have to have the birthday cake without her!" You just have to trust. I wanted this scene between Lenny and Babe. I really saw it vividly—Lenny in the ecstasy of joy and Babe in the ecstasy of despair and then colliding with each other in the scene right before Lenny calls up Charlie and right before Babe goes to hang herself. I knew somehow that that was exactly right, but then I said, "Oops, now Babe is going to hang herself?" Luckily, I heard a thud from upstairs: it didn't work!

Interviewer: How did you decide to have Babe hit her head on the oven?

Henley: That was developed in performance because I realized a fallacy in the logic. Once Babe realizes that her mother killed herself because she was afraid of being alone, that would give her a reason to live because she understood something that she had been so afraid of. But then I couldn't have her get her head out of the oven because that wasn't as dramatic as Meg coming in and finding her with her head in the oven. So I had to have her say, "Oh I see!" like she had the idea and she would have gotten out but she got knocked out. Patricia Wettig, who was in "thirtysomething" dying of cancer last year, played Babe in that production, and she was so diligent, because we were going over the logic of it and she said, "Yes, but now I have to get out of the oven!" I'm saying, "No you don't. You've got to stay in the oven." I said, "Okay, so you hit your head." It's great to have really good actors because they challenge you and they're thinking things so specifically that it makes it good for you.

Interviewer: Do you give very specific stage directions to the actors in your plays, and has that changed from your earlier work to your later work?

Henley: I don't think I overdo stage directions too much. I have had productions in which the actors played it so dead wrong that then I tried to write heavy stage directions, but that really doesn't work, I've realized. I just try to have the stage directions give an essence of the whole feel. If this is funny, I try to make them a bit humorous; if this is dead serious, I try to tell the tone through stage directions.

Interviewer: There seem to be some links between *Crimes of the Heart* and *The Wake of Jamey Foster*. Could you talk about those a little bit?

Henley: There is a balance of characters that is similar, and they are getting back there for a tragic event. Caddy in *The Wake of Jamey Foster* is somehow another version of Chick in *Crimes of the Heart*. I felt like Chick was very one-dimensional, and I wanted to try and get more into a woman who was so controlling, so needing to be liked, and so needing to be perfect. Who was she really? That's what I tried to explore with Caddy.

Interviewer: Most of your plays focus on women and their relationships with each other and with society. Would you say that your plays are feminist or women-centered?

Henley: Do I have to pick one or the other?

Interviewer: No, you can pick something else entirely!

Henley: I just think they are about people. I don't necessarily think I'm going to write a women's play or a feminist play. I just think of a story I would like to tell, and whoever ends up being in the story, I'm grateful.

Interviewer: But you have said you are a feminist, haven't you?

Henley: Of course. People say, "Are you a feminist?" like I'm saying I'm a liberal or something; so I looked it up in a dictionary and it says that you believe women should have equal rights with men. No, I believe they should have less rights than men? Absolutely I'm a feminist, absolutely vehemently so.

Interviewer: Do you think there is a way that, because you're a woman playwright, you're sometimes asked to speak for all women?

Henley: Yes.

Interviewer: How does that make you feel?

Henley: I feel inept. I feel incapable. I sometimes feel I can hardly speak for myself. I think people have such a fear of not having things categorized, and a way to grab hold of things that they want is to say this is a woman writer, this is a southern writer, this is a black writer, this is a black woman southern writer. The more categories they can get you into, the more secure they feel so they won't have to feel what you wrote. I just feel sorry for them.

Interviewer: Some women playwrights have talked about how they feel that women's lives are changed through conversation and dialogue. Have you thought much about that? It seems that in *Crimes of the Heart* the sisters' lives are changed through their conversations with each other.

Henley: I don't know why it would be limited to women. I certainly think I've had some conversations with men that have spiritually enlightened my life, and I *know* I have enlightened theirs!

Interviewer: How would you characterize the bonds between the women in your plays? Have you drawn on the fact that you have three sisters in those relationships?

Henley: I think in *Crimes of the Heart* very much; growing up around women, I mean. Just having a family, I think, is different from not having a family. It is so strange how you can feel that the connection with these people is so primal and basic, although sometimes you would not be with them if they weren't your family. You are inextricably bound to them, concerned for them and enraged by them or enraptured by them. Families are a peculiar sort of situation.

Interviewer: Could you tell us a little about your early days with the Actors Theatre of Louisville?

Henley: That was my very first professional production, which was exciting for me in an almost unbearable way because I was so frightened. It was January and it was cold, and I remember standing in the parking lot watching people park their cars and walk into the theatre to see my play at a first preview and just crying because I couldn't believe they had gone out in the cold and gotten baby-sitters and were going to drive there and see my play. I just remember I've never felt like such a charlatan. I couldn't believe they were coming to see it, and it had been very rocky; the director had been fired and replaced by the producer of the theatre, who was also directing three other plays at the time, so we had to start rehearsal at 8:00 A.M. I was quite prepared for it to be a horrible debacle, but actually I was blessed by really having two of the greatest actresses I've ever ever worked with, Susan Kingsley and Kathy Bates, and they worked miracles, so I was very lucky.

Interviewer: Are any of your characters autobiographical?

Henley: Autobiographical? That implies that they are about me?

Interviewer: Yes.

Henley: I would say all of them, absolutely all of them.

Interviewer: Have any of your plays been performed in other countries, or have they been translated into other languages?

Henley: Yes, *Crimes of the Heart* being the most done, but even *The Debutante Ball* has been done in London and Germany quite a bit. My most exciting trip was when I went to see *Crimes of the Heart* done in China. That was just spectacular. It didn't go over; but it was the year before Tienanmen Square, and everyone was so alive. There was just this wildness about it.

Interviewer: When you go to write a play, do you think stylistically? Do you try to put it in a category—that it's comedy or satire or a particular kind of play—or do you think more eclectically about the play?

Henley: I think more specifically, in that it's almost like a smell I get or a feeling I get about a play, rather than in a generalized category. It's just much more intricate than that. Getting the tone of *Control Freaks* was quite difficult. Once I got it it was very blocky, but I didn't think in any broad category.

Interviewer: What writers, dramatic and nondramatic, are you influenced by?

Henley: I love T. S. Eliot, but I wouldn't defame him by claiming to be influenced by him. I quite love reading Flannery O'Connor; I think it's been a revelation to me. Willa Cather, William Styron, Dostoyevsky (not to be pretentious, but I do love those Russians). Gorky was in my childhood. I like to read. I'm reading now this wonderful man named Denis Johnson that I just found out about, and Richard Ford is a big favorite of mine from Mississippi as well. I have to say I was particularly influenced by Reynolds Price and John Kennedy Toole from getting to work so closely trying to adapt their books into screenplays. I feel a special kinship to them.

Interviewer: What dramatic writers do you like?

Henley: Chekhov and Shakespeare and O'Neill, Tennessee Williams and Beckett and David Mamet. Ibsen has become a new favorite of mine. I just saw this amazing production of *Hedda Gabler* in London and this amazing production of *Wild Duck*, and I was just enthralled by how absolutely stunning he is.

Interviewer: Do you have any favorite women dramatists?

Henley: Weren't there any women on that list? I guess Lillian Hellman would be my favorite, and Carson McCullers. *The Member of the Wedding* is a beautiful play, but it's a beautiful book as well. I love *A Taste of Honey;* that's a beautiful play. So I suppose there are some.

Interviewer: Is there a drama critic whose opinion you respect?

Henley: Well, I guess it would have to be someone like an Edmund Wilson or George Bernard Shaw.

David Henry Hwang

Photo courtesy of Writers and Artists Agency

David Henry Hwang was born in 1957 in Los Angeles. He graduated from Stanford University and attended the Yale School of Drama. His plays are F.O.B. *(1978),* The Dance and the Railroad *(1981),* Family Devotions *(1981),* The House of Sleeping Beauties *(1983),* The Sound of a Voice *(1983),* Rich Relations *(1986),* As the Crow Flies *(1986),* M. Butterfly *(1988),* Bondage *(1991), and* Face Value *(1992). His television play* My American Son *was broadcast on HBO in 1987; and he has provided the librettos for two operas by Philip Glass,* 1000 Airplanes on the Roof *(1988) and* The Voyage *(1992). He received the Obie Award for* F.O.B. *and the Tony Award and the Outer Critics Circle Award for* M. Butterfly. *He has also been awarded two Drama-Logue Awards, a Rockefeller playwright-in-residence award, a National Endowment for the Arts artistic associate fellowship, a Guggenheim Fellowship, and fellowships from the National*

Endowment for the Arts and the New York State Council on the Arts. This interview took place on February 15, 1992.

▶ ————————————————————————— ◀

Interviewer: You have an unusual mix of very serious subjects and humor in your writing. Do you feel there is some angst that drives you to write, or are you not a pained writer? Can pain be funny?

Hwang: I think that many people would argue that pain is the source of a lot of comedy, and I would probably agree with that. It basically has to do with being aware of a certain amount of angst, I suppose, and also being unaware of a great amount of it. I think it's sometimes really the subconscious degree of angst which drives the work. I don't normally consider myself that much of a pained individual. I don't think I go through life feeling that I'm under that much of a weight, but through my work I find out that there are various things which are bothering me, perhaps at an unconscious level. The work has always helped me to bring that to my conscious mind, so there's an interaction and a dynamic between my personal exploration and the work. The work helps me know more about myself and vice versa.

Interviewer: With the things that come up out of your subconscious that you had to push away for a while, can you feel them when they're first emerging?

Hwang: When *M. Butterfly* came out, a lot of people said, "Wow, that's a really angry play, the way in which the Asian man humiliates the white man at the end." I was always really uncomfortable with that interpretation because I didn't want to feel that that degree of anger, that degree of angst or whatever, came out of me. For a long time, it was important for me to kind of laugh that off and say, "No, that's not really what it's about; I think that both sides are really humiliating each other"—which is true. But more recently, I've had to admit to the fact that probably it did reflect some of my own anxieties, my anger and angst about being Asian in a predominantly Caucasian world.

Interviewer: Is there a positive way to use that anger, or do you think it's something that every minority has to go through to get to somewhere else?

Hwang: I think the acknowledgment of the anger is positive and that using it to write plays is at least more positive than going out and knifing people or something. Essentially, it is the acknowledgment of the anger which allows me to work past it and through it and get to the point where I understand that, okay, these are the things that have influenced me. Some of them I'm not very happy about, but there it is. Once I've acknowledged that, I think it's possible then to ask myself how I can incorporate that into my personality in a more positive sense than before.

Interviewer: If what people were saying was that the Asian man humiliated the white man, was there any resistance to the play being produced?

Hwang: No, the commercial experience with *M. Butterfly* was really fortunate and probably somewhat unique in the sense that we never really had any conversations about what was commercial. There were certain artistic questions that we wanted to address, but the idea of making the play less political or less sexual or something in order to go toward a commercial audience never really happened. There was a point at which some of the financers got a little worried, and there was a certain amount of pressure from that, but in terms of my day-to-day working relationship with Stuart Ostrow, the producer, those questions never came up. I think it just goes to show you that you don't ultimately know what's commercial or what's not commercial. This is a play which presumably didn't have any of those commercial elements, and yet it turned out to be the most successful Broadway play in however many years.

Interviewer: Do you think that's an oddity? Did you just get lucky, or can that happen to anybody?

Hwang: A lot of it is luck. If you look at the construct of the commercial theatre, particularly with nonmusicals, a lot of it just depends on the opinion of the *New York Times*. You have to concede the fact that there is a certain amount of tossing the dice up in the air and seeing how it lands, but I do feel that I happened to get hooked up with a particularly sensitive group of collaborators who chose to take this big gamble.

Interviewer: Is there a way around the situation with the *New York Times* that everybody seems to be miffed about?

Hwang: I don't think anyone's come up with a way around it. There's the exception, a play like *I'm Not Rappaport* for instance, which got a poor review in the *New York Times* but continued to run and won a Tony and all that, so it does happen; but certainly the influence of the *Times* at this point in New York theatrical history is huge, and I don't know quite how to get around that.

Interviewer: Is that any incentive, then, to have your plays done outside of New York?

Hwang: The regional theatre movement is very helpful in that regard, and that's why so many of the things that have eventually come to New York in the past few years have come out of the not-for-profit theatre. On the other hand, for better or worse I think there is still a New York cachet. There's still the situation where, if you have a play produced in New York and it's successful, you're probably going to get other productions of that play; whereas if you have the play produced in Los Angeles or Seattle or Louisville and it's successful, it doesn't mean that other theatres are going to produce it with the same amount of regularity that a New York production would guarantee.

Interviewer: In the New York or regional theatre, whose work do you like to see?

Hwang: It really goes on a sort of play-by-play basis. The last play that I saw in New York that I really was crazy about was *Six Degrees of Separation*. August Wilson's work I admire a great deal, and Wendy Wasserstein's work, too. Basically, I think I'm looking for work which addresses contemporary social themes and deals with the fabric of the world we live in but does it with a certain amount of theatricality. There was this whole thing called theatricalism in the seventies, and that term isn't really used that much any more. It's the idea that this is something which can be done better onstage than on television or film. Maybe because I grew up in a media generation, I don't go to the theatre as often. I'm sure I go slightly more often than perhaps others in my generation do, but I still have that bias, I think, toward all these other forms. When I go to the theatre, I want to see something which works better onstage than if I saw it in a movie or on television. Things that incorporate a dance or music or asides to the audience or that sort of thing: those are all things that you can do in the theatre that don't make sense in the other mediums.

Interviewer: When you take something like *M. Butterfly* that you wrote for the stage, where presumably it works best, and translate it to the screen, what is that like?

Hwang: That's an interesting experience because it is something I can see one way and say, "Well, I tried to make this as theatrical as I could. Now, can I make it filmic with the same effect?" I've tried to do that, and it remains to be seen whether people will feel that it has the same effect. Essentially, it's trying to achieve the same task but using different muscles. The clearest difference, I suppose, between film and stage is that in theatre the dialogue essentially drives the action and the visuals generally support that. In film it's rather the reverse: The visuals drive the action and the dialogue usually supports that. The dialogue is often interchangeable, and the actors improvise it. I hate to say it works, because I'm a writer, but I have to concede that sometimes that works in a film, just to have the actors improvise the dialogue if they know what's going on. I tried to find filmic equivalents for all sorts of stage devices that we used in *M. Butterfly*, and we'll see if I was successful.

Interviewer: When you say you let the actors improvise dialogue when you're writing for the screen, is that something you would let happen onstage?

Hwang: No, I would never let that happen in the theatre. Again, it's because the word is so important in the theatre. There are various filmwriters for whom the word is more important than others. Woody Allen is very dialogue-driven, but even Woody Allen, when he makes his films, allows a certain amount of improvisation and gives his actors free rein with the script. It's just that the demands of the form are different.

Interviewer: When you start writing for the stage, do you start with a visual image?

Hwang: I generally start with ideas rather than images, but at different points in my writing career this has gone differently. Right now I generally feel I need to know what the beginning of the play is and what the end of the play is, and the fun of writing them becomes a way to navigate between the two points. Sometimes I compare writing to a road trip. I know I'm going to go from L.A. to Louisville, but I don't know how I'm going to get there, and the fun is finding the road. I do feel like I want to know what those two anchors are so that I don't go completely off base.

Interviewer: Have you ever just scrapped where you thought you were going or where you began, if it got out of control?

Hwang: That's a good question. I don't think so. It's certainly true that I've taken some real wild tangents to get to Louisville, as it were; and sometimes when I get there it's a place that I don't quite recognize. Let's say I have a structure in which two characters are going to change places by the end of the play. By the time that happens, it may happen in a different way than I imagined it when I began writing the play, but essentially it follows the thrust that I set out when I began to write.

Interviewer: Do you have optional endings when you start out to write, or are those fixed points always there?

Hwang: I guess there is some variation. At the risk of totally belaboring this analogy, I could go to Louisville or I could go to Nashville but probably I wouldn't go to San Francisco, because it's a totally different place. Let's take *Butterfly* as an example. I felt that at the beginning of the play the Frenchman would fantasize that he was Pinkerton from the opera *Madame Butterfly*, and he'd found his Butterfly. By the end of the play, the Frenchman would realize that it was he in fact who was Butterfly, and that it was he who had been sacrificed for love, and the Chinese spy who perpetrated that deceit was therefore the real Pinkerton. I didn't know, however, if that meant that the French diplomat was going to commit suicide the way that Butterfly does in the opera, and that's something I kind of left open. So there's a certain amount of variation within that structure.

Interviewer: How did you get started as a playwright?

Hwang: I was a freshman in college, and I saw a play at ACT in San Francisco. I think it was *The Matchmaker*. I thought, "I think I can do that," so I started trying to write. I found a professor at Stanford, where I was going to college, who was teaching an introduction to drama class, so I took his class and started writing some plays. I showed them to the teacher, and he said they were really horrible, which they were, and that my problem was that I was trying to write in a vacuum, that I had the desire to write plays but that I didn't actually know anything about the theatre. So I spent the next two or three years trying to read as many plays and see as many plays as I could. I'd go up to San Francisco to the Magic and see all the Sam Shepard premieres that were going on at the time, for instance.

A couple of years later I wrote a play to be done in my dorm called *F.O.B.*, which stands for Fresh Off the Boat, and we performed that in the dorm. It later went to the 1979 O'Neill International Playwrights Conference in Connecticut, and Joe Papp picked it up. He produced it in 1980 in New York, it won an Obie Award, and I kind of had a career. I think there was something about the desire to create worlds and see them appear physically in front of me that seemed to be exciting to me. I'm not sure that it's such a great thing really; there's something megalomaniacal about it. My friend Harry Kondoleon, the playwright, says that playwriting is the ultimate arrogance because you're literally putting words in other people's mouths. For whatever reason, it appealed to me as soon as I saw it. To some degree it's a substitute or compensation for the fact that you don't actually have that much control over people in life. I don't know if it's psychologically the most healthy thing, but it seems somewhat more constructive than beating up people, so I guess it's a good thing.

Interviewer: Weren't you twenty or twenty-one when *F.O.B.* was done at the O'Neill?

Hwang: I was twenty-one when *F.O.B.* was at the O'Neill and twenty-two when it was done at the Public Theater.

Interviewer: Did it surprise you that success came in that way, or didn't you have anything to compare it to?

Hwang: No matter how good you think your play is, there's a shoot-your-arrow-into-the-sky-and-hope-it-falls-on-the-bullseye factor, so there's a certain amount of just being in the right place at the right time. Obviously, I think I am a good writer, but some of this involves luck.

Interviewer: What was the difference between putting a play on in your dorm, then going to a professional workshop situation, and then on to a place like the Public?

Hwang: When I was doing it in the dorm, the scary thing about that was that my parents decided to come see it. That was a severe critics situation! My father at that time wasn't totally sold on the idea of my being a playwright, so he told my mother, "We'll go and see this play, and if we like it we'll encourage him, and if we don't we'll tell him to stop." So actually, the stakes were rather high at that performance! Fortunately they liked it. At the O'Neill one of the things I learned to do was filter criticism. There was me and there were a couple hundred theatre professionals, and after the play they sat around and told you how you should rewrite your play. I at the time felt that I'm new and these people are well-meaning and professionals so they must be right. So I spent the next couple of weeks trying to rewrite the play along those lines. Eventually I threw all that stuff out. It just helped me learn that you have to listen to everything but that some of it will land in a useful place in your mind and the rest is not really that helpful.

Interviewer: Speaking of filtering criticism, was that exacerbated by the fact that your work was culturally rooted in the Chinese American immigrant experience and there weren't five hundred Chinese American theatre professionals there?

Hwang: There probably weren't a whole lot of Asian American theatre professionals at that event. That's true to some degree. I think there's work that comes from a particular cultural perspective, and that has to be taken into account; but I don't tend to believe, though, that the only people who should be able to appreciate the work or completely understand it therefore are people from the same cultural group. If that were true, there's no reason really to have Athol Fugard, an author I respect, or somebody like that. Ultimately, it's the careful attention to the specifics of the cultural situation that allows the work to be universal, and therefore it's very useful to have a "general audience" because I think it allows you to find out whether or not you're communicating the details of the culture specifically enough so that they become accessible to everybody.

Interviewer: Did you work early on with other Asian Americans?

Hwang: I went through a period that I now call my isolationist/nationalist period where I just worked with other Asians. The Asian

American Theatre Company in San Francisco was one that I was pretty closely hooked up with, but always, even during these periods, it has been important for me to have an outlet into the general theatrical community. I do feel that ultimately, although it's useful to work with members of your own group—particularly in terms of building up self-esteem or a self-image that's been lost—ultimately the goal is to communicate between different groups. That's why it's always been important for me to have some sort of outlet.

Interviewer: How do your ideas for plays come to you? Is it something you read, something you think about?

Hwang: Ultimately, I suppose, whatever I'm thinking about in terms of different issues in my life or different political issues ends up becoming what inspires the play; but, in terms of what the sort of hair trigger is or the spark that causes the actual idea for the dramatic work to be formed, I think lately that has tended to come a lot through real-life incidents. Earlier in my career, I think they were mostly personal questions that I was dealing with. I'd go to a family reunion, and I'd think something really strange happened there, and I would want to write about that. But lately I've been reading a lot of things in the newspaper. Obviously, *M. Butterfly* was taken from a real-life incident. A couple of days ago on the plane I was reading an article in *Vanity Fair,* and it made me think that that's a type of character I would want to write about or write a monologue about; so it tends to get sparked by things I'm reading.

Interviewer: But are those things that sparked you something that's already there?

Hwang: Yes, I think that the instant provides a fulcrum for a lot of different concerns or issues that I've been dealing with in general and that have been swimming around in my mind. I'm looking for a place to focus them—in a particular character or a particular story.

Interviewer: From your first production experience through the eight or ten plays that you've done, how has that varied? Is it always different?

Hwang: I think it is always different. I don't know that you necessarily get better at this as you go along. By that I mean that every production experience, it seems to me, is a new one. You have to redefine the rules of the engagement as well as the rules of your own part in the collaboration, given the different dynamics that different sets of people represent. It's not as if you can say, "I've had five production experiences and this is how I want to act; this is the way to work in the situation and everything will turn out fine." There's no guarantee of that. It's the same way that every time you write, every time you decide to put pen to page, it's a completely new experience. It's informed by things that have happened in your past, and maybe you have a larger repertory of things to draw from; but ultimately you have to confront the page and confront the rehearsal process as if it was the first time. At least I do.

Interviewer: Is there a point at which it's harder to let go of your play? Is the first time you show your draft to somebody difficult?

Hwang: Yes. I found, for instance, on *Face Value*, the new Broadway show, that I had been working on a first draft for a long time. It took four or five months, which for me was an eternity, and at the end I was really reluctant to show it because there is a relationship that I develop with my own work which is very intimate and which has nothing to do with anything else. Once I show it to somebody else, you start this whole other side of the process which is more public. Everybody starts to express their opinions on it, and you start to think about commercial considerations. You start to think about casting it. You can hold on to the intimacy of that relationship with your script to some degree, but it's ultimately going to be affected by the different factors that are coming in. I was very reluctant to show it to people. I was talking to Wendy Wasserstein about this because we both finished our new plays at the same time; on both our parts we sort of diddled around for weeks and weeks and changed the dots on the *i*'s for a while before we were willing to say, "Okay, let's get it out there."

Interviewer: Does that come, do you think, from both you and Wendy Wasserstein having had large successes? Was there a fear factor?

Hwang: Yes, that this is my first full-length play after *Butterfly* is a big factor. Failure is wonderful in some sense because it's so liberating. Once you fail and you exist, you are aware of who you are. Failure gives you complete freedom just to do whatever you want. Previous to *M. Butterfly* I had a play called *Rich Relations* which was my first really big flop; and after that I realized, "Gosh, I still like this play and I'm still really glad I did it." It gave me this tremendous freedom to say, "I can do whatever I want." Success is wonderful, obviously, in its own ways; but it's also restricting because there's something discouraging about the fact that whatever I do next is probably going to be perceived as a failure relative to what I just did. It's unlikely that you get two big hits in a row. I think that's why it's been four or five years between major plays for me; it's just taken me a while to get over that and get back to a place where I can feel like I just have to write for myself and I just have to write something that I like. The odds of it being a success are fifty-fifty either way. It doesn't make it more of a success if I try to make it more commercial.

Interviewer: With *Rich Relations* or any of your plays which had successful productions but not on the scale of *M. Butterfly*, are you interested in seeing that work done again in subsequent productions? Is it hard to let go of your attachment to the original production?

Hwang: I've always felt that at a certain point you have to let the kid go into the world. I tend to be rather protective of my plays for the initial production. I want to see one major production as I would like it to be seen, and then after that I really feel it's pretty much open for people to do what they like with it. There's a play that I wrote called *The Sound of a Voice* which we did at the Public in 1983 and then an L.A.–based director who I think is wonderful, and a great genius in some sense, decided to do it at the L.A. Theatre Center and did a deconstructed version. That's when you do Shakespeare and you put the beginning at the end and all that stuff; I thought it was fine. I didn't quite understand what it had to do with the text that I had written, but I thought it was really interesting.

Interviewer: In this supposedly collaborative effort, are there people that you feel closer to than others? What do you get from an actor that's different from, let's say, a director that's different from a designer?

Hwang: The director-playwright relationship is the basic fulcrum on which the production hinges. Sometimes there is a director-playwright-producer (or artistic director) relationship, particularly in the commercial theatre. I want to have a certain input with the actors, and I like to deal with them in a rehearsal situation where the actors feel free to comment on the text. I like to hear all that stuff, which is not to say that I'll necessarily go along with it, but I do want to get all the input and see which of it seems to land true. But essentially I think that my relationship is with the director.

Interviewer: Do you work now with younger playwrights or newer play-wrights?

Hwang: Work in what sense?

Interviewer: Work in any kind of mentor sense or teach at all?

Hwang: I do teach on occasion. I do playwriting workshops. The East Coast Players, which is the oldest Asian American theatre in the country, have set up a playwriting institute and they named it after me; so I show up every now and then, and that's fun. My problem with teaching is that I can do it for about three sessions and then I feel like I don't have anything really useful to say; I'm just treading water. I can fill the hour, but I feel like it's some sort of scam. There are things which have been useful to me in the past in terms of freeing up the subconscious and utilizing that in my writing that I can pass on; but I wouldn't say I had any consistent relation-ship with younger playwrights that I mentor.

Interviewer: Do you think that's because ultimately it's just something you've got to go do?

Hwang: Yes, I think you just have to do it. There's a certain amount an older playwright or a more experienced playwright can convey, but it's really very limited.

Interviewer: To what extent do you think that people should write what they know, or is the artist's imagination something that is boundless?

Hwang: I think that it depends on how you define "know." Ultimately, you do write what you know; it's just that you may know things that are not apparent in the most superficial sense. You don't have to murder someone in order to write about a murderer; but there may be some part of you that is in touch with that sort of evil, and it's a matter of probing that within yourself. You have to write about stuff that you are intimately and emotionally familiar with, but it may be things that are surprising; you may know things that you don't know you know.

Interviewer: With your first play, *F.O.B.*, you were talking about your parents, and most of your early work is very personally as well as culturally autobiographical. Was there any embarrassment in revealing family secrets that were either your own secrets or Chinese American or Asian American secrets?

Hwang: In terms of my family, I've never felt that bad about exposing family secrets. My dad is essentially of the school that it's better that they write bad things about you than they don't write at all, so I think he's always been kind of pleased no matter how he turns out in the plays. But in terms of the larger Asian American community, I've always gotten a certain amount of flak from the left and from the right. The right tends to feel the dirty laundry issues, whereas for the left the fact that I've been relatively successful in a mainstream market has always made me somewhat politically suspect. I've "whited-out" too much, as it were. When *F.O.B.* was produced, there was a review in an Asian American paper that said it set Asian America back ten years, and that sort of bugged me at the time. Now it's twelve years later, and I've gotten so much of it over the years that you realize it just comes with the turf. It's part of the job description.

Interviewer: Do you think that there is an American theatre, or is there New York which is separate from what else is out there?

Hwang: No, there is definitely an American theatre. New York represents a platform where it ends up being seen generally by a larger segment; there's a spotlight on New York. It's like when you have a main stage, everybody's going to look at the work; but the work that actually gets to the main stage is produced first in workshops or on the second stage. A lot of the important work is done at the other places, so it seems to me there is definitely a connection. The American theatre does essentially reside now in the not-for-profits, with Broadway as a place with the big light on it that sometimes you get to go to.

Interviewer: Is there an aesthetic that ties all of these disparate places together in this pluralistic country, or is that not applicable in the way it might be in another country that's more homogeneous?

Hwang: I'd like to think that there is definitely an American aesthetic, and that it encompasses a recognition of the differences and of a certain amount of fragmentation and yet there is a community underneath it all. I'd like to think that the varied heterogeneity of the culture gives rise to a certain aesthetic which is different from what you would have in the more clannish European or Asian countries.

Interviewer: What role do you feel that your ethnicity plays in what you write?

Hwang: I think my ethnicity plays a huge part in the work, but it's simplistic to say that because I'm an Asian American that that would mean I would necessarily always write about Asian American characters. Nonetheless, I think my perspective is shaped a great deal by the fact that I'm Asian American in the same way that it is shaped by my being a man and being from Southern California. There's a lot of different things that go into making us who we are, and the experience of being Asian American, the experience of being a minority group on the one hand and on the other hand growing up very upper-middle-class, creates a balance there that contributes a lot to my seeing the world. At various points I've taken a very explicitly rebellious stance and said, "Just because I'm Asian American I shouldn't necessarily have to write about Asian characters." In the case of *Rich Relations*, I essentially did it wrong; I wrote an autobiographical play about my family, but I made them all white. That's not where it's at either. On the other hand, with a piece like *1000 Airplanes* or the other Glass collaboration or some of the movies I'm working on, they are not explicitly Asian American; but I recognize I do come from a particular perspective that helps me see the world in a certain way and that goes into the work.

Interviewer: Has being an Asian American in the theatre changed in the ten or so years that you've been working?

Hwang: Ten years ago, when you said someone was an Asian American writer or a black writer or a Latino writer, there was much more of a sense of second-class literary citizenship. When I first began writing, there was the notion that Chinese American or Asian American literature represented something that had sociological importance, something that had political importance. It was useful if you were going to work in Chinatown, but it somehow didn't achieve the same kind of literary heights or the same universality as "mainstream" work did (mainstream equaling Caucasian culture). I think that that's changed a lot in the last ten years; there's much more of a recognition now that American literature encompasses a great many groups. With someone like August Wilson, for example, most people feel that his work is just as valid and just as universal as a work by someone of the ethnic group called European; so I think that's changed.

Interviewer: Has the makeup of the theatre companies you see on stage changed, and is it driven by there being an August Wilson or there being a you?

Hwang: We get into some of the cross-casting issues with that question. There's been a lot of lip service paid to color-blind casting, cross-cultural casting, whatever you call it, over the past x number of years; but the fact remains that 90 percent of the stage productions in this country still employ all-white casts, and in any other industry we'd have to say that's a pretty rotten minority hiring record. That question needs to be addressed because Caucasians are increasingly becoming a plurality rather than a majority in this country, and you don't want to get into a sort of artistic apartheid situation where a minority of people control a majority of the artistic resources simply on the basis of some self-defined aesthetic superiority.

Interviewer: Is the answer, then, color-blind and nontraditional casting? What do those words mean?

Hwang: In the *Miss Saigon* controversy which I was involved with, it seems to me that ultimately Jonathan Pryce should be able to play anything he wants. B. D. Wong should be able to play Jewish and James Earl Jones should be able to play Italian; that's where you want to get to. You want to say that acting is acting. We're at a certain point in the evolution of that right now, but we're not there. It's useful now to say that when a role comes along for a minority we should cast it with a minority, because otherwise these people aren't getting employed. But ultimately you do want to get to a place where you suspend your disbelief. It is theatre; it is metaphor. We're used to seeing *The King and I* with somebody who's not Asian; we say, "Okay, I guess he's supposed to be Asian," and we accept that. I don't see why the reverse can't be true as well.

Interviewer: You would feel that way, then, about your own plays, if we were in the best of all possible worlds?

Hwang: In the best of all possible worlds, yes. There should be enough of a cultural understanding so that different people should be able to play anything they want; but I would stress the idea of cultural understanding in the sense that, if you're playing another race, without a certain amount of knowledge of and sensitivity to that race there's the unconscious desire to resort to stereotypes. If I'm a white person and I'm playing black, what does "black" mean? Or what does "Asian" mean? Do I associate it with a series of images which are ultimately stereotypical, and do I try to play those images? There's a lot more cross-cultural understanding that needs to take place before that can really be achieved.

Interviewer: You've said that there is no race and that there's a mythology of race that we often conspire to agree upon.

Hwang: Right. I'm sort of playing with the notion that maybe race has lost its usefulness as a construct in this day and age. What we're essentially talking about when we talk about race is culture. We're saying that if we associate different races with different behaviors we're not associating the color of the skin as much as we are the culture of that root country. I don't know why it's necessarily true that skin color and culture need to go hand in hand. Ultimately, our cultures are much more personal than we have let on so far. Our cultures are essentially the personal histories that we have, and those elements of that personal history that we can share with other people and form a group become a culture. Consequently, the whole idea of skin color doesn't seem to me to be that useful anymore. I'm playing with this idea; it comes out a lot in *Face Value,* and it comes out to some degree in *Bondage.* We have these mythologies that skin color should mean certain things, that we can gain information about the essence of a person by observing certain things in their exterior. I don't know that that's necessarily true, because a lot of times what would be information that you infer from looking at someone's outward features may be completely at odds with what their interior actually holds.

Interviewer: In *M. Butterfly,* in *Bondage,* and in *Face Value,* there's this idea of surface and how surface is mutable or not and what's underneath. How much of those surfaces are related to the truth, and how do they dictate our perceptions of the truth so much that we can't escape them?

Hwang: Sometimes when Asian Americans read Amy Tan, Maxine Hong Kingston, or my work, they try to say, "Gee, there's supposed to be some stuff here that's supposed to be Chinese American. Is it really Chinese American, or is it just that we think it's Chinese American because we grew up in America and this is some stuff that we've been told?" The information that we get becomes so inextricably linked with whatever the "truth" of the root culture is that for all practical purposes it becomes indistinguishable. I don't know to what extent it's possible to separate those two things. Again, culture has to be taken in a more personal sense.

As an Asian American, I've grown up with American influences at least as much as I've grown up with any root-culture Asian influences. I have to deal with those things, and some of them may or may not be true in terms of what the root culture would say; but I'm not in the root culture. I'm in this country, those are my influences, and I have to deal with them.

Interviewer: In M. *Butterfly,* ultimately the man kills himself. When the illusion is gone, he can't go on. Do you think that's a parallel to what's going on in this country where people are clinging to these mythologies because they've had them so long that they don't know what else to do?

Hwang: I hadn't thought of it that way, but I think that that's a good point. We're going through this weird transition right now. America's always been a country that's dominated by Euro-Americans, Americans of European descent, and in another twenty or thirty years Euro-Americans will be a minority. The whole question of what is American is being redefined right now, and our respective roles in this new country are also to some degree up for grabs. There is a desire to reach back for something that feels secure, that has the weight of tradition and inertia behind it. That's one of the reasons why now you see this kind of split taking place in the culture where you have some people you would call progressive who accept the notion that it's going to be a slightly different country and then you have a whole reactionary wing that's resisting the change. Somehow, traditional values are supposed to save us. Traditional values are values that were thought up in another contemporary culture, so I don't know that the weight of history necessarily gives them any added value.

Interviewer: Do you think that that's particularly true with slightly to the left playwrights, people in the arts, or people who listen to NPR or whatever, and that that's not going on in the culture at large?

Hwang: I think the discussion is going on in the culture at large. It's just that those of us who are more on the left don't like some of the discussions. David Duke is discussing these things; I happen to think he's completely wrong, but the thing that allows a David Duke to exist is very much these issues that we're talking about. People are talking about these issues all over the place in one form or another.

Interviewer: Where does the theatre fit into this discussion?

Hwang: I think that the discussion is really important, but I happen to come from a particular perspective and I hate to say, "That means all of you should think it's important." You either do or you don't. How does the theatre fit in? Something like the *Miss Saigon* debate, for instance, definitely encapsulates a lot of these different cross-cultural multicultural issues, which is one of the reasons it ended up attracting so much attention. It was a very esoteric debate, and yet it made the front pages around the world for two weeks. I think that's because there are certain issues which act as lightning rods for other tensions in the culture and become a focus for things that people are thinking about anyway, and this was one of those times. In general, I think that all the issues that are in society we have to deal with in the theatre in one sense or another.

Interviewer: One of the fascinating things for me in *M. Butterfly* is the issue of gender bending, how a lot of people play with the idea of gender, and the way it's tied to race. How do those two things work in conjunction for you?

Hwang: When I was in college, there were third-world identity movements. People used to say, "Feminism is a white woman's thing"; of course, all the people who were saying this were third-world men! One of the things that I learned from *M. Butterfly* is the universality of the other, as it were. Whether we talk about it in terms of race or whether we talk about it in terms of gender or imperialism or whatever, there is a desire to degrade the person who is not like yourself and to feel somehow superior, to feel that you have power over them. The interrelationships of the gender issues and the race issues are really important, and it's something I discovered as I was writing about it.

Interviewer: In that play you also talk about the rape mentality, not necessarily between men and women but between East and West. Can you expound upon that or is it expounded upon in the play enough?

Hwang: I guess it's just that this sort of "her mouth says no, her eyes say yes" thing would seem to apply to imperialism as well. It would seem to apply to cultures. It still wipes me out that there is this idea that the English or Spanish just go someplace, plant a flag, and say, "This is ours now." It's a wild concept when you think about it, and certain countries weren't as happy as others about having a flag planted on them. In China, for instance, the English introduced opium and got the Chinese population in on drug dealing, made a lot of money, and expanded their sphere of influence that way. I just think that there is this desire for conquest. By the way, I don't mean to imply that it's only the West that does this to the East. Over the last five hundred years, we've been in a particular phase where that's taken place; but certainly there is a universal human desire on the part of different cultures to try and dominate other cultures. China's done it, Japan's done it; certainly it's not just a Western-Eastern thing, but it has been that more recently.

Interviewer: With multiculturalism or interculturalism or whatever it is that we're working to, is there a way to get beyond that? Is that just a human desire?

Hwang: Of all people, Jimmy Walker had a remark that I thought was great. He was saying that in the States we've got this thing between blacks and whites; then, when he went to Ireland, he saw the same thing between Protestants and Catholics and he said, "You know, if people don't have an enemy they'll improvise." There does seem to be this basic human desire to create an in group and an out group, and it's often easy to do that along racial lines or along gender lines, things that are more superficially different. I don't know quite how one necessarily evolves past that stage. Certainly, dealing with one another doesn't hurt in the sense that it was maybe easier to have a lot of rigid dealings with the other as nonhuman during those ages when people never went outside of a radius of ten miles from where they were born. I do tend to contend it's a little harder to bomb people when you can also fax them. But you can get into these little Hatfield and McCoy situations where you hate the people who live on the other mountain because a couple of hundred years ago they stole this pot. So I'm not really sure. We're asking some fundamental questions about why it is that people go to war and why there is hate. Maybe what I'm saying is that it's a little simplistic to organize those hatreds along the most superficial lines: you look different from me, so I hate you.

Interviewer: You've said that your plays before and including *M. Butterfly* did not have happy endings and were not optimistic. You've also said that it's a little hard to write happy endings. Why is that?

Hwang: Up to *M. Butterfly*, every romance that I ever wrote ended in somebody killing themselves. In one play, they both killed themselves; in another, one woman hung herself and the guy was a zombie; and in *M. Butterfly*, the guy knifed himself and the other person seemed really bereft. It seemed to me kind of important to write a romance with a happy ending, but the happy endings are harder to get to. If they have any reality to them, they take a lot of work, because it is easier for me to assume that something's going to end badly. To be able to take all the variables which exist in all relationships that would make them end badly and try and work through them and work past them to a place where there is some hope seems to me to be a much longer journey, and it's something that I find has been more difficult. But I do like the happy endings that I've gotten to in the two plays that I've written more recently, so we'll see.

Interviewer: Do you have anything sitting in your drawer that you've never gotten to the stage?

Hwang: Oh, yes. There's all sorts of stuff that's really embarrassing. *The Dance and the Railroad,* which is a two-character play we did at the Public in 1981, started out as a completely other play called "The Dance and the Railroad" which I modeled after Edward Bond's *Lear*. It was also set on the transcontinental railroad in the 1860s, and, as in *Lear,* there is a character who keeps coming in who's more dead or deteriorating every time he comes in. It probably still exists someplace in somebody's drawer, but it didn't work for me, so I took the situation and the title and wrote a completely new play that became *The Dance and the Railroad,* which was produced. Writing's like fishing: you go out and cast your line and try to catch a fish. Sometimes you do and sometimes you don't, and sometimes you catch a really ugly deformed fish and you have to throw it back.

Interviewer: Are there things that are sitting around that you think you'll go back to, or once you've tried something and it hasn't worked do you throw it away?

Hwang: Generally that's been my pattern. If I don't feel I've gotten something important the first time out, I just toss it back.

Interviewer: Is there something else you would like to do, or do you always see yourself writing for the theatre?

Hwang: I'm interested in film, and I'm working in film a fair amount of the time now. Writing plays is a great thing to do—to be able to write and see the work performed and make a living at it. I can't imagine anything that would be better.

Interviewer: Is there something that you get with your filmwriting that helps you with your playwriting, or are they separate?

Hwang: I tend to feel that one feeds the other. In filmwriting there is such an emphasis on story—being able just to spin a tale—as opposed to a lot of playwriting when you can just deal with the relationships in the plot, and the development becomes a little vague. I don't know if the amount of storytelling that takes place in something like *M. Butterfly* would have been possible if I hadn't done some filmwriting before that and had become more familiar with the structure of storytelling.

Interviewer: The money is there and there's more work for writers in movies and television, but is there a way to get that system to feed back into the theatre?

Hwang: I know that there's this feeling that somehow if we paid writers more money in the theatre that they wouldn't write films, but I think that's a myth. I think that if a writer is not interested in film he or she is not writing a lot of films anyway and that, if anything, the fact that you can make so much money in film liberates you not to have to worry about the economic consequences so much when you write for the stage. I think people write for the stage because they love the stage and that that love doesn't have that much to do with the money factor. I do feel that there has to be a certain minimal wage level that you're able to earn in the theatre so that you're at least able to survive, but over and above that I think that, for me anyway, the interaction between theatre and film is a good one. It's nice for me to know that if *Face Value* is a complete flop on Broadway I'll have some other place to go to make some money.

Interviewer: Do you think that the theatre is being changed by the media generation? Is that changing the kind of plays we have now?

Hwang: People talk a lot about the way that plays have gotten to be a short blackout kind of thing, and that seems to be influenced a lot by the media. Other than that, I would like to feel that developments in the media force us to be more theatrical. What can we do on the stage that we can't do in these other mediums, and how can we exploit those elements to a greater degree than we are able to do in film or television?

Interviewer: Have you ever done anything else in the theatre besides write?

Hwang: I direct now and then.

Interviewer: How do you find that?

Hwang: I don't like having to show up at rehearsals every day. It's really a lot of work. Maybe because I've been a writer all my adult life, I don't like the idea that I have to be someplace at 10:00 A.M. every day; so that's the hardest part, just getting to work. Other than that, it's fun. I find that I've never lost my temper as a playwright, but as a director I usually lose my temper once in the process: "God, I'm responsible for so many things, and you're just responsible for one thing, and you didn't do it!" It makes me mad for some reason.

Interviewer: Have you directed your own work?

Hwang: Mostly I've directed my own work. I directed that first dorm production of *F.O.B.,* and that was a perfectly nice experience. Recently I directed a revival of *F.O.B.* off-Broadway. That was fun because it had been ten years since the original play had been done off-Broadway, and it was interesting for me to go back and look at myself as a writer then. I also think, relative to this question of what it means to follow up on a big success, that I needed to be more in touch with some of the things that had made me start writing in the first place. It was useful for me to go back and direct my first play to get in touch with some of those values again.

Interviewer: Do you think that you could direct a premiere, or do you need distance?

Hwang: I don't think I would want to direct a premiere at this point in my life. Who knows in the future, but I feel that it's so much work just premiering a new play as a writer that I don't also want to have the directorial burden. Also, I want to have someone that I can interact with, someone that I can trust and bounce things off of; so at this point in my life I wouldn't want to direct a premiere.

Interviewer: If a person comes to you with an idea for a play, do you sometimes take that idea and work with that person, or do you just use ideas that you view from society? If you do converse with someone who has an idea for a play, what is the process?

Hwang: Actually there have been times that I've gotten ideas from people, and generally I've ripped them off. I heard the *Butterfly* story at a party. Somebody told me, "Have you heard about this French diplomat who had an affair for twenty years with a Chinese actress and she turned out to be a man?" In that case, it's not as if then we went and collaborated on it. It was a party story that I wrote up. I'm trying to think of instances where somebody has brought a story to me and we collaborated on it. I think the only collaborations I've done really are the ones with Philip Glass. Here at Louisville we're doing two one-acts, my play *Bondage* and Suzan-Lori Parks's *Devotees in the Garden of Love*. We spent a lot of time discussing the ideas beforehand, and then we went off to our separate corners and wrote our individual plays. I would be open to the idea of collaborating with somebody who was another writer or somebody who had an idea, but it's not something I've ever done before. It can be tricky in terms of how you define that relationship down the line. It's very important that it be made clear in the beginning, if it's a co-writing situation or whatever, that both people are going to get credit.

Interviewer: Have you ever found yourself laughing at a story or a joke that you later realized was fraught with incorrect political content?

Hwang: I think that that does happen to all of us, and I don't think that that's necessarily such a bad thing. Let's not get too guilted out about it, because the fact is that, while it's not the nicest thing in the world to be laughing at anybody for something that they can't control, the fact is that there is a lot of tension in the culture about issues of race and gender, and sometimes laughter is a way to release that. I make jokes in my own plays that depend on that. In *M. Butterfly* the whole idea that the child would be named Long Dong is a really cheap shot, but the fact is that the humorous response to that comes out of something that exists in the culture and something which is a little bit of a put-down of another culture. This is not to say that having recognized that this joke may be insulting to somebody doesn't mean you want to go on now and perpetrate it because you're "just relieving the tensions of the culture." There are times when we're all going to laugh at things that we're not that proud of; we should recognize it for what it is and go on, but there is no reason to get mired in guilt.

Interviewer: Can you remember the most interesting or unusual response to *M. Butterfly* that you received, either in person or through the mail?

Hwang: When we first did *M. Butterfly* in Washington, D.C., nobody knew what it was. There are a few things that happened the day of the first preview that I think are notable. One is that in the scene where Song gets disrobed, when B. D. Wong dropped his drawers, the audience literally screamed. It was really cool. It was like when Glenn Close came out of the water in *Fatal Attraction*. That's an experience which has never been duplicated, but I always really treasure it. At that same performance, somebody was coming out of the lobby and overheard a woman say to her husband, "You said it was going to be *Madame Butterfly*, and there wasn't a single song."

Interviewer: When you were speaking about the deconstructive production of *The Sound of a Voice* in L.A., you said that was fine. Would that have been fine if that had been the production that premiered the play in New York? What do you expect from a director the first time around, both in terms of the text and the intentions behind the text, whether it's completely realized or not?

Hwang: No, it wouldn't have been fine if it had been the first production in New York; or even if the first production of the play had happened to be in L.A., it wouldn't have been fine either. There is always a point for me when it changes, where I've seen the production that I want to see and I say, "Now let's see what other people can do with it." Up until I get to that point, I do expect that the director has an obligation to work with me and present the vision that I've conceived when I put it on the page. The L.A. version worked for me because it came after the point when I had already, as it were, seen my own production realized.

Interviewer: You've worked at the O'Neill and now at Louisville. What do you think is the role of these kinds of places in developing new playwrights and in the future of American theatre?

Hwang: I don't mean to do PR for these institutions, but I do think they're incredibly important. When I wrote *F.O.B.*, I sent it to a number of different theatres. The O'Neill picked it up and everybody else rejected it. Then one of the artistic directors of these theatres saw me at the O'Neill and said, "Wow! Why didn't you send your play to us?" It was one of those wonderful times in a writer's life that only happens every twenty years, and I said, "I did and you turned it down!" The point of that tale is that, while there is a certain amount of lip service being paid to the production of new American plays at a number of American theatres (it's good for grantsmanship, and it's good for all the PR stuff), it's very important to have institutions that actually are dedicated to new American plays, whether that be the O'Neill, the Humana Festival, or a number of different organizations whose raison d'être is really new American works.

Interviewer: You've talked a little bit about working with directors and actors. How do you feel about the writer-dramaturg relationship?

Hwang: I've been known to make some disparaging comments about dramaturgs, so, first of all, I'd like to apologize for the general tone of my hostility. Let's ask ourselves, "Where does this come from in David's psychology?" I'm going to get in trouble for saying this, but when I was at Yale in the Drama program, I think that it was structured in such a way that people who were not yet accustomed to the production process were asked to become part of it. At Yale, because it was a school, that's how they essentially learned what it meant to be part of the production process; but for those of us who had to teach them, sometimes we got a little irritated. My basic point is that sometimes in certain situations (certainly not here in Louisville!) the dramaturg tends to be a little result-oriented and not understand what the process is. It's like when you get a nondirector talking to actors and not speaking the actors' language. I'm sort of twisted, and I may be hostile to dramaturgs for life, but I'm working on that in therapy.

Interviewer: When you choose a director for your play, do you try to get someone with a slightly different take on reality—to expand the universality—or is that not a consideration?

Hwang: I have to say I've not worked with a whole lot of Asian American directors, and I think that that's an area where maybe I've been a bit remiss. On the one hand, it makes sense to me because I feel like my work does come from a particular perspective and I want to have somebody else from another perspective to bounce off of as a collaborator to make sure that the work is accessible. On the other hand, I guess that what I look for more in a director is somebody, of whatever background, from whatever culture they happen to come from, that I feel has both a certain active interest in what I'm trying to say and another perspective on it. I feel like I have a greater treasure chest to work with when I have a director who comes from that perspective.

Interviewer: Could you talk a little bit about *Bondage,* particularly in light of your comment earlier about happy endings, especially in terms of what the breakthrough or the insight is for the characters in this play that allows them to get to that ending?

Hwang: *Bondage* is a romance that's set in an s-and-m bondage parlor; it's a two-character play. The two characters are covered from head to toe in leather so we don't see any of their skin, and they play these ethnic games with each other and use that to humiliate each other, as in "I'm a black woman and you're a white man" or "I'm an Asian man and you're a white woman." They humiliate each other with stereotypes of race. I guess that the play is fairly hopeful at the end because to some degree the characters are able to get past a lot of those superficial images of one another and realize, perhaps through the process of having played so many races over the years, that the idea of race starts to become blurry. The mythology of race becomes less connected, again, to the particular color of the skin and more connected to the particular hopeful choices that are being made. What the play's trying to do is realize that you have to acknowledge ethnic differences and at the same time that you have to be willing to get past them to the human essence. It's too simplistic to say we are all the same and there are no cultural differences at all. There are some cultural differences; we come from different backgrounds, but the essential universal humanity is ultimately something you can get to from having acknowledged these differences.

Interviewer: You said earlier that, in an ideal theatre world, any race could play any other another race and that the audience would buy into the believability of that. I wonder if in *Bondage,* by creating a situation in which the audience has no idea what the race of these two characters is, you are trying to get at this?

Hwang: I hadn't thought of it that way, but I think that's a good point. Basically, because we hopefully don't know the races of the actual actors when we're seeing the play, it allows us to say, when they say, "I'm a white woman; you're a black man," "Maybe that actress is a black woman; maybe the actor is a white man." It allows us to begin playing with this notion of the interchangeability of skin colors and how they do or do not relate to particular behavior. As a matter of fact, going a step further, actually the director and I were talking about the notion that this play could have a completely color-blind cast. Here at Louisville we're doing it with an Asian man and a Caucasian woman. Maybe it could be done with any combination of races. It could be done with a black woman and a white man or whatever. It's another way to get past this notion that this information, the information about the skin, ultimately doesn't tell us anything useful about the individual.

Interviewer: In talking about the different ways in which you have addressed race relations, are you more apt to present relations as they actually are, or do you tend to lean more toward an idealized view of what they could be or should be? Do you think the theatre has a responsibility either way in dealing with those issues?

Hwang: I guess I tend to like to present things as they are but hopefully, at least more recently, to get to some place that's a little more evolved relative to where we actually are. Do I think that the theatre has a responsibility to present one or the other? I don't really think that the theatre has that much of a responsibility to present anything that a playwright or a creator doesn't happen to feel is important. I'm keen on the idea of having a little more equal employment opportunities in the theatre, but other than that I'm a bit loath to set out any sort of aesthetic or political agenda for the theatre. I'm more interested in seeing what people happen to come up with up with in their own lives. I think that's the most vital material.

Larry L. King

Larry L. King was born in Putnam, Texas, in 1929. After serving in the army, he attended Texas Technological College and began a career as a newspaper and radio journalist. In 1955 he came to Washington, where he served as an administrative assistant to congressmen J. T. Rutherford and James Wright. His novel The One-Eyed Man *appeared in 1966. His nonfiction books, several drawn from his long career as a free-lance journalist, include . . .* And Other Dirty Stories *(1968),* Confessions of a White Racist *(1971),* The Old Man and Other Lesser Mortals *(1974),* Of Outlaws, Con Men, Whores, Politicians, and Other Artists *(1980),* Warning: Writer at Work *(1985), and* None But a Blockhead *(1986). He co-wrote the book for the musicals* The Best Little Whorehouse in Texas *(1978) and* The Best Little Whorehouse Goes Public *(1994) and is co-author of the play* The Kingfish *(1979). His play* The Night Hank Williams Died *(1985) won the Helen*

Hayes Award; and he is also the author of The Golden Shadows Old West Museum *(1985). His work has been honored with the Stanley Walker Journalism Award, an Emmy for TV documentary writing, and the Mary Goldwater Award for playwriting; and he has been a Nieman Fellow at Harvard University, a fellow of Communications at Duke University, and Ferris Professor of Journalism and Creative Writing at Princeton University. This interview took place on December 4, 1991.*

▶ ── ◀

Interviewer: What appeals to you particularly about being a playwright?

King: I like writing dialogue, and I like seeing the story come alive. Actors and directors can bring their talents to you. Actors can do a lot with gestures and pauses; directors can find things in the subtext that the author may not have known. They help you tell the story, and you get to see your work come alive in front of your eyes. You get to see the audience react to it. I've never caught anybody reading any of my books, so it's kind of fun to see people's reactions to one's work.

Interviewer: That implies that you enjoy the production part of it.

King: Oh yes, very much. In fact, I think the most enjoyable time really is from rehearsal onward when you're around the stage company and doing your rewrites, cutting, all that. That's the best part. That's more fun than being in a room with yourself and blank paper.

Interviewer: What terrifies you?

King: Being onstage and forgetting lines, or having somebody forget lines, or, in the case of one fellow who played in one of my plays off-Broadway, having an actor invent dialogue as he goes along which doesn't even approximate what it was supposed to be. I had to replace him after two weeks and go on myself. It's horrifying to sit there and see that sort of thing happen.

Interviewer: *The Best Little Whorehouse in Texas* started out as a magazine article, didn't it?

King: Yes, it was a freak deal. I wrote it as an article for *Playboy* magazine. It was just one of many articles I wrote to make a living, and I didn't think much of the piece one way or another. About two years later, Peter Masterson, an actor and director who was playing on Broadway in *That Championship Season*, went out between shows on a matinee day. When he came back, through the mysterious will of the fates, this two-year-old *Playboy* was in his dressing room, and he started reading that article. About halfway through it, he says, he immediately thought—musical. He didn't know me, although we were both "New York Texans." But he knew Carol Hall, the composer-lyricist, and she knew us both. Carol called me, said Pete had this idea, told me who he was, and said, "Let's all get together and make a musical out of this." I thought they were crazy and told them so. I didn't know anything about musical theatre. I believe my response was, "Carol, I've seen three musicals in my life, hated all of them, and I believe they were all hits." That's the truth; it was *Oklahoma!*, *Finian's Rainbow*, and *How to Succeed in Business Without Really Trying*. I didn't like any of them. Anyhow, they persuaded me to do it, and I did it because I thought that might be kind of fun to try. The truth is, I really did it because I thought I could have a little adventure and then write a magazine article about it and sell it for five or six thousand dollars—about shooting for Broadway and missing by about ten miles. I never got to write that one.

Interviewer: What about some of the things you'd done before that, among them working in oil fields? You were a letter carrier for the Post Office, you were an administrative aide on the Hill at one point, a teacher, and you did a comic strip with Pat Oliphant.

King: Pat and I wrote a comic strip together that we thought Universal Syndicate was going to love. It was about a paper boy, Toby. Toby would sell papers, but he could also make them into paper airplanes and fly in them wherever he wanted to go. It was sort of a fantasy deal heavy on politics. Oliphant's syndicate thought we were crazy and turned it down, but we had lots of fun.

Interviewer: Those are a lot of different things, and none of those things sound like playwriting.

King: I was not, as someone said of George Bush, born on third base and thought I hit a triple. I had to get out there and work to make a living. But I wanted to be a writer from the time I was six years old. One of the things that really decided me to push on to become a writer was working on a farm, on ranches, and in oil fields. It just occurred to me one day that no law in the world said I had to do grunt work the rest of my life. Some of my friends say to me now, "You know, you don't ski and you don't boat and you don't do this, that, and the other. Why don't you like outdoor sports?" I say, "Listen, I spent twenty-one years trying to get in the house, and I'm not interested in going back out!" That's pretty much the story.

Interviewer: When you started writing, you started as a journalist. You did that for a few years, and then you went to Washington.

King: I came here to Washington because my family had a habit. They had a habit of wanting to eat three times a day. We about starved to death on Texas newspapers. They paid us just in titles down there. I had four or five titles. Every once in a while they'd lay a new title on me, but no money. You can't eat titles. I always liked politics, but I really came to Washington, one, for the money, but, two, I was trying to work my way back to New York and to publishing places. In Texas in those days (we're going back to the Eisenhower administration, the very early part of it), there was no place to publish in Texas. It did not have, as it does now, a lot of regional houses and magazines and so forth.

Interviewer: Initially you did a lot of interviews, didn't you? One of the things that you said about interviewing people was that you had to live with them for a week or two before you could get to know them well enough to talk with them. Is that so?

King: I had a sneaky technique. I interviewed a lot of politicians, a lot of sports stars, show-biz figures, people who were very experienced at being interviewed. The first thing you have to make them do is forget you're there, because they've all got an image to maintain. They've got handlers putting spins on things, and all you're going to get is the same thing they've told a thousand other people. Why are you *there* if you can't beat that? I always went in and just chatted with them, didn't make a note, just hung around and asked casual conversational questions, and got to know the people as I observed them. Finally they forgot why I was there and they'd start talking; then I'd start sneaking off to the restroom and taking notes.

Interviewer: Was that useful in writing plays, that kind of observation and hobnobbing?

King: I think so. I was the kind of journalist who learned through observation more often than not. I could not simply walk in with a list of twenty questions and sit down and say to someone, "Do you sleep in the nude?" or all those questions that conventional journalists asked. I didn't know what to ask till I had watched them a while, been around them, seen them in their natural state more or less. It was calculated: I wanted them to forget what I was doing so they'd relax and talk to me; but the other thing was that I simply couldn't go in and ask the questions cold because I didn't know what to ask yet.

Interviewer: If you're creating a character, do you begin with questions about the character? Does he simply appear to you? Does he start talking to you?

King: That sounds like I believe in spiritualism or something, but it really does happen. I hear voices; Mama always suspected I did. *The Night Hank Williams Died* came from one day when I was walking to lunch at Duke

Zeibert's restaurant. I had nothing on my mind but my hat, and suddenly I heard this voice say (with the accent and everything), "Gus, if they was giving away free tumbleweeds, I couldn't afford the wind to get mine home." I thought, "I wonder who that is and what they're trying to say?" I stopped and wrote it down on a piece of paper. I'd look at it periodically, pull it out of the mess on my desk, and finally one morning I decided to try to find out who that was and why. It turns out the fellow who put the line in my head was a young guy who wanted to be the next Hank Williams, a big-time country-western singer. He was a man of limited talents and abilities and didn't have that much adventure in his soul; so I had the story right away of a kid trying to break out of a Texas town, young, dreaming. It was kind of autobiographical. I was the same way, you see. I had in the past thought about doing a play using some country music in it as part of the plot, so that original line fit that. Of all the rewriting, and God knows there always is a lot of it done, I never had to change that line; it stayed in. It clued the audience early on as to my protagonist's socioeconomic circumstance.

Interviewer: Are all of the plays somewhat autobiographical? Were you ever at the Chicken Ranch?

King: No, I got my education in that regard along the Mexican border. They apparently didn't need me. Everybody I've met, every male just about except for a few priests, have claimed that they were there. I don't think the Chicken Ranch would have gone out of business if that many people had gone there. I had never been there until I went down to write the story of its closing, and I was alerted to that by an old friend who had called me and said, "There's a story down here that's got your name on it." I wasn't too interested, but I hadn't seen my friend in a while and he promised me we'd get drunk together; so I called *Playboy,* sold them on the idea, and I went down there.

Interviewer: Why did it have your name on it? Because it was Texas?

King: Because it was Texas and politics. The sheriff was involved, the governor, the media was involved—all the things that he knew I could take and have fun with.

Interviewer: Texas and politics are the two things that keep showing up, certainly the South and politics, in all of your plays, don't they?

King: I think so. Politics has always been a big influence in my life. I think it influences all of our lives more than most people stop to think about and know or we wouldn't keep electing the wretched people that we do. A lot of this had to do with being a journalist in Texas. When I was a young man, there always was a political machine in those little towns. It was almost always headed up by a sheriff who was not totally admirable and could usually retire in six years if he wanted to because he had gotten too rich for the twenty-four-hundred-dollars-a-year job. Seeing that sort of raw power and corruption going on, well, hell, that makes good drama. There's just not any doubt, there's a story in that. Power is quite often misused against the helpless, and that's what a lot of my work is about, too: *Confessions of a White Racist, Hank Williams, Golden Shadows,* even *Whorehouse.*

Interviewer: You said at one point in an interview about eleven years ago that the assassination of JFK caused you to rethink things, to go into more fictional writing.

King: Yes, I had long wanted to be a "writer." I had wanted to be a novelist, but unfortunately I never did turn out to be a very good one. I got in politics, one, because I liked it, two, because I wanted to get out of West Texas and, as I say, I needed the money; but I only intended to stay about three years, and I wound up staying ten years. When the assassination of Kennedy happened, it was terribly traumatic to me—and it happening in Texas made it even more traumatic. I worked for a Texas congressman, Jim Wright, at the time and I suddenly thought, "Wait a minute, I *knew* John F. Kennedy, and he was young and handsome and rich, and powerful— and he's dead at forty-six." I also thought, "Well, at least he did a lot of the things he set out to do." He had realized a lot of his dreams and I had not, and I was no longer the twenty-five-year-old boy who had come to work in Congress. I was almost thirty-five, and I decided that if I really intended to do what I set out to do that I had to start; so shortly thereafter I just quit the job and started free-lancing.

Interviewer: What was the first literary project you worked on? Was it a novel right away?

King: I sold a political novel right away, called *The One-Eyed Man,* which did not live up to my expectations; but it was published and had a fair reception—it was a book club alternate—and some good things happened, including a new book contract. Then I supported myself for a long time, as I wrote other books, by writing magazine articles largely about politics, and with side journeys into autobiographical pieces—things about Texas, music, family ties, and that sort of thing.

Interviewer: Essentially *The Best Little Whorehouse* changed that when you were asked to do the musical, didn't it?

King: Yes, it changed my life. It's hard to make a decent living as a free-lance writer. I had some good money years for a writer—eighty or ninety thousand dollars—but if you're spending $110,000 partying it doesn't work out too well. I don't do any of that anymore, incidentally. I got all of my wild oats over with finally. But suddenly I had more money than God, and of course I felt guilty about that because if you're rich you're "corrupt," right? I couldn't live with it comfortably, so I took what I refer to now as a whiskey sabbatical, took a couple of years out and didn't do much except drink. Fortunately, or unfortunately, that led to my alcoholic rehabilitation, with the encouragement of my wife, and then I went back to work.

Interviewer: How long after the play was a success on Broadway did it became a movie? It was just a couple of years, wasn't it?

King: Yes, it opened in 1978, and the movie, I believe, was released in 1982; but we knew there'd be a movie all along. What happened was, a person buying properties for Universal Pictures saw our workshop production of *Whorehouse* at Actors Studio and wanted to buy it for the movies. Our position was, we were trying to get it onstage, so in order to get the movie rights they agreed to open it off-Broadway and, if it did well, move it to Broadway—and it did well.

Interviewer: Did it affect the way you wrote the script for the stage— because you knew it was going to become a movie?

King: No, we had our basic script when the movie people saw the show. We did rewrite; we slicked it up and tricked it up after Actors Studio. It used to be more of a story and less music until they said, "If you're going to have a musical shooting for Broadway, you've got to have more music and dancing in it." So we hired Tommy Tune and changed it a lot that way. I, of course, fought it every lick of the way. I made the complaint that every time one of my characters was trying to talk somebody would dance on him or sing on him. It seemed to me that all they cut was dialogue and they kept adding songs and dances. I'd never been through that before; I'd never collaborated with anybody and it was very painful. To tell you the truth, I think I kind of made a pain of myself. I'm not too proud of some of my conduct, including the night before we opened. They got everybody together—the collaborators, Tommy Tune, and the producers and everybody else—in the theatre lobby. I looked at my watch and reminded them that it was 6:14 or whatever it was, and told them the day and the month it was, because I wanted them to remember *that* was the exact time and place when I told them I had delivered them a good play that they had danced on and sung on and tricked it up until the God-damned thing was going to close quicker than a switchblade. Of course, twenty-four hours later we had rave reviews, and I denied that I'd even been to the theatre the previous night, much less said those things! I liked the play a lot better at that point, too, the money tending to mitigate what I had seen as artistic failings.

Interviewer: When you were recasting it as a movie, were you suddenly having to write for Dolly Parton and Burt Reynolds?

King: I got fired pretty early for running afoul of Mr. Reynolds and his director, so I never even got to go out on location. Mr. Reynolds said he would not play, and I'm quoting Mr. Reynolds, the sheriff "as an old fart," that it would be bad for his image. It was Dolly's first movie, and she didn't quite know what to do, so she kind of went along with Burt, and they got the director Burt wanted. I tried to talk to Mr. Reynolds and said, "Look, you know you're the leading box office star for the past seven years, but you can do more than you have done, and I know you can just be a wonderful actor and win all these prizes and whatnot if you'll extend your range." He nodded and beamed, and I thought I had impressed him; by the time I had got back to my hotel, he had demanded that I be fired, and I was. Then they took the script over and rewrote the thing pretty much as they wanted to. On stage, under the Dramatists Guild contract, the author has the power. They can't cut or change *anything* unless the author agrees; in the movies, the author has the power to buy a ticket to get in to see the movie unless Mr. Reynolds doesn't want him to.

Interviewer: Have any of your other works been optioned for films?

King: *Hank Williams* has been optioned and reoptioned now for about the last three years. We're running into the same old problem: I refuse to sell it to the big movie companies. I want a small independent producer who'll promise me they won't hire a big star and spend several million dollars. I want a modest movie, and the people who optioned the thing agreed to all that, and we agreed to a five- or six-million-dollar movie. I wrote what I thought was a good script, then they decided maybe they ought to have an eleven-million-dollar movie, and at that point they began to take it around to the majors, and the major studios began to say, "But the characters aren't lovable and we need a sweeter ending." When the producers came back to me, I said, "I'll tell you what. Instead of doing a movie called *The Night Hank Williams Died,* why don't you all do one called 'The Night Hank Williams Had a Sick Headache but Made a Hit Record Anyway?' Y'all just do it and I won't have anything to do with it." That's the last I heard from them; their option is up January second, so I don't think there's going to be a movie.

Interviewer: How about Broadway? You had *Best Little Whorehouse* on Broadway, but the rest of the plays you've done have been off-Broadway.

King: I cannot knock the Broadway experience, despite all of the things I said about it before it happened. It turned out real fine for me, and I think

Whorehouse was good entertainment. Off-Broadway is very tough in terms of tickets, in terms of making any money. Theatre is in desperate shape in most of the country—straight plays—whether it's off-Broadway or on Broadway. I think playwrights now more or less have to depend on, and should depend on, and there's nothing *wrong* with depending on, regional theatres. You're not ever going to get rich, but you can see your work done very well and to some satisfaction. I loved doing things here in Washington at New Playwrights', a small theatre with 125 seats. I liked that kind of thing.

I've really decided that I don't want another play off-Broadway because you get up there and you run into directors and producers who want to put an actor in because of the actor's name more than the actor's talent or whether he fits the role. It's a little bit like Hollywood in that respect. People just won't turn out to see drama very much in New York compared to musicals. *Hank Williams* was a pretty good play. The *New York Times* couldn't have written a more rave review. A lot of people invested a lot of money in that show, and it ran and it got published and we optioned it to the movies; but the investors lost a lot of money, because just not enough people came to see the stage show. You can't recoup a half-million-dollar investment in a 280-seat theatre unless you're SRO every night for two years, and we lasted five or six months. It's very hard to get audiences these days. You've got cable TV, VCRs, and all that kind of stuff. People seem to feel if they go to the theatre, at least in large numbers in New York, they want to see musicals.

Interviewer: What's the trick? How do you get them back? You've written several plays since then.

King: Yes, and I prefer writing plays to writing musicals. I've got nothing against writing musicals, but my soul simply isn't in them. Musicals are craft, not art. I don't like to collaborate as well as I like to sail my ship alone. After *Hank Williams* and *Golden Shadows* (mainly *Hank*), suddenly Broadway producers again got interested in me, but not as a playwright in terms of *plays*, but to write books for musicals. We just finished drafting a sequel to *Whorehouse, The Best Little Whorehouse Goes Public.* Tommy Tune's going to do it, and Universal is putting up the money again. It's not as silly as it sounds; I think it's going to turn out pretty good. Then there's another one; I've always wanted to write about Harry Truman. It's kind of a weird notion; it's a musical about Harry Truman defeating Dewey in 1948 against great odds. The only thing is, I'm not going to allow a *dancing* Harry Truman. They can have other folks dance around him. I've just started working on that, though, for the producer Rocco Landesman. It's several years away at best. Musicals eat up your years, your life.

Interviewer: The most recent play that you've had in New York was also about a political figure—*The Kingfish,* which is about Huey Long. It was originally produced here at New Playwrights' Theatre in 1979, which means it took twelve years to get it to New York. Was there a reason it took so long?

King: Nobody in New York asked for it. Ben Z. Grant was born and raised in Louisiana but saw his opportunity to go to Texas and find a job without having to get honest work—he got elected to the Texas legislature. Ben is a good writer, and he came to me with the idea: let's collaborate and do a one-man show about Huey Long. I liked the subject, but I didn't particularly like the one-man-show idea. I said, "Let's write it so that he interacts with a bunch of invisible people so that he won't just be standing there giving a monologue most of the way. Maybe we can attract some producers." After all, *Whorehouse* had just been a big hit, so I was thinking "musical." We did it down here at this small theatre, and my wife-lawyer-agent, Barbara Blaine, produced it for ten thousand dollars in '79. We just hired New Playwrights' facilities for a month and did it ourselves. I invited all these big producers from New York, but we were on the wrong side of the George Washington Bridge, I guess. They felt they couldn't come down to the provinces, Washington. Three or four of them sent down people who did not apparently see the potential for a musical. Mike Nichols was interested in it for fifteen minutes. Time passed, years passed, and some fellows down in Louisiana heard about the play and got in touch with me; so they toured Louisiana and much of the South with it. Then they finally took it to New York last year. It ran about three years down South before they took it to New York, and there again it by and large got pretty good reviews—hell, even John Simon liked it—although Mel Gussow didn't care for this one in the *New York Times.* It only lasted five weeks or something, again because just not enough folks bought tickets. Off-Broadway's tough; it's very tough.

Interviewer: This leads me to a question. Critics liking or disliking something, particularly in New York, makes a big difference, doesn't it?

King: It makes a heck of a difference, the difference between a play running or not running, usually.

Interviewer: Some say that critics almost invariably praise a director and an actor for finding wonderful sides to characters and damn the playwright for not writing more full characters. Has that been your experience in general? I noticed in the reviews for *Kingfish* that almost to a man the New York critics said you didn't manage to distinguish between the bad side of Huey Long and the good side.

King: Yes, they said the same thing here in Washington, too. We had to make a decision when we wrote that show: are we on Huey's side or are we *not* on Huey's side? He was a rascal of a politician but, I thought, an intriguing one. Ben and I were more on his side than not: yellow-dog Democrats. Also, if we hoped, as I then hoped in vain, to make a musical out of it, you didn't want to make your musical about a villain; you wanted a person that you could have songs sung about other than hanging him. So we showed the good side; that charge has never bothered me the way it's bothered some critics. We used some of Huey's own language and actions, and some we invented for him; but I thought we were true to the historical record. I thought it was quite clear in the play that Long busted the heads of anybody who got in his way. Some critics said we made the man too funny when, indeed, he was a dangerous man. To that I say, "Yeah, we plead guilty, but we didn't have him arrest anybody; we just made people laugh."

Interviewer: Do you listen to critics?

King: More than I want to. I don't *like* to listen to any of them, but it's hard not to. It's strange, but good reviews do not make me feel as good as bad reviews make me feel bad, and I don't know why. When Mel Gussow turned flips over *Hank Williams,* that's fine and wonderful—I liked that— but I couldn't right now quote anything from his review. He just hated *The Kingfish,* and I could sit here and quote verbatim from that review. But we don't pay any attention to critics! Right?

Interviewer: A critic always thinks that he's contributing to a dialogue in some way, that there are people who have not yet seen the play who will see it soon and will therefore have a different appreciation of it if you give them something to think about on the way in. I guess what I'm curious about is whether critics affect the work in some way. Have you ever had a play open and then because of what the critics said you had the audience take it differently? Have you ever reworked something because the audience wasn't responding right to it anymore?

King: I don't think so as to your first question, but there's one thing that happens that I detest. I have had directors say to me, "The critics will kill us if you have him do that or say that." That was one of the things about *Whorehouse*; people said it had a sad ending and therefore wouldn't work. Look at what we'd done: we had brought the audience to the point that they were going to cheer for what would generally be the villains. They're cheering for women who sell themselves, a woman who manages women who sells themselves, and a sheriff who permits them to do that and takes "campaign contributions" for it. Yet we made *them* the good guys and the Austin politicians and the media the bad guys. We were successful; the folks cheered for the "wrong" people. They cared that the whorehouse closes, though they had a lot of fun on the way. But Carol Hall kept saying, "Larry, they're going to chuck rocks at us. We can't go to the theatre because the audience will stone us if we actually close the whorehouse and the critics are going to get us." I said, "Well, what are you going to do otherwise? It closed in real life!" Hell, it's like that Hank Williams movie script. Hollywood wanted it to be sweet at the end; life *ain't* sweet at the end. How we got around it in *Whorehouse*, is Tommy Tune came up with the idea that the minute the show was over and the applause starts, we counter with the biggest upbeat dancing tune possible, and everybody comes out twirling ropes, shooting six-guns, and all that stuff. Folks forgot the sad ending they'd just seen. You don't give them time to dwell on it; it's a matter of psychology, that's all.

Interviewer: It's interesting, the more I listen to you, the more I get the feeling that it's sort of a frustrating profession for you. You get these things up there and then somebody mutilates your work. It's very difficult to get productions to work off-Broadway anymore; why do you do this? You don't have to anymore.

King: Oh, maybe I kind of like being contentious and contrary with folks, like fussing. As I said earlier, I *do* like the collaborative process, in a way, because it gets lonely in a room with just blank paper. That's one of the things I like about the theatre process; it's a lot of fun to go back and forth. I get mad, everybody gets mad. It's defending your turf. Tommy Tune wants everything to be a dance, Carol Hall wants everybody to sing songs; that's natural. I don't want them getting in the way of my story; that's natural. What saves you is your director. He will just finally say, "Wait a minute here. We've got to have some of each, and no, you can't have forty-six songs, and no, you can't have twenty-nine dances, and no, you can't have two hours of dialogue." You go from there. It's frustrating but it's fascinating.

Interviewer: Besides the collaboration, why do plays? Wouldn't it be easier and certainly more lucrative to write nothing but television scripts?

King: Because you don't have any control, and I'm a control freak. When you get on film, I don't care if it's television or if it's movies, writers lose control to directors and stars. If I'd wanted to be a director or a star, I would've set out to try to be one. I didn't; I set out to be a writer. I want to work in a medium where the writer is the final arbiter of his or her work.

Interviewer: One of the things that strikes me about you as a writer is that you've also done a good deal of acting. You were onstage for two weeks replacing Henderson Forsythe in *Best Little Whorehouse* on Broadway, and I saw you in *The Night Hank Williams Died* here at New Playwrights'.

Is it different when you do your own work? When you hear a laugh, are you proud as a writer or are you proud as a performer at that point?

King: I don't think about it up there onstage; it's a technical pause. When you hear a laugh, you just wait it out. I learned that in *Whorehouse*. That's the first one of my shows I'd ever played in. I'd played in other people's plays, and I was aware of the laugh lines. I was aware of the laugh lines in *Whorehouse* when I sat in the audience. That gave me satisfaction when people laughed. But when I was in the play and in character, I didn't find any pride in the laugh. It was just: don't start your next line until they get through laughing, that sort of technical reaction. Quite frankly, I felt very detached. In both my plays that I've been in, I've felt much more detached from the work as an actor than I did sitting in the audience watching other people do it.

Interviewer: How did you feel singing?

King: Terrible. I was *terrified* of singing. I've not often been requested to sing. My loved ones used to request that I sit down and *not* sing in bars late at night, but I wanted to play the part. What author or playwright would not want to play on Broadway in his own show? So when they asked me if I'd do it, I nearly ran over them getting up there. Then I realized I had to sing, and I'm not a natural singing talent, shall we say. Fortunately, the song was written for Henderson Forsythe during rehearsal when it was discovered that Henderson Forsythe couldn't sing either. He was a hell of an actor, but no singer. So they wrote a song that was not too complicated to sing; it was almost a talk song. Still, it terrified me.

I remember my opening night. I won't get into the complexities of it, but union rules are such that I never did get to sing with the band until my opening night. You have one piano player that you sing with during your rehearsal period, then suddenly you've got a whole band and they give you *one* rehearsal with the band onstage an hour and a half before the show! So, suddenly, we're onstage an hour and a half before I open, and I look out there and it looked like a hundred people (they were all employees of the theatre, gathered in the back). I thought, "They expect me to sing to those folks?" I turned around to the fiddler, Ernie Reed, and I said, "Ernie, do I have the right to ask those folks to leave?" He said, "Oh hell, I guess you can, but in an hour you'll be singing to fifteen hundred more people than that and they'll have paid thirty-five dollars apiece." That was no comfort at all! I went off and had the dry heaves and staggered through the song.

After my second performance, Carlin Glynn, a fine actress who played the madam, called me aside and said, "Now Larry, don't worry about that song. You've done it twice now and nobody threw rocks. You got through it. Just relax and enjoy it and have something to tell your grandkids." So I decided I was going to rear back and thrill them in the far reaches of the balcony. I was really going to sing some! I was all ready, and just as I was about to rear back and come on like an opera singer—it was a matinee, and there were a lot of little blue-haired ladies sitting there with their shopping bags rustling—suddenly one of them said, "Oh my God, he's going to try to *sing!*" You could have heard her in Baltimore! Well, I got all befuddled. The music began, I started with the second verse, and then I had to decide if I go back to the first verse or on to the third verse. Then I thought, "Quit thinking about it or you can't sing any verses and you'll break down and cry." So I went back and picked up the first verse and then did the third verse. When the performance was over, I went up to the bandleader and said, "Craig, I'm real sorry about the song." He said, "Oh hell, I didn't think it was any worse than usual. All we're trying to do is keep you in time and in gear." After that, I didn't worry a whole lot about singing!

Interviewer: You wrote a document one time called *Confessions of a White Racist,* didn't you?

King: It was a book. It was about being raised in a racist society in Texas. When I went in the army, I had a lucky thing happen to me. This was the mid-1940s, and I was in one of about eight, I believe it was, units that the government very quietly decided to integrate—half black and half white—to see how it worked for a year. We were all called in and told by officers that this has got to work and be on your good behavior, etc. For the first time, I came to know black people as *people,* not just as stereotypes, and for the first time I had day-to-day contact with them as equals. It changed my thinking and my attitudes and I became very conscious of racism then. This book was about all that, racism down to the present time or at least until 1971 when the book was published. It was nominated for the National Book Award, got great reviews and all that, and sold twelve copies, actually seven thousand but that's nothing. My publisher lost about twenty thousand dollars on that book.

Interviewer: Have you ever written a role that could not be played by a black actor?

King: Yes, several. When we were starting to do *Hank Williams* at New Playwrights', the artistic director, Peter Frisch, asked if I would object to nontraditional casting. I said I normally wouldn't but if you're doing a play about a small Texas town in 1952—and believe me, I had *lived* in small towns in Texas in 1952—you could do violence to the play if you had a minority person playing a conventional role. They used some racial terms in the play which reflected the racial attitudes of the time; so I told him that I didn't think *Hank* was the play to do it in. Later on, I told him it was fine to do it in *Golden Shadows,* but I don't think any minorities showed up for the auditions. I think that it's generally fine, but I think that, when you're depicting a time of racism, I don't believe that your audience can be that color-blind. I believe that it's going to hurt your play because people are going to see a black person or a Chinese person or a Latin person, or whatever, rather than seeing a redneck bartender in this town in 1952. We are *conditioned* that way. I'm uncomfortable with what I'm saying, and I'm uncomfortable with the decision that I made in *Hank Williams.* At the same time, my plays, not my musicals, are about realism, about how things really *are.* If it's going to be true to the period and the place and I'm trying to transport people back there, then I'm just not ready to run the risk of nontraditional casting.

Interviewer: As a novelist and a journalist, how do you teach yourself to be a playwright? It's a different sort of writing, isn't it?

King: I can't answer for anybody but myself. I was fortunate in that I had acted in a lot of amateur plays in Texas as a youngster. I always liked being in theatre, I always liked writing dialogue; I knew the form. It wasn't like I was trying to learn a new form of math or anything. It was a pretty easy transition, and since dialogue was really sort of my strong point anyway, it wasn't that difficult.

Interviewer: You're a very successful playwright. Is it still difficult for you to get things on?

King: Oh God, yes. All the begging comes from my side. It's difficult to get my straight plays on; that's what bugs me, because I care more about them.

Interviewer: Can you get your plays done in regional theatres without much trouble, or is that not easy?

King: I think I probably could now that I know a little bit better how to approach them, since *Hank,* and also since we're coming back with the *Whorehouse* sequel and it's common knowledge that I'm going to do Harry Truman and all that. The thing that happened with *Whorehouse* was that, in terms of the theatrical community, none of us were known. Our producer was not known, it was Hollywood money; we were never really accepted in the theatrical community by theatrical people, and the whole thing was looked at as a freak show, as an accident. A lot of folks in the New York theatre community really didn't like that. I remember that the distinguished Roger Stevens wouldn't let it play the Kennedy Center or the National, which he was then controlling, because he said it was too vaudeville and uncouth. So we brought it in here twice and let the poor old rickety Warner Theatre get rich off it while the distinguished Mr. Stevens and the National were sitting there damn well dark—and I enjoyed their discomfort. But I think, quite frankly, that *Hank Williams* kind of revived me again in the eyes of theatre folk and made me semilegitimate—so they started coming to me.

Interviewer: Was there any kind of moral or religious backlash because of the subject matter of *Whorehouse?*

King: Oh sure, the religious nuts got up in arms every time, and that was wonderful. When we were in San Antonio, the Moral Majority prayed around the clock for a month in front of the theatre. A San Antonio columnist captured it best when he said, "*The Best Little Whorehouse in Texas* left town last night after thirty days, and the Moral Majority showed its strength by helping them sell twelve million dollars worth of tickets and twenty million dollars worth of whiskey in the lobby." I don't think those figures were quite right, but the *thrust* of it was right. I love for those folks to come and picket; everywhere they do we just get bigger audiences. And it's a great satisfaction to frustrate them. With the sequel we're working on now, I'm a little more worried. In this age of AIDS, running a whorehouse ain't really funny any more. What we have tried to do in this sequel, without having somebody come out onstage and make a speech about it, is have a little stuff about safe sex. We bring that point up in the guise of comedy, or as close as you can come to comedy on that. But I am a little skittish about it.

Interviewer: Have you heard any new voices, and are there any modern-day figures worth writing about?

King: I've been hearing voices from the grave. I've been hearing Lyndon Johnson and Richard Nixon in the spiritual world on the other side as they're in a holding pen waiting for eternal judgment to be passed on them. We see 'em each try to outdo each other and get close to God and all that. They can't even get in to *see* God, and they're going crazy. I think it's going to work. I'm writing it under the title "The Dead Presidents' Club."

Interviewer: Talk a little bit about the feel of Texas as a subject. It's been a long time since you lived there, but you keep returning to it in the plays. What about it other than the political part appeals to you, and why is it in all your plays?

King: I guess "write what you know" is an old adage which is probably pretty true. My formative years were lived in Texas, but I wanted to get away because I thought there was no material there and I had to get where stories were happening. Many years later I understood what had occurred: what I had seen as the aimless meanderings of oil field roughnecks was really the change of Texas becoming a superpower economically at the time, after World War II, when it converted very rapidly from agrarian and rural to industrial and urban. There were a lot of social changes happening that I didn't see or understand or know the significance of at the time; I saw it change from a horse culture to a mechanized culture. Hell, I rode a horse to school as a kid; a lot of my compadres did. We farmed with horses and mules, and but a few years after that everybody used tractors and mechanical cottonpickers.

When I realized *what* I had seen and been through, then I could run it through the memory machine. It suddenly became apparent in some historical context. I don't write much about modern Texas, today's urbanized Texas; I don't live there, I don't know it. I *go* there. I go to theatres and colleges and make speeches and visit friends, but I don't *know* day-to-day life there anymore. I really see myself as a kind of a sign painter. I passed this way then, and this is what I found and saw; this was my time and place and how it was. I'm sort of an instant historian, I guess. Of course, all of this has been refined through a sensibility that I did not then have. When I was there as part of it as a young man, I didn't think anything was happening. All kinds of things were happening; it just took me a long time to know that.

I grew up in an oral culture, where oral history was much more valued than written history. I came from a redneck family, working people; nobody had an education, nobody read much. My father, thank God, was a wonderful talker. He only had a third-grade education, used bad grammar, but God, he could talk and tell stories, and I listened to him all my life. I grew up listening to country poets, as I now think of them. I didn't know they were at the time; I just thought they were durn interesting old men. Some years later, in 1966, Willie Morris and I were sitting in a bar in Brewster County, New York, drinking, and Willie looked at me and said, "Larry, what is not happening in this bar that would be happening in Texas or Mississippi?" Mississippi is his original state. I knew immediately what Willie meant. I said, "Nobody's telling colorful stories, nobody's talking like we hear our people-poets talk." They were there and they were conversing, but they didn't have the color and the flavor of what we had grown up with.

Interviewer: What were the main influences that got you out of that rural redneck scene?

King: Strangely enough, I believe the United States Army. Getting in the army, meeting people from all over, and then having the experience of going in a racially experimental unit. It just taught me an awful lot about the different kinds of people in the world. It taught me things I never suspected about their similarities *and* their differences, about the difficulties in communication and yet that it could be done. I wanted to be a writer from the time that I was six years old when my mother took *The Adventures of Tom Sawyer* out of the library and read it to me the summer I had whooping cough. I asked her if that fellow Twain had written any more books, and she got me *The Prince and the Pauper.* I fell in love with Mr. Twain, and I decided I wanted to write stories that gave people pleasure the way his had given me.

Even at that early age I loved language. I remember I had a little cousin named Kenneth, and I often said, "Kenneth, I don't want to go play. I want to hang around and listen to these old men talk." Kenneth would say, "All they ever talk about is who got married, who had a baby, and who died." I remember thinking, "That ain't a bad thing to learn either. What else is there?"

I was interested in reading and listening and learning, and so I guess that's how I pulled my escape. The other thing was, by the time I went in the army at the age of seventeen, I had had my fill of heavy lifting—farming, ranch work, the oil fields. It wasn't for me. Too many Kings had already done that. I wanted to work indoors, aided by soft lights.

Interviewer: Does the fact that the plays are regional, that they're about Texas, affect the way they are perceived in urban theatres? Do they play better in regional theatres?

King: I think that's true. There's probably a whole lot of folks in New York as well as Washington that just really aren't going to rush out and see a play set in a West Texas bar. I know that *Golden Shadows* was better received (although it was better done, too) at Arkansas Repertory and Memphis State University than it was here. It is, after all, set in an old folks' home in Texas and more indigenous than not to regional climes. My plays can get hurt in New York when they cast a twangy redneck with a sissy or an actor who speaks Brooklyn.

Interviewer: Has *Best Little Whorehouse* been done outside the United States?

King: It's been done in every English-speaking country in the world that I know of. It ran a long time in Australia, New Zealand, England, Canada, South Africa, everywhere. There's been a production in Mexico; I never did see it. We've sold rights to the Japanese and the Germans. I'm told the Germans couldn't handle the translation of the text. I don't read German, but I saw a copy of the translation and it had words four feet long in it! I could see where they might have problems. Apparently it didn't make much sense. I can't remember the details, but I knew somebody who knew somebody who worked at the Library of Congress who spoke German, and I got a few pages translated, and they weren't even close, especially the laugh lines. I don't think the Japanese ever did it; if they did they never sent royalties, so I guess they didn't.

Interviewer: What is your writing process? Do you hear the voices first and then you see the characters? Is that how it proceeds? Where do you write?

King: I have a little office at home. I work on a manual typewriter. I hate modern machinery. I don't get to hear voices all the time. My mama did that. She heard a lot from Jesus; she really did, and it was kind of spooky. I've heard voices a couple of times, but with most of my plays and my short stories I don't ever really have a full plot. I kind of have a vague notion of where I want to go, and generally there is maybe something close to a voice in that a lead sentence or something will pop into my mind or a sentence that turns out to be fairly important to the story. It's hard to explain. It makes me sound a little sick, superstitious, or goofy or something; but I don't like to think about it too much or analyze it because I'm afraid it will go away. So I ain't going to tell you because I don't know, that's the thing.

Interviewer: Since you've been a successful playwright, has that affected your offers for free-lance journalism, and have you ever considered putting some of the people you interviewed in a play?

King: Not really. I wrote journalism about Richard Nixon and Lyndon Johnson, and I *am* fictionalizing them on the Other Side. Other than that, no. The other thing was, yeah, it's really strange, whenever one of my plays does well or gets good notices, editors who act like I've been dead for two years suddenly get on the phone and offer me more money than usual for free-lance stuff, and that's nice and that's sweet. Sometimes I take it and sometimes I don't. I had to write so many magazine articles for so many years in order to make a living that I got very tired of doing that so I try to be selective. I don't go out chasing "personalities" anymore. My general rule is, if I can write it out of memory and my own knowledge, I'll do it. If I've got to go talk to somebody, find yourself another boy.

Interviewer: Do you have any advice for aspiring playwrights?

King: Marry a very rich lawyer, one that has good earning power; that's what I did. I really enjoy writing plays, but God a'mighty, getting them *produced!* I've been lucky; I've never written a play so far, knock on wood, that hasn't been produced, but so many playwrights do. I knew a kid who was a really good writer. He's not a kid anymore; he was a kid when I taught him twenty years ago in a writing course. He's written three or four, maybe five, really good plays, and he's had readings at good theatres in New York and around, but he can't get a production. More and more, especially in commercial theatre, money's just getting hard as hell to find, especially for straight plays or new talent.

I would say for most playwrights regional theatres are the way to go rather than shooting for New York. I don't know what else to tell them. Hell, just keep writing and struggling, I guess. For plays, there's no central place you can send them. With the regional theatres, you've got to use the scattergun approach. If I want to send a play to Cincinnati Playhouse or the Louisville Actors Theatre or whatever, I've got to deal with each one of those sources. If you want your play to go forty-seven places, you've got to send out forty-seven copies and keep track of what's happening with forty-seven people and all of that business. The distribution system is lousy. The only way you beat that is, after the play is a success, Samuel French or one of the other publishing houses sells your rights and collects your royalties and makes all those dismal arrangements.

Interviewer: What is there about politics that you dislike the most, and what is there about politics that you consider noble?

King: I find very little nobility in it. Politics is interesting and fascinating to me but not often admirable. I would not have the patience or the stomach or whatever it takes to do what politicians have to do, which is pander to masses of people and pander to groups. I hate that kind of thing. I understand that's the democratic process and that there's not a better way; I find it interesting to be into that but very distasteful. I was a "second banana" politician, helping and observing; I kind of enjoyed that, but being out front and actually doing the ass kissing, I don't know how anybody tolerates it—of any party, of any dogma. It's not a thing it seems to me that grown people ought to do, but I guess somebody's got to do it.

Interviewer: Are there political figures today you could write a play about, a one-man show, for example?

King: It'd be very hard to do because everybody now is trying to homogenize themselves. Everybody is very concerned about image. Increasingly, people get wiser about sound bites and television, and there's no longer colorful people rising up in the parties. The parties have no influence anymore as such over members of Congress. The political money is raised through PACs by the individual members of the House or Senate, so the party has no hold over them. I used to think that it would be a very freeing thing if politicians could be more independent and not be controlled by a party. But now I think the balkanization of politics, the breaking of it into all these little individual principalities, has not only taken a lot of color out of politics, but it's taken a lot of the efficiency out of it, and it's made it very, very hard to do anything as a partisan unit because everybody runs their own show. It gets harder and harder to distinguish between Republicans and Democrats, except for the few extremists.

Interviewer: Isn't what you say about politicians and sound bites also true of the playwright? Don't you have to come up with a series of very clever lines during the course of an evening?

King: Yes, but the fate of the country's not going to ride on it. Our *personal* fates may, as playwrights, but not the nation's. So I find you guilty of a very bad analogy.

Jerome Lawrence

Photo © R. J. Osborn

Jerome Lawrence was born in Cleveland, Ohio, in 1915. After graduating from Ohio State University and brief careers in journalism and radio, in 1942 he began a playwriting collaboration with Robert E. Lee. Among their plays are The Crocodile Smile *(1952),* Inherit the Wind *(1955),* Auntie Mame *(1956),* The Gang's All Here *(1959),* Only in America *(1959),* A Call on Kuprin *(1961),* Live Spelled Backwards *(1966),* Sparks Fly Upward *(1967),* The Incomparable Max *(1969),* The Night Thoreau Spent in Jail *(1970),* Jabberwock *(1972),* First Monday in October *(1975), and* Whisper in the Mind *(1991). They also have provided books for the musicals* Look, Ma, I'm Dancin'! *(1948),* Shangri-La *(1956),* Mame *(1966), and* Dear World *(1969). Lawrence, the author of* Actor *(1974), a biography of Paul Muni, and of a novel,* A Golden Circle *(1993), is the recipient of a New York Press Club Award (1942), two* Radio–TV *Life Awards (1948,*

1952), *two Peabody Awards (1949, 1952), two* Radio–TV Mirror *Awards* *(1952, 1953), a Donaldson Award (1955), an Outer Critics Circle Award* *(1955), the British Drama Critics Award (1960), the Moss Hart Memorial* *Award (1967), the William Inge Award (1983), and several honorary* *degrees. He is also a member of the Theatre Hall of Fame. This interview* *took place on October 30, 1991.*

▶ ─────────────────────────────── ◀

Interviewer: Why did you become a playwright?

Lawrence: Actually, I began as a newspaperman, but I realized what a great social adventure the theatre is: living, breathing actors bring your words to life and meet living breathing audiences. That's the greatest thrill in the world. Also, theatre has so much influence. When our plays are in Washington we talk to Supreme Court justices and Presidents in our audiences. In effect, we have a public forum. My whole impulse in writing plays is to grab every watcher-listener by the shoulders and say, "Listen, there is something in my heart, in my gut, in my playwriting soul, that I want to get across to you." I demand something from every play I see. I want to wake up the next morning and say, "Wow! Something happened to me. I am a changed person, my soul has been sandpapered." The greatest experience as a playwright is to have your words sandpaper other people's souls.

Interviewer: So the experience of production is not fearful but an exciting thing for you?

Lawrence: Absolutely. We've been very lucky; we've been produced in thirty-four languages all over the world.

Interviewer: You don't feel like O'Neill, who hated to see his plays done because he hated to see what people did with them? You don't feel that kind of fear?

Lawrence: Sometimes people do things that we don't like to our plays, but we're totally different from O'Neill. We hate it if our plays are *not* being produced! We write big plays with large casts, and it's difficult to get them produced at the moment.

Interviewer: You're a playwright who has almost always worked with a collaborator. Would you talk a little bit about how that's been?

Lawrence: We each know that we could do it by ourselves, but it's better if we do it together. We play tennis. We laugh, and we cry. We usually start writing on yellow legal pads, then we dictate it into a tape recorder and listen to it. If it sounds good, we put it onto a computer. We write prose separately; you can't write that together. But dialogue is meant to be played. Actors tell us that our lines seem already rehearsed, and they were; they'd been performed at our typewriters and word processors. First—and this is terribly important—we get to know our characters. If they are historical, we do as much research as possible, and then we throw it out and write a play. We get to know our characters so well that they sit down next to us and say, "Lawrence and Lee said that; we didn't." We try to get ourselves out of the way and let our characters live. We also have something which we call the UN veto. Each one of us has the right to say no to anything—an idea for a whole play, a sentence, a comma, a character's name. But the one who says no has the obligation to come up with something better that the other will say yes to. You can't just be negative; at least it must be a *positive* negative. Most writers have to wear two hats. One is your playwriting hat, and the other is your critic's hat. Being a team, we have the dual process simultaneously. And it's worked for fifty years very well. Mostly it means having respect for each other, being gentlemen.

Interviewer: Can you say, when you look back at a script, "Bob wrote that line, I wrote that line?"

Lawrence: We never know, and if we did know, we forget about it. It's the end result that's important, not the individual line, or whose idea it was. Playwriting has to be a shared passion. I don't mean it has to deliver a message or a sermon, but it's got to have a reason for being. If you ask most young playwrights, "What's your play about?" all they can honestly say is, "It's about two and a half hours long." Then it's two and a half hours *too* long!

Interviewer: The plays you haven't musicalized or dramatized from another source, like *Inherit the Wind, First Monday in October,* and others, are very much built around political and social issues; that is, political with a small *p.* Is that part of your desire to grab the audience, that you're always dealing with an issue?

Lawrence: Absolutely! Most of them have been done here in Washington—and very happily for us. A play we did in New York called *The Gang's All Here* back in 1959 was about the Harding administration, but fictionalized. The year after that, on the eve of the Nixon-Kennedy election, the Arena Stage did it as the first production of their season, and it really shook the place. There on the cusp of Camelot was a play about political corruption and about the presidency which all the top people in Washington came and heard. It's a thrill for us to accomplish that.

Interviewer: When you say a play must be about something other than two and a half hours long, do you mean about a social issue or about a political issue?

Lawrence: Not necessarily. Most of our plays are on the same subject, the dignity of the individual mind, the individual human being. *Inherit the Wind* is being done now right in a courthouse in Philadelphia, in honor of the two-hundredth anniversary of the signing of the Bill of Rights. That's shaking up the place, too. Posters all over town say THE RIGHT TO THINK. We need that message today more than ever.

Interviewer: So what starts out as topical at a certain time stays topical forever?

Lawrence: If it's *about* something.

Interviewer: What terrifies you?

Lawrence: The direction our government is going at the very time the Soviet Union is becoming free. I worry a lot about our First Amendment rights. I find too much censorship around, and I worry about it.

Interviewer: Do you see that pervading the theatre?

Lawrence: In the theatre, it takes the guise of economic censorship, where government agencies don't give plays on certain subjects any support. I'm afraid that's going to silence producers and some playwrights. It sure as hell isn't going to silence *us*, but I'm afraid it's going to make others "play it safe."

Interviewer: The message of your plays is more pertinent today than it's ever been, isn't it?

Lawrence: We feel it is.

Interviewer: What have you been doing lately?

Lawrence: We have a new play which we wrote based upon material uncovered by Norman Cousins. We tried it out last fall in Tempe, Arizona. It's called *Whisper in the Mind*. It's about an unknown but historically fascinating encounter between Mesmer and Benjamin Franklin. We're very excited about it. Michael York played Mesmer and E. G. Marshall was Franklin. We're going on from there—soon.

Interviewer: You and Bob Lee really began in radio, didn't you?

Lawrence: As I said, I really began as a newspaperman, and then we got into radio. Bob Lee was in advertising originally. For young playwrights, radio drama today is, unfortunately, almost nonexistent. In writing for the ear, the *words* were important, the *ideas* were important. I'm not talking about soap operas, but good dramatic programming. We learned a lot working in that arena of communication.

Interviewer: Lawrence and Lee work in all these different areas. It's not just radio, it's not just drama. They both teach. Bob Lee writes plays for the church. Jerry wrote a perfectly marvelous book called *Actor,* a biography of Paul Muni. It gives you a remarkable picture of the Yiddish theatre of New York, where not only Paul Muni began but also Tony Curtis. There is a great sweep in this fascinating picture of New York in the twenties and the thirties. Tell that marvelous story about Paul Muni.

Lawrence: It's slightly dirty, but I hope you won't mind, because I want to tell you what he thinks about your importance as an audience. I tell it to all my playwriting students. He said he was in a play called *Rock Me Julie*; it was a terrible work, with a couple of schlock producers. One day during rehearsal, suddenly a very sexy girl appeared as a member of the cast; and the rest of the actors whispered, "She must be sleeping with one of the producers." About a week later, she appeared with two pages of dialogue; then everybody speculated, "Now she must be sleeping with the playwright." A week after that, the director stopped the rehearsal and said, "That lovely girl's way upstage behind the furniture. Come downstage, honey," and he gave her several pieces of business. Then everybody observed, "Now she's sleeping with the director." One day she came up to Paul Muni, who was always boning up on his script, and said, "Oh, Mr. Muni, you've had all these years in the theatre. This is my first play. Isn't there some basic rule, some universal truth about the theatre, I should know?" He looked her up and down and said, "Yes, my dear young lady, there is one basic truth I think you should know. You can't screw an audience!" It's true; you know when the actors, but especially the playwright, are telling you lies. You, as an audience, demand some truth, that you take something away from the theatre that will sandpaper your soul.

Interviewer: Yes. A play without an audience may be literature and that's all right in its place; you can read it. But without the audience, the play is only half alive. When you feel the audience getting with the play, that is truly exciting, and you don't find it in film. Much as one can enjoy the films of your plays, it's nothing like the experience of having been there when it was totally alive, and being a part of that life.

Lawrence: Good actors make every performance the first time. You must think it's really happening. Now! The actors and the director have to make that work. Wouldn't it be terrible if you and I were sitting here talking to empty seats? The audience is the vital part.

Interviewer: *Inherit the Wind* had some wonderful adventures here in Washington. Zelda Fichandler did it at Arena Stage, and then it was taken to the Soviet Union as Arena Stage's first venture abroad.

Lawrence: Actually, it was the first time American plays were ever produced on the stage of the legendary Moscow Art Theatre. They took Thornton Wilder's *Our Town*, which Alan Schneider directed, and *Inherit the Wind*, which Zelda directed. They caused a sensation there, and we were very, very happy about that theatre milestone.

Interviewer: Does a large part of the script for *Inherit the Wind* come directly from the transcript of the actual trial?

Lawrence: No. The transcript is pretty dull. There are only four lines in the play from the actual transcript. We read every word of it. A couple of lines from the Bryan character we called Brady were so fatuous that we had to use them, like when he says, "I am more interested in the Rock of Ages than the age of rocks." We couldn't leave that out. I did my master's thesis on Maxwell Anderson, mostly about *Winterset*, which is a wonderful play. I wish somebody would revive it. It's about the aftermath of the Sacco-Vanzetti case, but Anderson took the poetic license and the license of a dramatist to write a *play*, a passionate play, about what happened to the son of just one of the two, as if only one person had been Sacco and Vanzetti combined. When we came to find a parable from the past to parallel McCarthyism and thought control, we said, "Why don't we use the Scopes trial for the play's genesis but use dramatic and poetic license for the play's exodus?" It's got a lot of poetic license. I don't know if you realize that Hornbeck's dialogue is in iambic pentameter because he loved to dance with language. As a matter of fact, that's how Gene Kelly got cast in the film. Stanley Kramer called us and said, "How do you see Hornbeck?" And we said, "Get Tony Randall." And he said, "No, I want somebody who's more of a star." He said, "How do you see him? What's his character?" We said, "He dances with language." So he hired Gene Kelly! As for the Henry Drummond role, it is an amalgam of *three* lawyers for the defense: Clarence Darrow, Arthur Garfield Hays, and Dudley Field Malone.

Interviewer: Why was the character of Rachel Brown added?

Lawrence: She is the whole arc of the play. Brady putting her on the stand shows what an unfeeling bastard he was. There's no play without her; she is the whole town. The town is on trial. She is the one who goes from being a conformist, and parodying her father, the minister, to opening her eyes, her ears, her mind—and there's no play without that.

Interviewer: But the play can also use an all-male cast, can't it?

Lawrence: The only reason we did that was because *Waiting for Godot* had had its best audience and production at San Quentin Prison, and they called us up and said, "Please, could we do your play with an all-male cast, without putting one or two of our prisoners in drag?" We said, "We want it done there," and it was so successful that we did an all-male version in print. It's not used very often, so we've withdrawn it. Cates's "best friend," who in that version is called "Richard," is not nearly as effective as the emotionally charged Rachel.

Interviewer: Did I read that two of your plays, *Inherit the Wind* and *The Night Thoreau Spent in Jail*, have sold five hundred thousand copies each?

Lawrence: A half million copies as of last month for *Inherit the Wind*, 480,000 for *Thoreau*.

Interviewer: That doesn't often happen with a play, so I congratulate you. How do you two start to write a play?

Lawrence: Thank you. With *First Monday in October,* we got up one morning, and one of us called the other and said, "What would happen if a woman were appointed to the Supreme Court? And what would happen if she were a rabid conservative from Orange County and she had a head-on collision with a liberal justice similar to William O. Douglas?" We didn't stop until that play was on the stage of the Eisenhower Theatre. Then, when Sandra Day O'Connor was appointed, Dick Coe wrote a wonderful article saying Lawrence and Lee "wrote history before it happened." We were awfully excited about that.

Interviewer: You've spent most of your career working in the commercial theatre, but now that theatre is disappearing. How do you get a play done nowadays?

Lawrence: When I go to Broadway now, I want to place wreaths—not only on the newsstands, because when we started there were eight newspapers—but on theatres, too. For the last six months, major theatres that used to do serious plays are empty—the Broadhurst, the Music Box, the Plymouth, the Royale, the Golden. It breaks my heart. Twenty years ago, Bob and I decided we had to do something about getting new plays, especially plays of ideas, done someplace other than New York. We formed the American Playwrights Theater, not "warming up for Broadway" but *instead* of Broadway. Deliberately, *Thoreau* never went to Broadway because we wanted to say a play can make it without the Good Housekeeping Seal of Approval of New York. That helped, and so did the American College Theatre Festival, to give birth to new playwrights.

Interviewer: Do you still teach? How many years have you been doing that?

Lawrence: Since 1969, and for the last seven years at the University of Southern California. I've also done it in Salzburg at Harvard's Seminar in American Studies, at Baylor in Texas, at Ohio State, and as master playwright at NYU for three years. I always demand that my students' plays are professionally produced, not by fellow students or even by their professors. Fortunately out in Los Angeles, where USC is, we get the best directors, the top actors, and they flock to do these plays. It's the most wonderful experience teaching these twenty-first-century playwrights. I say often that if you want just a shred of immortality, do three things: write, teach, have children. My partner is luckier than I am; he's got all three, including biological children. But I say, "Wait a minute. All our plays are our children, too," And when my students produce healthy bouncing plays that are about something, that's like having grandchildren!

Interviewer: Don't you have them write plays about different characters from history?

Lawrence: Yes. The last five years of this program at USC we've asked them to write about famous people from history—because we've always subscribed to Santayana's almost cliché piece of philosophy: those who do not remember the past are condemned to repeat it, to relive it. So we want to make a connection. We say, "When you go to the past, have some parable for the present." So they write plays about Einstein, or about Schweitzer; this year, one's writing a play about Ring Lardner and F. Scott Fitzgerald. They're very exciting. You can't really teach playwriting, but it can be induced. You can guide them toward happy creative writing habits, and you can kick them in the butts and try to help them help themselves *be better.*

Interviewer: You and Bob have a unique relationship to the State of Ohio, the Buckeye State, don't you? You were both born in different parts of the state, and now you have a library there—at Ohio State.

Lawrence: We're archivists.

Interviewer: How did that come about?

Lawrence: Ohio State had collected over the years—just in secret little corners someplace—450,000 frames of microfilm of set designs and costume designs, and it was not being used. It was just there, and we donated lots of things to them; so they renamed it the Jerome Lawrence and Robert E. Lee Theater Research Institute. It is now the best research facility for theatre in the world. It's a very, very exciting place; if you're ever in Ohio, go visit it. Richard Coe here and fellow critic Elliot Norton were official dedicators in Columbus.

Interviewer: Although you and Bob Lee are primarily men of the theatre, you have been involved in Hollywood.

Lawrence: We haven't worked in pictures much; we prefer the theatre, where thanks to the Dramatists Guild the playwright has the clout. They can't change a word or a comma in theatre; in films and in television they change everything, unfortunately.

Interviewer: How do you stand on the problem of nontraditional casting? Is it a problem?

Lawrence: It's very difficult, but I think it works sometimes. It doesn't always; sometimes it hurts the play, sometimes it helps the play. I think you have to take each individual case.

Interviewer: Doesn't it depend really on the actors involved, their own particular gift?

Lawrence: Yes, and on the willing cooperation of the audience to use their imaginations, which they have to do anyhow. They are the best constructors of scenery we have.

Interviewer: Nowadays, our country has all these regional theatres. There are about one hundred theatres across this country with audiences that range from, say, four hundred to a thousand people a night. This is something that has never happened before in this particular way. There used to be road shows that would travel around, but that was before movies, but now we have these theatres all over the country. Margo Jones, who discovered you and Bob, was once the only person in the United States outside of New York who was doing only new plays, and it was wonderful. That was about 1946, wasn't it?

Lawrence: No, a little later, 1950 or 1951. We came there in 1955.

Interviewer: I thought she called it Theatre '47.

Lawrence: Maybe. I may be wrong. It was around that period, the end of World War II. Twelve million people in uniform had been roaming the world. They came back to their own country; in seeing the others they realized what we lacked. So from World War II came this great revival in interest in how to create this wonderful thing called theatre—which I like to think of as a craft rather than an art. Margo did this remarkable thing, by building this theatre in Texas and taking a chance on unknown playwrights. She did a truly remarkable thing, and now every regional theatre in the country has their new play. They don't have a season without one new script a year. That's a lot of plays.

Interviewer: Of course, the problem is that some of these new plays are terrible. Why are they so bad?

Lawrence: I'm going to go back to what I said at the beginning. Because they're not *about* anything. They also seem to be sketches; most of them are one-act plays at best. A one-act play is like a hundred-yard run. With a full-length play, you have to be an Olympic runner; you've got to run the distance. A full-length play is also like a symphony; it has many lines, many depths, many themes that have to be constructed. You also have to be a play architect. I built a house right on the shores of the Pacific Ocean, and I tell my students that if I had built it with every room in the house a toilet, that would be a terrible house. I couldn't live in it. Wouldn't that be awful, a great view of the Pacific Ocean, but still all toilets? That's how a lot of playwrights write plays: every moment of their play is a toilet. It's a trash can rather than a temple, which is where the theatre started. There's got to be some kind of nobility in this great, almost religion that is theatre.

I cook a lot. If I invited some guests, had beautiful crystal and candlelight and a solid silver tray, and I came to the table and they were all hungry and ready to eat, and on the silver platter all I'd served them was was salt and pepper, I'd be a hell of a host—and a terrible cook. That's what a lot of plays are, just salt and pepper, no meat. But you know what would be terrible, almost as bad? A wonderful cut of beef and no salt and pepper at all. There's got to be balance. I'm a very lucky amateur photographer. I photograph authors. I've photographed four hundred authors, and I have a sense of composition which is just intuitive from playwriting. A playwright has to have a sense of form, of architecture, and has to cook his play and serve his play well. That's the craft we were talking about. A lot of mixed metaphors there, but that's why they're so often bad. I'll admit with no fake humility that some of our plays have been terrible, too; but maybe that was because we were writing just to have another play on that year and we didn't really have a passion about the subject.

Interviewer: Has a critic ever affected how you make changes in a play?

Lawrence: Sure. Yes. Mainly Richard Coe and Elliot Norton. But let me tell you about another thing that happened with a critic. When *Auntie Mame* opened here in Washington thirty-five years ago, Dick Coe's headline was "Auntie Mame is a Whammy," and the man on the *Star* said, "'Auntie Mame' Is Another 'My Fair Lady.'" We got to New York and everybody loved it, every critic except Brooks Atkinson, the very important one on the *Times*. He said, "On the verge of an election, I want to vote for Rosalind Russell for President. She's wonderful, but the play would be a disaster without her. It would be nothing; she is the play." Well, three years later, he wrote a review of Bea Lillie in the role, telling about the fact that Lilabel Ibsen was playing in it in Norway and that five companies were running simultaneously, and he said, "I owe an apology to the play-wrights."

Interviewer: Do you try to be as eloquent writing stage directions as, say, George Bernard Shaw or J. M. Barrie?

Lawrence: Let me tell you about stage directions and how everything is useful—eventually. In the play of *Auntie Mame* after Beau dies—he falls off a "goddamn alp"—we put in the stage directions that Lindsay, who was her publisher, and Vera, who is her actress friend, are waiting for Mame to come back to Beekman Place, and we wrote: "Lindsay now looks like an aging Ronald Colman; Vera is now somewhere between forty and death." When we came to write the musical *Mame*, we said, "My God, we buried one of the best lines we ever wrote!" And we told Jerry Herman to take it and use it. It stops the show in "Bosom Buddies" as part of the lyric.

Another thing happened with stage directions. The most eloquent line of *Inherit the Wind* is not spoken. It's a stage direction at the end of the play when, after the big battle, Henry Drummond balances the two books, Darwin and the Bible, slaps them together side by side, puts them in his briefcase, and goes off to fight another battle for freedom of thought. I went to see it in Ankara, Turkey—about the thirtieth foreign production I'd seen—and the play ended and the actor didn't do that. I rushed up to the translator and said, "What happened to that business?" He said, "What business?" and I said, "Where's the part where he's supposed to balance the books?" "Oh," he said, "the director here insists that all direc-tions be cut out before the play is translated because he doesn't want any playwright to tell him how to direct *his* play." I made him put it back in. So if you're a playwright, make your stage directions clear, even if you have to say, "No, this is an important piece of business; read it, don't cut it." My partner Bob Lee says, "If I commit murder and am compelled to confess it and yet I don't want anybody to find out, put it in a stage direction; nobody will ever read it!"

Interviewer: Have you liked anything you've seen on Broadway lately?

Lawrence: The problem is there's nothing on Broadway now, except the long-running musicals, mostly British.

Interviewer: Brian Friel has a new play there, *Dancing at Lughnasa.*

Lawrence: Yes, I'm eager to see that. I know him and I love his plays, especially one he wrote called *Translations*. I love *Aristocrats*, and, of course, *Philadelphia, Here I Come!* is wonderful.

Interviewer: What about Mamet? How do you feel about Mamet?

Lawrence: He's a brilliant guy who is very dedicated to theatre and he writes good film scripts too. I like his work very much. I'm a little startled sometimes, like the eleven-minute first act in *Glengarry Glen Ross*. It's all right. I like him, I like him. There are wonderful playwrights in that age group—John Guare, Lanford Wilson.

Interviewer: What about the effect of television on playwriting today?

Lawrence: At the request of the *Dramatists Guild Quarterly* a couple of years ago we wrote "Ten Commandments for Playwrights"; it's been widely republished. We paraphrased each commandment. It started by being funny; the first was "There are no commandments for playwrights." When we came to taking the Lord's name in vain, we wrote, "Thou shalt not take the critics' names in vain, for if thou believest them when they praise thee, thou must also believe them when they pan thee." For the seventh commandment—and you know what that is!—we had to have a doozy that says, "Thou shalt not adulterate thy art, thou shalt not prostitute thy talent." So we came up with this: "Thou shalt not commit television." Of course, it's both refreshing and unusual when television writers come up with intelligent, mature work.

Interviewer: Is there a difference between propaganda and art?

Lawrence: I'll let the critics decide if something's a work of art, but I don't think any of our plays are propaganda. They're certainly not sermons; they're based on something that we believe in. We try to write it on a human scale. If it comes out like propaganda, I think it's the fault of the production.

Interviewer: What was it like to work with Patrick Tanner Dennis, author of *Auntie Mame* (the book)?

Lawrence: He was wonderful. He was one of the wittiest men I've ever known in my life. He himself tried to write a play of it, and the first act ran 320 pages! He was asked by *Woman's Home Companion*, which gave him thirty-four hundred dollars (an awful lot of money for an article in those days) to go out of town with the play and talk about all the backbiting and all the problems and how everything had to be rewritten in hotel rooms. We didn't do anything out of town except make a few small cuts, and Pat had to give the money back! Instead he wrote the preface to the published play in which he said, "I'm not responsible that it came across as a play." People think it's just a lot of sketches; it's a very carefully structured play. Pat Dennis appreciated that, and he was wonderful about it all.

Interviewer: Doesn't it seem that the movie versions of most plays never come out as well as the plays? *Mame* was terrible as a film.

Lawrence: The movie of *Auntie Mame* is a cult classic now. There are two theatres that for years did Saturday midnight shows where they would alternate three what they call "cult" movies: *Harold and Maude, The Rocky Horror Show,* and *Auntie Mame.* Everybody came dressed as the characters. Men and women alike, wielding long cigarette holders, would play the part of Mame. Everybody would recite the dialogue in unison with the screen. *Mame* as a movie musical is terrible, but I challenge you to find one decent stage musical that became a decent movie. *Man of La Mancha* is a disaster, *Dolly* is awful. They were great stage shows, and part of the reason they didn't work as movies is they were cast wrong. Somebody asked John Ford once, "Is it true that you said that a director's job is 90 percent finished if you cast a show correctly?" He said, "No, damn it, I didn't say that." They asked him, "What did you say?" And he said, "A director's job is ninety-*five* percent done if he casts correctly."

Interviewer: How do you evaluate the dialogue of very recent plays, which tends to be very open, profane, and shocking in terms of what passed for good taste fifty years ago?

Lawrence: Again, like with nontraditional casting, I don't want to be a censor, and I think when that character sitting down next to you is impelled to swear that it's passable; but if he's just swearing for the hell of it, then I think it's out of place.

Interviewer: Have rising production costs for union personnel such as electricians, stagehands, and musicians influenced the way you write and stage a play?

Lawrence: I know a lot of people who are getting pretty tired of two-character plays. I'm even more tired, with the possible exception of Julie Harris and Hal Holbrook, of one-character plays. What comes next, *no*-character plays? Just sit at home and think about it? I want to see a stage populated with people necessary to the concept. I don't approve of limitation. I think the number of characters in the play should be dictated by the subject matter. If the work calls for two people, fine. *Inherit the Wind* called for sixty-five people. The play at the courthouse, the actual courthouse in Philadelphia where it's playing right now, only requires twenty people because the space demands that. We're not going to write just for budgetary reasons, despite the fact our new play isn't on Broadway yet— because there are fourteen people in it.

Interviewer: In today's world, what is the biggest impediment toward a healthy theatre?

Lawrence: The censorship I mentioned earlier; people getting scared to speak out, to say things they really believe and are passionate about. I think it's the biggest danger. Part of it is economic censorship. When there is no money coming from certain sources, people are forced to write small plays. I want plays of size and meaning and ideas that change life. I think people get scared that their plays aren't going to get produced, and I'm sorry for them, because we were lucky enough to be in an era of theatre that could still afford to put up with a lot of costs. People suffering from a recession who don't have the price of a ticket: that's part of it, too. I recommend that you be adventurous. Don't take anybody else's recommendation. Go see what fascinates you and sit through it. What are you going to do if you walk out, go have a drink? You'll learn from what is bad as much as you learn from what's good. And support young playwrights and plays of ideas and meaning.

Terrence McNally

Photo courtesy of William Morris Agency

Terrence McNally was born in 1939 in St. Petersburg, Florida, and grew up in Corpus Christi, Texas. After graduating from Columbia University, he worked at the Actors Studio. His first play, There Is Something Out There *(later revised as* And Things That Go Bump in the Night*), was produced in 1962. Other plays include* The Lady of the Camellias *(adapted from a play by Giles Cooper; 1963),* Next *(1967),* Tour *(1967),* Botticelli *(1968),* Sweet Eros *(1968),* ¡Cuba Si! *(1968),* Witness *(1968),* Noon *(1968),* Last Gasps *(1969),* Bringing It All Back Home *(1969),* Where Has Tommy Flowers Gone? *(1971),* Bad Habits *(1971),* Whiskey *(1973),* The Ritz *(1973),* It's Only a Play *(1985),* Frankie and Johnny in the Clair de Lune *(1987),* The Lisbon Traviata *(1989),* Lips Together, Teeth Apart *(1991), and* A Perfect Ganesh *(1993). He has written books for the musicals* The Rink *(1985) and* Kiss of the Spider Woman *(1992) and has adapted* The

Ritz *and* Frankie and Johnny *for the movies. His book for* Kiss of the Spider Woman *won the 1993 Tony Award,* Bad Habits *won Obie and Dramatists Guild Hull Warriner awards, and McNally has also received two Guggenheim Fellowships, a citation from the American Academy of Arts and Letters, and the William Inge Award. This interview took place on November 13, 1991.*

▶ ──────────────────────────────── ◀

Interviewer: How did you become a playwright? There are so many easier ways to live.

McNally: I think it was to torment my parents. It made my father very nervous. I always liked writing, and for quite a while I thought I was going to be a journalist. But I think in my heart of hearts I always really wanted to be a playwright. I'm a great believer in taking young people to quality theatre if we're going to have a theatre that endures in the future, because our audiences are dwindling. My parents took me to New York to see *Annie Get Your Gun* with Ethel Merman when I was about five years old, and then when I was about ten or eleven they took me back to see Gertrude Lawrence in *The King and I.* I think these stayed in the back of my mind as something very, very special, and no movie ever affected me so much. Gertrude Lawrence died about a week after I saw the show, and I cried terribly; to this day, she and Yul Brynner dancing is more vivid than a play I saw last week, including some of my own. It just made this incredible impression on me, so it was always there.

My parents were both New Yorkers, though I pretty much grew up in Corpus Christi, Texas. They used to go to New York once a year to see friends and family, and they would always leave theatre programs on the coffee table for the next six months or so. People don't leave movie stubs on the coffee table; they don't even leave most novels on the table—so the theatre in our house was always something special. Although my parents maybe saw one play a year or two, they were always something very, very special; so I knew about it. I remember how affected my father was by *Death of a Salesman* and how much he loved *South Pacific* and *Kiss Me, Kate.* He would play those albums over and over and over. Growing up in Corpus Christi there was very little theatre. We had a little amateur theatre, and the only play I remember seeing was *Picnic,* because our speech teacher was playing the Rosalind Russell role. We were dying to see her rip the guy's shirt off and say, "Marry me, marry me!" Her name was Miss Birmeister, and the only reason we went to see this play was to see her do this big sexy scene.

Eventually I went off to college, to Columbia, when I was seventeen, and I started going to the theatre right away. I really enjoyed it; I think I saw every single play on Broadway. You used to be able to sit in the last row of a Broadway theatre for, I think, $1.90 or some pretty low price. I thought theatre was great entertainment, but I still was going to be a famous journalist. Part of my disillusionment with journalism began in Texas when I was working for our local newspaper. I was very aware of those cameras right there and tape. You're furiously writing the facts down while these other people are videotaping or audiotaping everything. You're driving back to the paper knowing that it's going to take you an hour to write the story, you're not going to get home until one o'clock in the morning, and it's already on the radio and TV. I didn't think I wanted to earn my living competing with a camera.

I also did an interview with Lyndon Johnson who was in Corpus Christi when he was a senator. He was talking to Lady Bird on the phone and he was flipping through the new issue of *Playboy,* which I put into my story because I thought it was very, very theatrical. Well, he didn't. He called the editor of the *Corpus Christi Caller Times* and said, "Who the hell was this kid you sent?" It was for a summer job in college when I did this interview with him. I loved the drama of him talking to Lady Bird about something boring domestically while he was flipping through *Playboy.* I had to get that into my story. The editor didn't think it would cause much of a fuss, but it did. I think then that I got my first taste of drama, getting an audience, readers, excited; and I liked that.

Then I was about to graduate from Columbia and they needed something called the Varsity Show. Columbia was probably one of the last universities to put on an all-male show (Columbia College was all male in my day), and they didn't have a writer for it. Rodgers and Hammerstein had written one, Rodgers and Hart had written one, and it was a great tradition; but the school paper said, "There's going to be no Varsity Show this year unless someone writes it." So, sort of like Judy and Mickey saving the day, I decided I would write the Varsity Show. The guy who wrote the music and lyrics was Ed Kleban, who went on to write *A Chorus Line,* and it was directed by Michael Kahn, who is now the head of your Shakespeare Theatre here in Washington. It's the one poster I have in my office; I treasure it. The best thing about it is, it says "Book by Terrence McNally, Lyrics by Ed Kleban"—no director. Michael went all over campus with a magic marker writing "Directed by Michael Kahn," so this poster is a true collector's item! They say, "Where's your poster for *Frankie and Johnny* or *Lips Together?*" And I say, "No, this is the one that inspires me!"

At any rate, I graduated and I went off to write. I thought all I could write was a novel, so I wrote about forty pages of this pretty dreadful novel, and then I wrote a play which I sent in to Actors Studio. I got a letter from a woman named Molly Kazan, who was Elia Kazan's wife. I'm giving a very long answer, I'm sorry. It's how things happen in life. In the movies you come to New York and you stand at the Statue of Liberty and shake your fist at the skyline and say, "I'm going to conquer you, you bitch." I don't think many writers have ever done that. Molly Kazan said, "You show an aptitude for dialogue but not much sense for stagecraft," because I had a scene where a woman was drenched in water and then there's a quick blackout, lights up, and she's in a totally different dress. She said to me, "Do you realize if you pour a bucket of water over a woman, her hair is going to get wet, her makeup will run, her dress will be ruined? You cannot have the lights come up a second later and it's a year later and she's totally changed herself. I think you should come here and just be a stage manager. Have you ever been backstage?" I said, "No." "Do you know any actors or directors?" I assumed she didn't count the Varsity Show at Columbia as a genuine experience, so I said no, and she said, "Here's this job."

So I was stage manager for two years at the Actors Studio. People say, "What was that like?" And I say, "Very menial work: sweeping up and stuff like that." But I kind of eavesdropped a lot, and I saw people like Kazan working with actors. In the playwrights' unit some very wonderful plays were developed, like *The Zoo Story* and *The Night of the Iguana*. It was really exciting, and I learned a lot just by being there, because that was my only practical theatre training. I was once asked to act, and I sure got over that bug. I was in a play with Jane Fonda; she and I were brother and sister, and Keir Dullea was my older brother. I thought I was not very good but okay. The day we did it my knees were literally shaking. I threw up. I came out, my eyes were blinking, I had tics, and it was the most horrible two hours of my life. But I think it's a good way to learn about playwriting—to be an actor and to think moment to moment the way an actor must. I wrote my first real play at the Actors Studio—*Things That Go Bump in the Night*. We did it, and sitting in the audience was someone called Arthur Balliett, who was developing a new Rockfeller program which was going to pay for two new productions of American plays at the Guthrie Theater. So my first play was done at the Guthrie Theater.

Interviewer: That's not bad.

McNally: This was in 1963 when everyone wanted to do new American plays, partially because *Virginia Woolf* was not only so successful on Broadway but was making so many people so much money. Everybody who was writing plays was getting done on Broadway, and my first play, the same play, was done on Broadway the following year, 1964, to probably the most disastrous reviews I've ever gotten. One review began, "The American theatre would be a better place today if Terrence McNally's parents had smothered him in his cradle." I don't think you can get worse than that! They haven't called for my actual death since the first play. I was kind of in shock, I must say. My family came up from Texas. They didn't understand that anyone could be so horrible to their beloved brother/son, and they left the next morning on a 6:00 A.M. flight. My brother said, "You have no place to go but up." That was true, so I went back and worked on a magazine; I had journalism as a thing to fall back on. The play did get one good review, to my memory, and that was in the *Village Voice*. I never quite understood the cruelty of those reviews. There's a lot wrong with the play: it's a first play; it's too long. It purports to tell you what's wrong with American society and with Western culture, and it foresees the end of the world. It's a very ambitious piece, as first plays are. I was going to combine *King Lear, Endgame,* and I think *The Oresteia* into one nice drawing room play.

I know why I went on writing plays: because we came in under budget, which is pretty unheard of, the producer, Ted Mann, said, "We have thirty thousand dollars left in the bank; instead of closing the play, I'm going to run it for two full weeks, and I'm going to charge two dollars for the orchestra seats and one dollar for the balcony, and at that price and with the thirty thousand dollars we have left we'll break even in two weeks." I still thought no one would come because the reviews were so derisive. Every performance was sold out, there were pickets in front of the theatre saying: "This is a wonderful new play; it should be seen." That, I think, is probably why I went on writing plays. Otherwise the experience would have been so devastating I don't know if I ever would have had the courage to do it again.

At any rate, I went back to the magazine, and in that period, I don't know what inspired me, chutzpah, or blind faith. I applied for a Guggenheim. I won one and quit my job at the magazine and started writing plays. I wrote *Next* in that period, which was my second play to be performed. It was very successful. It ran about three years, and that's where I met Jimmy Coco and Elaine May. Elaine directed it, and everything I learned about playwriting I learned from Elaine. We were in previews for six months with that show, and when it finally opened I couldn't get any friends to come. They said, "We've seen it six times already. Who's going to come?" The critics were going to come because this was in the days when the critics all came on opening night rather than to previews. The producer said, "The play is opening tonight," and I said, "It's not finished; I have work to do." She said, "I'm sorry. It's opening. I've had it with the previews." We opened, and it got very good reviews. Ever since then, I've earned a living as a playwright, though there were years when I've been very close to going under financially. But I haven't had to wait tables, drive a cab, or work for a magazine since the opening night of *Next,* which was in 1969.

Interviewer: In this country that's a pretty impressive record.

McNally: I'm very lucky; I count my blessings. I really do. I never decided to become a playwright. I sometimes still think: I could go to graduate school, I could become an architect. Seriously, what's the cutoff age of being accepted as a pre-med student? I think I've passed it, so I guess I have to do it now. I never really had that moment. I love being a playwright. One day I said I really like what I do for a living, or for my life, which is a wonderful feeling. I think the moment was when I saw Ethel Merman come out in that fringe outfit with a gun and I just didn't want to admit it for twenty years. That's where I wanted to be, in the theatre.

Interviewer: Could *Things That Go Bump in the Night* be produced now on Broadway?

McNally: I assume your question means if it was a brand new play, not a revival. The odds would be very, very remote. Last season there was one new play done on Broadway. There were about five plays done on Broadway to begin with, I have to say. Most plays done on Broadway come from either regional theatre or the not-for-profit arena; they're transfers. Producers used to read a script and say, "Boy, if I put this on Broadway I'll get some stars and a famous director and maybe it'll be a hit." That doesn't happen now; people go out to Seattle Rep, or the Alley Theatre, or come to Washington to the Arena to see a play, or they bring plays over from London. They want that protection. Very few theatres in New York are willing to take a chance on a brand new script, which I was very aware of when we did *Lips Together.* We did do a workshop production first, and we opened it cold. We did a workshop production of *Frankie and Johnny* first; with *Lisbon Traviata*, we did a workshop production first. Part of this is because the road has died out. It used to be, traditionally, plays went to three or four cities before they ever dared show their face in New York. Most plays take a real shakedown period. The production of *Lisbon Traviata* that we opened on the West Coast in San Francisco and L.A. was far superior to the New York one because it took me that long to get the text really where I wanted it to be. So, in answer to your question, for a young playwright now, who thinks his play is going to open on Broadway like mine did, the odds are one in a million.

Interviewer: It's opening night, the critics are all there, and you have to stop working on your play. When do you know it's the last brushstroke? When is the painting finished? And could you say something about how you work in the living theatre? Not necessarily what you do in your study in the morning, but what the process is like once you hit the rehearsal room, starting actually with casting?

McNally: When I write the play, it doesn't involve anyone; no one cares that you're off writing it. Once you've given it to the theatre and they say that they're going to put it on, then suddenly you're very connected with lots of people. Your whereabouts are really important; you can't disappear for five days, which is something I like to do, not when you have a play in rehearsal. I'm very involved in casting. I write plays for specific actors, and I've been very lucky for the most part getting those actors to be in these plays. I wrote *Frankie and Johnnie* for Kathy Bates and F. Murray Abraham, who really did create the play. Murray then decided to do a movie, as opposed to going on with a commercial run, so the vast majority of people who saw that play saw it with a wonderful actor, Kenneth Welsh. With *Lips Together,* four actors were in my mind when I wrote. Three created the roles, and Swoosie Kurtz was an actress that I had known. She was like family, I had seen so much of her work and loved it so much; it was very easy to have her come in.

I don't shop my things around. I go to the theatre a lot, and when I see a good actor I write their name down. I saw Nathan Lane ten years before anyone else did. I couldn't believe that, after his performance with George C. Scott in *Present Laughter,* he wasn't instantly given a leading role in a television series. With my good luck he stayed sort of a state secret until *Lisbon Traviata.* It was not my idea to cast him in *Lisbon Traviata* at all. I thought he was too young for the part; I didn't even think of him. Someone said, "What about Nathan Lane?" And I did say, "Oh, God, I think he's the best, but I think he's too young for this. But let him come in." He read three words, and he could have stopped right there. All he did was read the first sentences of the phone call when Mendy calls Discophile. Actors either hear you or they don't hear you, and if they don't hear you the play is doomed.

Chekhov had an experience kind of like I did with my first play. He was devastated. Someone found the script of *The Sea Gull* and showed it to Stanislavsky, who said, "This is wonderful; it was just not performed properly," and got him back into the theatre. I've been very lucky that way. Shakespeare must have had an extraordinary company of actors, and those Moscow Art Players must have been wonderful. I don't think a new play can survive a bad production. When you do *Three Sisters* now, Chekhov is really not being criticized, your production of it is; but on a new play what we see in the theatre's pretty much what you absorb, and that first person who walks out and says, "My name is Hamlet, Prince of Denmark," is how you accept the role. If he had been a bad actor, I don't think that Shakespeare would have wanted to stay in the theatre, and I think his play would not have been successful, and they would have vanished.

Interviewer: Yet if only those original actors can play those roles, then the play has a limited life. What would you say about that, about the possibility of a playwright's work being reinterpreted by many actors?

McNally: Well, I think it has to be. In a good play there are many ways, as the film of *Frankie and Johnny* shows. Michelle Pfeiffer's is, I think, a really magnificent performance, but it is a very different interpretation of Frankie, much darker actually than Kathy Bates, who was playing a very defensive hurt woman. Michelle's playing a woman with no self-worth, which I think in many ways is more painful. I think it's a more painful performance to experience.

Interviewer: Were the changes in the film *Frankie and Johnny* made for the actors, or were they for the form?

McNally: They were for the form. When I was writing the screenplay, I would have been thrilled if they had said Kathy was going to do the film. The change was made with that hope. I thought Kathy, and I always wanted Al Pacino to be in it. But it was the change of form. I thought, "They're paying me good money; here's a chance to write a screenplay."

Interviewer: Whose decision was it to cast Michelle Pfeiffer instead of Kathy Bates?

McNally: The decision to cast any film is never the screenwriter's. I have no rights. I do not have cast approval, nor does any screenwriter. It would be as if I bought your house and you came by a year later and were furious because I had painted it pink and put a lot of flamingos in the front yard. It's not your house anymore. Once you sell Hollywood your screenplay, they own it; they can put whoever they want in it. They certainly listened to me. Kathy was very much considered for the role, but finally Paramount, who was going to put up a lot of money to make the film, and Gary Marshall thought the combination of Al and Michelle was better box office, and that it would be a more interesting combination. The fact that Kathy had won an Oscar made her much more in the running than if she had never made *Misery*. Kathy, on the other hand, at the same time *Frankie and Johnny* was being made was doing the film version of *Road to Mecca*, in a role which was created in this country by Amy Irving. Hollywood is very much who's up, who's down this week, and that changes literally every Friday night. In theatre I take full responsibility for the cast; I have cast approval. In a movie, no screenwriter does. If I wanted to raise in excess of twenty-five million dollars to produce my own movie, then, yes, of course, I could hire anybody I wanted. You're dealing with megabucks here, and they have a lot to say about casting.

Interviewer: Had you ever written a screenplay before?

McNally: I wrote *The Ritz,* a play of mine, as a film. That play, though, is pretty much cinematic in its structure. It's as if we put the play on camera; we had very little to do.

Interviewer: But this was really major work. You changed the characters and the structure.

McNally: *Frankie and Johnny* is a two-character play in a tiny little room in real time. No one wants to see a movie like that. I don't want to see a movie like that; it would be boring. So I said, "Here's a chance; I'm going to put the play away. I'm not going to try to drag dialogue around." There's really very few lines from the play left in the screenplay. I wrote those lines for this small play which I thought would never be produced. It's the only play I ever wrote totally for myself; *Frankie and Johnny* is my little private chamber play. I thought no one would produce it, then Lynne Meadows said, "I'll put it on in the little theatre for three weeks," and then it moved to the bigger theatre, and then it moved to the commercial theatre. Actually, it's probably been the most accepted play of mine, the one done the most in other countries and all around the world.

Interviewer: Why do you think that is?

McNally: I have no idea. It's a good lesson to write what you really care about. If you start worrying about whether this will be a good scene for the people in Nebraska so if we do it at Nebraska Rep we'll have a reference, you can get in a lot of trouble. Then you'll start thinking the way Hollywood moguls think: it's all computers and "This is what our audiences want." Tell your story the way you see it. I think when writing is truthful it tends to interest other people. We all have a way of knowing when the person we're talking to is bullshitting us. Good writers can bullshit as well as the next person, and when our writing gets a little generalized people turn off. I think we should really say, "This is how I see it. I'm not trying to speak for you." I'm glad I'm a male writer, because a playwright like Wendy Wasserstein suddenly has to be this spokesman for women of her generation. Thank God, I don't have that weight on me. There's too many middle-aged male playwrights.

Interviewer: Does anyone ever ask you if you feel that you need to be the spokesman for gay American writers?

McNally: People have wanted me to be. It's an interesting issue, and I think about it a lot. When we did *Lisbon Traviata* last year in San Francisco, the gay community there is much more political. They don't seem to do anything in San Francisco but have opinions. No one has a job in San Francisco, they just sit around having opinions. *Lisbon Traviata* is not a politically correct play, which I was aware of, but I just think all one has to do is look at the art of the Soviet Union. Whenever artists are trying to obey a party line, I think that art vanishes fast. The stuff that was happening last year at the NEA I found terrifying. So many artists were quick to write letters to the Dramatists Guild, of which I'm vice-president, because I wrote this ringing editorial saying don't take the NEA grant if it has any strings. To say my new play examines life in Puritan America and it has nothing to do with these homoerotic issues so why should I care means they don't get it. We're all linked. All the arts are connected, and freedom of expression is terribly important.

I was speaking at a theatre convention about a week ago, and somebody told me that the President's new program to take education into the twenty-first century has four major study fields and the arts is not one of them. I didn't know this. As someone who works in the arts, I should know this and I should be doing something about it. That's appalling. We say, "Where are the new young audiences?" and the arts are not even going to be a priority in our educational system! *Lisbon Traviata* was enormously successful in New York City, and at the Mark Taper Forum you couldn't get a ticket for it. It was the biggest hit they ever had there. I think that's wonderful for what it says for an audience's willingness to sit and see a play about four gay men. I think that's a statement, frankly. I thought *The Ritz* said a lot fifteen years ago. It said it through farce; there wasn't a shrill voice in *The Ritz*.

Interviewer: Some people have said *Frankie and Johnny* is a play about the potential for commitment in the modern age or about one-night stands within the gay community.

McNally: No, *Frankie and Johnny* examines intimacy and what people who are over forty do about having a relationship. It's not *Romeo and Juliet*. It's not about people who meet and in one night say, "I'm going to love you forever." It's about love among the ashes, which was a subject that interested me as I got into my forties. I identify with that need, the feeling of loneliness, but also the feeling of wanting to be alone sometimes. When Frankie says, "I just want to be alone and eat ice cream," I understand that enormously. There are days when I don't want to talk to anybody. I just want to watch a really junky movie on HBO and eat lots of Häagen-Dazs; it doesn't make me a bad person. It makes me a human being, and certainly one of the impulses for writing *Frankie and Johnny* was being aware of the numbers of single men and single women on a Friday night in a video shop renting three or four movies. You know that's how they're going to spend the weekend. They're not going to go to a singles bar. You know they're not dating. They've got their four movies and the Sunday *Times* and that's how they're going to spend Saturday night. That kind of loneliness interested me in writing this play.

Interviewer: What usually gets you to start writing a play? Do you have to be bugged by something?

McNally: Deadlines. Looking at the bank account and saying, "I'd better go write something now." It's things like that, really, or sometimes an incident in real life. Sometimes a character interests me; sometimes a "what if" situation interests me. *Lips Together* I very much wanted to write for the four actors who agreed to show up April first of last year to rehearse it. Kathy Bates at the last minute got another movie, so Swoosie Kurtz came in; but very much part of the inspiration for that play was knowing I was going to have those four actors. Secretly I knew that if even one of them showed up I'd be very lucky, but to get three of them was great, and then to have Swoosie! Talk about a great replacement! She's someone I always wanted to write for, but when I wrote the play I heard Kathy saying the lines for sure.

Interviewer: Could you say something about how you feel about the casting of your plays after the first production vis-à-vis multiculturalism? How true should subsequent productions be to the play as written?

McNally: *Frankie and Johnny* with my enthusiastic approval has been done with a cast where both were black. I've also seen a production where Frankie was black, and I've seen a production where Johnny was black. I'm all for it. Part of that is because I come to theatre out of opera, which has been integrated since I first came to New York. I wouldn't even have trouble with a new play of mine being done with an interracial cast. There are other issues that interest me. I saw a *Frankie and Johnny* with a black actress, and the language did not come easily for her. She said, "It's very hard for me as a black woman; this is not how I speak." I was torn. I didn't want her to change the words, but I felt that she was constricted by the language, not opened up. I saw an all-black production of the play in Philadelphia where a few words had been changed, which I didn't like, but I felt the actors there were adding rhythms that were not mine because they very much wanted to make it their play. There are cultural differences, and I'm very ambivalent about it. Certain lines said one way didn't sound the same, or certain jokes were lost because the rhythm was different. These are real issues.

I'd like to feel more comfortable writing a black role. The few black roles I've written, I've had problems with the actors saying, "I wouldn't say this." There's a black role in *It's Only a Play,* and it's always very painful when somebody says, "A black man wouldn't say this" No one's ever said to me, "A woman wouldn't say this," or "A forty-year-old man wouldn't say this" or "An eight-year-old wouldn't say this." I would like to see our theatre reflect the multiculturalism of our society, but we've all got to be able to find a way to work together. It's tense. I think there are some wonderful black writers around. I wish more of their work was getting done in a larger arena. I think that every actor should feel that, if I'm up to it, I can play Hamlet, I can play Chekhov, and I can play Neil Simon—just as I should be able to write any character I want so long as it's truthful and my imagination allows me to go there. If we get bogged down in discussions about rhythms and speech and vocabulary, it's painful, but I can't really give you a tidy answer to this. It's something the theatre should be thinking about.

I was just at a seminar on color-blind casting which the Dramatists Guild sponsored. It was filled with actors, and there was only one other playwright there. I thought so many playwrights would be there. The audiences at my plays are mainly white, and I'm white, but that's not the world I live in, and I want to lose my inhibitions to write more black characters. I was very happy when I wrote my first black character, but it has not been easy whenever that play's been done. I'd like to find a way to get beyond that as a theatre artist, because, if our theatre doesn't start reflecting this country, what is called the theatre is going to drift more and more away from "the real world." That's one reason a lot of young audiences aren't interested in theatre. *Lips Together* takes place in sort of a ghetto, a white resort on an island, so no reality can intrude. They're three miles out in the Atlantic Ocean in that play. There's things I want to talk about in our culture, and I've got to find the courage and the freedom to do it with other theatre artists.

Interviewer: If the theatre does reflect what's going on in our society, then it's reasonable that that strain or tension would also be reflected in that theatre, isn't it?

McNally: I'd like it to be onstage in the play and not in the rehearsal room, is what I'm saying. That's no fun. Three weeks of rehearsal go by so quickly. I don't know if anyone who has not written or directed or acted in a play realizes how hard it is to get a play even remotely approaching anything decent. Those three weeks go by so quickly, and a waste of time in a rehearsal is a luxury that you can't afford.

Interviewer: What about directors? You've talked a lot about actors.

McNally: Do I like them? I've no desire to direct, so I'm very grateful for them. I work with a small group of directors I trust, and we can work in shorthand, which is nice. When I say how involved I am in rehearsals, there is a point where I cut off. When the leading lady comes up to the director and says, "Should I wear the red shoes or the blue shoes?" I would say, "I don't care. I'm busy, don't ask me!" but you have to say, "Oh, darling, maybe the blue." To the actress it's very important that she feel comfortable in the red or blue shoes. Also, if you get bored at rehearsals as a playwright you can leave. Directors are very patient people. I think they work very hard for their money, a good director does, I really do. I'm grateful to good directors.

I think, though, you find people you work well with. Geraldine Page did a play of mine, and she couldn't hear the way I write, nor could she inhabit the world I was trying to create. It was a disaster. I'd be one of the first to say she's one of the great actresses our country has ever produced, but she just didn't hear. She was reading the music from a different chart; she was singing somebody else's score. Someone like Nathan Lane, you know in three seconds; it's not a question of after three weeks of rehearsal. We knew in three words he was Mendy. More than that, I knew that this was an actor that I would want to work with the rest of my life, because the actors who hear you become an extension of you, and they also make you braver as a playwright. I think I took a lot of risks as a writer in *Lips Together,* but I had four actors I could trust not to make me look bad; they would know the transitions I meant.

I don't think I've written a a stage direction other than "Enters," "Leaves," or "Dies." You have to write those three. Otherwise, it gets very confusing. I don't say, "Sitting stage right and crossing his legs on that line." Who cares? In *Frankie and Johnny,* in the script I said they're in bed naked, but I never indicated when they got dressed. I went to see the first production of it in Houston with my mother and brother, and my mother said, "They're naked!" And I said, "It'll be over in a second." One hour later they're both still stark naked, for the whole first act! I said to the director, "They're naked." And she said, "You said they're naked." I said, "Yes, but they get dressed." She said, "You didn't put it in the script." So the audience sat there and there wasn't a laugh, not a titter, for the entire first act. I was so embarrassed. My mother now waits; she doesn't go to openings anymore. After the first play, she waited twenty-five years until I got a hit and went to see *Frankie and Johnny,* and I did it to her again!

Interviewer: In *Frankie and Johnny* you have Frankie spit out one four-letter word over and over again. Do we have to have that kind of language?

McNally: Do we have to? I think it implies that, when you come to see a play, I'm not going to do anything that upsets you, or my characters won't. That traditional notion of theatre I kind of reject. I go to the theatre to be appalled, to be stimulated, to be upset. I can't imagine four-letter words today being offensive to anyone. The theatre to me is not a sanctuary from the language, when people say the language you hear on the subway and in the streets. I don't think the theatre should be a sanctuary, but that's an aesthetic decision about what you want art to be. I want plays that try to deal with contemporary issues in a way that holds together. Otherwise you're doing revue sketches of what's on everybody's mind this day.

The fact you say "Do I have to?" implies that you expect something from the theatre that maybe I don't agree with. I was never bothered in the sixties and seventies when actors came out in the audience and confronted me. That was my generation, so I don't expect the theatre to be comfortable. In fact, one of the reasons that I rail so much against opera productions and the way Shakespeare is done is that it is so boring. Shakespeare is not a boring writer, but he's produced as a boring writer. Operas have been just stripped of any passion. I can't believe that someone like Puccini didn't want to rip your heart out with *La Bohème*. It was about young love, and dying at a time when a lot of people didn't live beyond twenty-five, and now we present *La Bohème* as an antiseptic experience.

I just saw a production of *Traviata* where Violetta had AIDS, and I thought it was a wonderful idea, if only for the last act where she was dying in a ward with other beds. That's what happens if you're poor, you know. In the libretto she says, "I have no money," but usually she's in a single room the size of the Metropolitan Opera House! If you have no money you don't get a room like that. I thought this director made the experience of death and being broke very, very real, and I think a young audience would say, "Hey, *Traviata* is about something which can affect my life. It's not just this boring nineteenth-century thing for my parents to go to."

Interviewer: How did you develop your love for the opera?

McNally: I didn't. It just happened. I heard three bars of Puccini and I loved it. I was at a parochial school with a very strange nun, I guess, because she let us listen to Puccini love duets every Friday. It was a very tormented convent, obviously. I thought it was very beautiful. Everybody else had paper clips and airplanes and was napping, and I just thought it was beautiful. Last summer I was going to Seattle to speak at an opera seminar, and the woman next to me said, "I heard you're going to speak at our opera company. It's one of the great opera companies in America. I really want to get into opera. How do you get to like opera?" I said, "I think it's like liver. You either like it or you don't. You're fine not liking opera. It doesn't make you a better person." You either think that it's wonderful that people sing about these things and get stabbed and sing about it for another ten minutes, or you think it's totally stupid and have no interest in it. I've never successfully gotten any of my friends to like opera. In fact, my parents now really hate opera, because ever since the sixth grade it was,

"Shut that door!" I started then saving all my money to buy opera records. Probably one of the reasons I write plays is because opera to me is theatre.

Interviewer: Could you tell us how you go about writing a play? What is your writing process?

McNally: It's very simple, really. You have to go to the typewriter, that's all you have to do. I have a word processor now, and you turn it on and something happens after a while, and that's all writing is to me. If I don't go to the typewriter I don't write. I'm not being facetious. I think it's a very practical thing, and deadlines help a lot. You realize that *Lips Together* opens April twelfth and it's December twelfth and you haven't written a word of the play. I carry them up in my head for a long time. That process is very hard to talk about. It's partially my unconscious. It's usually a year or two before I sit at the typewriter, but people say, "God, you write plays so quickly." Well, I think walking around with things in your head for two years is not exactly quickly. The typing part is pretty quick, if you really know what you're doing in a play. Once I know what my characters are doing, the play just comes very, very easily. I learned from Elaine May that playwriting is about what characters are doing, not what they are saying. My first play, *Things That Go Bump in the Night,* is just too conversational, people sitting around talking—which people seldom do in real life. This is a totally artificial situation right now; we're sitting around talking, but this is not real life. Elaine taught me: what are your characters doing? That's how she directed the actors. She never said, "You're feeling this here, Jimmy. You should be sensing that." She'd say, "You've got to open the door. You've got to go over there and do this." Theatre is not all that different from real life, and I think I'm usually doing something; so when I write a play I remember that it's not about two people sitting around having a conversation. It's about people doing something, and *Lips Together* is filled with the minutiae of daily life, but everybody's doing something. They're sweeping the deck or they're checking the chlorine in the pool, but they're not sitting around talking, even though it looks like they are. I'm glad I learned that at such an early age, because you can write ten plays before you learn anything about playwriting. I really give Elaine an enormous amount of credit, though if she had directed my second play we would still be in previews!

Interviewer: What is it like for you when you work on a musical?

McNally: Writing the book for a musical is very, very difficult. I find that it's not enough to love musicals to write a good book for one. I learned a lot working on the book of *The Rink.* It was a wonderful experience. I'd never worked with stars like Liza and Chita before. It was very much our show when it opened; it was a wonderful collaboration. It got a standing ovation at every preview. Then Frank Rich came and reviewed it and said, "I hate this show," and the audience stopped standing. They'd go, "I like it," under their breath. It was also a rare thing, an original musical. There are not many. Usually we're seeing a musical of *Romeo and Juliet*. It was one of the happiest theatre experiences I've ever had until the morning of the reviews. His review was very, very condemning. It was the kind of review that made audiences not enjoy the show anymore, if you know what I mean. He really profoundly disliked what the show was about. In a funny way, he never reviewed the craft of the songs, the script, the choreography, or the acting. I'm doing another musical now, an adaptation of *Kiss of the Spider Woman*. I'm finding again that everything I've learned about playwriting is gone when I try to write a musical.

Interviewer: Have you ever learned anything from a critic?

McNally: That's very hard to answer. Not the way I can say what I learned from Elaine May, what I learned from working with Chita Rivera, what I learned from all sorts of people. Critics are observers who are outside the glass window looking in; they don't go through the joy and agony of the rehearsal period. That's where you learn about your play. All you have to do is sit in the middle of the audience, and if the audience is enjoying it, you don't really need Frank Rich to tell you that. I can't say I've learned a lot. Now that I've written enough, someone occasionally will write kind of an overview essay about my work and point out themes, and I can see similarities.

Interviewer: Would the New York theatre be better if the critics were eliminated?

McNally: Maybe. I think it's going in circles; because you have playwrights saying the critics are the bane of our existence, yet if they like us then we spend fifty thousand dollars in the Sunday *New York Times* saying, "Wonderful! Fabulous! Brilliant!" One way to break the power of the *New York Times* is not to advertise in its pages. No one's willing to do that. In the meantime I don't think the standard of criticism is very high because people want a consumer tip—do I want to see this or not? The *New York Times* has started excerpting the news in a little box just this past week, like *USA Today*; so I'm pretty sure they'll do the same with criticism, as a service to their readers—so they don't have to read the review anymore. Frank Rich: yes, no. Good, got that dealt with. "Honey, we don't have to go see the new play, it's terrible." I don't envy the critics, because they're not allowed to have intelligent considered opinions. They have to say, "This is Mr. McNally's deepest and richest play yet," or it will read like they didn't like it. Every play I've ever seen I've liked things about and I've disliked things about, including *Hamlet*. I think *Hamlet* has some real bad stuff in it, but because it's *Hamlet* I can have a real opinion about it.

Interviewer: Why do you think the level of criticism has fallen?

McNally: I don't think the level of criticism has fallen. There are fewer papers. People are less willing to spend the money; they want some sort of guide. I found myself falling into it once. I was out of New York, and I came back and the paper said, "Martha Graham Ballet Performance Tonight, *Rite of Spring*," and she was ninety years old when she choreographed it. I called a friend and said, "What kind of reviews did Martha Graham's new ballet get?" As I said that, I realized that's what I'm objecting to. Martha Graham at age ninety with all of the masterpieces she's given the world hardly needs the approval of Anna Kisselgoff; but I was doing this because I felt I didn't know enough about modern dance and I needed a guide. Should I see it or not? Then I said, "Don't tell me, don't tell me!" I bought the tickets and I loved it.

Interviewer: Is there any way that one can make the audiences feel confident in their own judgment?

McNally: That's not the problem.

Interviewer: What about the price?

McNally: The price, of course, is very, very high. It's getting just people who love theatre. How many baseball games are interesting? Nine out of ten are incredibly boring, but you're a fan of baseball so you go for the game and it's exciting. That's why you go to the theatre, to say, "Hey, this is great." But unless you're developing a new audience the way I was hooked for life at age five, then you don't get a theatre audience. I think by the time we're teenagers we're so opinionated that it's almost too late. We've got to do something, as a theatre community. I don't think that we as a community are doing enough. Where are the five-year-olds at our theatres, the ten-year-olds?

Interviewer: What can we do about that? What can anybody do? Most people who come to the theatre want to have a good time; they didn't pay their money to have a bad time.

McNally: What's their expectation of theatre? We live increasingly in a society of such hype. You've got to be a musical like *Phantom of the Opera* or a play like *Death of a Salesman*. There's no room for anything less. The Hollywood mentality has seeped into the theatre, and people are only interested in producing blockbusting shows. At this theatre convention, all these producers were saying, "Do you know what it costs to do a big Broadway musical? A minimum of six and a half million dollars." But who said that's the only kind of theatre you can produce? You can produce a small two-character play off-off-Broadway; that's theatre. People are confusing Broadway with theatre. Theatre is very healthy in this country. Six blocks of real estate is not where the theatre is.

Interviewer: But it's not only the people in New York who need the theatre, and not only the people in New York who see the theatre, and not only the largest theatre in every city that is producing art. We all fall into those traps of thinking that our time is limited, our money is limited, our attention span is limited. Isn't it about people feeling confident themselves about art, instead of someone else having to tell them whether it's good or bad? Come and have some patience and see and be moved.

McNally: Something has happened to our audiences. The fact that Arthur Miller had to go to London to get his new play on, that Edward Albee has had a play now for six or seven years that is going to open in Houston: men who have created works like *Salesman* and *Virginia Woolf!* That they should have to go begging says something about the way the powers that be have rejected two of our most distinguished playwrights because they are not guaranteed money-making machines.

Interviewer: But New York is not America.

McNally: I can only talk about the New York theatre. Finally all theatre is regional. New York is a region. Its premier theatre for years and years was Broadway. Now you take away off-Broadway and New York has one play running, by Neil Simon, and ten musicals, most of which have been running for over six years, which everybody's seen now six times.

Interviewer: Are there plays that you particularly like, now?

McNally: Of mine?

Interviewer: No, not of yours. Productions that you've seen lately that you can recommend.

McNally: There are so few plays that are running in New York right now. I think that *Dancing at Lughnasa,* which is an Irish play, is very beautiful. I think it's wonderful. That's the only play that's opened on Broadway so far this year. Off-Broadway, the play at Circle Rep called *Babylon Gardens* was very unsuccessful, but I think that Timothy Mason is going to write a wonderful play. The reason he's going to write a wonderful play is because Tanya Berezin, the artistic director there, is committed to him, and she's doing his first three plays until he gets it right.

No one even remembers Arthur Miller's first play; Tennessee Williams's first play closed in Boston. Edward Albee was off-Broadway for ten years before he wrote *Virginia Woolf.* At the opening night of *Virginia Woolf* I remember that Abe Burrows came over to Edward and said, "Welcome to the theatre, young man." I just wanted to puke. But that was the attitude—welcome to the real theatre. At this theatre convention, the head of the Shuberts said, "You should try to put that play of yours in a big theatre and try to sell a thousand seats a night. You're in a three-hundred-seat theatre, and of course you can run for six months." Try to do a play in a real big theatre, as if, we're the big boys, give us the real estate.

The big producers keep saying, "Where are the playwrights?" The playwrights are everywhere. They don't want to know about the playwrights because it involves a risk and everyone is scared right now because of our economy, which I understand the reality of. Don't say, where are the playwrights? The question is, where are the producers? A producer used to be someone of vision and courage who said, "I'm going to put this playwright with this actress and this director and let's see what happens." He didn't sit around reading the papers and saying, "Oh, here's a play that got a good review. Let's go see about doing that." He created on an empty bare stage. They took chances, and you can still do that. You don't have to spend six million dollars. That's the Shuberts' idea of producing, to do another *Cats* or another *Phantom of the Opera*. They don't want to produce anymore.

There aren't many young producers. All the young people who are going into the theatre now out of the Yale Drama School program in theatre management are being absorbed by the not-for-profits, which are the healthy arena of the American theatre. Suddenly, they're at Seattle Rep, the Old Globe, the Mark Taper Forum. They're all working, and they're wonderful young minds, but they're working in the not-for-profit arena. We're not getting the new David Merricks, Rogers Stevenses, and Robert Whiteheads on Broadway. Joe Papp really was the end of an era. His plays said, "Joe Papp presents." They didn't say, "Joe Papp in association with Suntory, Mitsubishi, and ten other conglomerates presents." When *Frankie and Johnny* was moved commercially, it had twelve producers for a two-character play! *Nick and Nora* has many, many producers. It used to say "David Merrick presents" and it meant that the taste of David Merrick presents this evening, or the taste of Joe Papp; Joe Papp thinks this is a good play for you to see. No one is making those personal statements anymore. The producer was always a very, very strong force in theatre, and without him now we've drifted. Broadway is now competing with rock video, it's competing with restaurants. People say, "We've got to find a musical that the Japanese tourist will like. It's got to be very visual. With *Phantom of the Opera*, they know the plot going in, so we can run." My plays don't play well if you don't speak English. I'm sorry, I'll do my best next time.

Interviewer: Would you care to comment about whether playwriting is a craft or an art?

McNally: With questions like that you always wind up talking about semantics more than anything. Yes, it's a craft, and if it's good it's an art; but it's not some mystical thing. Writing plays is very practical. Theatre is the most practical art form I can think of. One, you have to deal with a lot of people, and it takes place in real time. A novelist or a screenwriter can jump cut from here to there. In the theatre, if I'm sitting here I have physically to get up and you have to watch me go through that curtain. That could be really boring to watch, but there's no other way for me to get back there. That's all craft. That's another reason I don't want to direct a play: actors say, "Should I come in stage left or right?" I don't know. I just wrote it, and I just say, "She enters"; I don't say, "stage left" or "stage right." It's not that I'm making fun of something I take very seriously, but I'm trying to convey that it's very, very practical. Yes, it's a craft; I think a good play, of course, is art; and other than that, I think we just get into semantics.

Interviewer: Do you write to discover what you feel about something?

McNally: That's not the motive to write something, but I do discover something and how I feel about things while I'm writing a play. But it's not the motive. I don't say, "Well, I'll write a play about suicide so I can see what it would be like to kill myself." Writing a play is not psychotherapy. But I do learn an awful lot about myself, and it makes me more aware of other people. I would like to think that my work is about equal parts autobiographical feeling, imagined feeling, and people I've observed. I've never created a character that I've had no empathy for, and I've never based a character one hundred percent on a person I've known in real life. It's a blend, and in the process you learn something about yourself.

Interviewer: Do you have a most and a least favorite piece of your own work, and why?

McNally: I definitely, quite objectively, think that *Lips Together, Teeth Apart* is my best play. I'm proudest of it. I think I'm more affectionate toward *Lisbon Traviata*. My least favorite? It's not the kind of thing I sit around making a list of. I have affection for the deluded immature person who wrote *Things That Go Bump in the Night*; he wasn't a bad person, he was just overambitious. I don't hate him for writing a play like that. I can't say I'd rush to see a revival of that play. *Where Has Tommy Flowers Gone?* I have enormous affection for; it's considered a sixties play, so it doesn't get done. Technically, in terms of the craft of playwriting, I thought a lot of *The Ritz*. It was very good writing. But because of AIDS *The Ritz* will probably never be done again. I think the second act of that play has some really wonderful farce situations.

I'd love to write another farce, but I don't have another three years of my life to devote to a play. Farce is the hardest form of theatre for the writer, and it's hard for the actors. Farce has to be boring for the first hour to get all the plots going, for it all to pay off. I spent the loneliest month of my life in Washington at the National Theatre getting *The Ritz* right. Fortunately, the President was gone, Congress was gone; there was no one in town—about twelve people and I wandered in to see this play. So we were very free to make huge changes. Actors went around carrying pages, but we found that play at the National Theatre one very dark December and January. We were here for four weeks. Farce really needs the out-of-town experience. I'd love to do another one. Just to have a line like "I think I'll go in the next room" bring down the house is so nice. It's not funny, but you know what they're going to see when they go in the next room. I've written another farce, called *Up in Saratoga,* which we tried out at the Old Globe Theatre, and I hope one day it will be done in New York. It has eighteen characters, it's in five acts, and it's a period piece. Needless to say, producers are not looking for eighteen-character five-act period plays right now.

Interviewer: Do you have any suggestions of where young playwrights should go to get the nurturing you mentioned?

McNally: Well, I got my early nurturing from actors. I would just see actors whose work I liked or off-off-Broadway theatre groups. I've never been a particularly naturalistic writer, so if a theatre company was well known for doing very naturalistic productions, it was not a good company for me to try and hang out with and get interested in my work. With *Next,* Jimmy Coco was an actor I saw in a play and I thought he was fabulous, so I wrote the play for him. He said, "Oh, that's great. I'm this character actor nobody's ever heard of. Who's going to do a play for me?" I don't know if you know *Next,* but it's very much a vehicle. He had this play which I thought would maybe never get produced, and I had left the magazine and was on my Guggenheim. He was off at summer stock doing a play, but the fourth play was canceled. So the producer hysterically said, "We don't have a fourth slot. Oh God, what are we going to do?" And Jimmy Coco said, "I've got this play," and that's how things get done in the theatre. Not through agents. So many young writers think they need an agent. No, network through actors, other playwrights, and up-and-coming theatre groups.

Somebody's doing *Bad Habits* in New York and begged me to come. I said, "I don't know if my nerves could take it." Once I'm done with a play, then I feel I have no business being in the theatre because I'm not working that night. I love being in rehearsal. I hate watching the play once it opens. The other night I went to see *Lips* because an understudy was on, and I really had to make myself stay. Once during the first act I walked out, and I missed the first ten minutes of Act II; but I said, "No, you've got to watch the performance." On opening night I'm sitting there right in the middle of the audience, and people say, "How can you sit there?" I don't feel nervous because I feel I'm working. But to criticize the understudy is the stage manager's and the director's job. I very seldom say anything to actors other than, "Where do you want to eat after the play?" or "You were terrific." I can think an actor is doing a scene wrong, but if I tell them and the director tells them, then he's had two different versions of what he's supposed to do. I learned early on that you're sabotaging your own play if you start criticizing the actor.

Interviewer: When you saw that Geraldine Page was wrong for the part in your play, did you sit quietly or did you do something?

McNally: We had a lot of fights. We had made a mistake. She was the star of the play, so we weren't going to fire her. What can I say? I was in agony for the three weeks. It wasn't fun; I didn't look forward to being in rehearsal, because there was no collaboration. She wasn't having joy speaking my lines, and I wasn't having joy listening to her speak them; so I had no impetus to go home and make it better or enrich it. It was just painful. It's a play called *It's Only a Play,* which closed out of town. It was a Broadway play that closed in Philadelphia. Manhattan Theatre Club redid the play a few years later with Christine Baranski (the first time I worked with her) and the play was quite successful then.

It's not just because of Geraldine Page that this production worked whereas the original production didn't; it was a series of things. I should have known from Geraldine Page's other work that she was not the kind of actress for my plays. They're too artificial for someone as naturalistic as Geraldine Page. Kathy Bates is not a naturalistic actress. People kept saying about *Frankie and Johnny,* "You've written your first naturalistic play." An audience can be fooled that if you eat meat loaf and make an omelet onstage that it's naturalism. *Frankie and Johnny* is a very artificial play. That's why so much of the dialogue had to go in the screen version, because a movie is automatically naturalistic, unless it's a total fantasy. With Geraldine Page, it was bad casting and we used bad judgment, but it was a star who wants to be in your play, and that means it's going to Broadway. I was thrilled the day she agreed to do it. It was only after the first day of rehearsal that I thought that this may not be the ideal combination of actress and role.

Interviewer: What terrifies you?

McNally: In theatre nothing terrifies me. I think it's very exciting. I think it's great fun. I did write a play called *It's Only a Play,* and I really try to keep reminding myself of that. The point is to write the next one. People in this country get so worried about topping themselves, about overcoming a failure. Just go on and write the next one. Shakespeare is the best inspiration in the world. From hits to flops he's all over the place; it's a roller coaster. He goes directly from *Hamlet* to *Timon of Athens*. Playwrights are only mortals. If you have actors who want to do your plays, consider yourself lucky and get on with it; so I'm not terrified. I think it's challenging, I think it's fun. I'm fifty-two years old as of last week, and I do this because it's fun. No one makes you write plays; the world could sort of get along without me turning out a play every year, so I do this because I enjoy it enormously. It gives me great pleasure, and working in the theatre is, I think, its own reward. I think people always want to know how much playwrights earn. Well, most years it's very, very, very little. If you have a success, you earn quite a bit.

You have to enjoy the collaborative process to work in the theatre. If you don't, you're going to be unhappy as an actor or director, or as a ticket taker. It's body contact in the theatre, and if you don't enjoy that go off to your desert island and write your novel or your sheaf of poems. You have huge fights in rehearsals sometimes, but they're healthy fights because it's family fighting; it's trying to make it better. An actor who I really trust and work well with (the four that were in this last play) can say, "This line doesn't work for me," and I don't take it as a personal statement like "I don't like you, Terrence." They're saying, "This line doesn't work for me" and we try to make it better. It's family, it's trying to find a continuity in your work. That's why I work with the same people over and over as much as I can, and I go to the theatre a lot. I'd never met Kathy Bates when I wrote *Frankie and Johnny* for her, but I'd seen her in three or four plays and I thought that she was one of the great actresses I'd ever seen. She was so present and physical for me, it was easy to write for her. Most of the actors I've written for I didn't know. Now they're friends. When I wrote the second part for Kathy she was a friend. With Nathan Lane, I can't believe it's taken ten years for America to recognize what I thought was the finest comic actor since Jimmy Coco. I'm just lucky I've had Nathan all to myself the last couple of years. Now the worlds of Hollywood and Broadway revivals have discovered him, but I hope Nathan and I can work together again soon.

Ntozake Shange

Photo courtesy of Ntozake Shange

Ntozake Shange was born in 1948 in Trenton, New Jersey, and raised in St. Louis, Missouri. She received her undergraduate degree from Barnard and an M.A. in American Studies from the University of Southern California and has taught at Sonoma State College, Mills College, Rice University, City College of New York, Douglass College, and the University of Houston. The author of fiction (Sassafras, Cypress and Indigo *[1983]* and Betsey Brown *[1985])* and poetry (Melissa and Smith *[1976],* Natural Disasters and Other Festive Occasions *[1977],* nappy edges *[1978],* A Daughter's Geography *[1983],* From Okra to Greens *[1984],* Ridin' the Moon West: Word Paintings *[1987],* and The Love Space Demands *(a continuing saga) [1991]), her first theatre piece,* for colored girls who have considered suicide when the rainbow is enuf, *was produced in New York in 1975. Her other dramatic works include* Negress *(1977),* a photograph *(1977), where* the mississippi meets the amazon (*1977*), Spell #7 (*1979*), Black and White Two-Dimensional Planes (*1979*), Boogie Woogie Landscapes (*1980*), Mother Courage and Her Children (*adapted from a play by Bertolt Brecht; 1980*), From Okra to Greens: A Different Kinda Love Story (*1982*), Three for a Full Moon, and Bocas (*1982*), Educating Rita (*adapted from a play by Willy Russell; 1983*), Betsey Brown (*1987*), *and* The Love Space Demands (*1991*). *She has been honored with the New York Drama Critics Circle Award (1977), two Obie Awards (1977, 1980), the Columbia University Medal of Excellence (1981), the* Los Angeles Times *Award for Poetry (1981), and a Guggenheim Fellowship (1981). This interview took place on December 10, 1993.*

▶ ─────────────────────────────────── ◀

Interviewer: I thought that where I would start would be with a question about *for colored girls.* I saw that play, I think, in five different cities. I saw it in New York, in St. Louis, in Detroit, in Los Angeles, in San Francisco, and I was really struck by how different it was depending on the audience. I think some of the actors changed in it, and I know that at one point you were actually in it, when it first started. Could you talk about its construction and how it came about? It's such an unconventional play, yet it took the audience by storm. People loved it, and I think part of the reason they loved it was because it was unexpected. There was something different, something immediate, about it. Could you talk about how you constructed that play?

Shange: This presents a real dilemma for me because I specifically called *for colored girls* a "choreopoem" because it's not a play. I wasn't trying to write a play, because I was primarily a poet at the time. I think I had only written two short stories in my life; all I had written was poetry, so that gets rid of the idea of how I constructed it. How it evolved is that I had worked myself up to being a featured poet at fairly important readings in the Bay area in the early seventies at some point. Since I was developing a following of some sort, people who would always come see me, I did two things: I wanted to have a new poem every time I went to read, because I knew that the people had seen me in the not too far distant past; and I also wanted to not scare them away, so that I would generally do fairly humorous or anecdotal kinds of poems and then in the middle of the reading start to go toward issues that were very serious and very hazardous to one's emotional health. That kind of art is essentially what I still do, because I'm not following a plot line so much as I'm following the surrender of my audience's emotions to the dynamic of the realities of my characters.

Interviewer: Can you remember what pieces from *colored girls* were the earliest poems?

Shange: Everything except "beau willie" and "Harlem" I wrote when I was in California.

Interviewer: So you did those as performances of your poetry?

Shange: Yes, and I worked with dancers and musicians. I had a big "for colored girls" show at Minnie's Can-Do Club in San Francisco and at the Bacchanal, a women's bar in Richmond, and in Alameda County before I came to New York. Then when we came to New York, Paula and I went to Studio Rivbea.

Interviewer: Who's Paula?

Shange: Paula Moss was my choreographer and my friend. She was my principal dancer when we were in California, along with Elvia Marta and her sister Cecilia. When we were in San Francisco, as far as Paula and I were concerned we belonged to a community of poets, musicians, and dancers. When I got to New York, we were also a part of the alternative jazz festival. We worked at Sam Rivers's Studio Rivbea that first summer; we did two shows, and I got a band together there with some guys I knew from Boston. Then I was going to go back to San Francisco because I had been back east about five months and I wanted to go home. I had done what I wanted to do; I had worked in New York and now it was time to go back. We'd also done a lot of readings at the Old Reliable on East Third Street. It was structured essentially the way I did it, which was that the dancers set pieces themselves and I didn't know about it. If they were doing improvs, I could follow that; and I would maybe do improvs in the middle of the poems. Then, through my sister Ifa, I was introduced to Oz Scott, who was working at the Public Theater. Oz and some actors that he knew introduced whatever formal conventions of theatre as we know it exist in *for colored girls.* I was never interested in it; I just thought it was so horrible that they wanted me to do the same poems in the same order every night. I said, "What in the world would you do that for? How is that supposed to be interesting to me?" I was still interested in making it interesting to me, and I just thought that was horrid.

Interviewer: So he essentially took the performances that you were doing that were expandable and changeable when you were doing them and made them set pieces?

Shange: Yeah, they were set pieces. Then the choreography got set, and then we had set blocking. We didn't change the text at all.

Interviewer: Did he rearrange the poems or decide what order they would go in?

Shange: I was continually rearranging poems because whatever the new poem was would disturb the order. I had this rule that I couldn't have a reading if I didn't have a new poem, so the order was constantly changing. What I was upset about was that the order was made static, but then after a while I got over that because I decided, "Well, these people can stay here all night and do these same poems if they want to, but I'm just going to write myself some more."

Interviewer: In a way, did you feel divorced from the Broadway production?

Shange: I left after three weeks; I just couldn't stand it. I wanted to go back downtown, either south of Houston Street or at least south of Fourteenth Street.

Interviewer: So it didn't seem to have the same kind of aliveness and vibrancy that you wanted it to have in these performances that engaged the audience?

Shange: No, it's not that. I was in the Broadway production and I think we did a wonderful job. I think the actresses did wonderful jobs, but there's two issues here. One is that when we work in small houses in neighborhoods that have a propensity for the avant-garde or the unusual, we're working for audiences that are very familiar with the kind of things we're talking about and that are essentially trying to give us back something. We become a whole as opposed to an audience and performers. When we went to the Public Theater, that changed a lot because there were a lot of people who didn't know anything about any images from California. We had to get rid of the one Puerto Rican we had in the show from Henry Street because white people and black people in New York couldn't understand what a Puerto Rican would be doing in a show that had black women in it. I mean it was that crude. Then when we went to Broadway, we were talking to people who didn't even know we existed.

Interviewer: Did *colored girls* change when you took it from the Public Theater to Broadway?

Shange: The text? No. Any space changes a show. It changed because of what Broadway audiences intended to see. I don't know what they intended to see; I don't have any idea. I just know that I didn't want to stay there and work on that up there. This was fifteen, sixteen years ago, but I came from the counterculture and I came from the Black Arts Movement and I really didn't understand what I was supposed to be so tickled about walking through Times Square, which at that time was not being renovated and gentrified. It was horrible; I hated it up there, and so I just wanted to get out and I did. I left after three weeks. I got sick; I got strep throat, and then I just never went back. I was protected in the show itself because in the show we were protected by the words. We could live inside the words, but me Zake the performer, me Zake the writer, I just needed a little less sense of isolation. At that point we were the first so-called serious black play since *Raisin in the Sun,* and that was a big burden for a twenty-five-year-old person to handle. So I just wanted to get out of the way.

Interviewer: Does that mean that there's some real antipathy on your part for Broadway, for taking a play to Broadway?

Shange: Oh, no, absolutely not. You see the thing is, having actresses do things that I would normally do by myself allows for all kinds of opportunities. One is that if a show does get to Broadway, I can still have my words go all around the country in first-string theatres and in amateur-string theatres for years and years, creating an audience I would never be able to reach otherwise, and I still didn't have to go—so that's really important. The other thing is that going to Broadway allows me, if the show works, so much financial independence that I can do any other thing I want to do. Those two things, I think, are very important. What bothers me is that we can work ourselves to death in Seattle or Houston or St. Louis and do fabulous work but because we're not getting national reviews from the *Washington Post* or *Time* or *Newsweek* or the *New York Times* it doesn't matter. That I resent. I really do resent that.

Interviewer: Is Broadway the only way you can get that kind of national attention?

Shange: Unless you go to the Louisville Festival of New Plays or go to the O'Neill, but then I have to go somewhere. Since I've been raising a child, it's very hard for me to just get up and go for ten weeks or go for six weeks. The child has to go to school.

Interviewer: So Broadway for you is really an economic issue and an issue of getting your work to more people?

Shange: Yes, more people.

Interviewer: It's not some kind of ultimate test of viability, then?

Shange: Oh, no. The test of viability is that people keep buying books. I think the difference between me and other playwrights is that I had books before I had plays; so my sense of longevity and validity has to do with my continual ability to produce books that people buy and want to read and want to hear me read from. I think trying to be a playwright is much too abstract for me. You can't take the play home, you can't video because Actors Equity wants so much money. You could say you had fifteen plays that were produced here, there, and the other; but you can't take pictures because the union won't let you—so you have no proof that you even did this. You see what I mean? So I really am very glad that I had books before I had productions.

Interviewer: When you say books, you don't mean just the books in which your plays are published?

Shange: No, I mean my novels and my poems.

Interviewer: What's the connection between the novels and your poetry and playwriting?

Shange: Usually, to write a piece as a poem is my first impulse, but I also write a lot of narrative poems. In some of these narrative poems, I've been able to find plot lines and characters which are implied but I might not have known it, so I can move them out and into something. I used to think that I started doing plays because it forced me to make people or feelings I had clear to audiences who may have never met these people or had these feelings. That's why I sort of did that. Also, I think that black and Latin people, at least in this country, are not as much a reading-based culture as, say, the Jewish American community is; so even if I did write a whole lot of books it doesn't mean any black people ever saw them. I know that we like to hear people perform. That's why Small's Paradise was a bar that had fifteen million brilliant famous people work there, because we like to see people do things.

Interviewer: I didn't know they performed at Small's.

Shange: Oh, yeah, singers and bands and everything. So I thought for sure that I needed to do that because I need to reach our people so that they know I'm out here. I want them to know that I'm investigating us and celebrating us and looking at our general complexity at the end of the twentieth century. Now, let me get back to the part about the novel. The reason I write novels is because writing plays and doing performance pieces and poetry readings leaves me in my fantasy world very much involved with a whole lot of other people who talk to me, who clap or don't clap, who want to give me my set design budget or don't want to give me my set design budget, who want me to edit out these two stanzas or want me not to edit those out, who want me to have comp tickets for only two nights instead of five nights. So it becomes too many people. I like to write long novels because I don't have to talk to anybody. I can stay in my house; I can make up seventeen million characters; I can have them go to bed when the sun comes up; I can do all kinds of outrageous things, because in a novel I have the control that a director and a writer have—and a producer, for that matter, because I can decide how lush the scenery is going to be and it won't cost me a cent!

Interviewer: In a way, then, writing plays for production actually interferes with your sense of creativity.

Shange: No, it doesn't. It's just that I can only do it for a certain amount of time.

Interviewer: When you take something to be performed, do you get involved in all the production aspects of it?

Shange: Usually for its first two or three productions, yes. I'm there every day in the first two or three productions. When I'm finished with it, I'm really finished with it. I haven't seen *for colored girls* in like twelve years. I just don't go. There's nothing I need to see about it, whereas I go see *photograph* every once in a while, I go see *Spell* sometimes, I see *Boogie-Woogie* sometimes. We still haven't gotten the rights to *Mother Courage* so I can't go see that. What else did I do? I'm going to go see *The Love Space Demands* in Chicago. I did that at Crossroads in New Brunswick, New Jersey, at the Painted Bride in Philadelphia, and at the Talawa Theatre in London, and it's time for me to let that go. I've done three whole shows of it.

Interviewer: What's the name of it?

Shange: *The Love Space Demands.* It's the piece we did at Crossroads a year and a half ago and I did it in London a year ago.

Interviewer: Are any of these more conventional plays than *for colored girls*?

Shange: No.

Interviewer: Are they done the same way, disparate pieces of all different kinds of writing?

Shange: What kinds do you mean?

Interviewer: Is there poetry or long narrative pieces?

Shange: There is a mixture of both. Everything except *Love Space* has characters with names who have real things they do in the real world; they don't just exist in my unconscious world. They're really real people. As a matter of fact, they turn out to be Negro performers.

Interviewer: Well, what did you write after *colored girls*? What was the next big thing that you produced for the theatre?

Shange: The next thing was *photograph*.

Interviewer: Can you describe for me the process by which you came to do that play?

Shange: When *for colored girls* had been up for about a year, I had a collection of poetry called *nappy edges* that hadn't come out yet. I was getting ready for galleys, and Joe Papp asked me what I wanted to do next, and I didn't know. I was going over the manuscript to get this thing ready for my editor, and I found a poem that I had written when I was in California that had had a very powerful effect on me. I had felt my hands starting to tremble and I thought I was levitating when I finished it.

Interviewer: What poem was it?

Shange: It's a poem called "cross oceans into my heart," and the first line is "all I need to know is his name is James or Jim shortened," and the last lines are "he is all my insanity anyone who loves me will understand." That became the female protagonist in *photograph*'s key monologue; so that's exactly how that happened. There were beautiful dance segments in *photograph* and a beautiful photographic montage. David Murray wrote the music for it. Even though that was a story that was episodic, it did have a plot. It had only five characters, who really did have to do what people really do when they are friends or lovers. It still was a little bit eccentric. Two things happened that I thought really funny. The black people in *photograph* are very bright and fairly worldly, and one of the critics in New York (I know it was a white male critic) said that these people couldn't even exist. I thought that was nice. You see, this is why I write poetry. When I write poetry, people don't tell me we aren't alive.

Interviewer: In other words, if it comes out of your own consciousness as a poem, people tend to accept the character; but if you put the character onstage, and say this is so, then white critics are more likely to question whether a black character exists?

Shange: Yes. "How did this happen? Where'd they come from?" And the other thing that somebody else said, which actually is sort of good, is that some of the scene changes came so quickly that in some ways it reminded him of soap opera. In a way that makes perfectly good sense, because I not only like soap operas but I also like the ideas of serials, of serial novels and novellas and things, and I like television. That one little thing, which I'm sure was meant to be a snide remark, let me open myself to go ahead and write for television. I said, "Why wouldn't I want to reach thirty million people instead of 175 in one night?"

Interviewer: Have you written for television?

Shange: I wrote something for Diana Ross, and we were nominated for an Emmy for that. That was a long, long time ago. Then I stopped and I didn't do that anymore because the television business was too brash for me, but now I think I've found a way to accommodate the hard elements of the industry that I didn't have before.

Interviewer: Is it a harder industry than Broadway to negotiate? Is it less or more respectful of you as a playwright, as a black woman?

Shange: I've been pretty protected by the directors I've been working with. If they did say, "This has to go" or "We can't use it," I didn't hear it. I just get suggestions about what we could change. I don't know if it's worse or less. I think in a way, because the Broadway community is so small, rejection or criticisms may be harder to take than in Los Angeles where you just assume they're going to throw the first draft out, whereas they wouldn't ever do that in New York. When they're talking to you in New York they're not ever going to throw the whole first act out; but when they do do something it probably hurts a lot more. On the other hand, I've estimated that it takes me a year to a year and a half to get a piece ready for the stage. That means to open for the critics, and that would include a couple of workshops, maybe, and some readings and rewrites and meet-ings with people and all that kind of thing—with no money transferring hands at all, maybe transportation money or something. Yet when we get a deal for television, we have to get an hour's worth of TV which is like sixty to seventy pages or half of somebody's play, right? You have to get that, and you just do it as quickly as you can, and it might go up in three months. We've never heard it, we've never watched people read it or anything, before all this is decided; so it's a very different process.

Interviewer: When you say "go up," does that mean actually appear on TV?

Shange: Go into production.

Interviewer: What's the difference with the money?

Shange: Oh, it's like a thousand percent more. I just directed a play at Ubu Repertory Theater—I was gone out of my house for three weeks—for a thousand dollars, and that's the going rate for off-Broadway directors. I lost money in those three weeks, but I would never have given it up. It makes me feel sort of stupid. I feel, "Why bother to do this? My child has to go to the dentist, too."

Interviewer: Why do you keep doing it?

Shange: Because, as I was telling somebody last night, it's what I do best. I've OD'ed myself on teaching, so I have to move in and out of these things that I can do, because when I burn myself out of one genre I have to go to the next one. I was working on TV and musical stuff all summer, and I wanted to go do a small, intense, emotional play. I needed to do it.

Interviewer: Is that what you just came back from doing? What is it?

Shange: It was called *Fire's Daughters* by Ina Césaire, Aimé Césaire's daughter.

Interviewer: You were the director. You've always done acting and playwriting and directing, but is this different now, your directing other people's plays?

Shange: I did Richard Wesley's *Mighty Gents* for the Mobile Unit for Joe Papp one summer, and I directed a piece by June Jordan. I trust myself more with other people's things than I do with mine. I still think that if I'm performing in the thing as well as having written it, that's all the hats I need to wear. If I'm not performing in a piece of mine I can direct it; but if I am performing in a piece of mine I cannot, because as an actress I get too involved with who I'm supposed to be onstage and I can't switch back out.

Interviewer: Are you working on any plays now of your own?

Shange: The novel I'm working on called "Resurrection of a Daughter" has three different kinds of writing in it. There are narrative chapters in the voices of many characters, there are dialogue scenes (including psychotherapy sessions), and there are poems. I'm listening now to see if any of those sections work by themselves, to see if I should just do a night of monologues all about the same person, or if I should do the monologues and the dialogue things, or can I put the poems with anybody. I'm experimenting to see what's stageworthy. I know they're stage-possible because the monologues are all from first person, and the only problem with the shrink sessions is that there is no action. If I could figure out how to get some action in those sessions, then I can probably just do a whole night of them—I've got ninety pages of it. So I'm going to be doing that at the Freedom Theatre here in Philadelphia and also at the Public Theater in New York. I'm going to be doing readings experimenting with the text as I have it.

Interviewer: How do you know when it's stage-ready and stageworthy?

Shange: When I get excited and get upset or when I start crying. I'm still always moving toward "We're going to start out very nice and you're going to feel very comfortable. The audience is going to trust me; they know they are going to have a really nice time because these are all such pretty things we're talking about and this is really nice." They relax, and they relax a little more, and then once they're relaxed like that, then we can go into the depths of hell—and they can't get out because they're relaxed already!

Interviewer: Where do you want to take them?

Shange: I want to take them to a place where they know that they have survived their own vulnerability and somebody else's. I think every time I can do that in America I help stop somebody from being shot, because this is a place of people just "frontin'" all the time. Hopefully, when they come see something I've written, that will have to go away. It might go away and it might get more belligerent but, see, then they'll stand out as being like really weird! Because they can't relax and just see how much this hurts whoever that was on the stage.

Interviewer: When you imagine a play like this, do you also imagine certain actors in it, or are there people that you would like to see in this new play that you are working on?

Shange: I'd like to work with all the women from *Fire's Daughters;* I'd like to see them in the new play. I have written specifically thinking about Laurie Carlos, and I've written specifically thinking about Avery Brooks, in terms of what qualities of actors that I want.

Interviewer: Who else?

Shange: I'm not really good with actors. If you asked me about musicians I've worked with, I could tell you.

Interviewer: Part of the reason I'm asking you is I think that black actors' names don't get out into the public very much.

Shange: Okay, then I should tell you the names of these women that I worked with just now. Harriet Foy, Darlene Bel Johnson, Ceecee Harshawn, and Alene Dawson. But I have difficulty with actors. By the time I let actors have anything, I've already played the part I wanted. I've done what I wanted to do with it, so I'm not feeling begrudging about that. I just have difficulty with actors, because I never know when they're not acting, and I never know when they don't want something from me. They can't go to work if people like me don't write things. That's why I enjoy the poets' conventions I go to so much more, because when we finish reading we're really finished; we go and have a nice time. At the theatre conventions, the actors are working every hour of the day, because they want to make sure that if we get something we think of them. I can't imagine trying to be a black actor in New York—or anywhere for that matter.

Interviewer: Is it worse than being a black playwright?

Shange: I think the hurtfulness of it is, yeah. Because they really need a production to go up, whereas a playwright can work at the post office and stack the stuff in the corner but you still have the experience of writing it and completing it. As an actor, if they don't get onstage, they can't feel themselves accomplishing anything. That's why I really try to let them explore and find what they can find in the text and not do a line-by-line directorial activity with them. They're sentient creatures!

Interviewer: As I listen to you, the thing I don't hear is you talking about the same bad experiences with any of these industries that I would expect somebody like Lorraine Hansberry or Alice Childress to talk about. I'm not trying to put this in your mouth, but I'm just saying I don't hear that. I hear you sounding much more authoritative and in control of what happens to you as a playwright.

Shange: Well, maybe. I can't speak for either one of them. I've taught both Alice and Lorraine's stuff. I think that may have to do with the fact that I've had the opportunity to work with a lot of women in arts administration—and not just white women, but black women as well, and Latin women—and I think at other places I've had producers who weren't strictly commercial producers. Joe Papp and Gordon Davidson are definitely interested in having a show work, and they want to have it make money, but they're also interested in off-beat, sort of wacky or intensely emotional work by people who might not be somebody that the Jujamcyn people want to bring in or somebody that the Shubert people want to bring from London. There used to be a difference between working for nonprofit theatres and working in commercial houses, because we used to be able to have workshops that weren't reviewed and that did run for three weeks with audiences, but that hasn't been true for almost twelve years. That would be the big difference: where you would actually get a chance to see the show, let audiences see it with you, talk about it and fix it up, and then do a whole full production. That never happens anymore.

Interviewer: It doesn't?

Shange: No, at least not in the same theatre. But the one difference between commercial and nonprofit houses is a sensibility of what could possibly go up in this place as opposed to a theatre group that definitely has got to find something that's going to go to Broadway next season.

Interviewer: In other words, a larger, more generous sensibility?

Shange: Yes, absolutely. Which is not to say that there aren't racist jackasses in that world either; there are. But when it gets weird, I just go write a book. That's probably why I don't have a lot of bad things to say, because when I see something getting ready to be funky, I just say, "Okay, well, I'm just going to write a novel for the next year and a half."

Interviewer: I have to ask you about critics, even though I am one, and get some reaction from you about what happens to your work in relationship to the critics, what happens to you as creator in relationship to the critics.

Shange: I have to deal with the fact that, if you get two bad reviews in any city, your show won't run anymore, it won't be picked up, and you might lose all your audiences besides subscriptions. In that sense, critics are very important. The shows can get better, they can have rewrites. All kinds of things can happen in the first two or three weeks of a run, but in cities where you can't afford to have previews (which is most places), your play is made or not made in one or two days, and it might be the first two or three days that the actors got to work in front of people. In that sense, critics are crucial, and they have got to be respected and dealt with on that level. As a writer, I don't pay attention to the newspaper critics so much. I'm more concerned about whether my show is going to stay open; that's all I can concentrate on about them. But you know, I'm a cultural historian, I went to school and learned how to do that, and I teach that; so I try to stay on top of literary criticism, especially of African American and women's writing in the Western Hemisphere. That means I run into myself when I'm picking up a book to read about other people, and I find those to be very helpful—if I don't get too involved with it and just really try to think through what the person is saying. It's helpful sometimes for me to know, number one, that I'm not out here by myself; number two, that I'm not the only person concerned about issues like this; and three, there might be a thematic or ideologic or aesthetic thread that I am following and I didn't know I was following, and I can maybe find out about it through whatever's in this collection of articles. So I read those. I like to read literary criticism, but I don't take very seriously the newspapers—except for the fact that the show either opens or closes.

Interviewer: Were there any good newspaper articles or criticisms on *colored girls*?

Shange: Oh, there were a whole bunch. I was going out with a guy, and I made him read all the papers; he started crying because he was older than me and he said he had never seen reviews like that in his life. That was good enough for me!

Interviewer: Do critics outside of New York—say, in cities like St. Louis or Detroit or Cleveland—have the same power that a New York critic has?

Shange: In that town they do.

Interviewer: In that town, to open or close a play?

Shange: They sure do. Not to close a play necessarily, but certainly to make your box office not worth your producer keeping you there. There are two different functions of a critic there. If Robert Ferris Thompson writes an essay about me, it's not going to shut anything down; it might change my image in history forever, right, but it's not going to close the show that's in New Haven right that minute. There are black people who get great reviews who unfortunately aren't in any so-called theatre history texts, and that's another one of those horrible ironies about being in this business. If I can keep my stamina up and I can keep functioning in these different literary genres that I'm functioning in, I'm not going to disappear. Because we do live in North America, I think there's a great danger of us being obliterated like they almost succeeded in obliterating the WPA art workers.

Interviewer: In a theatre history journal, how should Ntozake Shange be described at this point in her career?

Shange: Oh, as a passionate performer and a steady contributor of prose and poetry concerning survival mechanisms and dreams of people of color at the end of the twentieth century.

Interviewer: And how would you describe her from *colored girls* to now, in terms of any kinds of changes or development of your craft or of your themes or your ideas? Tell me something about that journey from that initial emergence to the present.

Shange: Let me see. I'm still a feminist. I still believe in ritual and magic. I still find being the only black person somewhere terrifying, but I have secured for myself a real sense that I can put together or bring together a group of people who will help me make whatever project I have to do manifest. I think for a little while I didn't always believe that. Because of the venomous environment that surrounded *for colored girls* in the late seventies, I didn't want to work with anybody or talk to anybody about anything, and I've been able to go back to my roots essentially of working in collectives and working in collaborations. I still try really hard not to hire sexist drummers or English chauvinists when I'm working on something, so I do have those barriers or boundaries. When *for colored girls* came out, I hadn't finished the novels and I hadn't written anything else; that was my only baby. Now I have real road marks for myself, and when I look at *Sassafrass,* at *nappy edges,* and at *A Daughter's Geography,* I can remember all the different stages of development of all those pieces. There's not one of those pieces that I haven't done in some way or another on some stage somewhere in the world, and that makes me feel pretty resilient.

Interviewer: What happens to your plays in other countries, outside of North America?

Shange: Oh, it's a big mess. We had a big edition of *for colored girls* in Japan, and it never sold one copy, not one. The press people told me that it couldn't be translated into French, but then they can turn around ten years later and translate *The Color Purple,* which was in Creole and English already. I don't know. *Colored girls* works really well in the English-speaking Caribbean, it works well in Puerto Rico, and in Brazil it's even worked well because just like in New York they didn't think that black Brazilian women could have thoughts like that. That's what the papers said. We continually run up against these racist ideas that make us disappear.

Interviewer: Do you remember what specific things they thought Brazilian women couldn't think?

Shange: Oh, gosh, that was a long time ago. In the four big love poems they thought the language was too sophisticated.

Interviewer: So mounting a play in other countries has these problems, too?

Shange: Yes. Americans exported racism with the Hershey bar.

Interviewer: Do you work on a word processor?

Shange: I have started to, but I also have a really good assistant because I don't like to go back over and check things. I check it when it's been checked.

Interviewer: What other playwrights do you feel a kinship with?

Shange: I feel really close to everybody from Thought Music, Robert Macauley, Jessica Hagedorn, and Laurie Carlos. Anna Deveare Smith I feel close to. I love Alice Childress's things. Then I would probably have to jump to poets and novelists, because that's where I get most of my intellectual and emotional nourishment. I also get enormous nourishment from black female dancers, specifically Mickey Davison and Diane McIntyre, and working with Diane Harvey and Beth Shorter was wonderful. I love to work with dancers; that's what gets me excited. I have a real problem being in an audience. That's one of the reasons I don't go to see a lot of plays. I like to see them in rehearsals. I don't like sitting in a room with all those people, so I have to really like somebody before I go out.

Interviewer: You don't actually like the theatre ambience, then, do you?

Shange: No, I get scared being in a dark room with people I don't know. That comes from being raised in situations where integration was very violent.

Interviewer: But you like workshop situations?

Shange: Oh, yeah, I like being onstage. I'm protected onstage. I just feel nervous in the audience. I'll do almost anything so I can just stand up in the back. My big reason is so I'll be able to get out. Why I need to be able to get out I don't know! I always tell ushers, "I need to get out."

Interviewer: This is what you actually do your writing for—to get other people to come into the situation which you're scared to be in?

Shange: But they want to do that; they want to come in there and do that. I have fits if they don't bring the lights down far enough. When I was doing *Crack Annie* at Crossroads last year, we were setting the light levels, and I almost started crying in the middle of my piece. I just said, "Stop, stop!" I knew it was tech, but I couldn't do it. I said, "These lights have got to come down more, because I can't look at these people when I'm trying to tell them that this man is screwing my daughter." My director Calvin Wilkes said, "Well, Zake, we don't want them to go all the way off," and I said, "If you want me to do this piece, you're going to get them all the way off."

Interviewer: This was a piece that you were acting in, but it was also one that you wrote; so you don't want to look at the audience when you're doing the performance?

Shange: Not certain characters. Some characters I can do it and it doesn't bother me, but for certain characters I can't because they're doing such awful stuff I have to just be talking to black space.

Neil Simon

Photo courtesy of Bill Evans

Neil Simon was born on the Fourth of July in 1927 in the Bronx, New York. After brief military service at the end of World War II, he began his writing career on radio and television in collaboration with his brother Danny. His first play was Come Blow Your Horn *(1961). In the thirty-three years since, his twenty-seven Broadway productions include the plays* Barefoot in the Park *(1963),* The Odd Couple *(1965),* The Star-Spangled Girl *(1966),* Plaza Suite *(1968),* Last of the Red-Hot Lovers *(1969),* The Gingerbread Lady *(1970),* The Prisoner of Second Avenue *(1971),* The Sunshine Boys *(1972),* The Good Doctor *(1973),* God's Favorite *(1974),* California Suite *(1977),* Chapter Two *(1977),* I Ought to Be in Pictures *(1980),* Fools *(1981),* Brighton Beach Memoirs *(1983),* Biloxi Blues *(1985),* Broadway Bound *(1986),* Rumors *(1988),* Lost in Yonkers *(1991),* Jake's Women *(1992), and* Laughter on the 23rd Floor *(1993), and the books for the musicals* Sweet Charity *(1966),* Promises, Promises *(1968),* They're Playing Our Song (1979), *and* The Goodbye Girl (1993). Biloxi Blues *and* Lost in Yonkers *won the Tony Award, and the latter also received the Pulitzer Prize for Drama. Besides adapting several of his plays for the movies, Simon has written the screenplays for* The Out-of-Towners, The Heartbreak Kid, Murder by Death, The Goodbye Girl, The Cheap Detective, Seems Like Old Times, Only When I Laugh, Max Dugan Returns, The Slugger's Wife, *and* The Marrying Man. *This interview took place on May 29, 1992.*

▶ ─────────────────────────────── ◀

Interviewer: What about playwriting, either when you started or now, appeals to you particularly?

Simon: That's a good question. I've never thought about it. From the first day I saw a play or a musical, the theatre was the way I wanted to express myself. When I started writing for myself as a young boy of thirteen, fourteen, or fifteen, I was writing dialogue, I wasn't writing prose. I think that maybe what attracted me to it was the immediate response that you get from an audience. They tell you right away whether they like it or are moved or appreciate the humor in it. I like the idea of it being live as opposed to it being filmed. The idea of being a screenwriter didn't appeal to me from the beginning as it does to most people who are growing up today and who have aspirations to be in the arts.

Interviewer: Since you've been writing plays, have you ever been tempted to do anything else—write a novel or write poetry?

Simon: Certainly not poetry. I couldn't see where I would get more satisfaction than from doing a play, its being so malleable that I could play around with it all the time during rehearsals or readings or whatever. With a novel, it seemed like such a lonely life; there's no one. It's between you and the person that buys the book. They're sitting someplace in Poughkeepsie reading this and you don't know what they think about it unless you get a letter. It's not that I need the approval. I just want to have that byplay between the two of us, that we are communicating in one way or another.

Interviewer: What about the collaborative aspects of theatre? Do you get a lot of satisfaction out of that, or is it a frustration? When the play begins to go into rehearsal and you're working with other people, is that part of the attraction of being a playwright?

Simon: Well, it works both ways. It is attractive when you have a really good director and you have a first-rate cast. Then you say, "I've got the best of everything." But there are days when you're sitting there and you say to yourself, "No, that's not what I meant at all," and you're frustrated. You don't want to say anything yet because you want to give them the time and the space. Sometimes I can jump in and say to the director, "No, that's not really what I wanted," and he will say, "Well, what do you want?" or "Let me try it this way and see." I keep forgetting that they have an overview more than I have because I've been on that play for a year and they may bring something new to it that I hadn't imagined, which is why I don't want to direct my own plays. Then I'm very grateful, but I would say, generally speaking, that when a play opens, 95 percent of what's up there is what I have approved of. With a film, I'm at the mercy of the director, and what comes out on the screen is about 10 percent of what I approved of.

Interviewer: With a play, what's the other 5 percent? Is the other 5 percent stuff you wished weren't there?

Simon: There's only 95 percent in anything in life.

Interviewer: Do you regard the rehearsal period as extremely significant to you as a playwright?

Simon: Yes, but with me it starts even before then. After everybody reads it—the director, the producer, the people that I'm concerned with for their opinion on it—we have a reading either a month or two months prior to rehearsals. So I have heard the play for the first time rather than waiting for that first day to find out that the second act doesn't work at all. If I'm going to find that out, which I have found out many times, I really have a good amount of time to sit down and correct it. With *Brighton Beach,* on the first day of reading, which was six weeks before rehearsal, I cut out a main character and put in another scene between the boy and the mother. That turned out to be the most important scene in the play, but I had the time to think about it and do it. Then, once I go into rehearsal, I have those four weeks. I don't have every minute of those four weeks; I figure I have the first two weeks to keep changing and improving, and then you've got to let the actors' and the director's work start to give it life. Then I go away for a few days and come back, and I'm looking at it much more objectively.

When you get out of town and you start to put it on the stage, the first couple of dress rehearsals look like garbage, and you don't want the curtain ever to go up. Then it goes up and, like the doctor coming out of the lab and giving you the results of your test, you find out all night long what's positive and what's negative. You get to fix that, but you have to be patient there, too, because maybe you got an audience one night that responded a certain way, as opposed to waiting for two, three, or four performances and seeing what regularly grabs the audience or when the coughing starts and they are not really with the play. You can even disregard what they're saying and pay attention to what you feel inside and say, "I don't like that." I'm very open to any changes as long as they make sense, not just to me. You hear it and you say, "Of course, that's a good idea," as opposed to just listening to anybody because you're so anxious to have it turn out to be a good result.

Interviewer: Do you think it's more a question of response because it's comedy?

Simon: Well, it's the easiest response. They laugh or they don't laugh, but sometimes it's the wrong kind of laugh. In *Plaza Suite*, when I did it first with Mike Nichols, they were laughing too much, and Mike and I kept cutting out laughs; but when we cut them out we got laughs in other places where we didn't mean to get them. They wanted to laugh because I had presented a very identifiable situation to them and it made them uncomfortable; sometimes when an audience is uncomfortable, they laugh. They laugh with it, they laugh from their own perspective. They're sitting next to their wife that they've had the same kind of argument with, and they're embarrassed by it, and rather than turn away they'll laugh at it as though it didn't mean them. It means other couples.

Interviewer: Do you sometimes get surprised by where you get laughs?

Simon: Many times I've sat in the back of the theatre with a director, and we'll hear this huge laugh, and we'll turn to each other and shrug our shoulders. There are laughs that I've had in plays that have run two or three years and I still don't know what they're laughing at. That doesn't happen a lot, but there are one or two lines where I say, "I don't get it." At first, I didn't get it in *Biloxi Blues* when the character Wykowski, one of the fellow soldiers who is not Jewish, was having some problems with Eugene and with the other boy, Epstein, and he said in a derogatory way, "It's always the Jews who wind up with the money." It got a big laugh from the audience, and I said, "Why are they laughing at that?" I meant that to be a real swipe, but the character who was saying it was such an obvious bigot you couldn't take him seriously. As he explained it, we're all kikes, wops, japs, niggers; he grew up on the streets, so none of those things were offensive to him and he could just easily say it. When the audience laughed at it, I said, "Are they laughing because they agree all Jews have the money or because of how obvious a bigot he was?" I still don't get it. Why are they laughing?

Interviewer: What about the opposite? Are there scenes where you wanted them to laugh but they didn't laugh?

Simon: Well, I have to examine that too because they may be very touched at that moment. You have to take into consideration what has preceded it; if they are in a frame of mind where they are very moved at what's happened, you could have the funniest line in the world and they're saying, "I don't want to laugh at that." It's as if someone just said to you, "I have terrible news. My mother just died," and I say, "Oh God, I'm so sorry," and you say something funny. They won't hear what's funny. Why you would want to be funny I don't know. It's possible that you might say something funny; but in terms of an audience hearing that, they don't want to have anything to do with it.

Interviewer: So you can be surprised by that in rehearsal or in the reading of a play, where you realize it wasn't the right time for that to happen?

Simon: One of the most tricky things that I ever wrote that came out really right was in *Lost in Yonkers*. The character named Bella, the sort of emotionally arrested girl, is trying to tell her mother and family that she wants to marry this young man who is obviously retarded and she wants to borrow five thousand dollars to open a restaurant. He is obviously illiterate, so it is sad, but there is a certain comical notion about it, and the rest of the family are being so difficult with her; they are standing instead of sitting. The audience is laughing and laughing until Bella says this one thing that just stops it. When her brother Louie asks, "What is this guy after? What more could he want?" she says, "He wants *me*! He wants to marry me." The audience stops laughing because they know that's when to stop. They know what she is going to say is going to be so powerful and poignant that you wouldn't dare laugh at it.

Interviewer: That brings up something else I was going to ask you. What does using comedy enable you to do as a playwright? Herb Gardner has said it gets the audience's attention so he can get the serious stuff across. That scene which you just describe is an example of that, isn't it? We're paying attention to Bella at that moment, so that when she does say something serious, it gets our attention.

Simon: Yes, I would say that would be an answer for me, too, except it sort of denigrates comedy. It's like saying it's just a setup to get to the more important things, and I don't think that's necessarily true. I think that comedy can be just as important as the drama in the play, because when you start puncturing those balloons of pomposity and the audiences laugh at it, you're also making some important points.

Interviewer: You've talked in other interviews about the irony in the humor you use. Would you say that that's the way you look at life and that that's the way the comedy comes through in the plays?

Simon: I think so. I think there is nothing as absurd in the world as life. The most incongruous things happen. I mean, you just watch where this country is going right now and you say, "Well, we're just heading for a crash. Why don't we turn right?" But we're not turning right. Or "Turn left" or whatever; but you see, we're going right into the sea. I'm putting that on a grand scale, but behavior interests me more than anything. I think in any play that I've ever written the people all have options to behave in another way; they don't, and that's what makes it so funny and so poignant. It's people who generally get themselves in all of the problems. There are the few who are going to get hit by the plane that falls out of the sky; some can say that they take that fatalistic approach by saying, "Well, they should've known better than to have been in that spot where the plane was going" or "It was destiny that you were going to get hit." I don't believe in that, but I do believe that 95 percent of the trouble that we do get into is caused by ourselves.

Interviewer: What gets you started on a play? Has that changed over the years? Do you hear something? Do you read something?

Simon: A seed is planted, and when the seed starts to flower a little bit, then you start to see what it's like. You can't start writing based on the seed; you say, "Oh, there's something in there." *Lost in Yonkers* was quite a different play when I first thought of the idea. I wrote twenty pages of it and I said, "It's not going anyplace," and I put it aside and went on to other things. It was starting to germinate and grow, so that the next time when I went back I realized what was wrong. In the first version, the girl was not retarded and the young boy who came to live there was alone, and I said, "Wait a minute. I need him to talk to somebody, so it might as well be two brothers who are in this predicament." Bella was just a spinster. When I made her the emotionally arrested person that she was, it was not for convenience, but it was because the grandmother had done this to them. So you started out thinking what nature had done to these people—or their environment or their background.

Interviewer: What was the germ of the idea that got you started on the play?

Simon: It takes a chain of events to happen. I thought about an uncle that I had never met who apparently was a bookkeeper in a garment business that was owned by some mafia people. One day he disappeared because he obviously knew too much. The character fascinated me; he was obviously not a gangster himself. He was just a bookkeeper, but he disappeared and the family never heard from him again. So I started to write about that; the play I was going to write was called "Louie the Gangster." Louie the Gangster now turned into that uncle who was really a gangster, and I said, "What if a kid was left by his father because the mother died, and he was being brought up in the house where the gangster lived who was corrupting the kid's morals, and the kid finally fought against it? Okay," I said, "there's something in there." But eventually that became only a very small part of the play; he didn't really corrupt the kids, but the brother was really needed there to show again what the grandmother had done to that family. He was the one who pushed and instigated Bella's ability to speak up against the family.

Interviewer: Is that typical of how the plays have started?

Simon: Yes.

Interviewer: Was *The Sunshine Boys* simply suggested by the career of Smith and Dale?

Simon: For years before I wrote *The Sunshine Boys,* I had wanted to write a play about two partners in business. I started three or four different plays about partners in business. They owned something in the garment center, they were in the furniture business; it was a really good idea. They were two partners who were both making equal amounts of money but one was living like a king. He had a great house on the beach, he had a great car; and the other guy had nothing. So after about twenty years he said, "I think this guy is stealing from me." I thought it was a great idea, but it evolved into these two vaudevillians who had nothing to do with money or one being richer than the other. Generally in a lot of my plays, two people are in major confrontation with each other, like in *The Odd Couple* or *Barefoot in the Park* or *The Sunshine Boys.* That's how that play evolved, but you never sit down and think of an idea and start writing it. At least I don't.

Interviewer: And it never ends up where it starts? Has there ever been a play where from start to finish of the writing process it stayed pretty much the same? *The Odd Couple,* for example, was essentially the same play from when it started to where it ended, wasn't it? It was the idea of writing about your brother, who had recently separated from his wife and was sharing an apartment with another man.

Simon: Yes, but I had the wives in it in the first draft. You go through all of these drafts and you don't go all the way through the play. You get to a certain point and you say, "Uh-oh, it just stopped; the light went out. It's going in the wrong way." And I kind of like that. The most dangerous play that I ever wrote was *Rumors,* because all I had in mind was that I wanted to write a farce, and I knew that farces had to be about wealthy people because they're never about poor people in trouble. There are some, of course, but the classic ones, the Molière farces, are primarily about the upper classes. So I pictured ten people or eight people dressed in black ties or gowns, because I knew that by the end of the evening they would be torn to shreds emotionally and physically. I went page by page setting up a situation not knowing where it was going until I got to the last scene. The interesting thing is, you do know where it's going, but it's something in the back of your mind that says, "I don't know what I'm not going to tell you yet, but just keep going and you'll get it."

Interviewer: Do the characters take over the play at certain times?

Simon: Yes, because if you're going to be truthful you can't start putting words in their mouth that you know they wouldn't say just because it's convenient for the plot. The minute something sounds wrong you know you're making it up (even though you know you're making it all up anyway). When that character is so well delineated and drawn so well, they can only say certain things; their minds will only take them to a certain level.

Interviewer: *The Sunshine Boys* is my favorite Simon play. That's why I keep talking about it.

Simon: I loved writing *The Sunshine Boys.* It was a play that allowed me to be outrageously funny but also dramatic at the same time, because these two old codgers were very poignant to me. They were tragic figures in a way, but they were so funny also. They really didn't know after a while whether what they were saying was funny or was from the act, because they talked in life in the same rhythms that they did in the act for forty-five or fifty years.

Interviewer: Wouldn't you say that's the kind of situation that you are always looking for, the kind of situation where you can be both poignant and comic? Isn't that the reason there are so many family plays, because families are by definition almost always both poignant and amusing?

Simon: I suppose so. I'm always looking for a comic idea that has a dramatic subtext to it. If it's just funny, I'm not really interested. I'm starting now to work on a play about when I worked on "Your Show of Shows" with Sid Caesar. There are seven or eight people in the play. They are all writers, and they are all funny in their own way, so I have a license to kill in a way. Eight really funny people could be too much, but underneath it there is some pain there about what's going on in their own lives, in what's going on in the life of the star, and also what's going on in the world. It was during the McCarthy era. One of them is Russian-born and makes jokes about it, but they are scary jokes. As long as I know I have that good solid foundation underneath it, then the humor is the gravy and you're still telling a story.

Interviewer: That's the irony, of course, isn't it—that at the same time it's funny there is something serious going on, and you can never forget either?

Simon: I know. People have told me that they've seen plays of mine in, let's say, dinner theatres and never gotten the subtext because the actors and the directors aren't good enough. As Mike Nichols or Gene Saks would say to the actors, "Okay, we've heard all the jokes on opening day; now we start playing this as a drama." At a dinner theatre they would play it as comedy; that subtext would be gone because they're just looking to get the laughs from the audience. A play can be destroyed, and that's why I would never go to see a play in a dinner theatre.

Interviewer: You never go see your plays in nonprofessional situations, do you?

Simon: No, I don't. I rarely go back to see my own play in the second year of the play when the third cast is playing. It's not fair to them; you may get somebody who's wonderful in it, but I don't have any more interest in the play. It's gone; it's like an ex-lover. She's gone and out of your life and you move on to something else. I don't want to see it again. I don't want to watch my movies, even the good ones. Once in a while I can watch a certain one. I like watching *The Goodbye Girl* a lot; it seems to hold up for me. But I don't even read my plays anymore.

Interviewer: Could you talk a little about the difference between being a playwright when you started and now? It's been thirty years and, obviously, getting the play on is more difficult now.

Simon: It was sheer terror in the beginning, especially with the first play. It was life or death: if the play failed, my career as a playwright was over because I had no money. I had quit television, which was subsidizing me and my family; and if *Come Blow Your Horn* had failed, I would have had to move to California (because all of television was moving to California), work in situation comedies, I guess, and maybe try to get into movies. But it paid enough for me to start to write the next one, which was *Barefoot in the Park. Barefoot* was a huge hit, but still I didn't feel comfortable. I lost all of the rights to *Barefoot* because I had a lawyer who advised me to sell the rights to Paramount Pictures, including the film rights to the next play I wrote, which was *The Odd Couple,* for some capital gains money because they said, "Look, you'll never write another play after this anyway; and, if you did, what chance would there be that it would be a hit? Who's going to write three hits in their life?" So I took the money, and I don't own *Barefoot in the Park* anymore, and I never received a single cent from all of *The Odd Couple* on television for five years! I never saw any of the millions of dollars that went with it; but *The Odd Couple* was even a bigger hit than *Barefoot,* so I said, "Okay, I'm going to stay in this business." But you still don't know when you're going to be secure and be able to make a living. Robert Anderson, who wrote *Tea and Sympathy,* said, "You can make a

killing in the theatre, but you can't make a living in it." I was determined to
stay in the theatre, and I went out and did some films, but I always came
back to the theatre, and I didn't have any flops for a long time. Even *The
Star-Spangled Girl,* which was not a well-received play, got its money
back. *Gingerbread Lady* finally got its money back; so I was making a
living, and then eventually making a killing. Then, when I suddenly felt,
"Okay, I'm secure now. I can do this," then comes the new feeling: "Well,
maybe it's going to start to go away now; you're not going to be able to do it
anymore."

Interviewer: Is that terrifying?

Simon: No, that's not terrifying anymore; there's anger that I still have to
face the *New York Times,* which never gives me a good review. I sort of
count on them; they're very dependable in that way. I don't think I'd put on
something that I thought didn't have some chance or didn't have some
major redeeming qualities; there's no point in doing it.

Interviewer: One thing that differentiates you from most playwrights is
that they depend on the regional theatres to get their plays started, and
many of them depend on the regional theatre even after their plays start—
to revive them and keep them in front of the public. Your plays are pretty
much Broadway plays. You try them out on the road, but once they go to
Broadway, that's it. Of course, they're done subsequently. That puts you in
a very different position from, say, a Wendy Wasserstein or a Herb
Gardner who need Seattle Rep working on their plays. How do you feel
about the repertory theatre system, even though you are really not part of
it?

Simon: I'm not part of it, but I think it's a great system. I love the
repertory theatre. *Jake's Women* would have been gone had I not done it in
a repertory theatre in San Diego—the Old Globe. I saw the faults and the
virtues in the play, and even though I lost money on it (because it was on
the way to Broadway, so the contracts were pre-Broadway contracts), I
believed in the play, and so we just did it again. The play was saved by
those enormous rewrites and by the recasting we did. One of the reasons I
don't go through the repertory route is because I subsidize at least half of
my own plays. I found out early on that people were making a ton of
money on plays like *The Odd Couple.* I was making my royalty, which was
good, but the backers were making more money than I was. I'm not a good
businessman, but I thought the only good investment is one which I could
control, so the plays I felt pretty good about I would put a certain amount
of money into, and the plays I felt really good about I'd put even more
money in. It was not only for me, it was for my family; I really put my
family's money in there, too, but there aren't many playwrights who can
afford to do that. I think Shakespeare did it.

Interviewer: But on a smaller scale.

Simon: Well, the shilling wasn't worth as much then.

Interviewer: There is another question we asked the other playwrights and, again, in your case it doesn't really apply: Is Broadway still your goal? A number of them said no. They didn't care anymore if their play was done on Broadway, if it got good productions at four or five major repertory theatres. Obviously, your aim with all of your plays still is to take it to New York and have it be a big success. Is there a reason for that?

Simon: Well, no. Sometimes I intended not to go that way, but I was sort of pushed. I never wanted *The Good Doctor* to go to Broadway; I thought it was an off-Broadway play. It was an adaptation of Chekhov's short stories, and I knew it was not going to be a big hit. I couldn't see lines around the block waiting to get in to see my adaptation of Chekhov's short stories, although I thought we did a good job with it. It does well in repertory theatres and with amateur companies now. Another play was *God's Favorite*, which was a play that I didn't think would be successful at all but was a play I wanted to write. It was sort of a dark version of the Book of Job and I wrote it shortly after my first wife, Joan, had died. It was a way for me to deal with the absurdity of a beautiful thirty-nine-year-old woman dying; it was a clash between me and God. Again I said, "I don't see the audiences lining up to see this dark comedy," but the producer and other people said, "They're going to like this. It should go on Broadway; you can't do this off-Broadway." I don't know how the critics would have treated me if I'd gone off-Broadway. They might have said, "Oh, he doesn't like this one well enough to do it on Broadway, so we assume it's not good enough," and I didn't want that obstacle, so we did it on Broadway. I don't regret it now, but I think the play maybe might have fared better had we not.

The standards for off-Broadway are different, not less; the quality has to be there, but sometimes you see an off-Broadway play and you say, "This is wonderful but it wouldn't make it on Broadway." *Driving Miss Daisy* is a perfect example, because it was all illusion; they just used chairs and made believe they were driving. On Broadway, they would have said, "Why don't they have the car?" They're spending more money, and they want to see the money spent on the sets. I don't know what that criterion is, but it's worse now than it's ever been. When I first started writing plays, there were many more avant-garde plays that today you would see off-Broadway that you would see on Broadway then because you didn't have to gross a lot to keep it running. You could run for a whole season doing half-a-house, but today it's hit or miss, and if you don't have a blockbuster hit you fail. Many of my earlier plays, with the exception of the really big hits, would not have lasted in today's world. *The Gingerbread Lady*, which was doing half-a-house all the time, ran a full season and won a Tony Award for

Maureen Stapleton. It's a different business now; it's like the movies. When I first went to the movies as a kid you went to the movies and that was it; you didn't care about how well the movie was doing. Now you open up the *New York Times,* and *Basic Instinct* did one hundred million dollars. Who cares? Does the public really care what that picture did? I don't understand it. It's all hype. It's because we have shows like "Entertainment Tonight" and people are just so needy to get show business news, I guess. It's all Cinderella stories: "Oh look, Sylvester Stallone is going to make twelve million dollars!" They resent him for making it, but they think that it's possible, it could happen to them, I suppose.

Interviewer: But it doesn't hurt you as a playwright that you've become a celebrity, does it? And isn't it kind of nice that a playwright can be a celebrity?

Simon: Well, there are very few playwrights that are celebrities, that are well known. Arthur Miller is well known; but unless you are on television a lot you don't become a celebrity—and the only way you become a celebrity in a sense is doing those talk shows.

Interviewer: Doesn't your celebrity status come from your work? It would seem that if playwrights can be celebrities, then somebody values what they do.

Simon: I think there is something special and unique in my story because it is kind of a Cinderella story. There's not a lot of people who really make it big in today's theatre world as a playwright. We have some wonderful playwrights, but they don't write a lot. The story is not that I've done something incredible; I just think that it's my job. I like writing the plays, but it's unusual that a playwright would become a celebrity. The celebrated writers in this country are mostly the novelists like Stephen King or the ones who write those love stories or, in other days, Ernest Hemingway or Scott Fitzgerald. Screenwriters nobody knows; they are just anonymous people.

Interviewer: Do you think, then, that the theatre as an art form is in trouble with the public, or do you think it's in a bad way or a good way in terms of its competition with the other arts?

Simon: I've heard that it's been in trouble for the last twenty years, and it's probably been in trouble for the last two hundred years or two thousand. It's in trouble now because the demands of making it a hit sometimes make one diminish the play to give the audiences something they want instead of being very artful about it. I don't know if that's a conscious effort on the part of the playwright or the producer or the director: let's go for the jugular, let's really make this a hit. One can do that a little bit easier, I think, with musicals because they are purely an entertainment form. A play that will probably win the Tony Award this year, *Dancing at Lughnasa,* I thought was a wonderful play, but it didn't have a long run on Broadway; it's still running, but hardly anybody is going to see it. The Tonys will help them, but I don't think the theatre could support a lot of plays like *Dancing at Lughnasa.* People want something bigger. Numbers are the name of the game now.

Interviewer: Do you think this spring has helped—with all of the serious plays that have opened—or is that just a coincidence?

Simon: What serious plays have opened this year apart from *Dancing at Lughnasa?*

Interviewer: *Death and the Maiden* is running, but that's because it has all those movie stars in it.

Simon: You couldn't get that play put on, not in America, without them. You could in England, but I don't think you could in America. That would be an off-Broadway play in America without those stars.

Interviewer: Talk a little bit about your actual writing process. Do you write every day? Do you work on more than one thing at a time?

Simon: Sometimes I have to work on more than one thing at a time because I get to a certain point with something. Let's say it's a film I'm working on, and I don't know if we're going to be doing the film, so I get sidetracked, and I go back to something I really want to do. I've been working on this play "Laughter on the 23rd Floor," and I was perturbed that I had to stop to go on to do something else. *Lost in Yonkers,* the film, is being made; I have to have meetings and auditions, so I stop working and I lose the run that I'm getting. Following that, we're doing *The Goodbye Girl,* the musical; I've been working on the book for that for a year with the composers. That doesn't mean you work every day for a year, but I took two months to do the first draft, and then I stopped to let them catch up and do the songs. I would go to see them in New York, and then I would get back to the play I'm writing. So I'm doing two or three things at the same time, but my mind is really only on the one thing until I really have to do *The Goodbye Girl.* Then all the attention and focus will go to that.

Interviewer: If you had your druthers, would you be working on one thing, or do you really enjoy working on lots of different things at once?

Simon: Well, if I had my druthers, I'd rather just write the play if it means forgoing doing the other things. I think I can do both, because the play doesn't have to go on next year and I could write it over a period of two or three years. *Brighton Beach* was written over a period of nine years. It didn't get put aside for other projects; I just got stuck on it, which is liable to happen when I get to the second act of "Laughter on the 23rd Floor." I haven't started it yet; I don't even know what's going to happen yet, so it may take me a while to get into it. Also, there's so many things that come at me now, offers to do things that are very promising, that sound like interesting projects or people. A prominent director wants to do a film of *Jake's Women*, and ordinarily I would think that would be a very difficult one to do. I'm not sure I will do it, but I'll have a meeting next week with the director. Because he's such a good director, maybe he can see a way of putting that on film; so I get sidetracked.

Interviewer: Do you consider yourself a kind of workaholic in that you really need to keep working to be happy?

Simon: Well, if you consider any man who goes to work five days a week on a job, doesn't work on the weekends, and doesn't work at nights a workaholic, than I'm a workaholic. I'm not working at night, I don't work on the weekends, I don't work on holidays, and I don't work nine to five. I work four hours a day, but I don't come into this office for any other reason but to work.

Interviewer: How have you changed your writing method over the years since you started writing plays?

Simon: When I started, I didn't know how to find my way. I didn't know how to start the play; I didn't know when I was on the wrong track. I was such a virgin at it that I always needed to go to someone and say, "Is this any good?" After ten or twelve pages, I was showing everybody! No one has seen a page of "Laughter on the 23rd Floor," and I'm finishing the first act. No one saw a page of *Lost in Yonkers* until I finished it; I just went ahead. I'm more reticent to show things to people now anyway, because, even if they love it, they put a responsibility on you: "This is great. What happens in the second act?" "Well, I don't know." I don't want to go through that, so I just show them the whole thing. I've written twenty-seven plays in thirty-one years. When I worked in television, I would do thirty-nine shows a year. Granted that it was with other writers like "Your Show of Shows"— because it was on thirty-nine weeks a year. Those were long seasons. I did that for years; working on "The Bilko Show," we did thirty-nine shows a year; they were half-hour shows, but they were tough. When I quit it all to write plays, I said, "A play a year? That's all I have to do? That sounds like a vacation." It was, comparatively; and even though sometimes they took me years to do and I would do them over and over again, I just kept at them. There have been playwrights that have written as many or more than I have: Tennessee Williams and maybe Sam Shepard—they've written in the twenties. Shakespeare wrote thirty-seven, I think; George Bernard Shaw wrote fifty-some plays. I don't think it's such an enormous output of work; it's just that people will say to you sometimes, "You've made enough money. Why do you keep doing it?" They miss the whole point of it. If Willie Mays could still play ball and hit .320, wouldn't he still be playing, not even for the money? If he could run back and catch the fly ball at fifty-six, he would do it, like in *Damn Yankees.*

Interviewer: Do you get unhappy if you can't work?

Simon: I admit to taking the pad with me on vacation. Lately, I've been trying to do other things when I go on vacations. I'll read more or take crossword puzzles or something to take my mind off of things, but it's hard for me not to do some work. I was going through my stuff the other day with my secretary, and I found on the stationery of Sandy Lane in the Bahamas that I wrote out the entire outline for *The Prisoner of Second Avenue.* I must have done it on the beach. My wife Joan was sitting on the beach reading a book then; and for me it was just as pleasurable to do this. I didn't feel I was working, but I was feeling young then and I had the energy to do it. The rest of the day we played tennis and went swimming.

Interviewer: Would you do that now?

Simon: Possibly, but not as much. If I were alone on the plane going to London for business, I might work; but I'm starting to do it less on airplanes. I'd rather read a book or something. I find I'd rather come back to the office. I am getting older, and I find it tiresome to be working that much. I want to be doing other things.

Interviewer: Is part of the reason for that that now you're more confident when you come in here you will have something to say? Then, if you didn't get it down while you were sitting on the beach, you might have thought that you wouldn't ever get it down. Now you know it will come eventually.

Simon: Yes, I think so. People say, "Why don't you get a word processor?" which I don't have. I have a typewriter over there. And I say, "Why?" And they say, "Well, you could work faster." The last thing that I want to do is work faster. I work fast enough as it is. I want to slow down the writing process so I can think about what I'm doing. I don't want to sit over the typewriter or any machine for hours, because it just ruins your back and your health if you don't get up and walk around. I'll walk around and sit in a chair with a writing pad and just sort of jot down things and write it out. There's the tactile beauty, I think, of coming down here and feeling the pen on the paper.

Interviewer: It's amazing how many writers still talk about that.

Simon: Yes, it's important. I think if you took the brush away from the painter, he would be miserable—even if there were another way to paint. I'm sure there is now, like you throw it at the canvas.

Interviewer: Well, we've got to talk about critics, not because I want to, but because we've talked about it with the other playwrights.

Simon: Now this gets to the R-rated part of the conversation!

Interviewer: You are a playwright whose work survives despite Frank Rich. Is there anything that can be done about the critical situation in this country?

Simon: This is hard to make clear to somebody because it's about negative reviews. I accept negative reviews, which I have received, when I see what they are saying. For example, Walter Kerr wrote of *The Star-Spangled Girl:* "Neil Simon didn't have an idea for a play this year, but he wrote it anyway." That was his first sentence, and I bought it completely. He was right, because I felt the idea I had was not really good. The producer I had at that time kept saying, "It's a wonderful idea." I could always write funny dialogue, and after ten pages he said, "This is wonderful," but I knew that the typewriter felt like each of the keys were ten pounds. I knew what I wrote was not really first-rate stuff. I will take that kind of criticism as productive and say, "Don't do that, Neil. Write something better, reach a little higher." The next play I did was *Plaza Suite* and I felt, "Okay, now I'm doing something worthwhile."

But when I come up against somebody like Frank Rich, who I think is a completely biased critic—a very intelligent man and a very good writer, but biased certainly against me and against other people and very pro other people (other playwrights, other actors, other directors)—for whatever reasons (they don't make any difference), I never learn anything about my plays. He never shows me where I went wrong or what I can do better, whereas Elliot Norton in Boston, when he saw *The Odd Couple* for the first time and I was sort of stuck in the second act, wrote: "Why don't you put those Pigeon sisters in there?" Of course, he was seeing something that was still in the working process as opposed to what Frank Rich sees. I said, "But of course, bring back the Pigeon sisters." That's a light comedy, and you can deal with that differently; but Frank Rich will tear the plays apart from his point of view of life, not "Is this a good play?" Maybe a critic can't write from any other place besides his point of view, but if I have one that is so diametrically opposed to how I see life I get maybe one good review in the last nine or ten plays from him—and almost all of those plays have been successful to one degree or another. John Simon doesn't bother me as much because he works on a rather esoteric magazine. People know reading that that it's not going to send people to the theatre or deter them from going; so I can sometimes learn more from John Simon, who is equally intelligent and sometimes more honest because he doesn't have to worry about the masses that Frank Rich is writing for. I'm as angry with the rave reviews that Frank Rich gives to plays that nobody seems to like—or acting performances or directors or concepts; it's the way he sees the theatre. He would rather that there were no Broadway with the exception of a few musicals; *Guys and Dolls* is fine to do, but when you do theatre you'd better do something really smart.

Interviewer: What makes a good critic?

Simon: A man who comes with a clean slate to the theatre; his mind is not prejudiced one way or the other. One who feels, "I hope I'm going to be entertained tonight, but if I'm not, I'll say so." If I can't predict what the critic is going to say, he's a good critic; but if I know before the show opens what his response will be, he's not a good critic. I can guarantee you, with the next three shows that I write, with the exception of one (I shouldn't say because I'll jinx it), I'll get a bad review from the *New York Times*; so I say he doesn't help me as a critic or he doesn't help me as a playwright, and I want to be helped always as a playwright. I want to say, "Ah, I see what he means. That's what I should be doing." I just have to forget about that, and I go by the ones who I think are intelligent. I'd feel the same way about somebody who was so pro-me that I learned nothing from him. I haven't found that critic yet, but if there was one who just loved everything I did, I'd say, "He doesn't really mean anything, and I can't learn from him."

Walter Kerr was always the guidepost because I guess I batted .500, which is not a bad average for him—fifty-fifty: half he liked and half he didn't like. Some of the ones he liked were some of the ones that none of the audiences liked, like *God's Favorite*. There's a man who's a devoted Catholic, a very religious man, who saw the absurdity of the Book of Job. The new kinds of critics seemingly want to make a name for themselves by being very negative to the establishment. I guess that's an ongoing thing for centuries. The minute that you become establishment you become a target. Sometimes the new gets a better shot at things than the establishment, unless the establishment gets so old and is about to die or about to quit that you have to say, "Hey, the guy's still got something in him"—like when Hemingway wrote *The Old Man and the Sea*.

Interviewer: What about other playwrights? I'm not talking about Shakespeare and Shaw and Chekhov, but I mean your contemporaries. Have you learned from other playwrights?

Simon: No, I can only learn from other plays, because I can't put any consistency on anybody's work including my own. There haven't been a lot of really good plays lately, but I like plays like *The Heidi Chronicles* and *I'm Not Rappaport*. I like August Wilson's plays a lot; probably I like him more consistently than any other contemporary playwright.

Interviewer: Why is that, do you think?

Simon: Well, because they are about a race that I'm not a member of except the human race, and that's the part I identify with. It's the fact that they're black and have a completely different cultural background from me, and it still affects me and I am pulled by it, and I see the honesty of his writing for the most part. Some things I don't always get, but the fact that he is a working playwright, that he turns them out all the time, that he set a goal for himself of writing maybe ten or twelve plays on the growth of black culture in this country, that he's at it all the time, and that the quality is always superior. He's never going to make millions of dollars from his plays because they're not lined up around the block and selling out, but they win prizes. He's won two Pulitzer Prizes, which he deserves.

Interviewer: What about the quality of them as plays appeals to you?

Simon: For one thing, they are both very dramatic and very funny. I haven't seen any of them that weren't funny, and the humor is so rich. In *Fences* I was very moved, and there's wonderful humor in *The Piano Lesson*; it's very touching and moving and terrific drama and a wonderful story. It's like sitting around a campfire and listening to a man tell the story of life.

Interviewer: You've also mentioned Peter Shaffer in earlier interviews.

Simon: I'm a major fan of Peter Shaffer's. One of the reasons I wrote *Rumors* is because he said on a television show, when somebody asked him why he wrote *Black Comedy*, that every playwright wants to write one farce in his lifetime. Here is the man who wrote *Royal Hunt of the Sun* and *Five-Finger Exercise*; you could go down the list of them and, of course, *Amadeus*. I think he's a major playwright. I liked *Lettice and Lovage*; the critics said that it wasn't big enough. I really identified with that because it's a terrific play. I wished I had written that play. It's very English, but he was writing about the decay of our society, the breaking down of, not the status quo, God knows, but of the things that are beautiful in life and fighting out against it. He loves London as I love New York. He sees London decaying, as I see New York and, God knows, Los Angeles (that I don't love that much to begin with) decaying. I think Peter Shaffer is first-rank.

Interviewer: Let me give you a sentence that we gave to other playwrights. "The biggest impediment to a healthy theatre scene today is—"

Simon: No people.

Interviewer: No audiences coming, you mean?

Simon: I don't like questions like that, because I have to answer. It's like saying, "All right, I'll tell you what's wrong with the American theatre." I don't think there is anything wrong with the American theatre. You just show me the play, and I'll tell you what I think is right or wrong about that play. The American theatre is made up of all these different parts—playwrights and actors and everything else.

Interviewer: Do you think if a good play is written, people come to see it?

Simon: Oh, sure. There's August Wilson's plays. They're on Broadway, and they've also had the benefit of touring around the country. He re-writes, he fixes them up, and they have long lives. They'll be playing those plays forever. As long as somebody like him can be around and profit in the American theatre, there's nothing totally wrong with the American the-atre.

Interviewer: Do you picture an audience when you write a play, or is that kind of a destructive thing to do?

Simon: I picture an ideal audience. They don't always show up—some nights they do—but they're the ones who give you a fair shake and can tell you the truth. I don't think a play keeps running if the audience doesn't like it; there's no name big enough to keep an audience coming all the time. For example, with the slams that *Death and the Maiden* got: I know a lot of people want to see those stars, but if that play were directed and acted badly, the people wouldn't be coming. I think there's a lot of quality up on that stage. I do write for an audience. I picture in my mind very tough people sitting there. I don't think that I'm someplace in the San Fernando Valley where they just want to see *Encino Man* or something. I'm thinking of a really sophisticated audience. I tried out my last two plays in Winston-Salem, North Carolina—both *Lost in Yonkers* and *Jake's Women*. With the new play, "Laughter on the 23rd Floor," by the nature of the material—they are twenty-six-, twenty-seven-, twenty-eight-year-old young men sitting in a room—the language is going to be salty, to say the least. I don't think I would go down there, because the last time we went down there a woman said of Helen Shaver in *Jake's Women* that she would've liked it better if her skirt weren't so short.

Interviewer: So you basically, in a sense, visualize a New York audience, which is a tough audience, a sophisticated theatre audience?

Simon: They are tough and sophisticated, but you can give them the corniest musical in the world and they probably will go to that longer than they will go to the sophisticated play.

Interviewer: But, in a way, you have two New York audiences. You have a tourist audience and you have a New York audience. There is a hard core New York audience who have been going to the serious theatre for years, and there are the tourists who are primarily going to the musicals.

Simon: They do seem to stay consistent. The ones that came twenty-five years ago to *Barefoot in the Park* and *The Odd Couple* come now to *Lost in Yonkers* and *Jake's Women*. They're the same people, only their children have grown up and their children are going to the theatre now. They have the same responses. I loved the audiences that came to *The Odd Couple*, but it must have been in the play. It was a very fresh play at that time, that kind of comedy; we didn't have a conventional love story in the play, which was fairly new then. That's the kind of audience I hope I can get, but you get theatre parties, and you need them because you can't exist without them. Half the audience is theatre parties. They come mainly because it's a social event. The men aren't interested in being there. Most of the time they don't know what play is playing or if it's a musical even; so they're not as good as the ones who line up and buy tickets. If you could just get a fresh audience every night who bought tickets because they want to see this play, that's the best audience you can get; and you can get them in New York.

Jean-Claude van Itallie

Photo © Susan Johann

Jean-Claude van Itallie was born in Brussels, Belgium, in 1936 and moved to the United States in 1940. He graduated from Harvard University and studied acting at the Neighborhood Playhouse. He has taught at the Yale School of Drama, Princeton University, the New School for Social Research, New York University, Amherst College, Columbia University, the American Repertory Theatre, Harvard University, and the Naropa Institute. His plays include War *(1963),* The Hunter and the Bird *(1964),* I'm Really Here *(1964),* Almost Like Being *(1965),* The First Fool *(1965),* The Girl and the Soldier *(1965),* Interview *(1965),* TV *(1965),* Motel *(1965),* Where Is de Queen? *(1965),* Thoughts on the Instant of Greeting a Friend on the Street *(1967),* The Serpent *(1968),* Take a Deep Breath *(1968),* Photographs: Mary and Howard *(1969),* Eat Cake *(1971),* Harold *(1973),* The King of the United States *(1972),* Mystery Play *(1973),* Nightwalk *(with Megan Terry and Sam Shepard; 1973)*, A Fable *(1975)*, Rosary *(1975)*, Bag Lady *(1979)*, Naropa *(1982)*, Sunset Freeway *(1983)*, Final Orders *(1983)*, The Tibetan Book of the Dead *(1983)*, Pride *(1985)*, The Traveller *(1987)*, Paradise Ghetto *(1987)*, Struck Dumb *(1989)*, *and* Ancient Boys *(1991)*. *He has also adapted plays by Chekhov* (The Sea Gull *[1973]*; The Cherry Orchard *[1977]*; Three Sisters *[1970]*; Uncle Vanya *[1983]*), *by Euripides* (Medea *[1979]*), *and by Genet* (The Balcony *[1989]*). *His awards include a Rockefeller Grant (1962), a Vernon Rice Award (1967), an Outer Critics Circle Award (1967), an Obie Award (1968), Guggenheim Fellowships (1973, 1980), a Creative Artists Public Service grant (1973), an honorary doctorate from Kent State University (1977), and a National Endowment for the Arts Fellowship (1986). This interview took place on December 27, 1992.*

▶ ━━━━━━━━━━━━━━━━━━━━━━━━━━━━━━━ ◀

Interviewer: Although you've become established, how much of a struggle is it still for you to get a new play produced?

van Itallie: Every birth is a struggle. It's a struggle to write something which is new in form, new in emotional content for me. It's then a struggle to find the appropriate director and the appropriate venue for the first workshop production, and then to move on from there to a larger production and so forth. I believe that's how most playwrights do it these days—start small and move toward a larger production. It's not as if I go to someone and I say, "Here's my script; please hand me a production on a silver platter." That is a child/parent view of the playwright and the producer. I need to be working with a director and producer with whom I am trusting, trustful, and trusted. We are peers, collaborators; we need to work together. There is a way in which I am part director and part producer, and I need to find friends to work with, to advise, to help. And like every venture out into the world, never success without pain.

Interviewer: Is Broadway—or some kind of New York production—still your goal, the final test of a play's viability?

van Itallie: It seems to be necessary to eventually have a New York production. That doesn't mean there might not be a wonderful production somewhere else. It's more congenial and safer to have a production elsewhere before New York. But, yes, it seems necessary to have a New York production. Without New York reviews it's difficult to get the play published even in an acting edition because the publicity of the New York review is a necessary ingredient in the stew of a play's national success. To get more productions around the country and the world, a play needs to pass through New York. I'm not pleased about that, but it's true.

Interviewer: What are the pros and cons of the nonprofit theatre network as a testing ground and developmental laboratory for your work?

van Itallie: As far as I understand what the nonprofit theatre network is, it's completely essential. It's where my friends are, it's where I have always worked, and it is necessary as a breeding ground.

Interviewer: How respectful is Hollywood of playwrights? Why do so many plays suffer in the transfer to the big screen?

van Itallie: If you've had a successful play, you're a hot item in Hollywood; but usually what they are respectful of is your success, not the content or form of what you've written. So you've had a successful play, you go to Hollywood, you are courted, and perhaps if you're lucky and play your cards right you leave Hollywood with some money. Typically, you leave Hollywood with some scars as well. The theatre and film are different media. Video is yet a third medium. The theatre has as its distinguishing positive value the presence of the live actor; film can detail visually. Film is the director's medium, not the writer's. Theatre, one can hope, is still the writer's medium, or the playwright/director/actor's medium. Certainly the writer has greater control in the theatre than she or he does in film. You're bound to be put into a film box when you work for film. If I had my druthers, I would write for the theatre and direct for films.

Interviewer: Who do you write for? When you picture the typical audience member, if you do, who is it?

van Itallie: I've asked myself that question for years. The answer seems to be: I write for friends—friends I know and friends I don't know. In other words, I write for like-hearted people. It's important—that question: "Who do you write for?"—in terms of how the audience feels when they view a play. The audience can sense what the playwright and actors feel about them. If you're condescending to an audience, it will feel condescended to. If you assume the audience to be friends, then they will feel like friends, open to the production.

Interviewer: Why are you a playwright? Why not a poet or a novelist? What about playwriting specifically appeals to you?

van Itallie: I question what I do. I seem to have been writing plays for over a quarter century. That doesn't mean I will never write a novel or that I don't write poems or dance and paint. On emotional ground, to choose to be a playwright is to choose to work alone, and at the same time to choose to work with people. If you're a poet or a novelist, you choose to work alone only. The theatre is a social art, it is collaborative. As a playwright, I choose to work alone, but also I choose to work with others.

Interviewer: What's your opinion of critics? Do you ever learn anything from them?

van Itallie: I learn from them that they are powerful. From reviewers who publish in newspapers and magazines, you learn to respect their power. The system is rigged: You need good reviews to publicize your play. More often than not, the reviewer's allegiance is primarily to the medium for which they write. They are trying to sell more newspapers, make an exciting TV show. So they oversensationalize. They make a play seem more terribly bad or terribly good than it is. They don't simply tell you, "I like this play or I don't." They paint the play in sensational ways so that their viewers or readers will be excited by their review. The playwright, the theatre, and the arts are generally caught and tossed up in this process and don't often get the chance to fight back.

It seems to be socially acceptable for reviewers to take often vicious potshots at playwrights. The playwright usually gets blamed for anything that doesn't work in a production. I think in actuality it's hard for anyone to tell the difference between directing, acting, and writing in a production. I find it difficult. But reviewers do it all the time, picking out who's to blame for what's wrong—and they most often blame the playwright. I'm amazed sometimes at how much blood can be scratched from a playwright's body by a reviewer—and this is socially acceptable. It doesn't seem to be that way in the other arts. But you know that when you enter the arena. You can't be thin-skinned or you can't be a playwright.

You must respect a critic's power to get people to come and see your play. Critics are powerful; to pretend that they're not is doom. On the other hand, do I have to respect their intelligence? No more than the intelligence of other theatregoers. Critics have no special crown of authority. They are not creators, and they don't see from a creative point of view. They are fixed in their roles of people who sit in armchairs at a certain distance from the stage, judge results, and are never part of the process. I think the critic is frequently too removed. Unless a critic happens to be a friend whom I respect, I don't learn more from a critic than I learn from any sympathetic, intelligent, heartful viewer.

Interviewer: How do you feel about the production aspect of theatre? How involved are you in mounting the first production of a new play? Do you see yourself as a collaborator in that process, or in charge of it?

van Itallie: I am as involved as I can be in the first production of a new play. I see myself as a collaborator in that process and, yes, secretly I probably feel in charge of it. I don't believe that playwrights can't be directors, even of their own plays, and I do believe that playwrights learn tremendously from being actors, not necessarily in their own plays. I think there's an overlap in the functions of playwright and director and actor in the theatre. Actors can contribute tremendously, from their intellectual knowledge of the theatre. I think directors need to know what it's like to be an actor and/or a playwright, and a playwright needs to know what it's like to be an actor or a director.

Each new production involves new chemistry. I need to work collaboratively with the director, if I'm not that director myself; and if there is a tremendous disagreement, the director needs to go. I hope to be in a position—along with the producer—to do that. The best thing is, of course, that whatever disagreements come up become creative and bring about new solutions. I do not believe in handing a director a script and then coming on the opening night and seeing what she or he has done with that script. That to me would be like being in the last stages of pregnancy, going to a hospital and being put out, waking up, and finding your baby in your arms. You would've been robbed of the entire process, however painful it is, of giving birth. I believe in natural childbirth for plays as well as babies.

Interviewer: What have you learned from other playwrights—living or dead?

van Itallie: I believe that playwrights inherit a lineage, a family lineage, of great playwrights. We don't suddenly pop into the world as if we had no antecedents. I visualize it as on a Tibetan tanka, the teachers of the central figure lined up on top of her/his head. I see all the great playwrights that I admire sitting on each other's shoulders on top of or in my head. I actually honor and acknowledge each of those antecedent playwrights. For Chekhov, I wrote new English versions, translations. I've created a new text for *Medea,* directed Shakespeare. In an imaginative way, you enter into the process of your antecedents, the masters whom you admire—in my case Shakespeare, Chekhov, Beckett, the Greeks, to name the obvious ones. I learn from them by creating new versions of their work, imaginatively identifying with them, directing their plays. Then they enter my bloodstream. Brecht I've learned from. Pinter, who is alive, I have learned from. I've learned from them by studying their plays, then entering imaginatively into what I believe their process to be. What one learns are not specific adages. Rather one learns to explore one's own mind, those corners of it which were previously illuminated by those great playwrights. We have a larger mental and emotional space from which to work. We have many rooms in the house of our imagination. Finally, of course, it's you that's alive, and they who are alive in you now, today.

Interviewer: Has Artaud influenced your ideas on ritualistic theatre or with regard to your work on *Motel*?

van Itallie: Yes, Artaud was an influence on me. It's hard to know exactly how. Gordon Craig was also an influence on *Motel.* From reading Artaud and about Gordon Craig, I got the idea for those large puppets. The desire to shock was probably stimulated by reading Artaud; the desire for the stage to be someplace wild and savage and fierce came from reading Artaud, and it gave permission (although I may not have known too consciously that this is what I was doing) for the angry elements in me to express themselves theatrically. A door was opened to a demon which turned out to be positive. Onstage, demons are encouraged, especially by Artaud.

Interviewer: Recently, you've been translating plays by Chekhov, Genet, Ionesco, and Euripides. How has translation helped make you a better playwright?

van Itallie: It's not only recently. I've been doing that for a long time. I started working on the Chekhov plays, I guess, in the early seventies. *Medea* was also, I believe, in the seventies. Ionesco may have been in the early eighties, and Genet in the eighties. For a playwright to do a translation is in a sense like an actor performing a part. You become that part, and an aspect of you becomes enriched. Forevermore it's as if you've thrown light into a room of your being that was previously dark. For a playwright to translate is the same thing. You "osmose" something from the writer that you're working on, as well as, of course, bringing something to that writer. If you work on Chekhov, you become aware of how Chekhov expresses reality in a theatrical way. In Chekhov's case, I became aware of how things are funny and poignant at the same time, not necessarily in alternation; and I learned his depth and simplicity. From Shakespeare— not from translating, obviously, but from directing some Shakespeare and from making *The Tempest* into a musical—I learned how to transfer expression from one of the five senses to another. Shakespeare often sees what people usually think they hear, and hears what people touch and so forth. (I could expand on that, but I won't.)

Genet allowed me to be in touch with my daring, with my strength as an outsider, as a gay man; and it confirmed to me that portraying evil is a powerful force within the benevolent context of the theatre. I wrote an essay, "The Healing Power of Theatre," for the program notes of my translation of *The Balcony* (at the American Repertory Theatre, directed by JoAnne Akalaitis), in which I talk about how if you put that which is your own nightmare on the stage and that nightmare is recognized as its own by the audience, it is brought into consciousness and healed. In the same way, something brought into consciousness in psychotherapy is healed; you bring the light of consciousness to it (Artaud talks about that, too), but you have to go through the often painful emotional experience of *feeling* what's wrong before that consciousness signifies.

There is a way in which all creativity is translation, including all creativity in the theatre. There is a value in the playwright seeing himself as vessel, seismograph, channel, or medium. Translation is allowing reality to pass through yourself and to express it for the stage. In a sense, creativity is the same thing. You don't make something out of nothing (a really scary Western concept of creativity). Rather, you clear yourself as a channel and let flow through you as clearly as possible impulses you feel arising from the earth beneath your feet. You let it flow through your heart, and through your hands or whatever, to create something. Your effort is not to impose yourself on what you're translating or creating. You want to be careful not to impose ego. Rather, you let the energy pass through you with as much ease as possible. Somehow, in the passing through you, a certain style becomes evident, but there is no effort to create a style. The work is not to impose ego but to let clarity happen. The image is of clear water; you're clarifying the water.

In working on Chekhov, I always worked with the spoken word. I worked with an assistant, to whom I dictated and who would read back to me what I had just let pass through me and spoken as Chekhov. I would look at a "trot" made for me because I don't speak Russian, or I would look at the French, and I would let the essence and rhythm of the idea pass through me as Chekhov. I became an actor. I'd be Chekhov, I'd be a doctor, a charming, humorous, intelligent guy for a moment, and then I would let the idea flow through me. I would say the words, and they would be read back to me, and I would listen to hear if the idea, the rhythm, was clear. Clarity was always my standard. Those are very useful things to be doing when you're writing a play as well. The theatre is about the spoken word, not the written word. I know this better as I work on translations.

Interviewer: What gets you started on a play?

van Itallie: I feel the start of the creative process, the seed, is an image, a visual image. The seed of a play seems to be a visual image which is provocative to me, which has some mystery about it, and which I can turn like a prism or a crystal in the light. That image becomes like a question, but not an intellectual question. It's an image which comes from a dream and remains with me in my conscious day. The questionings of that image are the beginnings of the play.

Interviewer: What led up to *War*, your first theatrical effort?

van Itallie: What led up to *War* was *Children on the Shore*, a play I wrote when I was first in New York City, a play which was probably my attempt to conform to the desires of establishment theatre and write in a relatively conventional way. *Children on the Shore* is not a bad play, it's just not a very good play. It got me an agent and several very nice rejection letters from producers. This was around '59 or '60, and then I emotionally threw up my hands and wrote "directly from the heart." I wrote *War* and *Motel*;

they were written probably in '61 or '62. At this time I gave myself a directive not to write anything if it didn't excite me on the page. I would only permit myself to write a minute or two a day if that's all I could write with interest, and I was always trying to surprise myself. I had read that Diaghilev had said to Cocteau, "Surprise me."

I read both *War* and *Motel* aloud to my mother and father, probably in '62. They were appalled that I had written plays that were so inaccessible, and they doubtless thought, "Oh my God, what's going to happen to our son? How will he ever earn a living?" They were angry and disturbed. A year later, after my mother's death, on her birthday, December twenty-second, the year that she died (1963), *War* became my first play performed, at the Barr-Albee Playwrights Unit. My father sat in the audience and wept. He asked me afterwards, "How could you write such an autobiographical play? How could you be so personal and put it on the stage?" So, with hindsight, *War* was a play about me, my father, my brother, and my mother; but I was not conscious of that while I was writing it—which probably gave it strength. I was more conscious of the images I was creating. Ellen Stewart of the Cafe La Mama, my theatrical mother, reminded me not long ago that the creative question is, "What do you want to see up there on the stage? What is visually exciting?"

Interviewer: What are your writing habits? Where do you work? For how long? What time of day? Do you use a word processor? Do you work on only one play or project at a time?

van Itallie: That's a good question, in a sense the most important question. I work at home, wherever home is currently for me. That's usually my farmhouse in Massachusetts; sometimes it's my apartment in New York. I work at my desk. I also sometimes work with actors, which means going back and forth between desk and workshop space. I wish I could say I work five days a week four or five hours a day at the word processor. I'm attempting to establish that discipline. What more often happens is that there will be periods of time when I work little, occasionally jot down notes, and then other times when I'll sit at the word processor six, seven, eight hours a day (which is not healthy, not good for the eyes or back). Ideally I work during the morning and afternoon. It's best to work at a set time. I don't always manage it. The earlier in the day I work, usually the better work I do. I seem to be more alert and awake in the morning.

Do I use a word processor? Yes, but not exclusively. What I do not use is a typewriter. I'm so glad I live in an era when the typewriter is gone from my life. The typewriter is a product of the Industrial Revolution. You write along a horizontal line, and then it's as if you drop off the end of a cliff; you have to move back, and that makes you think in horizontal lines. As Marshall McLuhan pointed out, people who work in factories begin to think in terms of putting the right-shaped object into the right-shaped hole. One thinks rectangularly with a typewriter. I think there's a lot of blank-paper fear about filling in those horizontal lines. It's a masculine, patriarchal way of thinking that the typewriter encourages, and I'm glad it's gone. The word processor, on the other hand, seems more circular, more feminine. You don't have to worry about the end of the line. It seems to be closer to the way the mind works. I love that I can lift a section from here and put it there. On the other hand, the danger of a word processor is that it is in a sense too easy, by which I mean it can be too mental. It seems to facilitate principally the head, and not so much the gut and the heart. There need to be rest breaks. One has to remember one is a physical being, to breathe.

Last summer I worked *not* at the word processor for two projects. I dictated into a tape machine and had the words transcribed. I'm editing on the word processor. Editing is a good thing to do on a word processor, because the word processor encourages obsessive polishing and changing, mental tasks. Being able to dictate is wonderful because you can be walking along a country road, as I do, paying attention to your breathing, to your physical body. Writers need to remember that writing is a physical act. You can't do it without a physical body. You need to breathe while you're writing, while you're thinking. The rhythm of your breathing, how you hold your body and what shape your body is in, matters to your writing. We are not simply cut-off heads. Do I work at only one play at a time? No. Perhaps I should, but I don't. One project at a time? No. I'm a Gemini.

Interviewer: How much of a play do you know when you're writing it—the end, a general outline of where it's going?

van Itallie: That's a good question, and it strikes fear into me. I feel I should know more about it than I do. It depends on the length of the play. I have a tendency to plunge in without knowing too much, which makes me write effective short plays. I think that a play is in a sense like a dream, it has the shape of a dream; you rarely know the end when you are at the beginning. I was relieved to discover that Chekhov did a lot of cutting and pasting. But I sometimes feel guilty about too much cutting and pasting and feel I should know more than I do about the end when I'm still at the beginning. But sometimes I feel imprisoned by what I've predecided, and I need to change it.

What I do know is that the planning and critical processes are left or logical brain processes, and that the writing part is a more right or creative brain process. You need both in writing a play: you need to plan, and you also need to let go and write within that plan. Later you go back to using your left brain and criticize, see what works and what doesn't work or change your plan. What you do at your peril, and usually paralysis, is to try to use both sides of the brain at the same time. I find I can't be critic/planner at the same time as creator. That doesn't work. It doesn't work to use right and left brain at the same moment. It encourages paralysis; the judge becomes too powerful during creativity.

Interviewer: Who reads your play before it goes into rehearsal, or while you're writing it?

van Itallie: I read my play before it goes into rehearsal and while I'm writing it. One excellent way to edit is to read aloud what I've written. I do that as early in the process as possible. As I've said, the theatre is for the spoken, not the written, word. Sometime early in the process I speak aloud what I'm writing. Sometimes I actually start by speaking it aloud into a tape recorder. If I'm writing at the word processor, I read what I've written aloud as soon as possible. What it sounds like tells me if it works or doesn't work. When I've written a scene, I read it aloud to myself. The parts that I enjoy reading, I know are good. When I find myself speeding through something to get to another part, that's a sure sign it needs changing or cutting. The next step is to read to sympathetic friends. You learn by doing that, because you are a performer when you read, and if you find yourself reading something you don't enjoy reading, are speeding through, and are bored by—cut it. If you find something that you really love reading, usually you'll get a very positive response from friends.

Interviewer: In writing a play, do your characters ever take over, or are you always in control?

van Itallie: Ideally, you're working on the boundary between your control and theirs. If you've built them carefully, sympathetically, and imaginatively enough, the characters will take control—whatever taking control means. As I said earlier, I think a good way to view oneself as a playwright is as a seismograph, as a vessel, a channel, or a medium; the characters speak through you. I think that's an excellent way to think of it. It tends to make good work.

Interviewer: How much rewriting do you do—before and during rehearsals?

van Itallie: I do a lot of rewriting. When I'm first writing, I let myself go and go. I write more than I finally use. A lot of my work is to cut from the large amount of writing that I've done. I'm relieved to get into rehearsal because then I can hear the words coming out of actors' mouths and can rewrite for them. I like the experience of writing with and for actors. I like to be like a tailor cutting cloth to order. Sometimes I cut, sometimes I add. I enjoy that process, even after the play is up. I rewrite and repolish for the published edition. I stop when the play gets published, although I do change it again sometimes for later editions. A play is never completely finished; it's never engraved in stone. We know Shakespeare's plays aren't, and neither are mine.

Interviewer: I understand that you plan to rewrite *TV.* If so, why?

van Itallie: Stephanie Sills, the original producer of *America Hurrah,* suggested rewriting *TV.* I'm delighted to have *America Hurrah* revived. The producer feels that *Motel* and *Interview* work as they are but that *TV* is dated. There was a recent production of *TV* all by itself in Rome, and it worked quite well. I translated the reviews for Stephanie but didn't convince her. There is a quality of *TV* being dated, but that brings up the question of can I rewrite the play or a part of the play and still call it *America Hurrah?* What I'm doing now is to work on what is the effect of TV in our lives, with a group of actors called the Working Playground, attempting to write a new play on TV and leave the old one alone, or use elements of the old one and write a new one. The form is not dated, and the relevance of TV in our lives is not dated—just a bit of the content. TV has grown enormously in importance in our lives in the last twenty-five years. I'm learning about why I'm rewriting *TV* as I rewrite it; I don't know what the final result will be.

Interviewer: Do you write with specific actors or actresses in mind? And what is your general opinion of actors?

van Itallie: Sometimes I write with performers in mind. It's a pleasure to do that. I think that acting is a high art. Actors who are conscious of what they are doing are spiritually, emotionally, and physically aware at the same time. Their presence on the stage is an act of consciousness. Maybe the highest calling is to be a stand-up comic, or an actor. I regret I didn't, at an earlier time in my life, work through my fears and be on the stage. I am working on it now. I couldn't respect actors more; I detest the idea of actors as stupid bodies to be pushed around as much as I detest the idea of writers and directors as cut-off heads and hands only good at thinking and manipulating. We are all persons of the theatre. I have a holistic view of the theatre and of us who work in it.

Interviewer: Which of the plays that you have written are you most fond of, and why do you feel more comfortable with those plays?

van Itallie: I don't know that I have favorite children. I don't know. It's a whimsical question. I'm attached to the early plays. I'm attached to *War,* and yet I reread it recently and I don't think the dialogue is very good—but the shape of the play is really good, and the images are good. I'm attached to certain speeches in early plays. I like the Queen's speech in *Where Is de*

Queen? and like to read it aloud. I love reading my work aloud. I love reading anything aloud. I'm really a performer, and if I can read aloud it's fun. I am, of course, fond of the plays that have brought money. I'm fond of the successful plays. I'm fond of those plays which have gone out into the world and have their own lives, just as children go out into the world and have their lives. I'm glad when someone tells me that they've had a good experience performing in a play of mine or seeing a play of mine. That's wonderful. But I'm most involved with the play that I'm writing now, always.

Interviewer: You have experimented with form extensively in your career. The forms of your plays range from Theatre of Cruelty to realism. Do you feel that this search for form and structure has improved your writing?

van Itallie: The search for form and structure *is* my writing. Each new play is a necessary reinvention of form. That's the way I write. The categories Theatre of Cruelty and realism are critical categories, not creative ones. One can look at theatre from the point of view of critic, and one can look at theatre from the point of view of creator, and I prefer creator. It's usually not useful for me to be critic. I'm trying to fall into it now in order to answer your question. There's always a questioning in everything that I write. Questioning is part of the process—even when the play is finally up on the stage. If you think you're giving the audience answers, you're usually being patronizing. Each new form, new play, is a different language. I believe in knowing as many literal and figurative languages as possible. If you're raised in more than one literal language, you're lucky because then you realize that reality is not contained in any single language. In a sense, when you're inventing a new form for a play, a new play, you've invented a new language.

Interviewer: What terrifies you?

van Itallie: Oh Lord. At different moments, different things. Death. Old age. An opening night. Dancing onstage in a bikini in front of three hundred people. I did that a couple of years ago in a dance piece by my friend Nancy Spanier, and it wasn't so terrifying. The stage fright beforehand was terrifying. In moments, I can be overwhelmed by anxiety; at other moments when I'm centered, I am relatively fearless or able to transform fear into other energy.

Interviewer: Although you've spent considerable time with form and structure, your plays also explore important social issues, such as homelessness, nuclear proliferation, the hypocrisy of the medical profession, and the influence of the media on our lives. Do you see some of your plays as significant social statements about contemporary society?

van Itallie: To answer the last question first, yes, I do see my plays as statements about contemporary society. But implied in this question is a duality between the form of a play on the one hand and the social content on the other. I believe *Motel* is a political play and also an adventurous foray into theatrical form. A play ideally should be political, personal, and innovative in theatrical form all at once. That's important to me. Form and content are not separate. I don't approach them separately. They connect on a deep dream level. Which brings us back to Artaud. In the first chapter of Artaud's *The Theatre and Its Double*, the Viceroy of Sardinia has a dream. He dreams in depth that he's suffering from the plague. He really suffers horribly, but he doesn't know that it's the plague. Then he wakes up, and somehow he has the knowledge to forbid a distressed ship from landing in Sardinia. Later we learn the ship carried the plague to Marseilles. The question is, what is the nature of the communication between the ship and the Viceroy? I ask my classes this.

Plays are like dreams, but not dreams in an airy, ethereal way. Plays are the dreams of society. Dreams are knowledge which needs to be brought into consciousness, exorcised. I think important political knowledge is personal. If something is personal to a writer, it is usually personal to members of an audience. It's curious: if you set out to write something political which will be generally acceptable, it's usually not interesting; but if you write something uniquely personal (not self-indulgent), it's usually meaningful to others and political. Look at Brecht, *The Good Woman of Setzuan*. Look at plays like that, which are original in form and yet simultaneously are important in their political implications. Political and personal at a deep level are not separable.

Interviewer: How has Buddhism influenced the content of several of your recent plays?

van Itallie: From the creator's point of view, although you plan with one part of your brain and fulfill with another, nonetheless, form and content are inseparable. *Struck Dumb* is a very Buddhist play; so is *Bag Lady*. In Zen koans, questions asked students are meant to be answered not literally, but to shake the mind of its habits. The best answer to a Zen koan might be laughter from a deep place: knowledge of being has been transmitted on a wordless level. Perhaps Buddhism has taught me that words are the important tip of an iceberg of feeling, that words are the top of something deep and wordless, so you must respect and leave space for that. It may be that Buddhism has taught me the importance of leaving space around words.

You've asked me how Buddhism has influenced content, and I'm answering how Buddhism has influenced form. I hope that I never preach, Buddhism or anything else, in my plays. The theatre doesn't work as a pulpit. Obviously, *The Tibetan Book of the Dead* deals with Buddhist texts, is an expression of human experience seen through the eyes of Buddhist masters. It talks about the moments before and after death. I was careful in that to use language available to the audience. I don't use Sanskrit or Tibetan words. I don't think I even use the word "Buddha" in it. If a play is not present to its present audience, it's not present at all. In translating Tibetan texts for the stage, as in translating Chekhov, you want to make sure the content comes through as clearly as possible. The text must be neither as obscure and creaking as a museum piece, nor clunkingly contemporary.

Interviewer: What have you been working on during the past two years, and what are your future playwriting plans?

van Itallie: The moment somebody asks me what it is I'm working on, I think I'm not working on anything. I'm working on a new short play, a playwriting textbook; I'm working on memoirs of off-off Broadway, which is becoming a larger type of memoir book—so I'm working on two books. I'm working on rewriting *TV*; I'm working on a production of Bulgakov's *Master and Margarita* in New York; and I continue to teach.

Interviewer: During the past thirty years, you have witnessed the evolution of American drama. What trends do you see occurring in contemporary American theatre? How would you appraise the current status of American theatre?

van Itallie: To place myself in the critical position is uncomfortable, because it's not where creators are at their best. There are cycles. Just as Artaud was reacting against the too great mannerism in plays, and felt that that had to be broken out of in his time, so then what he had taught was to some degree absorbed into mainstream theatre. By the time we came around in the early sixties, something had to be again broken. Then some of what we learned in the sixties became evident on Broadway: *Chorus Line*, which was in part based on my play *Interview* in terms of form, and *Hair*, which was written by Jerry Ragni, who was in my first play *War* and who was at the Open Theatre. *Hair* took a lot of the stuff that we were all working on at the Open Theatre and popularized it. I was moved when I saw on television recently that, during the bombing of Sarajevo by the Serbians, people risked their lives to go and see a lunchtime production of *Hair*. Then the cycle comes full circle, and it's time again to break form and to create new form from the shards.

If you're lucky you're at the right place at the right time for the creation of the new forms. In the sixties we were in the right place at the right time, and I feel fortunate about that. One always has to look out for when some previously new impulse becomes stultified and stylized. Some of the stuff that Bob Wilson was doing twenty-five years ago came right after the Open Theatre work. Bob had his first job in the theatre making the dolls for *Motel,* and I was in one of his plays as an actor. Bob's work, which was so original in terms of stretching space and time in the early days, has now become visually perfect, but to me not as interesting as his early work, because it is mostly cerebral. The theatre needs to appeal to all the chakras—your gut chakra, your sexual chakra, your heart chakra, your throat communicative chakra, and also to your mind and your eye—but not *only* to the mind and the eye. Something which has no heart in it is as uninteresting to me as something that's purely corn and sentimentality. I hope that a minimalist, visual, heartless, bloodless theatre which started in the avant-garde has reached the end of its cycle. I'm hoping that we break through that.

Theatre is the most social of arts, so it is impossible to notice where theatre is at without noticing where the society is at. It's interesting that solo performance is a viable and reverberant form these days. I taught a class this fall in solo performance at Playwrights Horizons. I've been teaching actor-writers how to make plays out of their own material. I'm moved to do that myself. It seems appropriate today to dig deep inside oneself, to express what is politically relevant. There's a gay play called *The Night Larry Kramer Kissed Me* which is a good example of that. It's not a great play, but it comes from inside somebody and has a lot of political reverberation in the world. As it seems more difficult for people to communicate with each other, maybe the rise of the solo performer means you can't be communicating with other people unless you know who you are yourself. Solo performance seems a rich process, a regeneration of self, and a validation of one's anger, one's fear, one's personal experiences. You need to know yourself first before you can communicate with others. The individual explorer of inner space seems to be a strong suit in the theatre at this moment.

The integration of the arts is an important thing that's happening. I'm not much interested in any play now that's not very rhythmical and doesn't have some music in it. This time, the end of this century, if it's about anything good at all, is about breaking through categories of thinking that we used to have. The separation of theatre and dance and music is breaking down. Those are no longer singular compartments. Those are areas which overlap. Ideas about separate body and mind are also breaking down, as are some differences between actor, writer, and director. People can act, write, and direct their own piece. The only factors that keep these things in separate compartments are the way that we think. It doesn't make the critic's job any easier—or the academician's, or anybody who's trying to categorize anything—but it's great for creativity, and I think it's great for human beings, that these categories are overlapping. Science and art are overlapping, physics and metaphysics. The physicists are exploring deeper and deeper into smaller and smaller places, and there they are discovering God, and they are naming things "joy" and "truth."

So it's an exciting time if one goes with the flow, which is, after all, one's only choice. You can go with time and space and your own mortality, or you can fight it. And you fight it at your peril. To go with it is painful, and it means letting go of ways of thinking, habits of being. We're going toward theatrical events which include many more elements and which are more personal and more individual. I'm not talking about chaotically mixing together a lot of media. I'm talking about organically reaching deep into the human soul and human emotion and coming up with spirituality expressed rhythmically as well as in words, in the music of being. I find myself singing and dancing for pleasure. I've also gotten into painting—calligraphy, to be precise—and that comes directly from the dancing. This overlapping of form, I think, is good.

Wendy Wasserstein

Photo courtesy of Royce Carleton, Inc.

Wendy Wasserstein was born in 1950 in Brooklyn, New York. A graduate of Mount Holyoke College and the Yale School of Drama, she is the author of Any Woman Can't *(1973),* Happy Birthday, Montpelier Pizz-zazz *(1974),* When Dinah Shore Ruled the Earth *(with Christopher Durang; 1975),* Uncommon Women and Others *(1977),* Isn't It Romantic *(1981),* Tender Offer *(1983),* The Man in a Case *(adapted from a Chekhov story; 1986),* Miami *(1986),* The Heidi Chronicles *(1988), and* The Sisters Rosensweig *(1992).* The Heidi Chronicles *received the Pulitzer Prize, the Tony Award, and the New York Drama Critics Award; and* The Sisters Rosensweig *was awarded the Outer Critics Circle Award. She adapted John Cheever's story "The Sorrows of Gin" for the PBS "Great Performances" series. Her book of essays,* Bachelor Girls, *was published in 1990. In 1993 she received the William Inge Award. This interview took place on October 9, 1991.*

Interviewer: If you think back to your home life and your upbringing, what are the things that sort of pulled you to the theatre?

Wasserstein: Gosh, I think a lot of it has to do with my mother, Lola, who's a dancer. I grew up taking dancing classes at the June Taylor School of the Dance. They were the dancers on the old Jackie Gleason Show. I've often said that my two theatrical mentors were June Taylor and Bob Brustein! I grew up with chorus girls, and it was show biz. My parents took me to Broadway matinees. I love theatres; I love being inside theatres. There's a certain calm to me before the storm. I love plays and the immediacy of them. My grandfather wrote Yiddish plays, and my mother sort of has a theatricality to her. People named Lola who dance often do! She's quite a funny woman actually.

It's interesting about people's parents. My dad owned a textile factory; supposedly he invented velveteen. All I remember was was that there was a color called Wendy Blue that was a discontinued line. I remember at Playwrights Horizons people always said that the signature of a Playwrights Horizons play through all those years was sort of bright urban comedies, sometimes Ivy League, and I think actually they're wrong. The signature is, all the flats in those plays are black velveteen from Wasserstein Ribbons! Even Stephen Sondheim or Alfred Uhry, they all had the black velveteen! I remember when I would go down to *The Heidi Chronicles* to check on the play, it reminded me very much of my father going to his factory. We were both in production, and that interested me. I think it's also interesting thinking in terms of who's creative in the world; it broadens your idea of who's creative. I remember when I was in college I always thought I couldn't grow up to be an artist or in the theatre because women in the theatre wore black and had Pre-Raphaelite hair, the silver earrings, the shawl, the cheekbones, and the Fred Braun sandals, and I was never one of those people. I think knowing that about the velveteen and my father sort of changes that a little bit.

Interviewer: Why do you write comedies? Do you think that's just the way you think? Are they comedies?

Wasserstein: I think they are serious plays that are funny. I'm a very unpretentious person, and I can't say that something is right or wrong. Comedy allows you to see either side of the issue, and it also makes it more pleasant to be in the theatre, I think.

Interviewer: You once said that you thought comedy covered up the pain. Is that it?

Wasserstein: Very much so. I think that you can go deeper being funny. I think that we have a limited vocabulary in terms of comedy. A lot of us think that comedy has to be farce, and I don't think that's true. I think that if you're writing character, comedy is humane.

Interviewer: Do you have a lot of pain to cover up?

Wasserstein: Probably. But it's not mine, it's the characters', and I think they do.

Interviewer: In one of the essays in *Bachelor Girls* you said something about your therapist wanting you to think sometimes a little more seriously and to try to come to terms with things rather than covering them up in your life with comedy. Do you feel you're doing that in your plays?

Wasserstein: I think the idea that something that's serious is not funny is ridiculous!

Interviewer: Or something that's funny not being serious either?

Wasserstein: Yes, exactly. If you look at Chris Durang's plays, at the darkness of the vision, that's what makes them funny.

Interviewer: Do you think that the humor in your plays might ever cause people to underestimate what's really going on?

Wasserstein: I thought that with *Isn't It Romantic*, which I thought was a far more commercial idea for a play than *The Heidi Chronicles*. You don't think, "I'm going to write a play about a feminist art historian who becomes sad, and it's going to become *Barefoot in the Park*." *Isn't It Romantic* is more in the shape of a boulevard comedy, but it has serious things in it. A girl says in it, "I make choices based on an idea that doesn't exist anymore," and that's interesting to me. Isn't it Woody Allen who says that if you write comedy you sit at the children's table, and if you write tragedy you sit at the adults' table? There's something sort of flippant and easy about comedy. It's the hardest thing in the world; it's much harder. If you write a play which you think is funny and nobody's laughing—I've had that experience when I've been at previews of my own plays and I'm a lone voice in the wilderness going ha-ha-ha and nobody else is laughing—it is awful. It is truly awful. What's really scary is that, if you're comedically agile and suddenly you believe that you're a serious playwright, sometimes you can lose your comic voice. My favorite playwright is Chekhov, and I'm always taken with the fact that *The Cherry Orchard* is called a comedy.

Interviewer: Has success spoiled you?

Wasserstein: No.

Interviewer: Has it changed you?

Wasserstein: Well, in a sense. I remember, when I won the Pulitzer, Marsha Norman called me up and said, "It's like a rock," and she was right. On days when I beat myself up or look at my new play and think it's not good, it's not this, it's not that, I think, "Just take it easy, Wendy, it's okay." In that way, the success of the previous plays helps.

Interviewer: Has success freed you artistically? Is it easier or harder?

Wasserstein: Every single play that you write comes along with the burden of when you're writing it, what the story is. When I was writing *Isn't It Romantic*, my second play, I talked to people about the burden of a second play. I think every single one has its own little story behind it.

Interviewer: How did you get your first play produced off-Broadway?

Wasserstein: Actually, how my first play got done is very funny. When I got out of Mount Holyoke, I took writing classes at City College with Joseph Heller and Israel Horovitz, and I also had a job at the Board of Education taking inventory. It was a really good job. They sent me from place to place with a measuring stick, but what they didn't realize was that one Steelcase desk has the same measurements as another. Anyway, what happened was, I wrote a play called *Any Woman Can't* in Israel Horovitz's class, which happily none of you will ever see again. It was about a girl from Smith College who comes to New York and makes an unfortunate marriage. My mother, Lola, was walking down the street, and she ran into this woman Louise Roberts, who used to be the receptionist at the June Taylor School of the Dance, and Louise said to Lola, "What's Wendy doing?" Lola started hyperventilating and said, "Wendy, I don't know. She's not a lawyer, she's not married to a lawyer, she's crazy, and she's writing plays. I don't know." I think Louise, really just to calm this woman down, said, "I work at a new dancing school, and it's across the hall from a new theatre called Playwrights Horizons, so why don't you give me Wendy's play and I'll give it to them." And that's how my first play was read in 1973! It's true, and I've been associated with Playwrights ever since. This was even before André came to Playwrights; this is when Bob Moss ran the theatre. That's how that got done.

Then I went to the Yale School of Drama and, with *Uncommon Women*, I sent it out to twelve theatres. My favorite was when it got returned to me postage due from one theatre; that was nice. I sent it back to Playwrights Horizons; they had remembered me, and we did a reading of it, and then I rewrote the play from a one-act to a two-act form and submitted it to the O'Neill, and it was done that following summer at the O'Neill. I think the thing about playwriting is that the theatre world is small and you don't have to know Mike Nichols or whoever to become part of it. Your mother runs into the old receptionist from the June Taylor School of the Dance. I think you don't have to know the artistic director of the theatre; that's not how things really happen. I always advise playwrights that if someone wants to do a reading of your play, let your play be read, because you never know. It's as my mother says, "You never know who you're going to meet." She's right.

Interviewer: Is it more difficult or easier for you to be produced now?

Wasserstein: In some ways if you have been produced and well received, you sit there and you think, "Oh, this poor play, they're going to kill it." You worry about what you're doing next in a way. I think what I'm good at is writing plays; as I said before, I love being inside theatres. I remember when *Heidi* was running I used to come to the theatre quite a bit just to hang out. But I don't know any playwright, really, who just writes plays now. Plays take a long time to write; they take a while to put on. Who knows if you got the right production, who knows if it will get good reviews; there's a lot of things going on. And filmwriting is interesting, television writing is interesting. They're different crafts from playwriting, but still I believe that ideas disseminate from plays. I think talking to different playwrights, you would have different answers about this.

Interviewer: Do you feel that you have less control with films?

Wasserstein: You have much less control, because when you write a movie you are an employee. When you write a play you own it, so whenever *The Heidi Chronicles* is done in perpetuity it is my play with words by Wendy. If you're hired to write a movie, they can hire and fire you thirty-seven times. If I had sold *The Heidi Chronicles* to a movie studio as opposed to independent producers, and they decided they didn't like my script, they would have the right to fire me and take me off the project and say, "Why is this woman an art historian? Why doesn't she become a pilot? *Days of Thunder* did really well; why doesn't she become a race-car driver?"

Interviewer: Do your ideas of the plays ever change on the basis of seeing them done differently?

Wasserstein: Not once it's finished. I think that you become so attached to plays that ultimately you have to withdraw and let them out into the universe.

Interviewer: What terrifies you?

Wasserstein: Not being able to write. Not writing well. Knowing that the writing isn't as good as I want it to be, or thinking that I didn't take good enough care of my play. Or if someday I didn't care about it as much as I know you need to care about it; that would terrify me. Not writing plays would terrify me.

Interviewer: What about your process as a writer? Do you keep a journal; do you work on several scripts concurrently; do you rewrite a lot as you go along, or after you've worked on something?

Wasserstein: My process is an arduous one; I always think I should become more efficient. I don't even work on a word processor. I'm driving a Model T. What I do is write in notebooks. I try not to write in my apartment, because the phone rings all the time, and if the phone wasn't ringing I'd make phone calls or I'd be at the refrigerator. So I go to the library and I write longhand in a college bound notebook, and then what I do is type it up on a typewriter. Revisions take quite a long time, and then I get it out to a typist. Plays tend to take me around nine months to write. I'm not as prolific as I would like to be; I always make mental notes to myself to become more prolific. But they end up with the same notes that say "Exercise more" and all of that stuff; they go to the same place. I'm just finishing a new play, and I had the idea for it in 1987 when I was finishing *The Heidi Chronicles*, but I never got around to it until last January. My plays tend to be semiautobiographical or come out of something that's irking me, and it's got to irk me long enough for me to commit to spend all that time alone writing and turn it into a play.

Interviewer: Once that first draft is there, what happens for you? How do you use the rehearsal process in terms of rewrites?

Wasserstein: The first thing is getting that first draft out of my house and giving it to someone to read, because I'm somebody who could pick at the play endlessly, and no one would ever see it. When I was at the Yale Drama School, they taught us about this woman Hrotsvit of Gandersheim who was supposedly the first woman playwright; she was an eighth-century canonist, and she wrote over seven hundred plays that were never produced. She was called a closet dramatist. I'm someone who could become a closet dramatist, only I wouldn't have seven hundred plays; I'd have five plays that nobody ever saw that were rewritten twenty-seven times. So I have to make the leap of getting it out of my apartment and giving it to someone to read. I'm very lucky because I've had a home at a wonderful theatre called Playwrights Horizons, in New York, and I've worked with the same producer, André Bishop, for a long time now, over ten years or so. Actually, they did my first play in 1973, so it's longer than that. I know I can give the play to André. And I have a very good relationship with Dan Sullivan, who runs the Seattle Rep and directed *The Heidi Chronicles*; I'm going to give my new play to him. It's pretty much getting the play out of the house to somebody to look at.

Then the next thing for me—and this is pretty true for most playwrights—is putting together a reading of the play, getting some actors together and just hearing the play out loud, because plays are written to be heard. I remember the first reading of *The Heidi Chronicles* was in some ways the best that play ever was, because it was when the play was born and it was very exciting to me. But you have to be very careful, because you can't really judge a play by a reading, because nobody has to do anything. I remember a friend of mine, Peter Parnell, wrote a play called *The Rise of Daniel Rocket* in which a character flies, so when you have a reading and you have actors sitting onstage and the stage manager says, "He flies," it sounds great, but basically you have to make this happen. I remember the same thing was true in *The Heidi Chronicles*; there's a scene in front of the Chicago Art Institute and, when I wrote it, it was out in front of the Chicago Art Institute in the rain. That's fine when someone reads this, but I remember Dan Sullivan said to me, "Well, how do you think we are going to do this in an off-Broadway theatre?" I said, "That's your problem." So there's that. You have an initial reading and you get a sense of your play.

I'll give you the history of what I did with *Heidi*. After that reading we did it as a workshop in Seattle with a two-week rehearsal and a three-day production period, and again it was really about the play. It's always been about the text; it's never been about "Boy, if we really fixed this up we can get it to Cher" or "If I fix this up, maybe it's a Broadway baby." That's never occurred to me either. It's always been, let's make this text as good as I can make it, and I want to tell the story; I want to tell it as well as I can. That's really what the workshop period in Seattle was about. And then I had another reading in New York, and then we went into production. My plays get revised quite a bit. I think it's because I don't write from an outline; I just start writing, I just start letting those characters talk, which again may be very different for different playwrights. I know that some playwrights have every scene on a different notecard, and they know exactly where everything's going. I'm in a state of "whoopee"; I just want to see what's going to happen to them.

Interviewer: Would you say, thinking of *The Heidi Chronicles* specifically, that that play changed substantially from that first read-through to the final product as it was seen in New York and around the country?

Wasserstein: That's interesting, because the structure of that play stayed the same. What happened was that a half an hour was cut out of the play; it was just too long. The speech that she gave at the Art Institute, for instance, the speech that she gives to the women's group, used to go on for eight pages; she just went on and on and on until the play became an hour on this woman—but I had a good time writing it. So in that way it changed, but the structure didn't change that much.

Interviewer: I'm wondering what you think about the concept of a female aesthetic and how you might relate to that.

Wasserstein: Boy, it's hard about female aesthetics. I remember when I was at college at Mount Holyoke and we were taking a course—it was the first actual feminism course given at Mount Holyoke—and we were reading about sexual politics and Freud and studying inner space and outer space and all of that stuff, and I just thought, "I hate this." I think that, being a writer who has come of age as a woman, you have had a different language, you have had a different experience. My plays are generally about women talking to each other. The sense of action is perhaps different than if I had come of age as a male playwright. Women are very good talkers. I remember when I first wrote *Uncommon Women*, which is a play about a reunion of Mount Holyoke graduates, I was a student at Yale and we were studying a lot of Jacobean drama. To me, basically, it was men kissing the skulls of women and then dropping dead from the poison, and I thought to myself, "Gee, this is really not familiar to me. It's not within my realm of experience." Simultaneously, there were all these posters for *Deliverance* around New Haven. I thought to myself, "I'd really like to write the flip side of *Deliverance*." I worked backwards and thought, "I want to see an all-female curtain call in the basement of the Yale School of Drama." It came from that. So in a way I do and I don't believe there's a feminine aesthetic.

Interviewer: Is it true that the new play that you are currently working on has a different structure?

Wasserstein: All my plays have episodic structures; they all break down into around eight scenes. For me they're fun to write because basically I know that within ten pages I'm out of this scene—so I'm not stuck there. In some ways you can move the action forward in that way, and also in a way you can make the action and the storytelling elliptical. I'm not that good at storytelling. I remember that, when I was at Yale, Richard Gilman was the playwriting teacher, and we'd bring in our plays, and he'd always say afterwards, "Well, I like the language." I've always thought that if I kept the language bright enough and the comedy bright enough no one could tell nothing's happened! One good way is to keep changing scenes. I'm also somebody who grew up watching a lot of television. It's interesting, because most playwrights are trying to break form and create new forms, but I'm trying to write a traditional living room play because I wanted to see if I could get these people on and off, and it's very hard to do. They have to say, "Oh, excuse me, I think the phone is ringing" or "Oh, I think I'll make some coffee now," and you try to think of the most ingenious ways you can devise for people to say good-bye or hello. At least when you write episodic plays you just cut to the next scene. A lot of my episodic scenes always end in singing and dancing!

Interviewer: There is a real craftsmanship to your language, and that's usually true in comedy.

Wasserstein: What you try to do, especially with comedy, is not write the underneath. If you're going to have somebody say, "I'm so lonely," you're going to punch it right at the moment, maybe at the funniest moment in the play. I always thought the best comic moment in *The Heidi Chronicles* was the saddest—when Heidi brings all of her belongings to the AIDS unit and Peter goes through her books, looks at Janson's history of art and Salvador Dali, and says, "Thank you, we don't have any of these." I always thought that allowed me the possibility to become even sadder, so the precision of that moment would upset me if it wasn't there. Sometimes I do look at playwriting very much like a craft and see myself first as an artist and then as a craftsperson, especially building comedy, I think.

Interviewer: Do you think, since *The Heidi Chronicles* deals with this, that the contemporary woman can have a successful ongoing relationship with a man and a successful and engrossing career simultaneously?

Wasserstein: Sure.

Interviewer: Okay, next question!

Wasserstein: I don't know. I mean it takes one to know one, I guess.

Interviewer: There's a lot of talk about either/or and not wanting it to be either/or, but yet there doesn't seem to be any alternative that shows a positive ongoing relationship between a man and a woman.

Wasserstein: I know that; it's interesting, because I thought about that even writing my new play. I thought, "God, these women are really out there; there's nothing sort of normal going on here!" I think it is possible, but I think you get into trouble when you think there is a paradigm or something for having a happy life. I think different people are able to do different things. Some people are incredibly well-organized, some people are not; some people are very fortunate to have met a wonderful and loving mate, some people are less fortunate. Some people have extremely fulfilling careers; some people don't find that. But I think where you get into trouble is saying, "I must have all of this and if I haven't had all of this I've done badly." That's a mistake, I think.

Interviewer: In regard to the feminist movement (thinking about that wonderful speech that used to be a half an hour and now is shorter in *The Heidi Chronicles*), do you feel that women are standing alone, sort of stranded? Do you feel that feminism is an idea that failed, or is it still with us?

Wasserstein: God, there was a picture in the *New York Times* today of those eight congresswomen walking into the Senate to protest the handling of Anita Hill's accusations, and I found myself very moved by it. There was something about seeing those women together. I think with women, God knows, that it's still a real issue. It's interesting when you deal with younger women and they say, "Oh, are you the *f* word, feminist?" and it's a bad thing to be. I'll go to panels and say that I am, that I can't imagine not being; how could you say, "Oh, I don't believe in the rights of women"? I'll never forget after *The Heidi Chronicles* I went out to dinner with a friend and his girlfriend who was first in her class at Radcliffe. She was a twenty-six-year-old girl who now is at the Columbia Business School. She went out with me and my roommate from Mount Holyoke, who were both forty, and her soon-to-be husband. She said to me, "Well, I loved your play, Wendy. It was so funny and good, but I have one question. What was the problem?" And I sort of thought, "Well, gee, we must have done good work if you don't think there's any problem anymore." But then again, maybe there's a big problem and it's still out there.

Interviewer: The *f* word seems to be one of the most highly charged words in our language these days.

Wasserstein: It's very charged. I know *The Heidi Chronicles* was a controversial play among many feminists. It was a play where some people thought I had sold out, because she had a baby at the end and I was saying that all women must have babies—run out and adopt a Panamanian tonight! I know that this happened, but from my point of view, what's political is that this play exists. What's political is that we can talk about this play that's about us—like it, don't like it; it's there, it exists, and that's the forward motion. When *Uncommon Women* was first done and got better reviews than *The Heidi Chronicles,* it ran for two and a half weeks at the Marymount Theatre in 1978 because commercial producers felt (and this was a play with Glenn Close, Jill Eikenberry, Swoosie Kurtz) an all-women's play could not be commercial. So that's how much things have changed in ten years.

Interviewer: Could you talk a little bit about what Heidi's choice meant to you?

Wasserstein: *The Heidi Chronicles* ends with Heidi adopting a baby alone. In my mind, when I was writing the play, that was always the end of the play. I remember that when I was coming to the end of the play I had called my agent, and she told me that an actress friend of mine had recently adopted a baby, and I thought, "That's right, that's what this is about." I would have changed the ending if it had been done in larger spaces before Broadway, much as August Wilson's plays are done, because I might have ended the play with her lecturing to fill the space, to bookend it. She would have still adopted the baby, but the final image might have been her lecturing. But I didn't have the time to go and do that. I always thought that I wouldn't change her; that was the right choice for Heidi, for her as a person. I know it was quite controversial. I talked at Cornell last year, and these two women art historians I met lit into me for forty-five minutes. Even as I explained it, they just stood there and said, "No, no, you're wrong. No, no." I can see where it would be controversial, and I could even see where me as an audience person, if I hadn't written that play, me as somebody who would identify with that generation in Heidi, could have seen that play and could have said, "Give me a break! Adopt a baby from Panama? No thank you." I could have gotten angry at it too. But as the playwright, and as someone who was logging that journey, to me it was the right journey for her. My new play is romantically uplifting; it's about the possibility of that anyway.

Interviewer: Do you think that because you are a woman playwright people expect you to speak for women in a way that a male playwright doesn't have to deal with?

Wasserstein: Absolutely, and also because I deal with feminist topics. Yes, you're always asked, "Are you a feminist, and how does this affect your work?" It would be nice if someone asked a man, "What are your feelings about women?" I guess they don't have to have them; I don't know. But it really would be an interesting thing to ask, because I'm asked both about men and women. "Why aren't there better men in *The Heidi Chronicles*?" I thought, "Why am I in charge of this? Ask David Mamet."

Interviewer: Do you think it's easier for women to be produced in general?

Wasserstein: I think it's opened up. I've been on a lot of grant commit-tees and stuff, and I think many more plays by women are being produced and many more women are writing plays. I think the atmosphere is much better.

Interviewer: Do you see the audience for plays getting smaller and more refined and more particularized over the years, or do you think theatre is always sort of struggling on the edge but always there?

Wasserstein: I think you always have to look at theatre from the widest possible notion. You have to look at it in America as a national art form. You certainly can't just look at Broadway; look at Washington. Look at the Arena Stage; look at the Kennedy Center; look at the smaller theatres. That's a wide variety. For the people who write dialogue of a certain kind, there's nothing like writing for the theatre; there's nothing like sitting through a preview when you're there with the director and the set designer, and it's a collaboration, and you're going to fix it. I think that for audiences, too, live theatre communicates in a particular way. It's quite interesting from my point of view that Murphy Brown is now pregnant and having a child alone. That's interesting because that's like *The Heidi Chronicles* three years ago. I think there are things you can do in theatre that you can't do anyplace else. And also, theatre is the voice of an individual writer. Movies are really a director's medium. Television is about producing; it's about manufacturing, though very well, and there is certainly, God knows, beautifully written television. But in terms of just the voice of a writer, that is most dominant in the theatre, I think.

Interviewer: Have you ever wanted to direct, or to direct one of your own plays?

Wasserstein: I really wouldn't be a very good director. I like the collaboration. Oddly enough, I've choreographed. I choreographed a rock musical version of *Das Rheingold* in a theatre that burned down. There was a theatre in New York called the Mercer Arts Theatre, and we were doing this play. Meatloaf was in it, and one day I came to rehearsal and the building had fallen down! I thought it was because of the musical version of *Das Rheingold*. I'm not very visually oriented. I really do respect actors. I think there is a real process, and when you've written a play and the actor says, "Well, what do you want here?" you just want to answer, "Oh, it's just funny; be funny." As a director, it's more complicated.

Interviewer: Are there favorite actors that you have?

Wasserstein: There's one actress, Alma Cuervo, who's been in every play of mine. She was at Yale when I was at Yale, and she was in *Uncommon Women*; she made the phone call to the doctor. She played Janie in *Isn't It Romantic,* and she recently was in *The Heidi Chronicles.* Unfortunately, I don't think there's a part for her in my new play, which makes me worry about it. But certainly one uses the same people. I adore Swoosie Kurtz; I think she's great; I'd do anything with Swoosie. When we did the first reading of *Heidi,* a lot of the women who were in it were people who had been in *Uncommon Women.* You tend to turn to the same people in a way. I love Joan Allen and Peter Freedman; I think they're just great.

Interviewer: Is there a kind of dialogue and an understanding, a vocabulary, that develops that you want to share with them?

Wasserstein: Absolutely. Particularly when you're writing a comedy, because you want the people who trust your work and know that what's funny comes from the character as opposed to what comes from being, quote, funny. I'll never forget when I went to see a production of *Uncommon Women* in Chicago, and the director had directed the actors every time something was funny to wink, and it was like everybody had this astigmatism. It was just terrible and I thought, "Why don't you trust the material, why is everybody winking here?" So you want people who know what works, who know that the writer has really thought about this carefully.

Interviewer: Is there something that is killing the theatre? What are the forces that you think are most destructive today?

Wasserstein: It's very hard to make a living in the theatre. It's very hard to be an artist in America, frankly. I remember I won a Guggenheim when it was time to rewrite *Isn't It Romantic,* and I was so happy. It gave me such a sense of self, a feeling of "do this." And I remember that it was for eighteen thousand dollars, which was to me in 1984 an amount of money; but you think about how much a first-year lawyer at a reputable law firm makes.

Interviewer: And you had an advanced degree and were like a doctor.

Wasserstein: Yeah, I think it's very hard, and I think, in terms of theatre, not only is it hard for actors to make a living but it's hard for everybody. It's hard for playwrights. You try casting a play during pilot season, and it's very hard to find an actor. In London, the television and theatre industry are all in the same city; here, people begin to choose between New York and Los Angeles, and at some point thirty-five-year-old people with children or whatever need to decide. I was watching the television show "Sisters" the other night, and there was Swoosie and there was David Dukes. These are great stage actors, not just good, so one has to think about that.

Interviewer: A lot of people, obviously, have uneasy relationships with critics in the theatre, and certainly there have been a lot of discussions about the relationship of the press to theatre. What do you feel about the critic's role in theatre today?

Wasserstein: It's very difficult, because on a scale from one to ten on a play that you've written, you always care ten. As soon as you care nine, you're out of the ballpark; and even if you care ten, that doesn't mean you're in the ballpark, that just means you can get your heart broken even worse. So on the night the critics come, you see all these people coming to your play to judge it or have an opinion, and it's very scary. I think it is part of the process of putting on a play. What always interests me is that when I speak at colleges they always ask about critics, and I always think critics are part of a process. Plays take a long time: you have to sit through a month of auditions to put on a play, you have to sit through five days of technical rehearsal. Critics come on one night, the reviews come out, and I wish that people understood that more; but it is how opinion on the play is disseminated. What happens is, often one wants plays to have a life so that audiences can have an opinion on them, too. What's scary about the critical process is that it is often new plays that are the most vulnerable to critics. If a Neil Simon play doesn't get particularly good notices, it's probably produced by a management that can pour enough money into it. People know the playwright, the play will have a life. It will hurt his feelings, I'm sure, but the play will have a life. With a new play by a young playwright that nobody knows about, it opens at an off-Broadway theatre in New York, and one doesn't know if that play's going to be done again or what's going to happen to that playwright.

Interviewer: Unfortunately, what seems to be happening in cities around the country is that one critical voice is taking the most powerful position.

Wasserstein: *The Heidi Chronicles* didn't get particularly good notices when it went on tour around the country, but because the play came in with all of those awards and I went on "Hello St. Paul" and "Midday Boston," we were able to sell the play. I believe in getting audiences to come and see plays.

Interviewer: Because your work is often autobiographical, do reviews affect it?

Wasserstein: It's hard. Sometimes you don't read them. If you know that they are bad and it's for no other purpose than to hurt your feelings, why would you read them? So it depends. If it's going to concern the life of your play, then you must read them. If everybody says the same thing and these are intelligent people who have come to your play, then something's not getting across; so I think that's important. But it's hard. Of course it hurts your feelings, it has to.

Interviewer: What's the worst thing that you can think of happening to you in the theatre?

Wasserstein: We talked about this earlier. It would be if I stopped writing plays. I would just be deeply disappointed in myself. I wrote a musical called *Miami* that didn't work out. We did it upstairs at Playwrights Horizons, and I cared every bit as much about *Miami* as about *The Heidi Chronicles*, but it didn't work. I believe plays have lives of their own and they have their own stories, and this play was just something where everything went wrong. When *Miami* didn't work, I had my niece come over and put everything related to *Miami* in the closet. I just put it away and only now am I beginning to deal with it a little bit; it's very painful, very painful.

Interviewer: When something like that happens to you in your process, do you think someday you'll take it out of the closet and fix it, or is it over and on to the next project?

Wasserstein: I'm thinking of fixing that now or doing something with it. I think sometimes it's over and sometimes it's not. If you see the right place for it, there might be something.

Interviewer: In musicals, often a song keeps getting shifted from show to show before it finds a home. Do you ever feel something that didn't work in one play might be in the next one?

Wasserstein: All the time. When we were doing *Isn't It Romantic* with Gerald Gutierrez, who's a wonderful director, he had me cut various lines because in fact *Isn't It Romantic* was too funny. You couldn't get to the character. There was one line that Janie said, when a man said to her, "You're clutching your purse." She said, "I have valuables." Gerry said, "You have to cut this line." And I said to him, "Gerry, this is important to the zeitgeist of the play and the hubris of the character." And he said, "What are you bullshitting about? You won't cut your joke." And I said, "Well, that's right." So we cut the joke. That joke is in *The Heidi Chronicles,* and I'll never forget when Gerry came to see the play and there was this howl when he heard the joke. You never throw away a good joke. Hold onto it for years to come.

Interviewer: When you are writing, do you imagine an audience? Do you feel the play is one half of a dialogue you're having with an audience and, if that's true, who is the other half?

Wasserstein: Sometimes I'll listen to music that I associate with the play; or I imagine moments of the play, and that makes me laugh actually. I don't know if I imagine the audience; that would make me nervous. I imagine the play itself and the production but, with my plays, I'm someone who sort of hangs around ladies' rooms for word of mouth all the time. That's one of the problems with becoming well known; suddenly they know who's loitering in the ladies' room. So you get, "I think it's wonderful. Would you like to meet my nephew?" And I'm thinking, "No, I don't. I just want to hear what you have to say about my play." But it's very interesting to see who comes to your plays, too.

Interviewer: Do you find that it's harder now, again because of the success, just to find the quiet time and space to work?

Wasserstein: Sure, a little bit. For someone who likes to escape writing, there are many more ways to escape, and you can say they're important. It's not like I'm off with a girl friend; I'm doing something serious and good, but what I'm really not at is my desk. So there's that, too.

Interviewer: Do you think a Jewish identity and a Jewish cultural upbringing inform your art in any way?

Wasserstein: Oh, very much so. My work extremely so, in terms of humor very much so, and in terms of a pathos, too, I think. It's interesting writing about Jewish subject matter as well. *Miami* was very much about Jews; it was about Miami Beach in 1959. There's a woman in it named Kitty Katz, and her boyfriend is named Murray Murray, and someone took me out after they saw the show and they said, "Wendy, can't you make this about Irish people? This isn't good for the Jews." I thought it would have to be worse when Kitty Katz comes out as an Irish woman! But it was an insight into what Philip Roth goes through. There is a part of me that thinks *The Heidi Chronicles* was taken more seriously because it was about a Gentile girl from Chicago. It wasn't about Wendy with the hips from New York, even if Wendy with the hips from New York had the same emotional life. It's a cynical point of view, but I partially believe that to be true. It was also interesting for me in *The Heidi Chronicles* to write Scoop Rosenbaum; I got to be the smart Jewish boy who tormented me all my life. I thought, "Now I get to be you," and it was fabulous; it was like revenge of the nerds. My new play is very much about being Jewish.

Interviewer: Do you find, going around the country to different cities that have different population makeups, that audiences react to your work differently?

Wasserstein: Well, I saw *Isn't It Romantic* in Tokyo, and it's the most Jewish of all my plays. It's about me and my mother basically, and it opens with this woman in a tie-dyed leotard singing "Sunrise, Sunset" to her daughter, asking her when she's going to get married. There I was in Tokyo, and this Japanese woman came out singing "Sunrise, Sunset" in Japanese, and I thought to myself, "That's my mother; good God, how weird!" It was really strange, but the play got the same laughs in Tokyo as it did in New York. Japanese audiences are not vociferous and what's interesting about them also is that they are 80 percent female. Women go to the theatre a lot, and a single woman in Tokyo over twenty-five is known as "a Christmas cake after Christmas." What played there was the emotional values of the play and the mother and daughter.

Interviewer: Do people in your life who know that your work is autobiographical react in ways that are different from the rest of us when they see themselves onstage?

Wasserstein: Well, my mother came to the opening of *Isn't It Romantic* and said, "Wendy, where did you get those shoes?" Sometimes they do and sometimes they don't. Oddly enough, in some ways *The Heidi Chronicles* is my least autobiographical play. In that play I'm more like the gay pediatrician in terms of his humor and in terms of his way of dealing with the world, except that I'm not him either. It is my coming of age, and my times, but the people in it have the least to do with me. But I was at the women's group where they screamed to me, "Either you shave your legs or you don't!" I remember that distinctly.

Interviewer: You've been writing a series of essays for various magazines, and the personal nature of those causes you to get a lot of interesting mail. Do you find that people sort of want you to be what they want you to be? How do you respond to that?

Wasserstein: When you write with a personal voice, you become immediately accessible so that people assume that they know you. *Bachelor Girls* has a lot in it about my mother and my brother and a bad affair and all of that. It's interesting for a playwright to use that "I" persona, because you can't have it onstage; it's got to become somebody else. In a way that's sort of fun, but on the other hand, people really do assume a familiarity with you, and they come up and talk to me in a way I don't think they do with other playwrights. I recently have lost some weight, and a stranger came up to me on the street and said, "Wendy, you've lost four hundred pounds!" I just thought, "Who are you? Why are you talking this way to me? I mean, nobody does this to August Wilson. I'm sure you wouldn't dare. Who does this to Marsha Norman?" I get these people; they're my special friends. In a way it's very nice because you feel a community, you feel in touch. There's this one essay, which I think is the best one in there, called "Jean Harlow's Wedding Night"; it's about growing up being funny, what that is, dealing with a bad personal experience and becoming compulsively funny to cover up the upset. That's been interesting because I walk down the street and women come up to me and say, "That happened to me." That is nice, except then you feel sad because you think, "Gee, in some ways I wish that it had only happened to me."

Interviewer: Do you get a lot of requests from young playwrights about how to get started? Do you try to help them, and how?

Wasserstein: I do. I've taught at Columbia and at NYU, and I work a lot with a group called the Young Playwrights Festival. We just had our tenth anniversary in New York; we do new plays by playwrights under eighteen. It's a national competition, and we get over a thousand plays. I think that's very important, to do that and to keep the life of the theatre alive. Also, I think a young woman or a young man believes they can become a playwright because you became a playwright; it becomes a possibility. For some reason, I go to girls' schools. I've spoken at every girls' school in New York. I'm the only person who flew from the Golan Heights to give the commencement speech at the Chapin School; I think that that was a first. I think it's very important because you basically look at someone and you say, "Gee, this isn't a person in black with the fur and the earrings; this is an accessible person and this is her job; this is what she does. If she was able to express herself in this way, then I can do that, too." I think that's great, really good, because Wendy never came to my school when I was in high school.

Interviewer: There actually weren't very many Wendys to do that back then.

Wasserstein: Right, exactly.

Interviewer: Is there anyone that you would say has been a really powerful influence on you and your work, other than your family? Another artist, another writer?

Wasserstein: I'm very influenced by my colleagues. I met Chris Durang when I was at the Yale Drama School, and he's been a great friend of mine. It's the closeness that you have to somebody who is also writing. Those sorts of friendships with people in the theatre—Peter Parnell I feel that way about, too—are very supportive at difficult times. I look at Betty Comden, who was in my play *Isn't It Romantic,* and now she's just won the Kennedy Center Honors, and I think, "When Betty was doing this in the fifties, it can't have been easy to have been Betty." I look at her and I think, "There is a woman of great gift and dignity." And André Bishop at Playwrights Horizons has been important for what he's given me and what he's given to other theatre writers too. And the directors I've worked with: Dan, and Gerry Gutierrez, Steven Rubin.

Interviewer: How involved are you with the director during the rehearsal process?

Wasserstein: The most important thing, actually, is working with the director, with someone you share a vision with, because if you sit down for an initial conversation and you're not on the same wavelength, it's not going to change. It's not going to get better, it can only go downhill from there. I tend to go to rehearsals just because I like to hear the play and I like to work during the rehearsal process. Any comments that I have I speak through the director, and he or she then speaks to the company. What I like about plays is that you can be around; when you write movies, you're not there at all, it's not up to you. The process of plays is, it begins with the writer, and then goes to the director, the director gives it to the actors, and the actors give it back to the audience, and ultimately it's about stage management. But it's very important to have a good relationship with the director.

Interviewer: When you're writing a play, how much of the world of the play beyond the words do you see? Do you know what your characters look like, where they go when they leave the stage, what the surroundings are like?

Wasserstein: Oh, gosh, they do start filling up my life. I wrote *The Heidi Chronicles* in London on a grant, and I remember it was a happy time. I was living in this horrible studio apartment with turned-over flowerpots for the decor. It was a place called the Nell Gwynn House or something. It was really awful. I had this grant for "midcareer stimulation." I didn't know what that was, but I was very happy. I remember writing the wedding scene at the Pierre in London, and I had never even been to a wedding at the Pierre, but I'd heard that it was the nicest place for a Jewish girl to get married. You can see why I've never been there! But there was something wonderful about being in that studio in London and imagining the Pierre and having for company Scoop and Heidi and Peter. I loved it. So in that way the characters *do* become real sometimes during the period that I'm writing them; I sort of merge with them in a way. That's both good and bad. Some nights I would see *The Heidi Chronicles* and be very moved by it and think, "I'm still that woman. I still feel stranded, too." And then some nights, she'd say, "Oh, I feel stranded," and I'd think, "Oh, just shut up and be happy. Stop whining." The characters become quite real to me, and I enjoy them. The plays become fun when they stop being autobiography. The characters who are the larger colors become more fun to me. I loved Kitty Katz because, in a sense, that someone like me who's somewhat demure got to be Kitty Katz for a while is great. Swoosie Kurtz in *Uncommon Women*, the girl who says, "I tasted my menstrual blood": that was great fun because I knew I'd never have to get up and say it. But it was fun to do.

Interviewer: What do you think about improvisation as a technique, not as an acting technique, but for you as a playwright? Do you ever like to see actors in character improvising and use that, or do you find that gets in the way?

Wasserstein: Not really, no. I think in some ways, especially with comedy, actually I should loosen up, but I find the work tends to be very precise. It works for certain reasons, so I'm not that interested in that, really.

Interviewer: Can you tell us a little bit more about your new play?

Wasserstein: It's hard to talk about the new play because I always think that if you talk too much about these things you don't know what will happen. The leads in the play are in their forties and fifties, so that the style is different. The writing is slightly different; it's more acerbic than my other plays, it's not as warm. I guess the model for it is more of a Chekhovian piece. I think it's an interesting play. It's not really done at the moment, but I'm happy to have written it, so I'll see.

Interviewer: How important to your development was your time at Yale Drama School?

Wasserstein: For me it was very important. I wasn't happy when I was there. I was very unhappy because drama school's a very hard thing. You're there for three years, and then you don't know what's going to become of you. It's not as if you get out of Yale and there's an ad in the *Times* that says, "Playwright wanted: $80,000 a year plus benefits." Plus you know it's very competitive; you have no idea if you're going to make a living, you have no idea if you're talented. So it was very hard for me, but looking back, for me it was very good that I went, because it made me feel one part of a community, meeting Chris Durang and Alma Cuervo and Ted Tally and all of those people and coming of age with them. Also, it made me take myself seriously as a theatre person, which was important to me because otherwise I maybe probably wouldn't have.

Interviewer: You've done a lot of traveling and talked to people all over the world. Do you have a sense that playwrights are regarded differently abroad from the way they are here, or is it pretty much the same?

Wasserstein: That's interesting. In England, people will go to the new Tom Stoppard play, they'll go to the new Stephen Poliakoff play, and it's not like a hit-or-miss thing: "Boy, he wrote a bomb; we don't care about him." I wish that was true more here. I wish it was less of "Is it a hit or is it a miss?" Theatre writing is a long career. You want a life in the theatre. You don't want, "Oh boy, she had one hit, let's dump her" or "Oh boy, she's a hit machine." What you want is for an artist to evolve. Even a career like Neil Simon's is a very successful career, but he is somebody who keeps writing plays.

Interviewer: Do you see a lot of young playwrights now who quit just for that reason—because there isn't such a market?

Wasserstein: Well, there is such an alternative in television and film and who that reaches. Many more people will be talking about Murphy Brown and that baby than *The Heidi Chronicles* and that baby.

Lanford Wilson

Lanford Wilson was born in 1937 in Lebanon, Missouri. After attending Southwest Missouri State College briefly and spending a year in San Diego and five years in Chicago, he came to New York in 1962. His initial plays, one-acts, were presented at the off-off-Broadway Caffe Cino. His first full-length play was Balm in Gilead *(1965). It was followed by* The Rimers of Eldritch *(1966),* The Gingham Dog *(1968),* Serenading Louie *(1970),* Lemon Sky *(1970),* The Hot l Baltimore *(1973),* The Mound Builders *(1975),* 5th of July *(1978; revised as* Fifth of July *[1979]),* Talley's Folly *(1979),* A Tale Told *(1981; revised as* Talley & Son *[1985]),* Angels Fall *(1982),* Burn This *(1986),* Redwood Curtain *(1992), and numerous one-acts.* The Rimers of Eldritch *received the Drama Desk Vernon Rice Award;* The Hot l Baltimore *received the New York Drama Critics Circle Award, the Obie Award, and the Outer Critics Circle Award;* The Mound Builders *received the Obie Award; and* Talley's Folly *was awarded the Pulitzer Prize,*

the New York Drama Critics Circle Award, and the Outer Critics Circle Award. Wilson is also the recipient of two Rockefeller Grants, an ABC–Yale Fellowship in motion picture writing, two Guggenheim Fellowships, the Brandeis University Creative Arts Achievement Award for Theatre, an award from the American Institute of Arts and Letters, the State of Missouri Outstanding Artist's Award, and an honorary degree from the University of Missouri. His translation of Chekhov's Three Sisters *premiered in 1984; he provided the libretto for Lee Hoiby's opera version of Tennessee Williams's* Summer and Smoke *in 1971;* The Migrants, *on which he collaborated with Williams, was presented on television's "Playhouse 90" in 1974; and his teleplay* Taxi! *was presented on "The Hallmark Hall of Fame" in 1978. In 1969 Wilson, along with director Marshall Mason (who has directed most of the first productions of Wilson's plays) and others, founded the Circle Repertory Company. This interview was conducted on May 20, 1993.*

▶ ── ◄

Interviewer: Even though you're an established playwright now, how much of a struggle is it still to get your plays done?

Wilson: It's not a struggle to get plays done, because I write for Circle Rep so I'm writing for a specific theatre, which I consider my theatre. I'm usually writing for specific people, so there's no problem there either; the problem is thinking of a play.

Interviewer: But *Redwood Curtain* didn't start at Circle Rep, did it? It started in Seattle and then was done in Philadelphia, wasn't it?

Wilson: I wrote it for Circle Rep, but Tanya Berezin, who runs the theatre, decided that it should be done on Broadway. It started in Seattle, but it was always a Circle Rep production. It took forever. As soon as Tanya decided they wanted to do it on Broadway, I just held my head and wept, practically, knowing all of the problems that it would engender.

Interviewer: Would you have been happier if that play had stayed away from Broadway, if it had been done at Circle Rep initially?

Wilson: Yes. It would have been done three years earlier.

Interviewer: What was the delay?

Wilson: When they decided they wanted to do it on Broadway, they said they also wanted to do it at a regional theatre first. Then Marshall and I both said that we wanted to see it at a regional theatre in a reading first to see if it held that large a stage. Very kindly we were offered the reading program at Seattle Rep, and we went out there almost a year before it was finally done. As soon as we did the reading, they said, "We love it. Can we do it in our regular season almost a year from now?" That's where it started its trip to New York.

Interviewer: What you're basically saying is it wouldn't have had this circuitous route had Broadway not been the ultimate aim.

Wilson: Exactly. We would never have had this route. We would have just done it at Circle Rep and let it run its six weeks and be done with the damn thing.

Interviewer: Following up on that, how do you feel about Broadway as a goal for your plays?

Wilson: I don't think it's a goal. I think the goal is to write a good play. You have to think with two heads and not simultaneously; one follows the other. First you just write a good play, and then you try to get it produced under the best possible circumstances. I never think Broadway is the best possible circumstance for a serious play. Broadway usually allows about one comedy and one, or maybe two, serious plays a year to sneak through, and they'd better be ballyhooed very heavily before they get in. That's about all the critics can cope with. That's their scope. This year we've had *Someone Who'll Watch over Me* as well as *Angels in America*.

Interviewer: Haven't you done very well with plays that have never gone to Broadway?

Wilson: I've done perfectly well with plays that have never gone to Broadway; but I've done better with the plays that have gone to Broadway, though, just financially speaking. *Redwood Curtain* is already scheduled to be done next season in seven theatres, I think.

Interviewer: And you think that's because it went to Broadway?

Wilson: I think so. *Angels Fall* was not done in that many.

Interviewer: What you're saying is that a failed Broadway production leads to more productions than a successful off-Broadway production?

Wilson: I think so.

Interviewer: Other playwrights say that one of the reasons to go to Broadway, although this would apply equally well to Circle Rep, is that then the play gets published. They say if a play stays out of New York, it's less likely to get published. In your case, most of your plays have gone to New York, although not necessarily to Broadway. That's fascinating that *Redwood Curtain*, despite its commercial failure, has gotten that much attention.

Wilson: I think it's a good play also, but *Mound Builders* has not got near that kind of play and it never went to Broadway. *Serenading Louie* has never got that sort of attention; it never went to Broadway. *Lemon Sky*, even with the television production, has not done well.

Interviewer: What do you think would have happened if *Redwood Curtain* had been done simply as a Circle Rep production and not gone to Broadway?

Wilson: It probably would have done about the same as *Mound Builders*. But that's all just airy speculation. Who knows; I have no idea.

Interviewer: On balance, what would you say you feel about the fact that it went to Broadway? On the one hand, it was a financial failure; but on the other hand, its life is extended now.

Wilson: People who saw it liked it very much, so I think many of the people who are doing it saw it along the way somewhere, especially if they saw it on Broadway, because it was gorgeous on Broadway. It was designed originally for that house. It was designed for that house a year and a half earlier, but it was designed for that house.

Interviewer: That leads to another similar question. What do you think are the pros and cons of the nonprofit theatre network as a kind of developmental laboratory—and I guess you'd include Circle Rep in there?

Wilson: It depends so much on who you are. I don't know if I should try to think as a new writer coming to New York, or as myself, or as a new writer anywhere in America really. You have to take the whole regional system as well as off-Broadway; off-Broadway is part of the American regional system. I believe that a success in New York, even off-Broadway or off-off Broadway, does have a better likelihood of an afterlife than a success at South Coast Rep, where they're also doing a lot of new plays, unless it's really an extraordinary play that catches on and people start seeing and carrying on over it and it gets done everywhere.

Interviewer: What about the regional theatre as a laboratory, in the sense of affording you the opportunity to work on a play? Talk about the Seattle experience with *Redwood Curtain*. Didn't that give you more opportunity to work on the play than if you'd had to open in New York?

Wilson: We were still changing things after we opened on Broadway. No matter where a play is done, if you have eyes in your head there are things you can tinker with and there are things you want to change and that you want to improve. It might just be one word or one line that you don't want in the play anymore, or a line that you've been trying to formulate for years and finally get. Just having the play on anywhere is an incredible benefit, even if it's just a lab show. We have a lab at Circle Rep that does, I guess, a play a week. Another branch of the lab does one reading a week, every

Friday, and that's an incredible benefit. There are a lot of people who don't take advantage of the discussion and what they learn there, but I certainly do. I think it's very important. I've always had my plays done in the Friday readings. There's usually been a rush to get it on so I've never had a lab production of one until just about six months ago. They did a lab production of my new play, and it wasn't finished. I've finished a draft of it now, and it's a play deliberately designed for a very small room—as a result of "the Redwood trek," I think!

Interviewer: You started by making a distinction between yourself and a new playwright. You had the luxury as Lanford Wilson of being able to rework *Redwood Curtain* right up until the end. But if you're a new playwright who's trying to get his or her play on, being able to do that in the relative privacy of Pittsburgh rather than Broadway is probably an advantage, isn't it?

Wilson: Oh, of course. That was the whole idea. Imagine the luxury of doing it with eight hundred people in the audience. It's just extraordinary to be able to have that feedback, to see people storm out, and you say, "Well, I certainly have to leave that line; that line is apparently wonderfully offensive." It's an incredible benefit. There's this odd thing that happens when you hear a play with an audience, even in the lab where there are only fifteen people in the audience. It's a brand-new play, you're very nervous about it, and they do it completely wrong. Nevertheless, these people who are listening are very well trained in making those adjustments. We also have a writer's workshop, here at my house, so you may have heard it here. We have two sessions a year, one in my apartment, where we read full-length plays just among ourselves. The writers do the reading, and sometimes we drag in a couple of actors to help.

Just hearing it with that audience you hear so much; you hear it with a different head. It's no longer in your head, it's being delivered to an audience; you hear the audience reaction and lack of reaction. In the discussions that follow—if they're at all the way Circle Rep handles the discussion—you learn so much about what the audience has received. In Circle Rep discussions, the writer's not allowed to answer any questions or you start talking about what you intended. What you are trying to understand is what the audience got, and your intentions be damned. If they did not receive what you intend, there's no point in you talking about your intentions for half an hour. Just hearing the way something was received and what it meant to someone, if they followed something as simple as the story of the play or not, is of incredible benefit in early development. Even reading series are very important to the development of a play.

Interviewer: When you write a play, do you picture an audience? Who do you write for?

Wilson: There's a circle of people, other writers and some actors—three or four actors that I like, and possibly the actors that I'm writing the parts for. I write specific challenges for actors from time to time, but whom do I write for? It's a circle of writers; but, you know, John Guare's sitting next to Chekhov who's sitting next to Ibsen who's sitting next to van Itallie. And Shakespeare's saying, "I did that four hundred years ago." And you're saying, "Yes, but it was never all that clear, Billy; shut up!" Chekhov is laughing his ass off, and someone else is saying, "I don't get it."

Interviewer: When the reading comes and somebody says, "I don't get it," then do you have to say to yourself, "Have I misjudged what an audience can hear?"

Wilson: Or "Have I just not been clear enough?" There's a strange development of my scripts: they get much longer. A lot of people cut. I end up cutting when it gets in production; but from the first draft it probably increases a quarter at least, with me just going back and trying to explain what the hell I was talking about, because to me the story, the theme, the metaphor, and all of the rest of it are all very clear in the first draft. I find often from the discussion that no one is really following me at all. In *Fifth of July*, for instance, if you don't begin by saying, "It's about this Vietnam veteran who is an English teacher," then I've not done it right. In the first draft no one said that; they didn't have a clue. They thought it was about selling the house or about God knows what. If we don't start with "It's about this English teacher who's in crisis," then I've missed it. In the first draft, Gwen ran off with the play completely. I had to cut some of the funniest lines that I've ever written because she was just trampling on the theme of the play.

Interviewer: What in your mind distinguishes a legitimate comment from an illegitimate comment?

Wilson: You have to know—by the time the play is finished; you may not know this until it's finished or until a short while after it's finished—what the hell you were after. I think, as a play is being written, as it's being developed in your mind and on paper, you begin to understand what you're writing and what you're trying to say. Writing, of course, is the process of understanding what you're feeling. You know generally what your play is about and what you're trying to say, and if a comment has nothing to do with that, you ignore it. There's a lot of things you hear that are irrelevant and you have to know that: "Yes, that's interesting, but it has nothing to do with the play I'm writing" or "Yes, it would probably make it a more commercial play or a more viable play for a cross-section of the American audience—whatever the hell that is—but it really has nothing to do with what I'm trying to say so therefore it's not interesting." In other words, you don't do something just to make it popular, just to make it funny, or just to make it accessible, unless you're making your theme or what you're trying to say more accessible.

Interviewer: Can you think of another example from a play where you made a change because you felt that it wasn't sufficiently clear?

Wilson: In *Redwood Curtain,* I did a lot of research about the lumber industry and had a great deal of business in the first draft which I thought was just fascinating. I thought it was fascinating because it was something I was just learning, but all of the details of that sale detracted so much from what the central image of the play was supposed to be that we just went off on a weird tangent that was completely unnecessary to the theme of the play. Much of that was cut back and simplified. A whole paragraph would go, and one sentence would become a phrase. The words "hostile takeover" took care of thousands of paragraphs of meticulous research. It just became much clearer to cut all of the details.

Interviewer: Using that case as an example, how did you realize that about *Redwood Curtain?* Was that something you, hearing the play on its feet, realized, or was that something someone else said to you?

Wilson: First, Claris Nelson, one of the writers who's important to me, who gives a better analysis of a play from a cold reading than just about anyone (and she knows business very, very well; she's a business person), was sitting there and she said, "You're losing me in this forest of the lumber industry. I'm not sure it's quite like that, I start arguing with it, and I get completely off of the track. All that's necessary is, what has this done to her? Because we're trying to talk about someone who no longer knows who she is." Of course, she was completely right and there went all of my meticulous research. She just hated it completely; and I thought she would be the one who would appreciate it the most because she understood business.

Interviewer: Basically, after you examined what she was saying, did you realize she was right?

Wilson: Oh, absolutely, especially after the first cold reading. It was absolutely clear—because all of that was left in for the cold reading—that it didn't belong there. It had nothing to do with the theme of the play, with what the play was trying to say.

Interviewer: Do you think that, if she hadn't mentioned it, you would have realized it anyway?

Wilson: I bet not, not for a long time, and it would have been so much more difficult to change all of that after we were in production or in rehearsal.

Interviewer: When that happens, is it more likely to come from someone else rather than from your own hearing of the play?

Wilson: Sometimes it is, because you're really quite deaf, especially to your meticulous research, but not when you can see an audience drift completely away from it. When you have a chance to question them, they say, "I was totally lost; I was so bored by that."

Interviewer: Have you ever had an instance when sitting there without anybody saying anything, without any audience reaction, you've said, "That's all wrong."

Wilson: Of course, all the time. Every line. As I say, just in the first reading of a play, you know if it doesn't sound right. The play that I'm working on now, which is a very small play and will not be done anywhere (I probably won't even ever allow it to be done) is about gigantic themes. I seem to be doing this more and more—writing very very small plays that are about huge things. But this one is a deliberately very small play about one of the most important things that's happened to mankind, and with the first reading I realized that we just don't spend enough time with the play, with the people; there's so much more information that we should have.

Interviewer: And you didn't realize that in writing it?

Wilson: Oh, not at all. I thought it was very dense and very crabbed and very excitingly circuitous and tight. Of course, it was much too tight; it needed to breathe, and the people needed to explain themselves. Then there were a few technical things. One of the reasons I had trouble working on the project in the past—it's something I've been intending to do for about ten years—is that the central character is a woman who influenced everyone but almost never spoke. She hated speaking, she didn't talk very much, and I finally came to the conclusion that, all right, goddamn it, this is the night that she speaks! We have this character who never ever speaks who is going to talk, and this guy is going to grill her until he finds out what makes her tick. The guy himself is in such crisis that she understands that he needs to talk or he needs to listen, so for this one time she does talk to him and does talk about herself. Although she's very self-effacing, we do get the information. Also it's just necessary to get the facts of her life in there somehow, and he just unashamedly grills the woman.

So the task, then, was to make you feel that this is a woman who rarely spoke but was so incredibly wonderful in the life that she lived that she influenced all of these people. Here is a woman who never speaks who has page after page of dialogue, and how do I get you to believe that this woman really is a very quiet woman? That was not completely successful in the first draft. You felt her going on, and I realized I had to emphasize her reluctance to talk even under the circumstances. She wrote four pages of an autobiography but then said, "Who cares? It's completely unimportant. We don't need another one of these; we don't need another story about a woman who lives this particular kind of life." So we have very little of her writing; she wrote a Christmas letter, mimeographed it, and sent it to all of her friends every year, and that's about all we have. But it's mostly about planting and the weather and what wildflowers bloomed and which didn't and very little about anything concrete; but that was her life, so there was a lot of that in it. That's why it's for a very small audience!

Interviewer: Is it a one-act play?

Wilson: It's a very long one-act play. In the first draft it's about thirty-five or forty minutes. In the second draft it was fifty-five, and it's going to be an hour and a half by the time I finish it. There's no intermission, there can't be one.

Interviewer: As you look back over your playwriting career, what sort of changes do you see? What have you learned to do better? How are the most recent plays different from the earliest ones?

Wilson: When I first started writing plays, I said, "Theatre should be a three-ring circus." I wanted a lot of people, all talking at once, creating life on the stage. After we formed the Circle Company, I became more responsible to the actor. I wanted to write deep, fully rounded people, beautiful language, roles an actor could sink his teeth into. The craft became less flamboyant, more subtle. The trick now is to get some of the old panache back into a beautifully constructed work.

Interviewer: Why are you a playwright? Why aren't you a poet or a novelist? What specifically about playwriting appeals to you?

Wilson: Well, I think we have different talents. I'm not compact enough to be a poet. I enjoy reading poetry sometimes, but sometimes I don't even enjoy reading it because it's so damned compact it goes past me; I don't get it. I think, however, I'm very strongly attracted to the craft of and the limitations of theatre. In a novel you can go on for pages about the psychological development of a person or the psychological ramifications or the political ramifications of a moment and on and on. You have to find a way to do that without saying it in the theatre, and that's just thrilling to me. The construction of a play is just incredibly difficult. Nowadays, the style is to do it without letting anyone know that you're doing it, because as soon as they see a construction they say, "Oh my God, I saw a symbol or I saw a metaphor," as though that wasn't what we have to build with. So you have to hide all of that with great facility, and that excites me.

When I was trying to write a screenplay, I realized what a totally different animal the contemporary screenplay is. It has so little introversion. Everything is extroverted. It's a generalization, but in the popular movie people say what they mean. In a movie they might say, "I love you"; in a play they might say, "Get out of my face!" It means exactly the same thing because of inhibitions and so on, but that doesn't read at all in a film. You're just working with a completely different agenda. Filmwriting is a very difficult medium for me because I've spent all of my professional life trying to hide the things that have to be very obvious in movies. Also exposition is handled in a completely different way—you see it or you can flash back or something like that—whereas that doesn't interest me at all. It's much more exciting to try to get someone's history into a scene while the scene is always in the present tense, without the audience knowing that they're getting exposition. They just think they're learning about what is happening between these two people. I love the limitations of theatre. While it has incredible possibilities, gigantic and wonderful possibilities, still it's beautifully limited.

Interviewer: What about Hollywood and playwrights? Hollywood is not terribly respectful of playwrights. Why do so many plays suffer when they are transferred to film?

Wilson: Because they shouldn't have been transferred, or else they should have been transferred a lot more cleverly. Sometimes it works wonderfully. There's the story of Tennessee working on *Streetcar*. Of course, that was the same director and the same author working on the screenplay. When they first imagined the movie, they thought it would be quite different from the play. They would open it out, they would go back to Belle Reve; it would just be a completely different experience. But as they started working on the film script, more and more it came back to just the play, and it ended with almost the text of the play. It can work but you have to be incredibly ballsy to do it. With *Virginia Woolf* they just cut a few of the profanities out, but other than that it's almost the script of the play. You have to be bold enough to do that or approach the story in a completely different way, but it's very difficult to tell the story and make it mean the same thing in a different medium.

A good play is a microcosm and a metaphor and has ramifications. If you start telling it in a different way, you lose one of those: you might lose the ramifications; you might keep the metaphor but you lose so much that you're better off not doing it. It's much easier to do a novel or a short story. The worse the novel is, the better off you are. A novel, generally speaking, has so much less dialogue in it that you're probably dealing with one-quarter of the lines and so you have all that room for story development. You can sit on a train for ten minutes with nothing happening, just sit looking at the ceiling. You can't do that when you're adapting a play

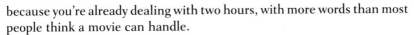

because you're already dealing with two hours, with more words than most people think a movie can handle.

Interviewer: How do you feel about the production aspects of playwriting? Some playwrights feel the play is done when they finish writing it; other playwrights say it's 50 percent done when they finish writing it and the other 50 percent happens in production. Where do you fall on that continuum?

Wilson: When I say it's finished, I'm about 90 percent done. I'll go through three or four drafts in a lab situation. Hearing it read to me or hearing it read to a small lab audience in the Friday readings is very important. I don't consider it finished until a couple of drafts after that. Then, when I do think we have a rehearsal script, probably 90 percent of it is there. Neither Marshall nor I feel that rehearsal is the place to rewrite a play, but we'll change small things. When we changed *A Tale Told* to *Talley & Son*, after I'd seen it in production there were a thousand things I wanted to do to it. It was beautifully produced and gorgeously acted, but it was all wrong. *A Tale Told* was a barn burner. It's a plotted play, it's deliberately a 1940s-style play with a lot of plot. In the first draft, the ghost of Timmy starts talking only in the second act and he starts telling about how he was killed. It's one of the best speeches I've written, but it's quite long and you just wanted to yank that kid off the stage because there was a plot going.

When you have that kind of a plot going, you're not going to stand around for something as irrelevant as how this guy got killed. That character is completely redone in *Talley & Son*. He was saying beautiful words and I'm sitting in the audience saying, "Will somebody please yank that kid." In the rewrite I had to find a balance of where we can put him in and how much of that story we can have. We had much less of it, and I used him also as a narrator to fill us in on a lot of the logistics of the play. I cut way back again on the business of the family, made the family wealthier because I just needed them larger. There were a lot of changes. We were working on that through all of the rehearsals. Timothy Busfield was playing Timmy out in California, and I had him sit on a stool just as if I were drawing him, so I could look at him and try to write a speech for him. I knew exactly what I wanted him to say, and I just could not get it. He sat on the stool and I sat at the typewriter looking at him and very slowly developed the quite brief speech that he was to say. He got up at one point, not really understanding what was going on, and I said, "Sit down! What are you doing? You can't move!" He was shocked that I was using him, but it was really very important to be looking at my material.

Interviewer: That's fascinating, because what you're saying is that, sitting in your study, you might not have been able to do that, but being confronted by the actor in a live situation you were able to work on that character more successfully.

Wilson: I couldn't have done it without that physical actor there. With the rehearsal going on in the other room, there was an urgency to the moment that fed beautifully into the work. But we didn't get the final moment of *Talley & Son* until we brought it back to New York and were in previews at Circle Rep. We were in previews before I realized that Timmy left and Lottie was onstage by herself. We did get that gradually she realizes he's there. He had talked to her a lot in *A Tale Told*; they had had conversations. They don't have in *Talley & Son* but, as he's talking to the audience toward the end of the play, he begins talking to her as well and we get the feeling that she's hearing it. When he walks off the stage, it's just an incredibly dramatic moment to leave her alone without that ghost that she's discovered. She's suddenly very, very lonely on that stage by herself, and I didn't understand that we had to end the play with just her until we were in previews.

Interviewer: Was that a result of physically seeing it and knowing it would make a wonderful dramatic moment?

Wilson: The play did not end. It was not fulfilling with the lights going down with both of them onstage looking at each other. But when he said all he had to say, wandered off to some other interest, and left her all by herself, it ended the play.

Interviewer: Do you think you could have realized that sitting in your study?

Wilson: Never.

Interviewer: Because you wouldn't have visualized it?

Wilson: I wouldn't have visualized it; it was a completely visual thing. We almost had him open the door, but then we decided, "No, we're not going to do that because as an audience we are imagining him not there and what she is seeing. She may be seeing a vague little shadow of him; but if he opens the door, it's too startling for that moment. For another play it would be fine, but for that moment it would look ridiculous because we're imagining him not there and those doors are opening by themselves." She has opened the door, and he hears the music from across the river and wanders out. She watches him going out, and he's gone.

Interviewer: It's almost like putting a note in a piece of music in the right place. It's a feeling that is beyond intellectualization in a situation like that, isn't it?

Wilson: It really is. It becomes theatre. You see plays all the time that you say, "No, that's just wrong." It's not wrong in the writing; it's wrong in the direction, and that becomes theatre. When you read a play as simple as *Hay Fever*, you know exactly the sound of their voices. You know exactly how this play has to be done. You see it and it's never done right. It never has the right sound, it never has the flip urbanity that that play demands. They get all bogged down in real moments that have nothing whatsoever to do with the movement and the sound of that play. You need to see something like the movie of *Blithe Spirit* to understand how the damn play has to be done. It can be done with different interpretations of all of the characters, but it still has to have that theatricality, that rhythm, that whatever. I've seen perfect casts of *Hay Fever* that should have done that play in a flick and they went way off, way off; they just ruined it, and you couldn't get a better cast.

And something can be right for one person and very wrong for another. I know when I saw the production that was generally bombed in New York of *Waiting for Godot* with Steve Martin and Robin Williams, I absolutely loved it. It did for me everything that that play had to do and I said, "I don't want to see this play again. I will never ever see this play again because now I've seen the play." I had seen a dozen productions of it that weren't funny, that didn't have the poignancy. It was just cast perfectly. The child that comes in with his little backbone sticking out was so small and so young—and that is exactly right. I've seen someone much too old in that part always and it gave you a completely different feeling. Also Steve Martin, whom I don't like in movies very often, walked onstage and it almost took your breath away to see someone walk onstage that casually. He walked onstage without a single ounce of theatrical performance rhythm. He walked onstage as someone would walk across a room. Well, that just doesn't happen; everyone has to perform walking across a stage. He didn't do that. He just waltzed onstage and started talking, and it took my breath away. I was with someone else from the theatre, I don't remember who, and we were spellbound throughout the entire thing, and audiences all around us were quoting the reviews: "Oh, look how self-indulgent Robin Williams is." I don't like Robin Williams at all in most of his films, but he was brilliant in this because it was written for a comedian and he's a comedian.

Interviewer: What have you learned from other playwrights living or dead?

Wilson: It was fun when off-off-Broadway was just starting; I've said this before, but it's so true. I think it became a pattern; when I lost all of those playwrights or when we all went wandering away, they stayed with me and just increased and added some of the other ones I respect and I admire. If Sam Shepard discovered something, it belonged to all of us. It was, "Oh, good, we can do that, that is possible." It was very much like we were inventing or discovering theatre for ourselves. If Megan Terry did something or Jean-Claude did something, it belonged to all of us suddenly.

I would never have written *This Is the Rill Speaking* if I had not read *You May Go Home Again* by David Starkweather, which was a completely nonrealistic play. *This Is the Rill Speaking* is essentially the same play. It's just *my* experience, *my* going home. David wrote a character named David who was very reluctant to go home to his sister's wedding because he didn't want to go home; he didn't want to go back there and get all embroiled in that nonsense again. The absurd mother, the absurd father, the ridiculous sister, and the even more ridiculous man that she was going to marry are all done very abstractly. The mother is mopping the floor throughout half of the play; the son is dressed as a Japanese executioner or something throughout the play and trying to cut the rope with a huge ax in his hand. He's off at a distance from them intellectualizing deeply and philosophizing deeply, and the mother's mopping the floor saying, "David, please, I've got a million things to do." At the end he makes them all bow down; he's going to execute them with his ax. And the mother says, "Even the child? Even the baby?" "Yes," he says, "all of you." They all bow down, and they say, "Oh, very well, but get on with it because we're really very busy, we've got so much to do." There's a roll of thunder and a blackout and a crash, and the lights come up immediately, and he's there in jacket and tie and ordinary shoes and a little suitcase, and they say, "Oh, you made it," and he says, "Oh, of course I would come home." and that's the end of the play. Oh Lord, it just ripped me apart. I saw it about fifty times, every time it was done at Caffe Cino. It made me realize that you can write about those experiences, about the incredible love that was in that play, which was filled with hate but was all about love. It was filled with horrible, horrible portraits that were all done so beautifully. That's what I took from that play.

From something of Claris's I took something else. In *Brontosaurus* I stole completely from a very minor play that Sam Shepard wrote. I don't remember anything about it at all except that at the end of the play, the lead guy turns to the audience and says, "And then I walked down the street and I kept walking and I started thinking and then I stopped thinking and I kept walking and then I stopped," and he freezes in position and the lights go out. Well, it was the most dynamic thing I'd ever seen in my life. In *Brontosaurus* the actor at the end of the play says, "And then I went down the street and this is the continuation of the story, then this happened to me." I had no idea you could do that.

I was working at the Phoenix Theatre and saw their production of *Next Time I'll Sing to You*, which was just a glorious production of James Saunders's play. He's still my favorite of all those British playwrights from back then. That and *A Scent of Flowers* are two of the most beautiful plays ever. One section, an entire page, was stolen verbatim by Tom Stoppard for *Rosencrantz and Guildenstern*. He just flat out stole one page of it because he needed it, I think. In *Next Time I'll Sing to You*, the second act begins with the longest, most ridiculous shaggy dog story you have ever heard in your life. Estelle Parsons sits on the edge of the stage, talks to the other character, and it goes on and on and on and on and on; really what it is it's a shaggy dog story. It has a ridiculous punch line. The guy's been coming on to her and she essentially is saying, "I think if someone is attracted to someone, it is perfectly all right for them to have a relationship. I see nothing wrong with that at all. If someone is attracted to someone, I think a relationship is a logical . . . " and it goes on and on and on like that and ends with, "The only problem is I'm not attracted to you." It's a fifteen-minute speech.

All of the shaggy dog stories in *Balm in Gilead* came from that realization; there the characters usually turn to the audience. Not the girl's long speech but all of the short speeches: "The difference between people in New York and Chicago is that in Chicago no one carries an umbrella and in New York they think nothing at all about an umbrella," which ends with "Consequently they get rained on a lot in Chicago"—all of that comes directly from that shaggy dog story in *Next Time I'll Sing to You*. I never would have thought of stopping the action and having a little entertaining speech with a punch line. It never would have crossed my mind. As I say, once you saw something back then, it belonged to all of us. I'm sure Megan Terry used that, and people were using things of mine as well—the simultaneous dialogue and all of that. And I don't have any idea where I got that.

Interviewer: As you have learned your craft, has that become less so now, or was it because of the particular moment in theatrical time where you were all going to see each other's plays?

Wilson: I think maybe I'm not as facile now. I'm not able to assimilate. I'm not as easily assimilated anymore.

Interviewer: Are you as easily impressed?

Wilson: Oh God, yes. If I'm not influenced by *Angels in America*, I'm not doing the right thing. I've already read both parts, and the first part (the second part's not finished yet) is one of the best plays written in America since what? Well, I think there is *Long Day's Journey*, then *Streetcar*, then *Virginia Woolf*, then *Hurlyburly* (in the rewritten script, not in the production), and now *Angels in America*. These are the really important poles in American theatre. *Angels in America* returns us right back to all of the theatrical possibilities of the stage and to the unabashed intelligence of the writer. It's just delicious! If I can't learn something from that, then I'm ossified—and it would be terrible to think that. My plays are getting more and more hard, more and more compact, like a black dwarf or something. They're getting denser and denser and denser and denser and I just have to explode. I have to get out of that. I've always felt this way. I was saying this when I wrote *Serenading Louie*. I'm never happy with how small the plays are; even when they're gigantic, I'm never happy with them.

Interviewer: Do you think that being more assimilable would help that?

Wilson: No, I think I was like that in *Balm in Gilead*, I was like that in *Lemon Sky*. I think *Burn This* was a great advance because I finally got some of that energy from *Balm in Gilead* and some of those other plays back onto the stage again, got it in a character in a realistic situation.

Interviewer: Do you see *Burn This* as a less dense play?

Wilson: No, the idea was to keep what I'd learned of character development and the psychology of the character and the ramifications of what I was trying to talk about but to get some of the good old-fashioned theatricality back onto the stage, even if it was just in one character, Pale.

Interviewer: What are your writing habits? Where do you work? For how long? At what time of day? Do you use a word processor or do you write out your work in longhand initially?

Wilson: First I have to bore all my friends to tears saying, "I don't have an idea for a play." This lasts anywhere from a year to about three. During that time I have no discipline at all. When I finally do settle down to work, I have a fairly set routine. I begin working about forty-five minutes after I get up. This could be nine in the morning or three in the afternoon. I begin by rereading what I wrote the day before—not editing too much— just to see where I was. Usually that tells me what I want to do next. I write for perhaps four or five hours, sometimes as little as three, sometimes as long as eight or nine, until I run out of gas and have no idea how to continue, or not the energy. As I work, I might make notes of things that are going to happen later—lines, events. I used to carry a notebook and I could write anywhere—on the subway, in a coffee shop, in a bar. Later I worked on a typewriter, either at the Circle Rep offices or at my apartment, or out in Sag Harbor at the house. *Fifth of July* was written mostly in Sag Harbor, *Burn This* mostly in the city at my apartment. I finally broke down and bought a primitive sort of word processor. I don't think I could write in longhand again or, for that matter, use a typewriter.

Interviewer: What gets you started on a play?

Wilson: God, I wish I knew. Sometimes it's an image, sometimes it's a character. With *Redwood Curtain* it was Lyman. I met him, I saw him, I couldn't figure him out; so I had to figure out what made him tick and why we had abandoned him. He was just such a palpable symbol for the collective mental block that we have with our history. With *Mound Builders,* it was a moment that never even got into the play. There were people talking, they leave the stage, and you realize there have been all of these crickets, frogs, and all of these night sounds all the way through. A stick breaks and it's all suddenly quiet; all the bugs and everything shut up. In other words, there's something out there that's going to get you. That was the image that I started with with *Mound Builders.* I think it's probably the only time I've written a play successfully where I really wrote what I intended to write. It didn't take me off in some weird place that wasn't the first impulse. First impulses are sometimes very good just to get you started, but with that play, I really wrote about what I intended to write about all the way through and stuck to it. I learned a lot along the way. I didn't know they were archeologists when I started; I thought they were real estate developers.

With *Hot l Baltimore,* I started with the image of the lost trains and all of those great abandoned railroad stations and this glorious hotel that was run down. But I didn't realize it was a whores' hotel, that it was whores and retired people, until April came down the stairs and the play snapped into focus instantly. It was just the character and her voice suddenly saying, "All right, all right, what's the story this time? Last night it was something wrong with the plumbing, the day before that it was something else." You can see it on the stage still; the play does not start until she comes down the stairs. It's almost right that it doesn't start until she comes down; she's the fourth character on, or maybe even the fifth. Marshall has said that he wants to throw away the first five pages of everything I write because it's just me trying to find my play. He's often very right. His direction of *Hot l* was one of the most glorious things I've ever seen in my life.

Interviewer: When you start a play, or when you're writing it, how much of it do you know? Do you know the end? Do you know a general outline of where it's going? Do you discover it as you go along, or does it vary from play to play?

Wilson: It varies some. Generally, I find out as I go along. I'm making little marginal notes as I go along, telling me things that I've discovered: "The first act will end like this." I may not know how the last act ends, but I get an image; or maybe I'll begin with a knowledge of how the first act ends. I have a dynamite first-act ending of a play and I don't even know what the play is, so I'll probably never write it—but it sure is a dynamite first-act ending. It's typical of my endings, these long dying falls that I end acts on instead of something dramatic. Generally, I'm discovering the play as I go along. The characters are telling me without me pushing them around too much where the play wants to go. I'm making a lot of plot notes at the same time. I don't know much about it. That's why it's so difficult to try to begin a play, because when you're thinking about a play you're thinking about the whole damn play. I haven't learned to just think about whatever it is that's going to start me writing something. I'm always thinking about the whole play. There are a dozen plays where I can see the whole play in my mind and I just don't want to write it. If I could learn where I start, I would be searching for that start rather than an entire play, because it's never an entire play that I have when I begin.

With *Burn This*, I started with Pale's tirade. It killed me when we finally cut the place where I started on Pale. The play was four hours long, and all we cut was Pale going on and on and on. I loved that four-hour version, but nobody wanted to do it except John Malkovich. When I started, I had the dancer. Then I did the tirade and said, "What in the hell was that?" and realized that I had a play that I was going to write for someone that I eventually decided I didn't want to work with. Years earlier I'd written the beginning of that play, and it was down there brooding in my subconscious somewhere. In that first speech that I wrote, he refers to his brother by name and I didn't even know what he was talking about. When I finally ran out of gas on that first speech, I said, "What in the hell is this?" Then I realized, "Oh, of course, that's a guy I was going to write for what's-his-name." I had the whole story. I said, "Oh, so she's the dancer and she has the boyfriend who's a movie producer and the roommate who works in advertising." So I had the whole damn play.

Interviewer: You mentioned earlier that you sometimes have written with specific actors or actresses in mind. Has that increased over the years?

Wilson: Less the last few years. In *Redwood Curtain*, I was writing this man that I had met. It was not an actor, but a person that I had in mind. I had an image that I had made up for the girl, and I was writing the aunt for Debra Monk. I knew what I was doing with her. I knew Debra's voice and all of that, but the other two, not. *Burn This* I wrote for Malkovich and Nancy Snyder, but Nancy decided she didn't want to act anymore. She wanted to have children, and we were just lucky enough to find Joan Allen. I also had in mind someone quite different from John Hogan, who ended up playing Burton.

Interviewer: But earlier on, you did much more writing for actors?

Wilson: We don't have the company that we did then. It was a result of having a company. The play that I want to write now, not the one that I've finished a draft of—that's called "Trinity," by the way, the play that I've finished a draft of—but the play that I want to write for Circle Rep I want to write for people who are in the lab because they're around and I know them. We have a lab membership of about 250 actors who are just incredibly good; they're very much like our original young company was. There's not more than four of the original company still in New York, probably. With the original company, I wrote not for what I thought they could do but for what I wanted to challenge them to do. Sometimes I took advantage of who they were. I wrote Wes specifically for Danny Stone because of a tiny little moment that I'd seen him do in a play called *Mrs. Murray's Farm,* a play that Roy London wrote which was commissioned for the Bicentennial. There was one moment where one of his bosses came in and said something and left and the other one came in and said something completely opposite and left. For one moment as the play went on, you were just left to decide which one of those he was going to do. And for one moment he went, "Uh, which one of those am I supposed to do?" And that was Wes. It was the only moment that Danny had like that, and I knew he could do that.

Interviewer: What is your opinion of critics? Do you ever learn anything from them? In your mind, what would be a description of the ideal reviewer? Does he or she exist?

Wilson: The theatre would be better off without critics. No, I've not learned anything from a critic, but they don't write to teach the author, thank God. I'm trying to ignore critics nowadays; I've stopped reading them unless I know the review is good, and of something I have seen and liked. My ideal reviewer is Harold Clurman, and we are unlikely to ever see his like again. What he did that the others don't do was try to understand the play. He also knew what acting was.

Interviewer: What terrifies you?

Wilson: There are a lot of things I'm troubled by. I am troubled by the idea that Circle Rep won't get a decent theatre, a larger theatre, and we need it desperately. What terrifies me is not being able to work. I'm at that age when most American playwrights stop, or start getting very strange. I have to focus now on the Arthur Millers and the ones who didn't stop and who didn't get very strange. Not being able to have another play put on, not writing another play, is always looming over you; it always has, because you don't know where in the hell it comes from. Flippantly, I say I never should have started this because now people expect me to continue doing it and I don't know what I'm doing. I never knew how to write a play to begin with and now they expect me to write another one. But beneath that, I really don't know where it comes from, and I really don't know if that muse is going to continue to buzz around and talk to me or not.

I really can't do much of anything else. I'm not a decent teacher; I can't stand up in front of people and talk, and I can't lecture. I suppose I could run an antiques store, but it wouldn't be nearly as much fun. So the idea of not being able to work terrifies me. I don't mean getting senile; that just happens. But until that point, not finding the next play scares me. I very often know what I want to write. I know what a play looks like and sounds like and generally should be, but I don't have any specifics at all. Getting the specifics is the entire thing, and so not being able to do that is very surprising.

I've never been able to write something just because I wanted to write something for someone. I was going to write something for Liz Sturges for years before I came up with Aunt Lottie. Finally, when I came up with Aunt Lottie, *Talley & Son* started with the image of a house where no one smokes; they smoke outside, they don't smoke inside. And they don't swear. Here is Liz Sturges walking through the room, smoking, saying, "Oh, kiss my ass." I didn't know another thing about it, and then it turned into one of the Talley plays. I grabbed onto that image so gratefully because I'd been wanting to write something for Liz Sturges for about ten years. The drill is to find a character, then say, "Who can play that?" and then aim the writing at a challenge to that actor or take advantage of something that they do very well. That's the method now. There's an actor in the lab now who's one of the great discoveries of our time. I think he's like discovering Jeff Daniels or discovering Bill Hurt or any of the other actors who have gone on to become very famous at Circle Rep. I want very much to write something for him, but I haven't been able to come up with anything because it's not the process. The process is finding the character and then finding the actor.

Index

About the Editor

Photo by R. J. Osborn

Jackson R. Bryer is a professor of English at the University of Maryland, where he has taught for thirty years. He has authored or edited over twenty-five books in the fields of American literature and modern drama.